Participatory and Self-Managed Firms

Participatory and Self-Managed Firms

Evaluating Economic Performance

Edited by
Derek C. Jones
Hamilton College
Jan Svejnar
Cornell University

LexingtonBooks
D.C. Heath and Company
Lexington, Massachusetts
Toronto

Library of Congress Cataloging in Publication Data

Main entry under title:
  Participatory and self-managed firms.

  Includes index.
  1. Employees' representation in management—Case studies. 2. Producer
cooperative—Case studies. I. Jones, Derek C. II. Svejnar, Jan.
HD5650.P3335   338.6   80-8612
ISBN 0-669-04328-1   AACR2

Copyright © 1982 by D.C. Heath and Company

Second printing, May 1983

Published simultaneously in Canada

Printed in the United States of America

International Standard Book Number: 0-669-04328-1

Library of Congress Catalog Card Number: 80-8612

Contents

Acknowledgments

Preliminary versions of some of the chapters in this book were first presented at the International Symposium on Economic Performance of Participatory and Self-Managed Firms, which was held at Hamilton College, from May 2-4 in 1980. The symposium was sponsored in part by funds provided by Proctor and Gamble and by the Program on Participation and Labor-Managed Systems at Cornell. Other chapters were especially written for this book. All chapters are previously unpublished.

Thanks are due to the editorial staff at Lexington, especially Margaret Zusky and Susan Lasser.

Several people helped with the typing of the manuscripts. We are particularly grateful to the efforts of June Darrow and Carmen Immink. Nathan Pyles provided valuable assistance in preparing the index.

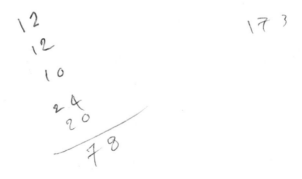

**Part I
Introduction**

1

The Economic Performance of Participatory and Self-Managed Firms: A Historical Perspective and a Review

Derek C. Jones and
Jan Svejnar

A Historical Perspective

The 1970s witnessed a reawakening of interest in organizational forms that are radical alternatives to capitalist and state-owned firms, principally the producer (worker/industrial) cooperative (PC) and the self-managed economic system of Yugoslavia. Interest also has blossomed in schemes providing for some degree of worker participation in decision making, and/or in ownership, and/or in the surplus (profits). Typical of these schemes, which usually—though not always—do not fundamentally challenge the existing structure of power, are employee stock-ownership plans and codetermination.[1]

Various factors have contributed to this recent development of interest. These include a desire for better industrial relations and a response to the "democratic imperative" (Bullock 1977, chapter 3). Increasing awareness of the apparent viability of long-established schemes, such as the U.S. plywood PCs and German codetermination, undoubtedly played a part too. Additionally, it was claimed that participatory firms not only preserved but also created jobs.

Most of these arguments, however, are not new. Sometimes, as with Christian socialists, anarchists, guild socialists, and industrial unionists, similar views were central features of influential doctrines and powerful social movements.[2] But in the past, most of these arguments, as well as the associated doctrines, have tended to be discredited. In part this results from early empirical analysis of participatory forms, such as that of Potter (1890) of early British PCs. These studies suggested that all participation schemes would inevitably be unsuccessful and short-lived. And indeed many did fail. For example, in the United Kingdom, the early self-governing workshops promoted by Christian Socialists, early PCs connected with labor unions, and guilds established by guildsmen all perished quickly. In the United States, too, most of the early well-known participatory ventures, such as

Knights of Labor PCs, tended soon to collapse. Connected with fluctuations in the birth rate of participatory organizations, some have observed
the not unrelated cycles of interest in worker participation (Buchannan
1978; Brannen et al. 1976). In the past, impulses for systematic study of participatory phenomena, including economic analysis, were never sustained.
Furthermore, in response to the claims made by the advocates of participation, there have always been counterarguments that seemed weightier to
most. In Britain and in the United States, for example, the Webbs and
Commons, respectively, championed collective bargaining as the most practical and expedient strategy for labor. These views were buttressed by the
development of doctrines that disdained workers' participation and self-
management, regarding such ventures as inherently unstable (Jones 1976).
But today the tide seems to have turned. Worker participation is an idea
that has captured the imagination and sustained the interest of a growing
number of academics and practitioners.[3]

In explaining the sustained recent interest in participation and labor-
managed firms (LMFs), six factors loom large. First, there is the productivity and unemployment crises faced by Western industrialized nations in the
1970s and early 1980s. In Britain and in the United States, recent years have
seen first a deceleration and then falls in productivity. Unemployment and
inflation have both reached what many regard as intolerably high levels.
Many societies are plagued by continuing concern over distributional questions. In less developed countries (LDCs), too, there is mounting evidence
that traditional models have not worked well. In both north and south there
is a search for alternative organizational models that might not only improve national productivity and employment but also help to produce more
generally acceptable income distributions.

Second, and differing from the largely pessimistic revived economic
doctrine of yesteryear, the 1970s saw the development of a body of formal
economic theory that was often optimistic as to the potential of participatory firms and LMFs.[4] Also there have been developments in other
disciplines that pointed to the potential for participatory firms under certain
conditions (Bernstein 1976; Pateman 1970; Rothschild-Whitt 1979). The
development of the outline of a new conceptual framework for the
theoretical analysis of participatory firms and self-managed economies is of
great significance in accounting for the burst of academic interest in the
area.

Third, support for the new optimistic position that was grounded in formal economic analysis was provided by early empirical studies that
documented the strong economic performance of the Yugoslav economy
(Balassa and Bertrand, in Vanek (ed) 1975; Horvat 1971). Also important
was the discovery of certain success stories within capitalist economies,
notably the Mondragon PCs in Spain (Oakeshott, in Vanek (ed) 1975), and

the U.S. plywood PCs (Berman 1967). These studies pointed to the potential for labor-managed sectors within industrialized Western economies. Under certain conditions PCs apparently could work well, though as many other studies have shown (Jones 1980) not all forms of the PC are effective, and PCs fall far short of being panaceas. Accounts also began to appear that suggested that substantial economic gains could flow from partial participatory experiments, such as autonomous work groups (U.S. D.H.E.W. 1973) and, more recently, "quality of worklife circles."

Fourth, there has been a major spurt in the rate at which participatory and self-managed firms have been established in the last decade. Even after allowance is made both for the exaggerated claims of some enthusiasts[5] and the fragility of available data, there remains an impressive documentation of the spread of the phenomenon of worker participation in recent years.[6] In particular, many countries have introduced legislation that requires worker representation on boards.[7]

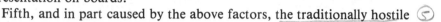

Fifth, and in part caused by the above factors, the traditionally hostile positions of many toward participation has been modified, and in some cases has been reversed. For example, in their representations to the Bullock Committee (see Bullock 1977) many British labor unions reversed traditionally antipathetic attitudes toward codetermination. The Welsh Trade Union Congress (TUC) is giving serious consideration to the question of committing union funds and its prestige to the establishment of PCs in Wales. In many Scandinavian countries too, trade unions now encourage codetermination. The position of many other groups on PCs is being intensely debated. Note in particular the debate in many cooperative movements on appropriate forms of cooperation (Laidlaw 1980). Various initiatives are being urged by many individuals prominent in different cooperative movements to stimulate the development of PCs, which for the most part have been the poor cousins in the cooperative family. Support by political parties for different species of participation seems to be growing. In Britain, for example, all major political parties have gone on record as favoring PCs of one kind or another. Of special interest in Italy is the conclusion of an accord among several parties, including the Communist Party and Communist labor unions, on measures designed to encourage the spread of cooperatives, including PCs. Developments in the United States are reviewed by Carnoy and Shearer (1980) and in *Employee Ownership* (1981), the principal publication of the National Center For Employee Ownership, that was established in 1981 and has attracted support from diverse groups that seldom align with one another.

But perhaps the central factor differentiating this period from that of others is the role of the state toward radical participatory forms such as the PC. In the past, the response of the state to calls for extensive worker participation has been the introduction of moderate reform programs, such as

Whitley committees in the United Kingdom following the shop-steward movement of the 1910s and the early 1920s. But the 1970s saw one government after another give ad hoc direct financial support for PCs. Best known in Britain was the establishment of the new worker cooperatives (the Benn PCs) with state aid. For the United States and Canada too, various federal and state agencies have provided assistance to PCs and worker-owned firms that were typically established following capitalist divestitures (Whyte and Blasi 1980). Among the best known U.S. cases are the Farmers Home Administration's assistance to Bates Manufacturing, the Economic Development Administration's assistance to South Bend Lathe, and, more recently, the $4.6 million loan provided by the Department of Housing and Urban Development to Rath Meatpacking. These initiatives have been accompanied by a series of more formalized ongoing legal measures such as the passage of the Industrial Common Ownership Act and the introduction of the Cooperative Development Agency in Britain as well as the establishment of the Cooperative Bank and the passage of various employee stock-ownership plan (ESOP) bills in the United States.[8] LDCs too have introduced various experiments and undertaken certain initiatives. Besides the schemes described in this volume these include the social-property sector in Peru, a PC sector in Chile during Allende's adminstration, industrial democracy in Maltese shipyards (Kester 1980), and the encouragement of PCs in Turkey (Uca 1979). The issue of worker participation has clearly become and is likely to remain a central one for public policy throughout the world.

Empirical Research on Participatory and Self-Managed Firms: A Review of the Book

In view of the fact that an increasing number of firms around the world are being managed in a participatory manner, the question of economic performance is a crucial one. At the same time, while many governments are establishing participatory ventures or formulating policies in this direction, until recently the available literature on the economic performance of participatory firms and SMFs has been slim, often diffuse, and usually not readily available.[9] Consequently the principal purpose of this book is to provide accessible evidence on the economic performance of participatory firms, sectors, and economies.

We hope not only to shed light on the range of institutional experiences in the area, but also to illustrate the scope and the nature of the work that has been and is being done on participatory firms and SMFs. We have endeavored to assemble a book that covers most of the recent major cases both in industrialized as well as in developing economies. Nearly all authors are seasoned empirical researchers in the field. All contributions include a review of the literature in a particular area. The bulk of this book reports new studies, and no contribution has been published elsewhere before.

This book has five major divisions. First, in part II, three chapters examine various issues in theory and in the meaning and measurement of
performance in participatory firms and SMFs both in industrialized countries and in LDCs. Although recently there have been some attempts to
review the theory of LMFs (Steinherr 1978), and the empirical implications
of that theory are by now fairly well known, Roger A. McCain's chapter in
this book is the first to focus on participatory firms and to do so by spell-
ing out empirical implications. McCain surveys the growing literature,
evaluates individual studies, and points out the existence of competing empirical predictions on many issues. In doing so he classifies the different
approaches and assumptions used and categorizes the existing literature
into several methodological streams; he is particularly critical of the so-
called "Texas school of thought." Even though the literature in this area
is growing rapidly, McCain shows that much theoretical work remains to
be done.

McBain

Henry Levin and Juan Guillermo Espinosa both point out the serious
and often neglected issues and problems in measuring the productivity and
evaluating performance of participatory firms and SMFs in developed
capitalist countries and LDCs. Levin first summarizes the differences in incentives and other organizational features that exist between traditional and
participatory firms. He then discusses the various concepts of productivity
and participation, the procedures for selecting comparable firms and the
associated selection bias, and the relevant accounting issues that arise in the
empirical comparisons. Although his analysis focuses on the two polar
cases, namely, the fully labor-managed and the traditional capitalist firms,
special references are made and a substantial part of Levin's chapter applies
to the intermediate participatory schemes as well.

Espinosa concentrates on the problems of evaluating the performance
of participatory firms and LMFs in the LDCs. He stresses the crucial impact
that the LDC environment, influenced by the international trade and
finance factors, has on the economic performance of domestic firms. He
also examines the different political factors, the various goals or objectives
of LMFs in LDCs, and the practical problems encountered in assessing
relative interfirm efficiency.

Most of this book is devoted to empirical studies, which are arranged
according to the level of development in the economy and the degree of de
jure participation in control enjoyed by workers. In part III are to be found
four essays that look at highly participatory situations for the best-known
cases of Yugoslavia and Mondragon. The chapter by Saul Estrin and
William Bartlett provides a welcome survey of much of the important empirical literature on Yugoslavia. The authors examine the available evidence
for the predictions from both the static and the dynamic economic theories.
For static theory they analyze findings with respect to allocative efficiency
at the level of the firm as well as the product and factor markets. Very few

testable propositions have been derived about the dynamic behavior of the labor-managed economies. As a result, Estrin and Bartlett focus on the existing national and international production function studies of the rate and patterns of growth. They argue convincingly that considerable scope remains for further empirical work in this area.

Stephen R. Sacks uses Yugoslav data to determine whether the labor-managed economy generates a greater or a lesser concentration of industrial power in the hands of a few giant corporations than do capitalist economies. Although the evidence at first appears self-contradictory, the paradox is resolved upon a closer examination of the concept of an enterprise or a firm.

Henk Thomas, and Keith Bradley and Alan Gelb, provide empirical evidence on issues relating to the economic performance of the Mondragon complex of PCs. Mondragon is widely considered to be the most important example of a growing, successful, and highly diversified conglomerate of "pure" PCs in the Western world. Yet very little systematic analysis of this Basque case has been performed to date. Focusing on the period 1967-1979, Thomas presents findings based on ratio analysis relating to productivity and profitability. He finds that the productivity and profitability indicators of Mondragon are superior to the corresponding indicators for the regional and national industrial sectors.

Bradley and Gelb use data from their questionnaire survey of about 1,200 Mondragon cooperateurs and 280 workers in two neighboring traditional firms to examine the replicability of cooperative undertakings and the sustainability of cooperative forms. In doing so they also assess the effects of PCs on industrial relations and efficiency. Contrary to a commonly held impression, this analytical study does not find Basque ethnicity to be a major factor accounting for the success and hence the difficulty of replicability of Mondragon's experience. Rather, the nature of the linkages with local communities and the limited labor mobility are found to be the critical factors in this arena.

In part IV are to be found four chapters that look at the productivity of PCs and of codetermined firms in Western economies. Derek C. Jones uses augmented production functions to estimate the separate effects on productivity of worker participation in control, in ownership, and in surplus within the British PCs in the printing, footwear, and clothing industries during 1948-1968. He finds important differences in the impact that the three variables have on productivity both among and within industries. In general, his preliminary results support the hypothesis that worker participation in decision making, ownership, and surplus has positive effects on productivity.

Jan Svejnar uses West German data from fourteen industries to test the impact of the 1951, 1952, and 1972 codetermination laws on productivity.

Combining the cross-section and time-series data, and measuring the impact of the laws as a disembodied productivity change, he finds that neither the 1951 Codetermination Law nor the 1952 and 1972 Works Constitution Acts had a noticeable effect on productivity.

Michael Conte provides a needed survey of recent studies that measure the impact of worker participation in control and in ownership on motivation and performance in participatory firms in North America. Conte's survey is interdisciplinary and finds that participation is positively related to individual motivation. Conte also shows convincingly that existing studies do not throw sufficient light on the question of whether the increased individual motivation leads to greater organizational efficiency.

Alberto Zevi analyzes the performance of large Italian PCs in manufacturing and construction. During 1975-1978, Italian PCs are shown to have had high growth rates, even faster than those for capitalist firms. PCs also recorded higher levels of profit and possibly better rates of growth of total factor productivity than did capitalist firms. Considerable differences exist between PCs in construction and those in manufacturing. In examining these phenomena, Zevi stresses many factors and attributes an important role to building consortia.

The three chapters in part V look at participation elsewhere, including participatory schemes in LDCs. Avner Ben-Ner presents an econometric study of the changing values and preferences in the communally organized Israeli kibbutzim. His study bears directly on the important issue of a survival potential of communal organizations. Using data from 1955 and 1965 the author finds a significant change toward decommunalization in preferences and in actual consumption (a switch to more private consumption on the part of the kibbutz members).

Peter Abell and Nicholas Mahoney examine the performance of small-scale PCs in India and Peru. Focusing on the so-called capital-starvation thesis of Vanek (1971, 1977) and Furubotn (1971), the authors find that the main problems of the PCs in their survey do not arise from lack of capital. Rather, the main problem encountered by the small PCs is how to manage their capital effectively. Abell and Mahoney conclude by supporting Vanek's (1970) idea that a support organization may be necessary to propagate a viable co-operative sector.

Vincent Richards and Allan N. Williams present institutional and economic aspects of the Jamaican sugar cooperatives. They first describe the intricate institutional arrangements and constraints under which the cooperatives operate and then analyze the employment, output, export, and land-use performance of the cooperatives. The projected and the actual performances in terms of profitability and productivity are compared. With all the information at their disposal, the authors evaluate the cooperatives' performance as moderately successful.

In the concluding part, Jaroslav Vanek, one of the pioneers of the theory of self-management, offers a critical and provocative commentary on much of the research that has been and is being done on participatory firms and SMFs. Vanek raises important issues, particularly concerning the appropriate role to be played by researchers in the field of worker participation and self-management.

Review and Conclusions

In reviewing the chapters in this book and other empirical work in the field, a number of themes become apparent. First, most authors contributing to this volume focus on technical rather than economic efficiency. Under the assumption of identical prices and objectives across firms, one can of course make inferences about economic efficiency on the basis of technical-efficiency results. However, since the objective function of the firm is likely to change with the degree of participation, inferences about allocative efficiency are difficult to make. But even existing approaches to allocative efficiency in profit-maximizing firms suffer from numerous restrictive assumptions. As a result, the emphasis on technical efficiency seems warranted. Several researchers use ratio (input-output or input-input) analysis. Although the shortcomings of this approach have become well known,[10] its use in the present context is dictated by the limited availability of data and/or the pilot nature of the research. This is the case with Abell and Mahoney, Zevi, Richards and Williams, and Thomas. It should be noted that until recently most studies on the relative efficiency of participatory and LMFs used this type of analysis. On U.S. PCs these studies include early publications of the American Economic Association (1887, 1888), Virtue (1905, 1932), Stockton (1931), Berman (1967), and Jones (1979). Other works of this type include the kibbutz study by Melman (in Horvat et al. (eds.) 1975); and the German codetermination study by Blumenthal (1956). For U.K. PCs the work of Potter (1890) and parts of Jones (1974) are relevant.

More recently, and in part prompted by the availability of more complete data sets, there is a growing tendency to attempt more sophisticated quantitative analyses and to test specific hypotheses. For the United States, Conte reviews the pioneering studies of this ilk. For German codetermination Svejnar's works on effects on wages (1977, 1981) and on productivity (this book) are the first studies of this kind. The major work on the kibbutz by Barkai (1977) has been extended by Ben-Ner (1981, this book), while Jones and Backus (1977) and Jones (this book) have undertaken the pioneering research for long-established British PCs. For Yugoslavia, as Estrin and Bartlett (this book) note, there have been important contributions by many, including Horvat, Jan Vanek, Jaroslav Vanek, Estrin,

Bartlett, and Sacks. Bradley and Gelb have done imaginative quantitative work both on the new British PCs and on Mondragon. The other major econometric analysis in the field is that by Espinosa and Zimbalist (1978) and by Cable and Fitzroy (1980a, 1980b).

In sum, these studies represent substantial contributions to knowledge. Although there are important historical antecedents, it is probably true that more has been learned about the theory and practice of worker participation and self-management in the last ten years than in the previous century. At the same time, the intellectual resources allocated to the area remain less than adequate, inhibiting further advances and contributing to the perpetuation of unresolved issues. On some issues, however, a growing volume of evidence has been produced and perhaps a consensus is emerging.

The chapters by Thomas and by Jones in this book support the view that by drawing on the work of Vanek, Horvat, and Bernstein a set of rules that are necessary for viable PCs or LMFs can be identified. As such this lends support to earlier studies, such as Jones (1979, 1980). But as the chapters within this book by Abell and Mahoney, Bradley and Gelb, and the remarks by Thomas on collective ownership suggest, there is still far from complete agreement both on whether all features are necessary and whether the sufficient set of conditions for a generally viable and reproducible model have been identified, or indeed whether such a task itself is feasible.

There is apparently consistent support for the view that worker participation in management causes higher productivity. This result is supported by a variety of methodological approaches, using diverse data and for disparate time periods, including the studies reviewed by Conte and those by Jones and by Zevi in this book. Previous studies by many including Cable and Fitzroy (1980a, 1980b) and Espinosa and Zimbalist (1978) found similar relationships. But this is not always the case, as Svejnar's work in this book illustrates. Nor as the methodological chapters by Espinosa and by Levin in this book suggest, should we always, under all conditions and for all forms of participation, expect to find a positive, sustained, and pronounced effect of participation on productivity. It is clear that on this and with other issues there is a need for additional careful empirical analysis.

One area deserving of more attention is the development of de facto measures of worker participation and the further investigation of the relationship between de jure and de facto indicates of participation. While the studies by Espinosa and Zimbalist (1978), Cable and Fitzroy (1980a, 1980b), and the IDE International Research Group (1981) have improved our understanding on these matters, many unanswered questions remain. Much work hitherto has focused on aspects of the internal organization of firms to the exclusion of external factors, which are stressed most by writers on LDCs such as Espinosa and Richards and Williams in this book. Ways need to be developed and adopted to assess the relative and absolute importance of these factors in understanding the behavior of participatory firms. In addition, more work is needed in developing accounting frameworks, and hence data sets, that are relevant in view of the special aims and purposes of PCs. Too often research instruments for studies of participatory firms are designed by borrowing from studies conceived for capitalist or state-owned firms. Furthermore, as stressed by Levin, when measuring performance in participatory firms and LMFs, criteria and indicators of success must be developed that are consistent with the specific goals of the firms under investigation and not simply borrowed from studies of conventional firms.

As noted by McCain, Conte, and Estrin and Bartlett, to begin addressing these and other questions will require further theoretical analysis and the development of testable hypotheses. While this will permit a diversity of approaches to be used, available research experience suggests that best results will likely require interdisciplinary theoretical and empirical work. More fruitful results are also likely to be obtained from studies that use behavioral theories of the firm, that are longitudinal in nature.

Notes

1. For example, codetermination in iron and steel and in coal in Germany in principle provides for an exact division of power between stockholders (and their representatives) and workers (and their representatives). Equally, many PCs in practice provide for worker participation in decision making that falls far short of giving workers the potential for self-determination.

2. For illustrations see Vanek (ed.) (1975), part I, and Horvat et al. (eds.) (1975), part I.

3. This has found practical expression in, among other things: (a) the establishment of various journals devoted to the subject, including *Economic Analysis and Workers' Management*, *Economic and Industrial Democracy*, and *Autogestion*; (b) the development of specialized academic programs, including the Program on Participation and Labor-Managed Systems at Cornell and the project for kibbutz studies at Harvard; (c) the appearance of various newsletters, including *Workplace Democracy* and *CICRA*; (d) a growth in the number of conferences devoted to the subject; (e) a growth in the volume of publications in the field, including special issues of established journals such as *Industrial Relations* (Fall 1979), *Journal of Comparative Economics* (June 1980), and the *Annals of Public and Cooperative Economy* (April-June 1978); (f) the multiplication of research

projects in this field; and (g) the establishment of specialist consultancy services such as the Industrial Cooperatives Association in the United States.

4. In particular see Vanek (1970, 1977); Horvat (1971, 1976b); Meade (1972); Ward (1967); and Dreze (1976). Also see Jay (1976); Clayre (ed.) (1980); Oakeshott (1978); Zwerdling (1978); and Carnoy and Shearer (1980).

5. For the British case, see Thornley (1981, chapter 1).

6. For PCs and employee-owned firms in the United States, see Frieden (1980). For European countries see Thornley (1981) and Oakeshott (1978).

7. For example, in 1980, legislation was introduced in Denmark that provided for board representation for workers.

8. For details and discussion of developments, see the chronicle section of *Economic and Industrial Democracy*, and the country reviews in *Economic Analysis and Workers' Management*.

9. For example, the early readers in this subject contain only two pieces of empirical economic research. (Balassa and Bertrand in Venek (ed.) 1975, and Melman in Horvat et al. (eds.) 1975).

10. See for instance Lau and Yotopoulos (1971, pp. 94-109).

Part II
Theory and Methodology

2

Empirical Implications of Worker Participation in Management

Roger A. McCain

Despite generations of hortatory, homiletic, and utopian discussions of worker management (self-management) (Vanek (ed.) 1975), economic theory took up the topic only in the late fifties. Though worker participation in management has a longer history (principally in Germany and the United Kingdom) its neglect by economic theorists continued until even more recently. Even now the literature of economic theory on worker participation in management is small and little known.

Worker participation in management comprises a wide range of arrangements. At the one extreme this encompasses minimal rights of consultation or being informed of management decisions within the context of the capitalist firm or state enterprise. On the other extreme is the extensive structure of codetermination on the supervisory board, workers' councils, labor unions, and the historic guild identity of the German Montanindustrie and, in posse, all other such institutions short of unilateral management by the workers' council. The variety of types offers a real opportunity for empirical work of a comparative sort. If the degree of participativeness can be roughly measured, then we may be able to find statistical relationships between participativeness and other dimensions of the firm's performance that can in turn shed some light on the comparative validity of rival theories of participation.[1]

This chapter will concentrate primarily on the few relatively formal theories of worker participation and the empirical hypotheses that they pose. I will first take up those that stress bargaining power as the distinguishing characteristic of the participatory firm.[2] These theories are generally limited in their scope to codetermination. Three studies (McCain 1980; Carson 1977; and Furubotn and Pejovich 1974) will then be taken up; each, in quite different ways, is intendedly applicable to participatory firms in general. McCain's paper, like some of the previous group, relies on a bargaining hypothesis to construct a decision function for the organization. In Carson's study the decision function for a firm of a particular type is taken as given, while Furubotn and Pejovich proceed from a hypothesis about the interests of employees qua employees. In the last major section I turn to some important discussions that are informal or that rely on ad-hoc theorizing or plausible conjectures that form or that suggest empirical hypotheses. Next I examine less formal studies, with particular attention to the property-rights literature (Pejovich (ed.) 1978; Gallaway in Pejovich (ed.) 1978; Jensen and Meckling 1979) and to ad-hoc hypotheses in some existing empirical studies. A brief summary concludes the chapter.

Bargaining-Power Hypotheses

A first task of any theory of the participatory firm is to distinguish that kind of firm from other kinds. Some observers of parity codetermination in the German Montanindustrie have suggested that the routine decisions of the joint board of supervisors (Aufsichtrat) are made by "Kuhhandel," that is, literally, cow trading (see Hallet 1973, p. 91). The equivalent phrase in idiomatic English is, of course, horse trading, and the technical term is bargaining. This suggests that we might approach the theory of parity codetermination by way of the theory of bargaining. Unfortunately, there is no received theory of bargaining, and it is often held that outcomes of bargaining are indeterminate. Thus, studies that assume that the decisions of the codetermined firm are determined by bargaining may draw different conclusions (both normative and empirical) insofar as they rely on different bargaining theories. Moreover, bargaining is not limited to codetermination. Collective bargaining between unions and management takes place in the absence of any labor participation in management. Thus it seems appropriate to indicate how codetermination would differ from collective bargaining.

We might begin with a model as much as possible like Ward's Illyria, if only for comparative purposes. We should then be examining the codetermined triplet (and the collective-bargaining quadruplet!) of Ward's Illyrian and capitalist twins. Thus we would posit a production function,

$$Q = f(K,N) \qquad (2.1)$$

and a firm demand price curve,

$$p = G(Q) \qquad (2.2)$$

with $dG/dQ \leq 0$ in general and $dG/dQ = 0$ in the case of perfect competition. The firm also faces a supply curve of labor that may or may not rise.

$$w \geq h(N) \qquad (2.3)$$

with $dh/dN \geq 0$. Here, $h(N)$ is the second-best alternative wage of the Nth worker. If the firm is perfectly competitive in labor markets, then $dh/dN = O$; otherwise it has monoposony power.[3]

The simplest widely accepted bargaining hypothesis is the Zeuthen-Nash hypothesis. The theory works as follows: Let U be the utility of shareholders and V be the utility of workers. Assume that, if there is no agreement, the shareholders can do no better than U_0 and the workers can do no better than V_0. The Zeuthen-Nash bargaining theory leads us to expect an outcome that will

$$\max (U - U_0) (V - V_0). \tag{2.4}$$

We must, then, make some judgment as to the nature of the utility functions and the identity of the threat points, U_0 and V_0. Again taking only the simplest possibilities, I identify U with the economic profit accruing to shareholders and U_0 *with zero*. Following the Illyrian literature, I also identify V with the wage, ex post the allocative decision w. Some new workers may be hired as a result of the allocative decision, but, not being part of the work force when the decision is made, they play no part in the decision. Accordingly I must identify V_0 with the second-best alternative, not of the marginal worker, but perhaps of the median man (Downs 1957)[4] among the workers employed ex ante the allocative decision. That is denoted by v, a constant.

Accordingly I then assume that the codetermined firm will

$$\max (pQ - wN - rK) (w - v), \tag{2.5}$$

where r is the rental cost of capital (presumably imputed) and the other variables are as before. I will not belabor the mathematical development, which is of the conventional Kuhn-Tucker type. Several cases are possible. Under conditions of pure competition, the necessary conditions for the maximum include

$$w = p \partial f / \partial N \tag{2.6a}$$

$$r = p \partial f / \partial K \tag{2.6b}$$

$$N(w - v) = pQ - wN - rK. \tag{2.6c}$$

Conditions 2.6a and 2.6b are familiar. Condition 2.6c is novel, and what it tells us is that the economic profits accruing to the firm are divided equally between the employers and the work force. From this it follows that, in the absence of profits, $w = v$ and the codetermined firm adopts policies identical to those adopted by the capitalist twin (and the Illyrian firm) in long-run equilibrium. If there are profits, $w > v$, and that implies that the codetermined form will hire less labor and use a more capital-intenstive technique than the "capitalist twin." In this case, the employment and output of the codetermined form are intermediate between those of its cousins, the capitalist and Illyrian firms, so that it shares some of the short-run inefficiency of the latter, though to a reduced degree.

These comments also apply *mutatis mutandis* to the case of monopoly power ($dG/dQ < 0$), but the case is quite different in the face of monopsony power ($dh/dN > 0$). There are two subcases. The labor-supply may or may not be binding on the codetermined firm. If profits per head are large, the labor-supply constraint will not be binding, and the necessary conditions will again have the form of 2.6 above, if $dG/dQ = 0$. In that case, however, the conditions for the capitalist firm are different—the labor-supply constraint must be binding on the capitalist firm, since it will never pay a higher wage than it must—and the codetermined firm hires more labor, produces more output, and pays a higher wage than does the capitalist firm. If the labor-supply constraint is binding, the case is more complicated, but the same conclusions follow. Since the Illyrian literature has tended to neglect monopsony, in this case it is not clear how the codetermined firm would compare with the Illyrian firm.

This model (which is taken from McCain 1977b) may serve as a basis for comparison and criticism, and thus as a point of departure. One virtue is that it is firmly in the Illyrian tradition and so serves to link that tradition to the discussions of worker participation that follow. This Illyrian model of codetermination has the following regrettable properties. (1) It does not admit of any distinction between codetermination and other forms in which bargaining determines the wage, and in particular, therefore, between codetermination and collective bargaining. (2) It does not address some issues that have been central to the policy-oriented discussions of codetermination: labor productivity, effort, working conditions, and the "alienation" of labor.[5] (3) The model imposes the assumption that the organizational form can have no impact on the productivity of the resources the firm uses, ceteris paribus. This assumption guards against a common fallacy of economic advocacy, namely, the comparison of an ideal form of one system with a subideal but realistic form of another. Still, the assumption is implausible, and it means that the theory cannot confront one of the issues that policy-oriented discussions of codetermination have stressed. Some advocates of codetermination[6] believe that codetermination, by establishing class harmony in the workplace, can improve both labor productivity and working conditions, and that is impossible unless codetermination is in some sense a superior organizational form. (4) The model embodies one of the most criticized assumptions of the Illyrian tradition: the assumption that the workers' collective would lay off some of its members in order to raise the incomes of the rest. McCain (1977a,b) offered some results from a model that differs on this score in that the workers veto any layoffs beyond a certain minimum labor force. This is expressed by an inequality constraint,

$$N \geq N_0, \tag{2.7}$$

where N_0 is an unknown constant. When this constraint is binding, it has the predictable result that output and employment are greater than they would otherwise be. (5) Finally, the model imposes the assumption that the bargaining powers of the two parties are in some sense equal, with the far from surprising result that the economic profits, if any, are equally divided between them. In a Zeuthen-Nash bargaining model, the bargaining powers depend only on the threat outcomes and risk aversion of the parties, and the explicit Illyrian assumption is that workers' utility is linear in wage income. The corresponding assumption is that the capitalists' utility is linear in profits. These assumptions, together with the designation of the second-best returns as the threat outcomes, imply equal division.

Svejnar (1977, 1980a, 1982) has proposed two models that, although they (independently) adopt the bargaining-theoretic approach, depart constructively from the Illyrian tradition. Svejnar's models are motivated quite directly by the search for empirical implications that may be tested by econometric methods, and in that sense his study is exemplary. First, in both models, Svejnar assumes that the bargaining powers of the parties may be unequal. He expresses this in the following way. In place of expression 2.4 above, in my notation, he assumes that the bargaining outcome will

$$\max (U - U_0)^{GS}(V - V_0)^{GL}, \tag{2.8}$$

where the exponents GS and GL express the relative bargaining power of the owners and the workers, respectively. Svejnar normalizes so that GS + GL = 1. This immediately admits of a hypothesis that distinguishes codetermination from collective bargaining: that codetermination shifts bargaining power from the owners to the workers. (Svejnar also proposes to introduce the interests of managers in a similar way). Moreover, this specification and hypothesis lead to some clear and econometrically convenient implications of fact.

In the light of bargaining theory, this specification, although precedented (Coddington 1968, pp. 37-40; and Pen 1952, pp. 24-42) appears somewhat ad hoc. However, Svejnar (1980b) has recently proposed a new bargaining theory, less restrictive than that of Nash, that allows for varying bargaining power, treating bargaining power more or less as a "black box." Although the "black box" bargaining power leaves one a bit unsatisfied (at least if one has a taste for bargaining theory), it suffices to generate the most econometrically advanced model of codetermination now available.

Svejnar (1977, 1980a, 1982) explores two models. The first of these, nearer the Illyrian tradition, assumes that the utility of workers depends only on individual or average wage income. Positive profits imply an Illyrian restriction of labor inputs and output in the most plausible case.[7] The economic profit of the firm is then distributed among the factors, labor, capital, and management, in proportion to their respective bargaining powers. That is, for example,

$$\frac{N\ (w - v)}{K\ (s - r)} = \frac{GL}{GS},\qquad (2.9a)$$

where r is the alternative cost of capital and s the rate of dividends that the firm chooses to pay. Equivalently,

$$\ln\left(\frac{w - v}{s - r}\right) = \ln\left(\frac{GL}{GK}\right) + \ln\left(\frac{K}{N}\right).\qquad (2.9b)$$

This suggests an immediate econometric hypothesis. Suppose that codetermination increases the bargaining power of labor. One would expect that, in a regression of the logarithm of excess wages on the logarithms of economic profit and the capital-labor ratio, a dummy variable for codetermination would have a positive coefficient. Unfortunately, the data for such an experiment would be difficult to come by. One would, therefore, have to look for indirect tests based on some related or derived relationships. One possibility is that different patterns of resource allocation would be implied. For example, greater bargaining power would imply a higher wage and, on the Illyrian pattern, that would have some effect on the allocation of resources within the firm. Intuition suggests that it would lead to a higher capital-output ratio, but Svejnar explores this possibility in detail and finds that the direction of the effect is indeterminate.

Notice that, if $GL = GS$, then 2.9a is identical to 2.6c. This suggests that it may not matter, in this context, whether owners' utility depends upon the rate of profits, or, as assumed in deriving 2.6c, absolute profits. This point has not been rigorously explored, however.

Svejnar's second model assumes that workers' utility depends upon the expected wage (or alternatively the wage bill), so that workers are interested in employment as well as wages. There is some precedent for this assumption in the study of collective bargaining (Law 1977, pp. 27-37; Fellner 1947, pp. 503-532). Owners may be interested in either absolute profits or the profit rate, without affecting the results. An important difference is that, in the second model, the bargaining outcome implies optimal factor demands, based on the alternative costs of the respective factors. Thus there is no Illyrian restriction of the labor input and of output, even if economic profits are positive. Again, the economic profits are divided in proportion to the bargaining power indexes, GL/GS, and Svejnar derives the following wage equation:

$$w = GL(pQ - vN - rK)/N + GSv. \qquad (2.10)$$

This equation is the basis for Svejnar's econometric study, though some further derivation is required due to limited data availability.

Aoki has proposed a model rather similar, in many ways, to Svejnar's. Like the preceding models, it is based on bargaining theory. Aoki begins his discussion by assuming that there is firm-specific human capital embodied in the skills and knowledge of long-term employees. This serves to justify the assumption that there are rents (or positive economic profits) that accrue to the firm even in long-run equilibrium. These economic profits are, as usual, relative to the alternative costs of the inputs used, not necessarily to the prices paid for them. For example, the entire economic profit might be paid to the workers in the form of wages, so that accounting profit would be zero even though economic profit is positive. This neatly disposes of the case of zero profits in long-run equilibrium, which has so diverted the attention of Illyrian economics, of McCain and of Svejnar.

Like Svejnar, Aoki (1980) allows for unequal bargaining power between labor and capital. He makes the utilities of both parties nonlinear in money payments and relies on differences in risk aversion to account for differences in bargaining power.[8] On the assumption that risk aversion is locally constant, Aoki derives a measure of "pure bargaining power" and an approximative form of the utility function of either party (Cobb-Douglas, again, of course), from which he concludes that the economic profits will be divided between the two parties in proportions determined by their respective bargaining power, that is,

$$\frac{(w - v) N}{pQ - wN - T} = \frac{a (1 + b)}{b (1 + a)}, \qquad (2.11)$$

where a is the measure of the pure bargaining power of the workers, b that for the shareholders, and T capital cost. Here, the Cobb-Douglas exponents are $a/1 + a$ and $b/1 + b$, so this result is the same as 2.9a insofar as they both are operational.

However, T is capital cost only in a broad sense, for Aoki's model is innovative also in his theory of the firm. There is no conventional production function. Output is in fixed proportions to the labor input, but a capital input is not explicitly mentioned, except for the informal discussion of firm-specific human capital. Instead, Aoki posits a given relationship between the firm's chosen growth rate and the "growth expenditure," that is, advertising, fixed investment, personnel training, and other similar expenditures not listed. If fixed investment were the only growth expenditure and the fixed proportions production function were assumed, then the relationship between growth and growth expenditure would be a proportionate one; so presumably the nonlinearity Aoki assumes for this relationsip reflects some of these other things.

Unfortunately, Aoki does not offer us a reference model of the profit-maximizing firm with this sort of growth-expenditure trade-off for comparison. Thus we do not know how the bargaining firm compares with the profit-maximizing firm. Aoki does, however, point out the effect of a change in the environment of the firm that strengthens the workers' bargaining power. If the price of output is unconstrained, that would tend to increase the planned rate of growth and the price. However Aoki, like Mc-Cain (1977a,b), takes it that the firm is constrained not to lay anyone off, and in Aoki's scheme that constraint is translated to a lower constraint on total sales and thus to an upper constraint on the price. If this price constraint is binding, then an increase in worker bargaining power will decrease the planned rate of growth. A higher planned rate of growth and consequent higher growth expenditure presumably corresponds, in Aoki's scheme, to a more capital-intensive mode of production in more nearly neoclassical models.

Furubotn (1978), in addition to his contributions to the property-rights approach—the Texas school of thought, which will be separately considered below—has constructed a model that is described as a model of codetermination and that rests upon the bargaining power that codetermination might provide to the workers. I say that the model is described as a model of codetermination because Furubotn does not mention collective bargaining and the model could as well be described as a model of collective bargaining. Indeed, however, Furubotn's paper contains two quite different models, each of the firm under some sort of bargaining and of the capitalist firm under profit maximization. This creativity seems to have its roots in Furubotn's initial misunderstanding of his own assumptions, but both models have some aspects that are of interest.

Furubotn begins from the supposition that codetermination may have something to do with worker alienation, which in turn depends upon the work environment. Thus in place of equation 2.1 he posits

$$Q = f(K,N,E) \qquad (2.12)$$

where E is an index of the working environment constructed in such a way that a larger E is preferable to a smaller, ceteris paribus, from the viewpoint of the workers. Furubotn also assumes that (at least beyond some point of diminishing returns) increasing E means decreasing Q, ceteris paribus. Thus we might identify E with (good) working conditions or (inversely) with effort, although Furubotn does not mention these possibilities. There is also a technological lower limit on E, which Furubotn treats as an inequality constraint additional to equation 2.12. Furubotn (1978, p. 146) tells us that the lower limit of E is the ideal, the best of all known technologies. This, of course, can be true only if the workers' preferences do not count. This may serve to explain why Furubotn changes models in midstream and actually provides us with two, quite different, sets of empirical implications.

Furubotn does not adopt the Zeuthen-Nash bargaining theory, nor indeed any bargaining theory. He assumes that the workers' bargaining power, under codetermination, sets a lower limit to the utility, or preference ranking, that they will accept. This lower level is greater than the second-best that they could obtain in some other activity. The second-best alternative of a worker is expressed, not simply as a wage but rather as the utility level attainable in the other activity, and thus as a functional relationship between the wage and the characteristics of the job. In fact, the functional relationship is precisely the economist's old friend, the indifference curve.[9]

Thus, in Furubotn's system, the worker's bargaining power is expressed only as a lower constraint on the realized utility of workers. This constraint is taken as given. Thus, Furubotn gives up any attempt to determine the distribution of profits endogenously. Thus, Furubotn's codetermined firm maximizes profits (shareholders' utility) subject to the constraint that workers' utility not be reduced below a given level. That is identically the formulation of a Pareto optimum, as among the associates of the firm, as a problem in constrained maximization.[10] However, this is not noted by Furubotn (1978, pp. 146-149), who points out that a traditional capitalist firm will choose the smallest feasible E and will hire labor at a competitive w, not negotiating over the exact E and w because the transactional or information cost of doing so is too high. Furubotn (1978, p. 148) then states that the wage will be higher with codetermination, the profit lower, and the output price higher.

In the context of Furubotn's model, all of this is mistaken. Consider figure 2-1, which is adapted from Furubotn's (1978) figure 7-1. In the figure, I, II, and III are successively higher indifference curves for the representative worker; z_1, z_2, and z_3 successively higher isoprofit curves; and E^* the technologically determined minimum of working conditions. Then assume that I is the second-best alternative of the representative worker. It follows that the traditional capitalist firm pays a wage of w_1 and achieves profits z_2. Assume that II is the given minimum of worker utility under codetermination. Then the codetermined firm pays a lower wage, gets more profit, and, with lower costs, may well charge a lower price. Even when the profit is reduced by codetermination, as it would be if III is the worker's minimum utility under codetermination, the wage can still be less, as w_2 is less than w_1. The first of these two cases raises the question why an enlightened profit-seeking firm would not adopt codetermination voluntarily,

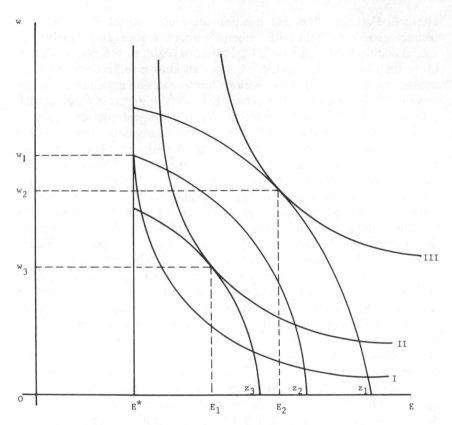

Figure 2-1. Furubotn's Model of Codetermination

rather than awaiting a change of corporate property law before doing so. It does, however, illustrate a clear empirical implication of Furubotn's first model: under codetermination, whether it is voluntary or mandatory to the firm, E will be greater than it would be under traditional capitalism and so the productivity of the firm's inputs will be less.

Furubotn's traditional capitalist firm fits the image of the sweatshop rather remarkably well. On (1978) pp. 149-150, Furubotn suddenly tumbles to this fact, and drops the first model like a hot potato. He then proposes a second model in which each worker faces a range of opportunities in various industries, with different combinations of wages and working conditions; but (this being a highly competitive economy, inhabited by workers who all have identical tastes and opportunities) these different opportunities all yield the same utility. Moreover, each of these workers will move in an instant if he or she is disappointed with the wage-working conditions vector. (Evidently there are no costs of transaction or information in getting reemployed in this world, although there are transaction costs that make the negotiation of working conditions prohibitive). Thus, the opportunities available to the worker trace out an indifference curve—let us say that it is indifference to curve II—that in turn is a lower constraint to the realized utility of the worker, and the untrammelled capitalist firm is now assumed to maximize its profits subject to that constraint.

In short, the constrained maximization model that Furubotn previously represented as a model of codetermination has now become his model of pure capitalism—and indeed it is a valid model of market equilibrium with varying working conditions in the absence of information or transaction costs or other market imperfections.[11] But then, how does codetermination differ? Why, only in getting a better deal for the workers. We now treat III as the constraint imposed by the workers under codetermination, and observe that III is greater than the second-best option available to the workers. All workers being alike, there must be many workers who would willingly take the jobs that yield that vector of wage and working conditions, and those many being excluded, we have inefficient restriction of the number hired—precisely the Illyrian conclusion, and precisely for the Illyrian reason. Profits will be lower under codetermination. Also, if we assume that tastes and the production function are sufficiently regular so that there are no inferior goods or inputs, wages will be higher, and E being higher, productivity will be less, as shown in figure 2-1. Also (Furubotn stresses) the lower profits will lead to reduced investment. These are, in principle, testable implications of Furubotn's second theory.

All these theories put bargaining power at the center of the theory of codetermination, and so one is hardly surprised that they tend to draw similar conclusions. All (except Furubotn's first model) conclude that the firm's policies must be Pareto optimal as among the members of the firm, but may or may not be efficient when nonassociates' potential gains are also considered. Save for Svejnar's second model, all conclude that when profits are nonzero, the workers' bargaining power will lead to an Illyrian-style restriction of the membership of the workers' collective associated with the firm and a consequent restriction of output. Except for Furubotn's models, all conclude that profits will be distributed in proportion to bargaining power. Thus, to shed light on the empirical validity of these theories, we might wish to examine the relationships among the wage, labor's alternative cost, economic profits, the capital-intensity of production, and the output. Codetermination implies that wages would be higher in proportion to profits, that excess wages and profits would be correlated under codetermination (Furubotn excepted), that wages and capital intensity would be positively correlated under codetermination and both inversely correlated with output (Svejnar's second model excepted).

More General Formal Hypotheses

The models in the previous section all share the shortcoming previously noted: They adopt the convention of the capitalist twin, thus excluding by assumption the possibility that the organizational form could affect the productivity with which the firm could use a given vector of resources. This effectiveness in using the resources at hand may be called X-efficiency, a term due to Leibenstein.

Like Furubotn and like McCain (1973, 1977a), McCain (1980) introduces the characteristics of work as independent variables in the production function. McCain begins with a reference model of a firm that sets wages by bargaining with a given trade-off between effort and productivity. The following empirical implications follow from this model: Under collective bargaining (or codetermination) wages and profit per head will be correlated, and both inversely correlated with productivity. One should add that there may be an identification problem in these associations, since high productivity may be a cause of high profits; and further, profit statistics may be hard to come by. Supposing that there are no inferior-good or -input complications, collective bargaining (or codetermination) will imply both higher wages and less effort than under "untrammelled capitalism," and either higher wages or less effort or both if there are inferior-good or -input complications.[12] The model provides no basis for any difference of outcome between collective bargaining and codetermination.

This reference model is meant only as an exploration of the implications of a given effort-productivity trade-off, that is, a given production function with effort as one of the inputs. McCain now addresses the determination of the effort-productivity trade-off, that is, of X-efficiency. Beginning from the facts that effort is actually multidimensional and that labor contracts are always incomplete (Leibenstein 1969), McCain first explores the necessary conditions for efficient multidimensional effort. McCain then digresses on game theory, defining a suboptimization game as a game in which payoffs depend on a multidimensional strategy vector of which some components must be predetermined, while others may be set later in the light of the known values of the predetermined strategy components. Suboptimization games do not generally give rise to efficient outcomes, but the nature of the outcome depends sensitively on the commitment structure of the game, that is, which variables are precommitted and which are free of precommitment. The free variables may be set opportunistically (see Klein et al. 1978), which may be inefficient in itself, but which also requires the players to anticipate opportunism as they determine the precommitted variables, and this anticipation may lead to inefficient precommitted strategies as well.

In the context of the reference model, for example, suppose that wages are precommitted by the workers, as a reservation price, while effort is a free variable under the control of the employers; and that once an employee has committed himself or herself to a firm, it is not practical to leave in the short term. This is Furubotn's first model. Then effort will be opportunistically set where the marginal productivity of effort is zero (ignoring long-run impacts of such a policy). Workers, anticipating that it will be so, demand wages high enough to compensate for the sweatshop conditions. Both of these are departures from ideal efficiency.

The incompleteness of labor contracts implies that effort determination is a suboptimization game. Under collective bargaining (or "individual bargaining") those dimensions of the work process that are negotiated are necessarily precommitted, while the rest are free variables determined unilaterally either by workers or by the employer. The inflexibility of the contract excludes some variables from contractual determination, while simple lack of foresight excludes others, and public-goods difficulties may exclude still others in the case of "individual bargaining." The possibility of opportunism in the determination of these free variables implies that only a second-best can be achieved. McCain treats the opportunistic setting of free variables (in the tradition of the theory of the second best) as constraints in the bargainers' joint maximization program (or as constraints on profit maximization in the case of "individual bargaining.") As in the general theory of the second best, these side constraints imply that the bargainers' constrained optimum is inefficient.

McCain argues that the different forms of the firm can be ranked in a hierarchy as follows: (1) "individual bargaining" (untrammelled capitalism, profit maximization); (2) collective bargaining; and (3) codetermination. In making the transition from untrammelled capitalism to collective bargaining, one allows for the joint determination of work characteristics that are public goods to the workers, and thus eliminates some free variables. Any variable that is free under collective bargaining is also free under untrammelled capitalism, but the converse is not so. Under codetermination, the joint administration determines all the employers' free variables, by bargaining, and so eliminates yet another set of free variables. At each stage, as the hierarchy is ascended, some of the constraints on the maximization program implied by opportunism are relaxed, and so[13] the objective function cannot decrease and in general will increase. In simple terms, as we ascend the hierarchy, the effort-productivity frontier shifts outward.

What this means is that the whole set of Illyrian predictions about the impact of codetermination must be reconsidered. Suppose that an industry makes the transition from "untrammelled capitalism" to codetermination. The bargaining-power hypotheses of the last section, and the reference model, would lead us to expect increased wages, decreased effort and productivity, decreased profit, and decreased employment and output (Svejnar's second model excepted). The suboptimization theory leads us to expect increased wages, increased productivity, decreased effort (improved working conditions), and either increased or decreased profit, employment, and output, depending on the relative impact of increased wages and increased productivity. Notice that the theory permits what optimistic advocates of codetermination have asserted, that is, improvements of both productivity and working conditions. By nesting these possibilities within a theory that allows for other possibilities as well (for example, the set of variables free under collective bargaining but jointly determined under codetermination may be null) the suboptimization theory points toward a test of the optimists' hypotheses.

Notice also that the suboptimization hypothesis can be broadened to consider other forms of worker participation in management than just paritatisches Mitbestimmung (parity codetermination). It is likely that in practice, any two distinct forms of firm organization would have different commitment structures and so would in general imply different effort-productivity trade-offs. For example, consultative workers' councils with a legal right to be informed of management decisions prior to their implementation, but without veto power, could still limit employer opportunism for some dimensions of the work effort, and so relax some suboptimization constraints and improve X-efficiency. Of course, the direct implication is negative: there is no capitalist twin. However, there is also a positive implication: participation is productive. If suboptimization is indeed a significant aspect of business and labor organization, then we may expect that the more participatory form will in general be less X-efficient.

One further comment is in order. McCain (1980) uses the Illyrian assumption that workers are interested in wages but not in employment. If, as Svejnar cogently argues, workers value employment as well as wages, then another important difference between collective bargaining and codetermination emerges. Under collective bargaining, employment is a free variable controlled by the employers. Under codetermination it is jointly determined. Intuition suggests that, that being so, employment under codetermination will be systematically greater than employment under collective bargaining. However, a formal analysis of this case is lacking.

Carson's model (1977) is a generalization on all the bargaining models in a significant way. Instead of taking a joint objective function as suggested by some bargaining hypothesis, Carson assumes that the "cooperative" maximizes a Pareto-type welfare function of the utilities of all members of all classes. Thus Carson's model could reflect not only bargained outcomes, but the outcomes of any other decision process capable of generating a well-defined decision function. Carson's model also allows for consumer as well as worker participation.

Carson's model allows for different classes of members within the same organization (for example, employees, shareholders, and consumers) with different interests, and for different classes of inputs and outputs, some outputs being sold only to members, some to the general public; and some inputs being bought only from members, and some from the general public. Carson's model also allows for intramarginal (lump-sum) transfers among the members of the organization. Work by Graaff (1957) in welfare economics tells us that any set of distributional norms can be attained without loss of efficiency if lump-sum transfers are possible, but that absent lump-sum transfers, full efficiency and arbitrary distributional norms, such as equality, may not be reconcilable. This can be illustrated by figure 2-2, which is highly simplified by comparison with Carson's model, but which is adapted from Scitovsky's (1971, chapter 24) analysis of collective bargaining. The figure is set up as an Edgeworth box diagram, with I and II indifference curves for one bargainer, oriented toward origin 0_i, and 1 and 2 indifference curves for the other bargainer, oriented toward origin 0_j, and *bcdef* is the contract curve. The bargainers begin from point X_0. Suppose that d is the point on the contract curve that the distributional norms (arrived at either by

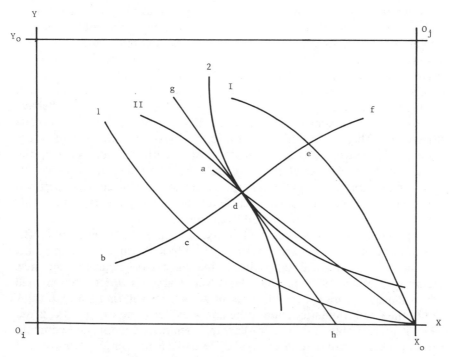

Figure 2-2. Analysis of Collective Bargaining

bargaining or by ethical reasoning) dictate, among all the points on the contract curve. Exchange between the parties at a single price, without
transfers, will not realize this outcome. For the price would have to be as
shown by line X_0a, but that is not the relative price that makes point d
mutually acceptable to the parties. The price represented by gh makes both
parties satisfied with d, but d and gh are not consistent with the original
distribution at X_0. Thus d is unattainable by exchange without a lump-sum
transfer. However, a lump-sum transfer of good X to party j, which moves
the initial endowment to h, followed by exchange at the price represented by
gh, will realize the outcome at d. If good Y is labor and good X is wage-
goods, then the transfer might be in the form of "fringe benefits" unrelated
to work time; if X is labor and Y wage goods, the transfer might take the
form of overtime rates; that is, intramarginal hours of labor might be sold
at a price lower than the marginal price, which is effectively equivalent to a
transfer of labor from the workers to the employer (Carson 1977, p. 568).

In general, efficiency and distributional objectives will be attained only
if the factors bought from members and the goods sold to members are
priced at their marginal products and costs, respectively, and the distributional difference is made up by lump-sum transfers. Thus, in effect, the
Carsonian firm acts as a profit-maximizing firm, with competitive markets
for the transactions among members, and distributes the profits (or losses)
as lump-sum payments (or membership fees) among the members. In particular, since the lump-sum transfers allow for unlimited discrimination
among the members, within as well as among classes, discrimination
between old and new members is possible. This implies that whenever the
admission of new members is Pareto-preferable, they will be admitted. In
the face of competitive markets, the Carsonian cooperative firm will behave
just as a profit-maximizer would, except that it will distribute the profits
differently. There is no Illyrian restriction of output when profits are
positive. Moreover, if some markets are imperfectly competitive, the
Carsonian firm will admit the potential victims of monopoly power as
members, expand its output and employment to the efficient (competitive)
level, and thus produce more output than the profit-maximizer would. This
Carson calls the full welfare-maximizing solution.

Of course, constraints on the lump-sum transfers can generate inefficiencies and different empirical results. The Illyrian firm is a case in point,
in that it is constrained from discriminating between current and new
members (Carson 1977, p. 578). However, Carson suspects that in real
labor-managed firms (LMFs) the present work force will find a way to carry
out optimal discrimination, admit the new members, and expand its output
when it is profitable to do so. For example, seniority benefits and compensation packages including salary-skill differentials and a large proportion of
"fringe benefits" could function as discriminatory lump-sum payments.

Formally, all these comments apply equally to codetermination and other partial forms of worker participation, though these would presumably imply different decision functions and so different patterns of lump-sum transfers.

Further, while the LMF would determine price and output exactly as would a "capitalist twin" under pure competition, it would distribute the profits differently, and this reasoning provides an empirical hypothesis about the distribution of profits. Since discrimination is a way of reconciling positive profits with efficiency, one would expect to see more of it when profits are higher, that is, the dispersion of (gross) wages would be positively associated with their level. Under worker participation, there would of course be a component of owner profit as well, and so there should presumably be a positive correlation between profit and the dispersion of the gross wage.

However, Carson (1977, p. 568) doubts the existence of the "capitalist twin." He argues that there would be differences in X-efficiency between cooperative and profit-maximizing firms. His arguments for this proposition are altogether informal and have little to do with his formal model, with one exception, and so will be deferred for now. The exception is the comment that cooperative firms would be more risk averse, since they would prevent efficient specialization in risk bearing. Here Carson seems to be arguing against his own model. If discriminatory means will be found to admit new workers, when it is profitable to do so, why would discriminatory means not be found to admit specialized risk-bearers to membership, when it is profitable to do so?[14] Anyway, if the Carsonian cooperative firm is less X-efficient, it will produce less output than an otherwise similar capitalist firm, and perhaps, in equilibrium, pay lower wages.[15]

One other formal model should be mentioned here; this is the Furubotn-Pejovich effect.[16] This is the shortening of the horizon of intertemporal planning in the case of worker ownership where the individual worker cannot appropriate the product of an investment after he or she has left the firm. In the context of worker management, Furubotn and Pejovich assume that the representative worker does not expect to remain with the firm for a period as long as the physical life of a representative capital good. Thus the representative worker will ignore the productivity of that capital good in the later period of its life, and will vote for a less-than-efficient program of investment out of retained earnings. If the worker can invest her or his income in a savings bank at a rate equal to the social marginal productivity of capital, she or he will prefer to do so, and will vote for an investment program only if the rate of return on that investment (over the foreshortened horizon) is much greater than the social marginal productivity of investment.

This is an assertion about the interests of workers in general and thus it may well apply to worker participation in general. Furubotn, Pejovich, and their epigones have asserted that it does.[17] They are mistaken in that, taking their own assumptions, the conclusion does not generalize to a simple and plausible model of codetermination, although, on the same assumptions, it would be valid of pure worker management with finance only out of retained earnings (McCain 1977a).

To explore the determinants of investment in retained earnings, at least a two-period model is required.[18] For a firm that invests out of retained earnings, shareholder dividends in period i are constrained by

$$D_i = pf(K_i, N_i) - w_iN_i - tB_i - R_i \quad \text{where } i = 0,1 \qquad (2.13)$$

where D_i is period i dividends, p the output price, f the production function, K_i and N_i the capital and labor inputs respectively in period i, B_i bonds outstanding in period i, R_i retained earnings in period i, w_i the wage paid in period i, and t the rate of interest on bonds. Without loss of generality one may assume that B_0 and R_1 are zero. Then suppose that the outcome of codetermination is determined by bargaining in such a way as to

$$\max UW \qquad (2.14)$$

where

$$W = w_0 - v + \frac{w_1 - v}{1 + s} \qquad (2.15)$$

and

$$U = D_0 + \frac{D_1}{1 + r} \qquad (2.16)$$

and r is the shareholders' rate of time preference, s is the workers' rate of time preference applicable to nonowned assets, and v is the worker's second-best alternative wage interpreted as a threat point. Thus the assumptions of this model agree with those of the simpler bargaining hypotheses above, to admit of easy comparison. A further constraint on the maximization program is

$$K_1 = K_0 + R_0 + B_1. \qquad (2.17)$$

For an interior solution, $r = t$ is required. This may reflect the owners privately optimal adjustment of their household consumption plans, which are not formally considered. Another necessary condition for an interior solution is

$$-W + \frac{W\,(p\partial f/\partial K)}{1 + r} = 0 \qquad\qquad (2.18)$$

or equivalently

$$\frac{p\partial f}{\partial K} = 1 + r \qquad\qquad (2.19)$$

Notice that the workers' rate of time preference does not enter at all into the determination of investment. Equation 2.19 reveals the formal reason why it does not: W, the workers' incremental utility, simply cancels out of the equation. The failure to construct fully specified models often leaves one open to the error of overlooking such small matters. The substantive meaning of the point is this. Equation 2.14 is a Pareto-type welfare function, so its maximum must correspond to a Pareto optimum so far as the parties to the agreement are concerned. Equation 2.19 is a necessary condition for that Pareto optimum. The same result would follow in the context of any Pareto-type decision function for a firm under worker participation in management, as Carson's analysis suggests.

Thus, the Furubotn-Pejovich effect does not in point of fact apply to worker participation in management in general, and the Texas School is mistaken in asserting that it does.[19] Indeed, it is not clear that the Furubotn-Pejovich effect applies to the worker-managed enterprise either. Carson's discussion casts it in the deepest doubt. If discrimination between present and future members is feasible, then the present members presumably can capture the full marginal product of the current investments from retained earnings by means of discriminatory payments to themselves. Ryland Taylor's revolving credit fund (1976, pp. 75-81), a proposal founded on the practice of agrarian and consumer cooperatives, enterprise bonds placed with the pension fund, and apartments supplied below cost to present members, built with a mortgage on future earnings of the workers' collective, and allocated according to seniority, are all examples of such "discriminatory" payments. The Furubotn-Pejovich effect is a formal point for which we should be alert in exploring the theory of worker participation, but it remains to be learned whether this applies to any fully specified model of worker participation in management validly based on a theory of rational action.

If it does so, then empirical implications are straightforward. Restriction of output and a less capital-intensive mode of operation for the participatory firm than for the nonparticipatory firm in comparable circumstances would be implied. The Ward-Vanek effect also implies restriction of output, and, in practice, the two models could be difficult to discriminate. A highly specified econometric model would presumably be required to discriminate between them; the data problems of such a model could well be insolvable.

Three other studies call for mention before proceeding to the informal studies. Severyn Bruyn and Litza Nicolaou-Smokovitis (1979, pp. 1-24) approach worker participation from a viewpoint of organizational psychology rather than from that of economics. Their study is not directly comparable to the economic-theoretical ones. It is not mathematically formal, but it is closely organized around a single logical concept, the psychosocial contract. The idea of the psychosocial contract is that workers meet needs other than strictly economic ones at work, and that a set of reciprocal expectations exists, between workers and employers, with respect to the meeting of those needs (Bruyn and Nicolaou 1929, p. 12, esp. footnote 1). This surely is a matter of social concern; in the economist's jargon, the social character of one's neighbors is surely a public good.

Here, however, we are concerned with empirical implications. Bruyn and Nicolaou devote considerable attention to a research plan, but as their approach is principally psychological, there is little here with direct empirical implications with which an economist can deal. However, their analysis does tend to suggest that participation may have a favorable impact on productivity. Indeed, Bruyn and Nicolaou are inspired by some evidence on that point (1979, p. 13, footnote 2). Moreover, their discussion of key variables might be helpful to economists in designing measures of partial participation for comparative studies (1979, pp. 14-17, 19).

Steinherr (1977) presents a model in which participation and profit sharing are assumed to have impacts on productivity, perhaps through some effort variable that plays no formal part in the model. Participation and profit sharing are direct arguments of the production function; also, participation is a direct argument of the utility functions of workers and managers. Participation is assumed to be measurable by a continuous variable on the interval [0, 1]. Steinherr does not assume anything about bargaining power or the objective function of the firm. Instead, he assumes only that the decisions of the firm are Pareto-optimal as among its members, and investigates properties that apply everywhere along the contract curve for managers and workers. (Since managers have unattenuated property rights in the residual, they seem to be owner-managers, though Steinherr also refers to the model as one of a managerial firm). Steinherr finds that in plausible cases, some participation and profit-sharing are optimal, but apart from that, his conclusions for comparisons are essentially the Illyrian ones.

Kleindorfer and Sertel (in Mitchell and Kleindorfer 1980, pp. 139-167) present a summary of a large series of models of labor-managed and codetermined firms with a distinctive concept of codetermination. They assume (or rather define codetermination by reference to the fact that) different classes of members of the codetermined firm set the levels of different inputs with reference to their own interests. These input levels are set noncooperatively; thus Kleindorfer and Sertel discuss Nashequilibria under various assignments of the control functions and various assumptions about profit sharing. Problems of agreement within interest groups and costs of enforcement are abstracted from (1980, p. 145, footnote 12). Output depends on capital, the number of employees, and "input" per worker. The "input" is not further defined, and while in one place it is referred to as effort (p. 159) it often seems to function more nearly as hours per worker might function. Anyway, "input" is a discommodity to the workers, and is always (bar the welfare-maximizing reference model) determined by them. Some peculiarities emerge in the model of the capitalist-managed firm. As with Furubotn's first model (and perhaps for the same reasons) workers consider employment offers only in terms of the wage, not the joint utility of the wage and "input." Moreover, the capitalist-managed firm pays a wage per unit of input (as it must, since by definition it does not share profits, and otherwise the workers would have no incentive to supply any "input"). A simplifying assumption is that the rate of pay per unit of input is linear and homogenous: that is, there are no intramarginal transfer (Carson) nor overtime wages, fringe benefits unrelated to hours worked, or such. This implies that the capitalist-managed firm will allocate an inefficiently small amount of "input," since the firm is, in effect, a monopsonist in the extraction of "input" from its own work force. This conclusion may depend sensitively on the assumption of the linear homogenous payment schedule, though there is no formal analysis of other payments schedules to which to refer to verify this conjecture. In the light of that open question, one might want to treat the comparisons of the capitalist-managed firm to other forms as tentative. Kleindorfer and Sertel also consider a worker-public codetermination in which the capital input is determined by a welfare-maximizing public official.

With some qualifications, the empirical implications are the Illyrian ones, in dilute form, once again. One qualification is that the worker-public codetermination case is less restrictionist than the worker-capitalist codetermination case and is comparable with the capitalist-managed case, which generally is less restrictionist than worker-capitalist codetermination or labor management. Where there is profit sharing, reduction of the labor share increases restrictiveness. All this is in the context of nonregulated natural monopoly, and as Vanek (1970) shows, monopoly is a particularly unfavorable case for the worker-managed enterprise. Kleindorfer and Sertel then consider the prospects for regulation of the natural monopoly, and find that the worker-public codetermined firm under effective price regulation will be less restrictive than it would be without regulation, and can be so regulated as to attain the efficient (welfare-maximizing) outcome.

What these various models seem to convey is that there is a wide variety of assumptions on which one can found a theory of worker participation in management, but the variety of conclusions is less wide. Many models support the conclusion that the participatory firm is simply intermediate between the Illyrian firm and the capitalist firm. Several suggest that the two kinds of firms may not face the same effort-productivity trade-off. If this difference favors the capitalist firm, it will tend to exaggerate the Illyrian restrictionism of the participatory firm; if it favors the participatory firm, it would offset it. In either case it might be expected to create observable differences in productivity. However, the Illyrian restrictionism itself depends on a narrow conception of worker goals (Svejnar) or on the absence of intramarginal transfers (Carson). There are plausible grounds for doubting that it will occur in any case.

Some Hypotheses from Informal Studies

This section will consider several strands of reasoning from ordinary-language studies of participation or from "common sense," which may or may not be distinct from the foregoing. Since ordinary language and "common sense" are elastic, some dispute may be possible as to the actual empirical implications of these hypotheses, or as to their proper interpretation. In many cases one can only state one's own interpretation of the comments of others; however, in some cases the empirical implications are clearly stated by the authors. Sources for such hypotheses include the discussion of statistical studies under way, in which empirical implications must be clearly stated, even if the theories themselves are not; obiter dicta in studies mainly concerned with other and more formal theory, and the work of theorists whose primary mode of reasoning is ordinary language.

There are, I think, two simple ordinary-language hypotheses about the relationship of participation to productivity. One we might call the "mice will play" theory. This we find, for example, in Carson (1977, p. 584). The hypothesis is that, since under participation both decision making and profits are widely shared among the workers (so far as they are shared at all), no one worker will gain very much from improved productivity. Thus, any dilution of the employer's authority and control will lead to X-inefficiency.

The opposite theory we might call the "working for themselves" theory, and we find a good statement of it in Cable and Fitzroy (1980a, pp. 101-102). In its more naive "common sense" form, this would hold that the workers in a participatory firm will work harder because they are working for themselves, not for somebody else, at least to some degree (McCain 1973a). Of course, in this form it is immediately subject to the rejoinder implicit in the "mice will play" hypothesis foregoing: The rewards of higher productivity are widely shared, but the costs in the form of individual effort are borne by the individual, and this is classically the condition for shirking. However, the rejoinder misconceives the point. We may grant that the increase of productivity resulting from one worker's increase of effort will be small, and that the individual worker's share of that incremental productivity will be a small proportion of it. Thus no one worker has an incentive to spontaneously make an optimum effort. However, even if worker A's share of the profit from an effort increase by one worker is not as great as the cost of that effort, it may be greater than the cost, to worker A, of reporting worker B's shirking, so that participation can bring about horizontal monitoring (Cable and Fitzroy 1980, p. 103). Moreover, informal social pressures within the working group can enforce activity in the group interest (Olson 1965) and under participation these may be mobilized for increased productivity, while absent participation they are likely to be mobilized against "rate-busters," that is, to limit productivity and so prevent layoffs. Indeed, the cost of reporting another employee's shirking probably depends more on informal social pressures than on anything else, another reason why it cannot be mobilized by the "untrammelled capitalist" firm.

One might also call on the reasoning offered by Brown and Medoff (1978, pp. 357-359) to explain the apparent productivity advantage of union-organized as against unorganized firms, as Svejnar does in his study in this volume. Those advantages may be even more fully realized with codetermination. Finally, Cable and Fitzroy argue, the existence of firm-specific human capital, and the fact that job definitions and similar managerial decisions have redistributive impact, imply the possibility of employer opportunism. By limiting this opportunism, participation can create an atmosphere of trust within which improved work organization can be more flexibly introduced. Some aspects of the opportunism problem were, of course, formalized in McCain's (1980) suboptimization hypothesis.

Each of these hypotheses implies differential X-efficiency as between participatory and nonparticipatory firms. That such differentials have implications for employment and output has already been mentioned in the previous section. Cable and Fitzroy estimate production functions, with an index of participativeness included as one independent variable. The empirical implication of their hypothesis is that participativeness would have a positive "marginal productivity."[20] Moreover, cross-sectional studies across industries with different degrees and kinds of participation, and time-series studies encompassing periods characterized by different degrees and kinds of participation, might be expected to show similar correlations of participation with productivity. This is the beginning-point for Svejnar's study in this volume.

Reference has already been made to the property-rights, or Texas, school of thought. The central doctrine of this school is informal and perhaps not susceptible of formalization. In respect of participation, it is this: under "untrammelled capitalism" the owners of a firm have unattenuated property rights in the capital of that firm. This is a necessary condition for efficiency. Any corporate form prescribed by any public authority, including participative ones, attenuates the owners' property right to organize as they may will, and so must be inefficient and undesirable.[21] Simply considered, this is a normative and not an empirical proposition, but the Texas School makes the normative-to-positive leap in its most naive and Panglossian form, supposing that whatever is must be socially optimal. There is an argument for this (Furubotn and Pejovich, 1974, p. 5), but it is quite fallacious, being firmly founded on the confusion of "Pareto optimal" with "Pareto preferable."[22] This form of reasoning leads the Texas School to conclude that the participatory firm must be inferior in inefficiency to the unfettered capitalist firm, except in those few cases where it is spontaneously adopted by the owners (Jensen and Meckling, 1979, p. 503). This would be an empirical implication if it followed validly from the theory, but it does not do so.

The members of the Texas School also offer any number of arguments for the preferability of the untrammelled capitalist firm that have nothing necessarily to do with property rights (Gallaway in Pejovich (ed.) 1978, pp. 175-176). Some of these, being formal, have already been discussed and their validity assessed. Gallaway offers a potpourri of comments, which, although decorated with the outward stigmata of mathematical economics, are informal and unconnected. His comments are generally restatements of results stressed by others, including the Illyrian theorists, having to do with increased capital-labor ratios, reduced saving ratios, and their consequences. Gallaway's contribution to all this is a series of equations based on the assumption of Cobb-Douglas production functions.

Jensen and Meckling offer a list of five "flaws" of the labor-managed firm (1979, p. 485) that, they assert (1979, p. 503), carry over to participation. Two have already been dealt with: the horizon problem and the "common-property" problem.[23] The impossibility of pure rental refers to a critique of the Ward-Vanek theory of the purely externally financed firm. Jensen and Meckling assert that intangible capital goods cannot be rented, and that that means that the Ward-Vanek theory must be wrong and so that the worker-managed (or participatory) firm must be inefficient. Here we see a confusion of necessary with sufficient conditions. The rental of capital goods is a sufficient condition: the necessary condition is that the cooperative's net worth be zero. Surely liabilities may be set against intangible as well as tangible assets on an enterprise's balance sheet.

The control problem is simply the problem of making collective decisions and enforcing them. Jensen and Meckling point out that this is a political problem, and thus they decline to say anything about it, except that it is a problem (Jensen and Meckling 1979, p. 488).

The nontransferability problem has to do with monitoring and finance. As Alchian and Demsetz (1972, pp. 777-795) point out, a condition for efficient monitoring is that the ultimate supervisor be the residual claimant. However, the residual claimant must also bear the residual risk (McCain 1981, chapter 15). Since the residual claimant may be risk averse, both efficient monitoring and efficient allocation of risk cannot be achieved simultaneously in a world of uncertainty (and neither problem arises at all in a world of certainty). Nothing whatever is known about the socially optimal trade-off between monitoring and risk allocation, and little enough about privately optimal trade-offs (Markusen 1978, pp. 405-410). Jensen and Meckling, quoting Dréze (1976, pp. 1125-1139) on this topic, make it out to be an argument against worker participation. Now this problem applies equally under "untrammelled capitalism." Jensen and Meckling assert that it does not arise there because the capitalist owners may sell their claims, and thus capture the discounted present value of increases of efficiency that result from better monitoring, while the employees cannot. However, that misconceives the problem. The problem is not with cashing in the gains, but with extracting them in the first place. Markusen (1978) has shown that the ultimate supervisor must receive 100 percent of the residual value created by the firm, for fully efficient monitoring. But that means the ultimate supervisor must also bear 100 percent of the risk, and any insurance of that risk whatever will dilute the incentive to monitor. This is true regardless of who monitors: the general assembly of the workers, or the capitalist owner. Precisely to the extent that the capitalist owner can insure by diversifying his portfolio, we would expect less monitoring and less X-efficiency under "untrammelled capitalism" than under participation. While this may be socially efficient the empirical implication will be the same in either case. Perhaps this supports Dréze's conjecture that codetermination is the optimum regime.

This sampling may serve to indicate that the Texas School doctrine is a purely polemical doctrine that, whatever its normative merits, has no empirical implications whatever.

Conclusion

Although the formal literature of economic theory of worker participation in management is small, it does contain a number of implications with respect to matters of fact. Of course differing hypotheses yield different implications. These implications center around factor-neutral efficiency (or X-efficiency), employment, output, and labor incomes. In principle, they admit of empirical test, often by standard econometric methods, although most of this work remains to be done. Discussions of informal hypotheses in the literature are less scarce, but, excepting the Texas School literature, less diverse. Again excepting the Texas School literature, these informal hypotheses are quite straightforward and amenable to empirical test. By contrast, the Texas School (so-called property-rights) literature is so inchoate and polemical in nature that it does not admit of any empirical implications that would distinguish it from the other bodies of literature on worker participation.

Notes

1. On the history and institutional background of the Montan-industrie, see Hallet (1973) and Moore (1978). For comparative studies see Bellas (1972), Bernstein (1976), and several studies in this volume.

2. See Furubotn (1978), McCain (1980), Svejnar (1977, 1980a, and 1982), and Aoki (1980). Aspects of McCain's reference model are also discussed in McCain (1973a,b). On bargaining in Svejnar's theory see Svejnar (1980b). For more general studies see Carson (1977), Furubotn and Pejovich (1974), Pejovich (in Pejovich (ed.), 1978), Gallaway (in Pejovich (ed.), 1978), and Jensen and Meckling (1979).

3. Notice that while an equality constraint would be acceptable in the case of capitalism, any of the other forms may choose to pay a wage above the alternative cost of labor, so the constraint must be treated as a lower bound of the wage to be paid. Domar (1966) seems to miss this point.

4. On the supply constraint see Domar (1966).

5. I am indebted to my colleague Paul Rappoport for pointing out the shortcomings of this model. For some flavor of the journalistic discussions of codetermination, see various articles in the *Economist* between November 1975 and February 1977.

6. See various *Economist* articles for examples and Jones's (1977) survey for further discussion of the point.

7. Svejnar also assumes that the rate of profits is maximized, rather than absolute profit. In the long run that means that capital input would also be inefficiently restricted, and the same is true of management. They would not be restricted to the same degree but to a greater or lesser degree depending upon the bargaining power of the three parties.

8. Note that Aoki (1980, p. 600) does not assert that there is any difference between codetermination and collective bargaining and he says that his model is a model of both, and also of conciliatory adjudication by the managers as in Japan.

9. For an earlier use of this device see McCain (1973b); for a more systematic discussion see McCain (1981, chapter 13).

10. See Lange (1942, pp. 215-228).

11. See McCain (1973b) and McCain (1981, chapter 13).

12. But compare Brown and Medoff (1978, pp. 355-378).

13. By the generalized Le Chatelier principle. See Samuelson (1965, pp. 36-39).

14. Compare Vanek (1977, pp. 213-231) and McCain (1977a).

15. Given the central role of the firm's objective function in this study and in the bargaining theory-based studies, some recent work in estimating the revealed preferences of government bureaucracies may be of interest. Perhaps the techniques used in those studies can be adapted to the participatory firm (or indeed to the firm under collective bargaining, or to the "untrammelled capitalist" firm if one can be found) and thus shed some empirical light on the objective functions of these organizations as well. See MacFadden (1975) and Barton (1979).

16. The term is from McCain (1973a); see Furubotn and Pejovich (eds.) (1974).

17. See Pejovich (ed.) (1978, p. 19); Furubotn (1978, pp. 153-154); Gallaway (in Pejovich 1978, p. 158); and Jensen and Meckling (1979, pp. 469-506).

18. The model sketched here owes something to McCain (1977a).

19. Compare Jensen and Meckling (1979, p. 483), footnote 16.

20. For similarly conceived earlier studies see Bellas (1972), Bernstein (1976), and Jones and Backus (1977).

21. Furubotn and Pejovich (1974, p. 7, 230, 274-275); Pejovich (ed.) (1978, p. 18); Furubotn (1978, pp. 158-159); and Jensen and Meckling (1979, p. 474).

22. For a discussion see Graaff (1957).

23. This is the Illyrian restriction of employment, though Jensen and Meckling do not cite the Illyrian literature on this point.

24. Compare McCain (1977a, p. 376).

3

Issues in Assessing the Comparative Productivity of Worker-Managed and Participatory Firms in Capitalist Societies

Henry Levin

A number of recent studies have suggested that firms with high levels of worker participation in decision making tend to have higher levels of productivity than conventional capitalist firms. The issues underlying such comparisons are complex, and in this paper I wish to explore them.

Two types of literature on the relation between participation and productivity exist. The first set of literature tends to examine productivity and the degree of worker participation among firms that have established participative practices (Cable and Fitzroy, 1980a, 1980b; Espinosa and Zimbalist 1978; and Jones and Backus 1977). These studies seek to determine how increases in worker participation are associated with higher productivity of enterprises among firms that have adopted substantial worker participation in decisions. They suggest that higher levels of participation among such firms are associated with higher levels of productivity.

A second literature tries to ascertain the degree to which firms that practice worker participation show differences in productivity relative to those with more conventional managerial practices. This literature includes various surveys of studies of productivity between firms with worker participation and those without such participation (for example, Blumberg 1968; Frieden 1980; U.S. DHEW 1973; and Zwerdling 1978) as well as between producer cooperatives (PCs) and their capitalist counterparts (Bellas 1972; Greenberg 1978; Jones 1979; Jones and Backus 1977; Levin 1980b, 1981; and Thomas and Logan 1980). These studies suggest considerable preliminary evidence that firms with a high degree of worker ownership and involvement in decision making show higher productivity than their more conventional counterparts.[1]

Neoclassical economists have been skeptical of such claims on purely theoretical grounds. For example, property-rights theorists have assumed that cooperative, labor-managed, and other participative firms must necessarily face the same production possibilities as capitalist firms. They have then gone on to argue that the labor bias will prevent Pareto-optimal

The author appreciates the suggestions of the editors and Michael Reich on an earlier draft.

production decisions, and they argue a priori against the possibility that labor-managed firms (LMFs) will be efficient (Jensen and Meckling 1979). Stiglitz (1975) even argues that a hierarchy of managerial control and worker compulsion on behalf of capital is actually desired by workers because it prevents fellow workers from shirking and thus provides a larger product and higher wages for all workers. It has also been argued that existing forms of capitalist hierarchy tend to be more efficient than other forms of work organization because of the lower information and transaction costs of getting worker compliance in the former (Alchian and Demsetz 1972).[2]

But, of course, what is ignored in such a priori arguments is the fact that workers in a worker-managed and worker-owned firm have strong incentives to monitor their fellow workers to make certain that they are not shirking, a phenomenon that is lacking in the capitalist firm (Levin 1980a, 1980b). In the capitalist firm the incentives to shirk are implicit in a wage contract that pays only for the time of the worker rather than for the worker's product. Accordingly, the shirker will minimize his work effort unless he is being observed by a supervisor. In the cooperative and LMF, the economic returns to workers will depend heavily on the collective success of the firm. Thus, workers in the latter firm will tend to reinforce the productivity and work efforts of their colleagues through both collegial support as well as peer pressures, and there are powerful forms of social sanction and disapproval for members who are not putting in a maximum effort.

Indeed, studies of PCs have found a number of ways in which they differ from conventional firms and provide bases for higher productivity (Levin 1980, 1981; Bradley and Gelb 1981). Of central relevance are the incentives for workers to contribute to the success of the firm. Since the workers own their own enterprises, they will share in the prosperity or failure of the collective entity. This feature provides enormous personal incentives to be productive as well as to create peer pressures on colleagues in these directions. Further, it contributes to low rates of worker turnover and absenteeism relative to capitalist firms, reducing the costs associated with these phenomena.

In addition, higher productivity seems to derive from reduced needs for supervisory and quality-control personnel, for workers have incentives to produce a good product. One recent study found that while cooperative plywood manufacturers in the United States used only one or two supervisors per shift, the comparable capitalist firms used six or seven (Greenberg 1978). A mill that had recently been converted from cooperative to capitalist ownership quadrupled the number of line supervisors and foremen. Other organizational reasons for higher productivity among cooperatives and LMFs are strong incentives for training members for a variety of work roles so that production bottlenecks are avoided and worker interest is enhanced; more efficient training arrangements in which workers instruct colleagues as a natural and continuing part of the work process; solicitation and utilization of worker-contributed ideas for improving the operations of the enterprise; and the tendency for workers to take much better care of their tools and equipment, prolonging the life and the usefulness of these implements.

Although there is an empirical basis for claims that participative firms generally and worker-owned and -managed firms specifically tend to be more productive than conventional capitalist firms and there is also some observations of differences in incentives and organizational features that support these claims, there is an increasing need to provide systematic evidence on these matters. The purpose of this chapter is to suggest some conceptual and empirical issues that must be addressed in making productivity comparisons between worker-managed and capitalist firms. In much of the existing literature on this subject, these issues are ignored. Yet, the unambiguous interpretation of productivity comparisons will require that they be addressed directly. More specifically, three broad classes of issues will be raised. First, what concepts of productivity and participation underlie the comparisons? Second, how should one choose firms for such comparisons, and what intrinsic biases are evident in that selection? And, third, what accounting issues arise in the comparisons?

One difficulty faced in assessing such comparisons is created by the widely different situations that are found under the terminology of worker participation, worker control, and industrial democracy. Typically these vary from management consultation with advisory councils of workers, worker representatives on boards of directors (codetermination), and profit sharing to full worker ownership and democratic management through direct participation in shop-floor decisions and worker election of managers or boards of trustees (Jenkins 1974; Zwerdling 1978). Clearly one would expect different results among different types of LMFs, a fact that mitigates against generalizations about the comparative productivity of such firms. Much of the discussion that follows will be based on comparisons between pure LMFs or PCs and capitalist firms. The former enterprises are characterized by full worker ownership and democratic forms of worker control. The latter are characterized by external ownership of the firm and the management of the firm according to the dictates of capital, with wage-labor being hired to carry out those imperatives. However, there are many types of possible arrangements between these two extremes, including capitalist firms with profit-sharing plans and limited forms of worker participation as well as LMFs that hire some wage-labor. Although most of the analysis will focus on the comparison between the two ends of the spectrum, much of the discussion will also have relevance to enterprises that fall between these two extremes.

Concepts of Productivity and Participation

Economists view productivity as deriving from the efficiency with which the firm uses its resources to produce market outputs. A firm is considered to be technically efficient if it derives the largest possible output for any given level of resource inputs; that is, if it is on its efficiency frontier (Farrell 1957). Further, firms can be ranked according to their technical efficiency or total factor productivity by comparing the amounts of output that they can produce for any given level of inputs. It is possible to rank productive organizations on a Farrell-type index where a value of 100 is given for firms that are maximally efficient or on their production frontiers, and values of less than 100 are given for less productive firms. Theoretically, then, it might be possible to rank labor-managed and conventional capitalist firms on such a scale to see which ones seem to be most productive.

However, such a technique for assessing productivity on the basis of technical efficiency presumes a well-defined output that can be represented by a single metric. Thus, it is possible to compare the amount of a particular commodity that can be produced by each of two firms with different modes of organization and similar resources. However, once one moves to the multiproduct case, the issue becomes more complicated (Pfouts 1961). In such a case one cannot simply compare productive efficiency for the conversion of inputs into a single output. Somehow it is necessary to set out a value function or set of prices that enable one to create a measure of output that can summarize in a single index the value of different combinations of outputs produced by different firms.

When all outputs have market prices, this problem is solved by evaluating output according to its market value. But this assumes that the objective function is similar between participative and nonparticipative firms. In the case of worker participation at least one of the outputs of the firm will be the value to the workers of participating in the decisions of the firm rather than being objects of compulsion by their managers. The implications of this become clearer with the following example.

Let us assume that both capitalist firms and LMFs have a production function as in equation 3.1:

$$(Y_1, \ Y_2) = f(X_1, \ X_2). \qquad (3.1)$$

Each firm is producing two outputs, a commodity or market output, Y_1, and a nonmarket output that we will call worker participation, Y_2. X_1 represents the input of labor and X_2 the other inputs. Further, assume that each worker will receive some share of each of these outputs so that the amounts received of each will simply be positive functions of the amount of the market output and the nonmarket output that are produced.

Each worker has a utility function (equation 3.2):

$$U_j = g(W_1, W_2) \qquad\qquad (3.2)$$

This utility function is composed of two arguments, the pecuniary income W_1 received from the worker's share of production of the commodity output Y_1, and the nonpecuniary income or satisfaction received from worker participation W_2.

Now let us assume that there are two types of firms in the world, those that practice rather traditional forms of managerial control and those that sponsor a significant degree of worker control. Workers are able to choose between these two types of firms according to the priorities between the two forms of income W_1 and W_2. Figure 3-1 shows this situation graphically. For a given level of resources, a firm faces the product transformation curve AA'. It is clear from the shape of the curve that the greater degree of worker participation that the firm practices, the smaller the amount of market output that can be produced. But, what is extremely important to note is that any point on AA' is on the production frontier. That is, movements along the curve reflect only different combinations of Y_1, Y_2. From the point of view of technical efficiency, all points on AA' are equally efficient.

Now assume that there are two types of workers, B_0 and B_1. B_0 has a very high priority for pecuniary income relative to worker participation, while B_1 would prefer relatively more worker participation while trading off pecuniary income in his utility function. Each one chooses an appropriate firm. B_0 chooses a firm that produces a relatively large amount of market output and a relatively small amount of worker participation at point E on the product-transformation schedule. B_1 chooses a firm with considerably lower market output and a high degree of worker participation at point F on the product-transformation schedule AA'. Not only is each individual working for an efficient firm, but the fact that each can choose the firm that meets his needs results in a Pareto optimum with respect to social welfare. This can be seen clearly if one assumes that B_1 were forced to choose the firm with the higher relative output of commodities Y_1 for greater pecuniary income. Such a choice would place B_1 on a lower indifference curve, B_2 that intersects point E on the product-transformation schedule. If both workers were forced to work in the same situation, total social welfare would be lower. Thus, from the perspectives of both technical efficiency and social-welfare efficiency, the choice of firm E for B_0 and of firm F for B_1 would be optimal.

However, most studies of productivity or productive efficiency do not take account of nonmarket ouputs. Rather, they measure only the production of market commodities. This must necessarily discriminate against firms that produce nonmarket outputs, especially when nonmarket outputs are highly valued by the workers so that they are willing to sacrifice

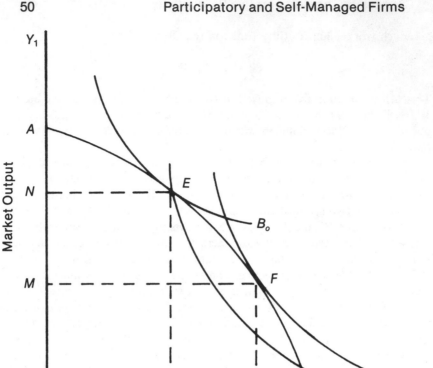

Figure 3-1. Production Frontier with Trade-offs between Worker Participation and Market Output

pecuniary income to obtain such nonpecuniary results. For example, if only the production of market output Y_1 is measured in comparative studies of productivity between conventional capitalist firms and LMFs, firm E with its traditional management will be found to be far more productive than firm F with its worker participation. With the same resources, firm E will be found to produce *ON* of output Y_1, which is about twice as much as the *OM* that is produced by firm F. Such a study would conclude that the conventional firm is far more productive than the LMF, a conclusion that would be erroneous when other outputs were taken into account. Indeed, both firms are on the same production frontier.

On the basis of this analysis, it becomes obvious that as long as both participative and nonparticipative firms are situated on the same production frontier in which participation and market outputs compete for the resources of the firm, the restriction of output measures to the market output will always understate the total output of the participative firm. From the perspective of social efficiency, both outputs ought to be taken into account, particularly if workers are willing to relinquish pecuniary income for the psychic benefits of greater participation. Of course, if the latter is true, the costs of the labor input will be lower in the participative firm; and this may compensate for the lower output of market commodities. But if the analysis is limited only to measures of technical efficiency, comparing physical inputs and market outputs, an important nonmarket output of the labor-managed firm will be ignored in productivity comparisons.[1]

Under what conditions would it be possible to find that the LMF provided not only the higher psychic outputs and incomes for workers, but also higher market output as well for any given level of resource inputs? Essentially, this is the case of complementary outputs, in which worker participation actually leads to a larger output of the market good. It is the case that has been argued in the previous literature, which suggests that worker control of production is more efficient in the use of resources for producing market outputs than more conventional forms of enterprise, and which is reflected in figure 3-2.

Based upon a reasonable interpretation of what seems to be known about the relation between worker participation and productivity, product-transformation schedule AA' suggests that there are three distinct relations.[4] At relatively low levels of participation, there is simply no effect on the production of market output Y_1. These minimally participative schemes are ones that are typically adopted by capitalist firms with the hope that traditional managerial prerogatives can be retained while increasing worker participation through advisory councils and worker representatives on corporate boards.[5] The actual control of the work setting is remarkably invariant, and so is the productivity of the firm within this minimal range of participation, OM'.

But as the degree of worker participation increases over the range $M'N'$, additional increments of the market output are also increasing. These types of worker participation may vary from worker councils with decision authority to firms that are fully worker-owned and worker-managed, but with heavy reliance on elected managers and representative democracy.[6] As workers have larger and larger intrinsic and extrinsic incentives to provide a high level of work effort and to work efficiently from an organizational perspective, the market output of the firm also rises.

However, once the worker participation level N' is reached, participation beyond this point can be accomplished only with a sacrifice of market output. This level may entail a much higher degree of direct participation in decisions and worker meetings, reducing the amount of time left for the work to be performed. Finally, as A' is approached the participation level

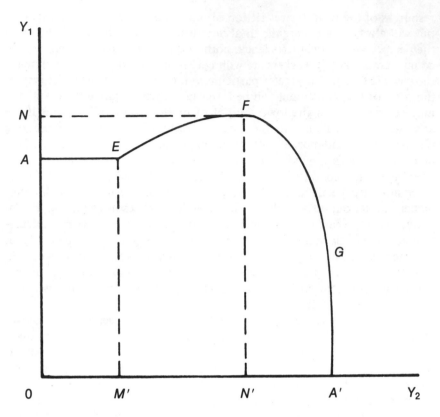

Figure 3-2. Production Frontier with Worker Participation Associated with Constant, Increasing, and Decreasing Levels of Market Output

becomes anarchistic, with drastic reduction in the amount of market output that will be produced. This represents an "irrational" range of production in that a small increase in worker participation will be associated with a precipitous decline in market ouptut and pecuniary income.[7]

If figure 3-2 represents a reasonable picture of the probable relations between worker participation and market output, one would obtain the following comparative results. A firm with no worker participation at point *A* would show about the same productivity with regard to the market output as a firm with modest levels of worker participation at point *E*. However, when firms at point *E* were compared with those at point *F*, there would be a rather strong effect of worker participation on productivity with respect to the market output. Comparisons of firms at *F* with those on the *FA'* segment of the transformation frontier would show a negative effect of worker participation on market output, with particularly profound trade-offs between G and A'.

The consequences of figure 3-2 are that comparisons between firms with different degrees of worker participation on their production of market outputs will depend crucially on the nature of the comparison. Comparisons between traditional capitalist firms and those with only modest attempts at worker participation may show no effects, while those of traditional and low-participation firms with LMFs may show rather large differences in market output in favor of the latter. However, at the highest stages of worker involvement there may be a decline in market outputs as workers are willing to trade off pecuniary income for the higher level of direct satisfaction created by their fuller participation.

Accordingly, studies of labor participation should be very careful to specify the nature of participation along various spectra that characterize the firms that are being compared. Obviously, the two major dimensions that must be considered are the nature and distribution of ownership of the firm among workers, and the nature and distribution of decision processes and powers. Fortunately, there has been major work considering the conceptualization and measurement of some of these issues (Bernstein 1976). But, most emphatically, comparative studies of traditional capitalist firms with PCs or other forms of labor-managed and participative firms should be explicit about the nature of the comparison with respect to the issues reflected in figure 3-2, and generalization across the range of worker control is probably not possible and may be highly misleading.

Choice of Firms for Comparison

In general, one would wish to compare the productivity of one form of organization with another, holding constant such factors as the nature of the product, market prices, and the external environment in which the firms must operate. That is, one would attempt to determine if the fact of worker control and participation, in themselves, alter the way in which the firm operates and the efficiency with which it uses its resources. The comparative situation can be seen more clearly if one draws an analogy with an experimental situation. According to this experiment, cooperative or labor-managed and traditional capitalist forms of organization would represent experimental treatments applied to productive enterprises to see which provides higher productivity. That is, one would wish to compare firms with identical resources and products in the same geographical areas. Such firms would be established only for purposes of the experiment, and they would be assigned randomly to the labor-managed or traditional mode of organization. Employees might be randomly allocated to firms according to skill needs, or one might permit self-selection in hiring according to the nature of the experiment.

There are two major difficulties with following through on the experimental analogy. First, the firms that we are able to observe were not established according to random assignment, but according to the specific historical forces that brought the firms into being. This means that there may be special factors determining the origin of each type of firm, and these may be confounded with their productivities. This is likely to be especially serious if LMFs are found predominantly among enterprises that are purchased by their workers as a last resort to maintain employment, after the capitalist owners have decided to terminate production and close the firms. That is, if LMFs are typically a product of worker takeovers of failing capitalist firms, a comparison of productivity will hardly be valid.

A second difficulty with the experimental analogy is the presumption of neutrality in the relation of the environments with respect to labor-managed versus conventional forms of enterprise. That is, if we are to compare the intrinsic merits of two modes of organization with respect to their productivity, it is important to separate out external factors that may impinge upon their performance. Yet, there is reason to believe that the treatment of traditional capitalist organizations by government, the financial community, and other social institutions is more supportive than the treatment of LMFs. For these two reasons, a comparison between the two forms of enterprise will tend to be biased against the labor-managed or highly participative firm. Let us explore these reasons in greater detail as well as their consequences.

Conditions under Which Labor-Managed Firms Are Established

What types of firms are likely to be labor-owned and -managed or to have a high degree of worker participation? Studies of worker-owned and -managed firms in the advanced capitalist societies suggest that in many cases the worker-owned and -managed firms arose as a response to a threatened closure of an enterprise or to other forms of employment insecurity.[8] The Basque cooperatives in Mondragon, Spain were a response to the poor economic opportunities in the Basque region created by the repressionist policies in postwar Spain under Franco (Thomas and Logan 1980). The plywood cooperatives of the U.S. Pacific Northwest were initiated in order to minimize the employment instabilities associated with the vicissitudes of the construction industry (Berman 1967). The Meriden Triumph Motorcycle Cooperative in Meriden, England was a worker response to the decision by a parent conglomerate to shut down what the workers believed was a viable enterprise (Carnoy and Levin 1976). This has also been true of Rath Meatpacking Co. (Gunn 1980), and most of the other documented cases in which workers have purchased their firms (Stern et al. 1979).

But capitalist owners do not close down firms that are highly profitable. At the very least, profits are below those that can be obtained by selling off the plant and equipment and investing these elsewhere while taking advantage of tax laws that make such an action profitable to a conglomerate. Most likely the parent enterprise has been disinvesting for a considerable time before the closure decision is announced. Typical actions include allowing capital to deteriorate and depreciate, ignoring research and development, draining away liquid assets for other endeavors, ignoring labor relations, and making long-range arrangements to shift production to other plants (in the event that production will be cheaper elsewhere), often in Asia and other third-world countries (Bluestone et al. 1981; Bluestone and Harrison 1980).

Indeed, one of the reasons that the workers are able to succeed in purchasing such firms is because other potential investors do not view them as profitable. Future viability may be demonstrably poor by virtue of all of the "disinvestment" that has taken place as well as a purchase price that is far greater than the economic worth of the capital (Bluestone and Harrison 1980; Gunn 1980; Carnoy and Levin 1976). But when workers are faced with a last-ditch effort to save their employment, they will tend to place a greater faith in their willingness to work hard and make the firm survive than might be justified by the hard data. Essentially, they will be taking responsibility for an entity that has been abandoned by its capitalist owners, who can obtain higher returns by investing elsewhere. Thus, many firms that are converted to worker ownership and management as a way of avoiding closure and unemployment are likely to be the most marginal of enterprises by the very circumstances under which labor management and ownership arise.

Even those firms that practice substantial worker participation under capitalist ownership may have similar properties. Again, one must ask under what conditions capitalist firms would increase the degree of worker control or participation in decision making. With the exception of those rare cases in which the capitalist owners and managers are motivated for purely humane reasons, it is likely that such reforms represent a way of improving productivity and reducing costs where these have been a persistent problem. That is, companies with the most serious productivity problems are the most likely to transfer some control to their employees, with the hope that this will increase output, product quality, and overall worker productivity while reducing worker turnover and absenteeism. A well-known case in which this was clearly the motive is the Volvo plant in Kalmar, Sweden (Gyllenhammar 1977).

Thus, the question of whether firms are worker-managed and participative or are based upon more traditional forms of capitalist organization is hardly determined by random influences. The conditions under which LMFs such as PCs or highly participative capitalist firms are established are likely to be ones in which low productivity or poor economic results were the driving forces that led to changes in ownership or work organization. The result is that comparative studies of productivity must somehow attempt to choose LMFs for comparison that were not established under these circumstances, or that overcame them in the quest for longer-run survival. Alternatively, the comparison might be one of assessing productivity both "before" and "after" the onset of worker management to ascertain the effects of changes in the organization of production, alone, on productivity. However, the "before" and "after" design suffers from the difficulties of controlling for changes over time in external factors that affect performance. Moreover, the external environment itself is not neutral between the two types of firms, a fact that leads to a second problem in making comparisons.

Bias and the External Environment

By external environment I refer to the existing forms of legal structures, access to capital, management training, education, and other institutions that serve to support the functioning of productive organizations. Every society promotes, both explicitly and tacitly, particular forms of productive organizations, while ignoring or even posing obstacles for the development of other types. At the extreme, socialist societies and capitalist societies sponsor schools, financial institutions, and laws for reproducing and sustaining forms of enterprise that are unique to those societies rather than attempting to create a "neutral" environment that would be supportive of any type of productive organization.

In a capitalist society, the supportive institutions have evolved to respond to the needs of capitalist enterprise, rather than worker-owned and worker-managed ones. As examples, matters of tax treatment, liability under the law, eligibility for government assistance, and social-insurance provisions are factors that may differently affect different organizational forms. The legal status of collective property is also an important issue in the case of labor-managed and labor-owned firms. However, the laws affecting these matters have never been established to accommodate LMFs. The result is that existing laws often conflict with the basic operational principles of such firms, while providing a more appropriate legal basis for the establishment and operation of capitalist firms (Ellerman 1980).

Access to financial capital has also been a matter in which the more traditional firm has been favored by financial insitutions. In addition to the possibility of outright discrimination against labor-managed and -owned firms, there are a number of reasons. Until very recently, most government programs such as the Small Business Administration would not lend to PCs. The financial community also prefers some measure of control over firms that it lends to, control that is easier to achieve over capitalist firms than labor-managed and labor-owned ones. Instead of transacting business with a proprietor, executive, or the officers and board of a corporate entity, lending institutions must deal in the labor-owned and -managed firm either with managers who are removable by the workers or boards that are elected by the workers. Indeed, members of the financial community are often elected to corporate boards to cement relations with financial institutions. Under such circumstances, the personal and institutional connections that can be established by capitalist firms and their managers with financial entities is difficult to establish for worker-run firms where there exist the possibilities of democratic changes in management. Further, the possibility of using the assets of the labor-owned and -managed firm for collateral is typically proscribed in the case where only workers may be owners. All these factors represent obstacles to obtaining capital for the LMF, even for short-term loans to cover temporary rises in inventories or seasonal cash-flow difficulties.

Likewise, the educational system and work experience in capitalist firms do not prepare workers for labor-managed workplaces (Gamson and Levin 1980). Participative problem-solving, decision-making, and work relations must be learned through experience in democratic organizations as well as training in cooperative settings. Existing schools and workplaces emphasize highly individualistic and competitive orientations, personality factors that can represent obstacles to participative and democratic functioning. The ability to participate democratically in the work setting is unlikely to be created by schools that function in a strictly hierarchical fashion where rules, regulations, and bureaucratic control characterize the learning and social process (Bowles and Gintis 1976; Levin 1980a). In contrast, these institutions will tend to correspond closely in their functioning with preparing labor for capitalist firms.

The result of all these factors is that it is virtually impossible to assess the intrinsic productivity of capitalist and LMFs in the absence of a "neutral" environment. If the labor-managed workplace were to be supported by an appropriate legal framework, access to capital, and workers with education and training that is pertinent to the functioning of democratic work organizations, a fairer comparison could be made of the effects on productivity of the different forms of organization. But under present arrangements, some of the differences that will be observed will reflect the greater ability of a capitalist society to reproduce the requirements for survival and expansion of capitalist firms than of non-capitalist enterprise. Alternatively, a labor-managed society would have institutions that support the need of labor-managed productive organizations, and traditional capitalist firms would be at a disadvantage. In general, then, a comparison of productivity in labor-managed and traditional capitalist firms within capitalist societies will tend to understate the potential of the LMF relative to a comparison in a society that is more supportive of such an enterprise. The result is that no comparison of intrinsic differences in productivity between the two types of organizations can be undertaken, without controlling for the degree to which each is supported or constrained by the external environment.

A final issue on the choice of firms for comparison is the rather small number of labor-managed or highly participative firms. In part, this is a result of the nonsupportive environment with respect to the establishment and survival of such firms (Jones 1979; Shirom 1972). And, of course, related to this environment is the fact that few persons have a broad enough vision that such enterprises are possible, given their rarity and the high transaction costs in establishing them in the absence of supportive institutions. But, whatever the reason, there are so few PCs and other forms of labor-managed and labor-owned firms, it is unlikely that one would be able to compare groups of these firms with similar groups of capitalist firms. The exceptions to this generalization have been the rather large group of plywood cooperatives (Bellas 1972)—about twenty-one at one time—the PCs of Mondragon, Spain (Thomas and Logan 1980), and some groups of PCs in Europe (Jones 1978, 1980; Jones and Backus 1977).

This means that the comparative study may necessarily take the form of comparing a single LMF with a traditional firm. Certainly, there is precedent for such analysis, if it is believed that the two firms are representative of their genres. However, representativeness must be clearly established so that the choice of particular entities does not, in itself, bias the comparison. For example, it would be inappropriate to compare an outstandingly successful PC with an average capitalist firm. Such a comparison would show only that PCs have the potential to be highly productive and possibly more productive than the average capitalist firm. However, the question that might be more central is whether the average worker-managed and -owned firm or highly participative firm is likely to be more productive than the average traditional firm. Clearly, the choice of entities for comparison must be sensitive to this issue, if the results are to address the appropriate question.

Furthermore, the choice of organizations for comparison should probably focus on mature and stable firms. All productive organizations have life cycles. The period of establishment is one in which organizational learning must take place for the firm to survive. It is not likely to be as productive a period as the later stage, when trial and error and "learning-by-doing" have taken place. Further, for LMFs this period may be characterized by lack of familiarity of most workers with democratic organizations and participation (Gamson and Levin 1980). Of course, counteracting this tendency is the possibility that workers in labor-owned and -managed enterprises provide greater effort in this period to assure the survival and prosperity of their firm. In fact, one difficulty in interpreting the superior performance of firms that incorporated participation during the early Allende period in Chile is that the fervor of the "revolution" and the new form of organization may have accounted for gains that would not be sustained as conditions became more routine (Espinosa and Zimbalist 1978). But the main point is that comparisons should be made between enterprises that are at similar points in their life cycles to avoid biases and problems in interpretation.

Accounting and Methodological Issues

Given the choice of outputs and nature of the comparisons as well as possible biases that might arise in the exercise, it is necessary to choose an appropriate methodology and accounting approach for the analysis of productivity.[9] In this section, I will review some of the issues that arise in selecting different procedures. First, I will address the use of standard econometric techniques for estimating production functions or production sets and their relation to this problem. And second, I will review some of the accounting problems that arise in measuring inputs of firms in this type of comparative study.

Production Function Approaches

A standard approach to looking for differences in efficiency among different types of firms has been that of estimating production functions that include variables to "catch" differences in efficiency created by some factor that is under scrutiny. Particularly, estimates of agricultural production functions have sought to ascertain the effects of management on the efficiency of farm production (Griliches 1957; Hoch 1962; Massell 1967; Mundlak 1961; Timmer 1971). In parallel fashion, estimates of production functions for participatory firms have incorporated measures of worker participation to capture the effects of that variable on productivity (Jones and Backus 1977; Cable and Fitzroy 1980a, 1980b; Espinosa and Zimbalist 1978; and Svejnar in this volume). A typical statistical form is the Cobb-Douglas equation in equation 3.3, which is transformed into the log-linear form 3.4 for purposes of estimation:

$$Y = a \, X_1^{b_1} X_2^{b_2} X_3^{b_3} \tag{3.3}$$

$$\log Y = \log a + b_1 \log X_1 + b_2 \log X_2 + b_3 \log X_3 + \log u \tag{3.4}$$

Assume that data on outputs and inputs are collected for a substantial number of firms across the participation spectrum. Equation 3.4 is estimated using ordinary least squares, where Y is a measure of physical output; a is the constant or intercept term; x_1 and x_2 refer to inputs of labor and capital, with estimated marginal products of b_1 and b_2, respectively; x_3 represents a variable measuring the degree of labor participation; and u signifies ,the residual term or unexplained variance.

But this approach has some major drawbacks that make it both difficult and even inappropriate to implement. First, physical capital and labor inputs are not homogeneous resources with simple measurement properties. In all but the simplest types of production, many different types of capital and labor are utilized. There are enormous difficulties in measuring and accounting for each type satisfactorily, and serious problems exist in combining them into aggregate measures of capital and labor. Second, the same is true of output. If the firms are producing more than one product or quality of product, an aggregate measure of output must be established that is appropriately weighted for this composition. Further, even if prices are used to create this aggregate measure, nonmarket outputs will be ignored. Third, the fact that there are so few LMFs in any industry in the United States means that the coefficient for b_3 may be based upon a bimodal distribution.

Fourth, the formulation in equation 3.4 makes a very strong assumption about the production set for enterprises with different levels of participation. It assumes that the marginal products for capital and labor are identical, and that differences in efficiency will be reflected in a shift in the variable for participation. That is, it assumes that differences in productivity are not reflected in the estimated effects on output of each of the inputs, but only in the overall effects of the production process. However, it is certainly reasonable to expect that the production set itself will differ; that is, each type of firm has its own production function.[10] One type of firm might have higher marginal products for all inputs than another type, or the relative magnitudes of the marginal products between enterprise types might depend upon which input is being considered.

For this reason, any approach that combines statistically both types of organizations and that looks for efficiency or productivity effects with a shift parameter may be inappropriate. For similar reasons, the use of mathematical programming techniques to estimate the production set for firms on the production frontier (to see the relative ranking of the two types of firms in productive efficiency using the frontier as a basis) will also be inappropriate (Aigner and Chu 1968; Timmer 1971). Rather, each type of firm will require separate estimates of the production function, and efficiency rankings would be made by comparing output for each type of firm for any given level of resource inputs on the basis of the pertinent production sets. But, of course, the relatively small number of LMFs in any industry may limit our ability to estimate a separate production function for that group. Given a large number of each type of firm and adequate accounting for inputs and outputs, the use of separate production functions is the most appropriate methodology. The estimated production sets can be compared on an input-by-input basis as well as for overall productive efficiency for any level of resource use, to establish productive claims by type of firm.

Accounting Issues

Given the difficulties mentioned above, a simpler method is to explore the overall efficiencies of the two types of firms by comparing the market values of inputs and outputs. That is, normally economists separate issues of technical efficiency from allocative efficiency. The former refers to the relation between physical inputs and outputs, while the latter is concerned with taking account of prices of inputs and outputs to make a comparison of the value of the inputs used in production with the value of the outputs or revenue that is produced.

   Presumably, it is possible that a firm that is technically efficient in terms of its transformation of physical inputs into outputs can be allocatively inefficient in obtaining the wrong combination of inputs or producing the wrong combination of outputs when their prices are taken into account. A firm is technically efficient if it produces the largest possible physical output for any set of inputs (Leibenstein 1966). A firm is allocatively efficient if it responds to prices in such a way that it produces the largest possible revenue for any given budget constraint. By comparing the monetary costs of the inputs with the value of output or revenue, it is possible to establish a ratio of total factor productivity for both types of firms in which the excess of revenues over costs is treated as profits for the capitalist firm and a surplus for the LMF.

   In the capitalist firm, the value of the labor input can be assessed according to the actual costs paid for wage-labor. However, for the LMF there may be only a remote relation between the wages paid to its employees and those paid in the labor market more generally. LMFs will generally have much flatter wage hierarchies, reflecting their more democratic organization. Even more important, the distribution between wages and the surplus of the firm after all costs are paid is a false distinction, when both types of returns benefit the employees. Thus, in some LMFs the worker may agree to relatively low weekly or monthly rates of pay in order to maximize the surplus at the end of the year, while in others the pay scales are set higher with less of a concern for the surplus.

In such cases, accounting for labor costs by measuring salaries and wages will not provide an accurate comparison between capitalist firms and LMFs or even among the latter. Rather, the cost of labor will have to be standardized by ascertaining the market value of labor for both types of firms. Even this may be inappropriate if workers in the LMF are willing to take lower wages because of a higher level of work satisfaction (Duncan 1976; Lucas 1977). This means that for the LMF, the evaluation must obtain data on quantity and quality of all labor inputs and set a market value on them. Such a cost of resource approach cannot rely exclusively on cost-accounting data, and it may require rather detailed records on the educational levels, experience, and skills of employees in LMFs as well as their actual hours of work (including unpaid hours). Even so, if there is a self-selection of workers for such firms that is not reflected in nominal worker characteristics, market wages may not be representative and there may be biases in inputing labor costs through this method.

Capital costs may be equally difficult to assess between the two types of enterprises. For example, the two types of firms may use different accounting methods for capital as well as different rates of depreciation and interest. The difficulty of obtaining access to capital markets may mean higher rates of interest for borrowing by worker-managed firms, which also may be using capital of different vintages so that standard accounting rules are misleading. For example, to the degree that LMFs have a bias toward labor utilization and have difficulties in obtaining loan capital, they may work with older equipment that is completely depreciated by the standard rules of capital consumption. In this case the capital may have no value in the general market for such equipment, or only salvage value. In addition, there is some evidence that capital is better maintained in worker-run and -owned firms, because the workers themselves have great incentives to sustain the life of equipment and avoid breakdowns in contrast to workers in capitalist firms (Levin 1980b, 1982). These differences suggest that the accounting for capital inputs cannot be easily routinized, and capital costs must be given as much attention as labor costs in comparisons between two types of enterprises.

Further, the time period over which comparisons are made is important. LMFs will tend to reduce their labor inputs less in periods of diminished product demand and expand them less in periods of high product demand. The principal reason for this is that stability of membership and employment is one of the motivating forces for establishing a worker-owned and -managed firm. Workers will be encouraged to reduce hours or increase hours as needed, and often slow periods will be used to attend to deferred maintenance such as painting and refurbishing of the plant (Berman and Berman 1978). Thus, during periods of low product demand, the labor input will be maintained at a relatively high level in comparison with product output, and vice versa. Depending upon the part of the business cycle in which a comparison is made between worker-managed and capitalist firms, there will tend to be a short-run "distortion" of the labor input in the former, in one direction or the other, which should not be used for a stable comparison. Rather it should be the average use of the labor over the business cycle that is relevant. This suggests that any comparative evaluation should be sensitive to the biases that would occur if the comparison were limited to a specific portion of the business cycle.

A second difficulty with comparisons at a point in time is the fact that investment always has a gestation period before it is reflected in higher output. That is, investment in plant and machinery will always require an outlay in advance of the actual increase in production that occurs. If one of the entities or group of entities in the comparison has made substantial investment very recently while the other has not, the comparison may bias the productivity statistics against the one whose recent investment has not become completely operative in increasing output. Thus, accounting comparisons of both inputs and outputs must take account of the biases created by the particular timing of the comparison.

Summary

In this chapter it was suggested that recent evidence on lower capital requirements, higher productivity, and greater worker involvement in worker-managed and participative firms has stimulated research on systematic comparisons of productivity and other facets of operations between such firms and their traditional capitalist counterparts. But, for a variety of reasons, such a research endeavor is not as straightforward as it might appear. The purpose of this chapter is to raise issues that must be addressed if such studies are to provide useful evidence on the matter. Of particular importance are the definitions and empirical choices of comparative entities as well as the measures of productive output. In addition, the effects of the external environment must be disentangled from intrinsic effects on productivity of the different modes of productive organization. Finally, there are numerous methodological and accounting obstacles that must be surmounted if such a comparison is to be unbiased and accurate.

Notes

1. For data on profitability and worker ownership, see Conte and Tannenbaum (1978). Greenberg (1980) found worker incomes that were 30 percent higher in cooperative plywood firms than in a comparable capitalist firm.

2. An excellent discussion of this issue is Reich and Devine (1981).

3. This may also explain the Leibenstein (1966) position on X-efficiency. Even more fundamental, the objective functions of LMFs may be based on the maximization of employment or employment stability (Berman and Berman 1978; Thomas and Logan 1980; Levin 1980b, 1982); and other nonpecuniary goals (Furubotn 1976) in contrast with the standard assumption of maximizing income per worker (Domar 1966; Steinherr 1978; Vanek 1970; Ward 1958).

4. See Steinherr (1977) for a discussion of theory that may underlie this relation. Steinherr does not consider the possibility that range *OM'* exists.

5. This conclusion is based upon two types of literature. With respect to codetermination, Batstone and Davies (1976) did an extensive survey and concluded that worker directors have had little effect on anything. Statistical confirmation of a lack of observable effect of the German practice of codetermination is found in Svejnar published in this volume. The lack of effect of superficial participative schemes is reflected in surveys of worker-productivity experiments. One shortcoming of this literature is that the experiments that found no effects rarely make their way into the literature, a fact emphasized by Katzell et al. (1977), p. 39. Many of the cosmetic approaches are found under the rubric of "job redesign." In a survey of effectiveness of job redesign on productivity the authors concluded: "Apparently job redesign is likely to fail unless there is a commitment, on the part of all concerned, to make it work; unless the redesign is more than super-ficial; and unless the program is congruent with other elements in the system—kinds of worker, technology, labor relations, etc. (ibid., p. 40)."

6. These include many of the established PCs as well as the cases of ex-tensive worker participation. Examples of the former are found in Greenberg (1980); Espinosa and Zimbalist (1978); Jones (1978, 1980); Levin (1980b, 1982). Examples of the latter are found in U.S. DHEW (1973).

7. This range is sometimes associated with some of the relatively small service collectives and PCs that are found in the major cities of the United States. For a survey of these firms, see Crain and Jackall (forthcoming); for case studies see Jackall (1980) and Margolis (1980); for an explanation of some of the reasons that participation may pose a threat to the survival of the firm under these conditions, see Gamson and Levin (1980).

8. While many contemporary PCs arose in this way, historically there are other causes as well (Jones 1978, 1979, 1980; Shirom 1972).

9. Although economists and laypersons use the word productivity as if it were a well-understood phenomenon, this is far from true. For a reflec-tion of the different conceptual, measurement, and accounting issues see Salter (1960) and Kendrick and Vaccaro (1980).

10. Evidence of such bias between average and efficient public-sector firms with respect to their production sets is presented in Levin (1976).

4

On the Problems of Estimating the Relative Efficiency of Participatory and Self-Managed Enterprises in Developing Countries: Some Illustrations from the Case of Chile

Juan Guillermo Espinosa

In studying the efficiency of self-managed firms (SMFs) and participatory enterprises, one can distinguish between two basic approaches. One approach is to study participatory enterprises with respect to each other in terms of various indicators such as income per worker, investment, absenteeism, productivity, days on strike, and level and distribution of income. The approach enables one to gauge the progress or the regression in efficiency of firms over time.[1] Another approach is to review the relative efficiency of participatory enterprises vis-à-vis traditional capitalist companies in the same region or economy in terms of their relative rate of production with respect to a given volume of inputs, or alternatively to determine which of these two kinds of enterprises minimize inputs required to meet a certain product level.

The extent to which one or the other methods is used will depend greatly on the environment or relative position that the enterprises concerned hold in the economy. For instance, if participation and self-management represent an official policy and the number of enterprises constitute an important and growing critical mass in the economy, then usually the first approach will be most appropriate. But if the participatory enterprises are isolated cases promoted under a program of controlled change, then a comparison with equivalent traditional enterprises in terms of size, activity, geographical location, technology, and other characteristics may be more appropriate. With reference to the experiences of Latin American and Caribbean countries during the last two decades, in the next section I discuss examples of the critical importance of the context of developing countries to the study of participatory firms.

The views expressed in this article are the exclusive responsibility of the author and do not necessarily represent those of the institutions to which he belongs.

The prevailing situation in most underdeveloped countries is one where isolated participatory enterprises exist in the market economies where capital ownership determines the overall management and control of the enterprise. Consequently, in the third section of this chapter, methodological problems encountered when trying to evaluate the technical efficiency of participatory enterprises are reviewed, and those problems that emerge when the approach adopted is to compare the performance of capitalist and participatory enterprises are emphasized. These problems are met whenever economists try to confront traditional theory with the actual world, which differs most significantly from the assumptions and constructions provided by standard theory. However, this discrepancy becomes more pronounced when the environment reviewed is that of a developing economy, where many departures from the idealized textbook economic systems are found. Nevertheless, traditional analysis usually proceeds by undertaking microeconomic comparisons of the relative efficiency of enterprises and considering only the productive features within the firms themselves. In other words, key external variables are overlooked, such as the characteristics of the market in which these enterprises operate, the overall economic policy that they face, the degree of openness of the economy, the reallocation of the economic activity among the various sectors, and the access to new technologies enjoyed by the different kinds of firms.

In the remainder of this chapter the foregoing discussion is extended. Arguments are developed based on the premise that the objective conditions prevailing in the finance and good markets in developing countries today mean that it is always extraordinarily difficult to attempt to evaluate the performance of participatory firms using traditional evaluative methods. For example, when endeavoring to gauge the relative interindustrial efficiency of participatory firms in a capitalist economy that is subject to a structural change and that is directed to apply the policies dictated by Western international trade theory, additional problems arise; these confine even further the possibility of analysis. Also, consideration of the anticipated influence that the internationalization of the economy will have on the future development of the organizations and economic structure in the underdeveloped countries is demanded. In the final sections these and similar issues will be examined.

The Efficiency of Enterprises and the Enveloping Context

To evaluate adequately the efficiency of participatory enterprises, one must begin by identifying the situations in which they may be found. The efficiency that firms attain depends on the extent of the obstacles or problems posed by the surrounding environment. In addition, efficiency is not an abstract concept that may be evaluated independently of the objectives sought. The objectives of participatory and SMFs vary according to the environmental circumstances and conditions facing them.

In developed countries the usual approach adopted by theory and policy makers is to identify mechanisms or tools that lessen their economic problems without changing the basic system. Therefore, worker participation often has been seen as a vehicle through which it would be possible to obtain some degree of improvement in performance and labor productivity.

On the other hand, in underdeveloped countries, since the crucial problems at hand are very high unemployment and underemployment and deep disparities in income distribution, participation and self-management have not been approached in the same light. Labor in these countries continues to press in search of production organization and management practices that may provide it additional stability in its sources of income, a more human creative environment in its means of work, and a more equitable remuneration commensurate with the minimum living conditions.

However, in practice the efficiency with which these objectives may be attained depends on the scope and extent of the change of the means of work and society. Therefore, it is necessary to identify at least three kinds of different and more frequent situations that have been observed in the last two decades in Latin America and the Caribbean.

First, there are experiences that have arisen out of the overall change of the economy and society. In these experiences there is an expanding of objectives far beyond a mere increase of production; this produces an effect upon the economic and social performance of the transformed enterprises. Although this expanding of objectives presumably seeks to establish a climate of liberty and progress for workers, there are a few studies in the countries of the region that have succeeded in undertaking an empirical analysis of the economic results of these enterprises. But most researchers agree that various favorable and positive effects have resulted, even though the analysis usually has been undertaken only in qualitative terms.[2] It is difficult to find in the literature on developing countries any economic arguments or solid evidence indicating a curbing in productivity or in results. Another dimension rarely considered in the analysis of participatory firms and SMFs when there is an overall change concerns the adversities and the restrictions that they are required to face. Almost invariably these arise in connection with inputs, foreign trade, or macroeconomic "austerity" politics mandated by the international financial, political, and commercial system of any economy attempting a change of this nature.[3]

Second, there are experiences arising out of or existing in a program of controlled change. These experiences, which to a greater or lesser extent enjoy official support or approval, have emerged in most countries in the rural sector and have hardly touched urban- or manufacturing-sector activities.

To attempt even a listing of the main initiatives of controlled change that have occurred in the countries in the region in past decades would be a lengthy exercise.[4] However, it may be noted that many have emerged in times of economic crises and violence, while others emerge in the midst of threats of rural risings or in view of fears of "communist progress." During these critical periods, sectors that never before had considered participation and self-management as a feasible way out of the existing situations of structural disparity endorse the cooperative idea. The opinion that producer cooperatives (PCs) would now be necessary to promote a more humane change, to attain a higher ideal of service, to fight exploitation, and to reach a new, more appropriate, and more equitable society is widely disseminated. This means that the cooperative ideal has been used in these programs for mainly political purposes. PCs are presented as a tool for directed or planned change that, according to this concept, can be used only with the assistance or "direction" of official agency experts and technicians.[5]

Within this clearly limited framework PCs may be pursued so long as they do not threaten the system. In day-to-day action emphasis will be given to various technical questions that, in most cases, are far from being applied in actual practices. Consequently, when analyzing the relative efficiency of these experiences, it must be remembered that there have always been various obstacles or limitations to the experiments. Most of these programs have a short life, and to a great extent this denies them the initially programmed support and contributes to the instability of their operation. Furthermore, controls and restrictions placed on these experimental enterprises cast doubts on their actually participatory or self-managed nature. Perhaps most significantly, these experiences usually orginiate in the more backward sectors, therefore imparting on them a comparative disadvantage that a traditional capitalist businessman would rarely accept.[7]

When controlled-change programs are interrupted, these experiences are faced with a situation that is similar to that of the third kind of experiences, those originating in isolation and as a result of the individual initiative of a group of workers in an existing enterprise.

Enterprises originating or existing alone have received significant attention in the past; consequently, I shall not discuss them at length here.[7] It seems interesting to recall merely some similarities that they exhibit vis-à-vis experiences originated under a program of controlled change. First, in both cases most analysts use as a basis a rarely examined assumption that these enterprises can live adequately in a market economy, of a capitalist nature, and with private ownership of the means of production. Alternatively, most neoclassicists would accept as a fact that a traditional capitalist enterprise would somehow see its efficiency reduced should it be required to exist in the midst of a centrally planned economy.

A second similarity is that in both kind of enterprises the main objective of the workers, at least until a stable level of activity is attained, is job security. However, in this case there seems to be a difference in the results of these two kinds of firms. In the enterprise orginated within a controlled transformation the level of worker participation in management always appears to be smaller than in the enterprise that is initiated in isolation. Therefore, when the former is abandoned a greater chance of a failure or bankruptcy is faced (Borda 1976; Hewitt 1976). On the contrary, the enterprise that arises in isolation from the outset is born with greater energy and vitality as a result of the number of obstacles that have to be overcome in order to come into being. In fact, its very existence is already a success and a proof of its greater relative entrepreneurial capacity to work under adverse conditions (Vanek 1970, 1973; Jones 1974).

Some Practical Problems in Assessing Relative Interfirm Efficiency in Underdeveloped Countries

In this section, major methodological problems involved in evaluating the efficiency of participatory firms in developing countries are reviewed.[8] One study that sought to arrive at the international comparison of economic efficiency at the microeconomic level in Latin American manufacturing industries (Knight 1974) concluded that the concept of efficiency, which is so fundamental to economic theory, is extremely difficult to implement in actual practice. Particular problems arise when comparing establishments producing more than one particular good; using various kinds of material inputs, labor and capital; and observing different price systems.

Notwithstanding the previous warnings many researchers, including this author, have tried to compile various data that would allow estimation of traditional one-factor productivity indexes, total factor-productivity indexes, production functions, and efficiency frontiers.[9] However, many restrictions prevented the compilation of even the very limited data that would have allowed such calculations. Because the limitations and characteristics of factor productivity indexes and production functions are quite well-known, only the limitations presented by the functions of the efficiency-frontier approach are included here.

It is useful to briefly review some of the assumptions that underlie the use of these techniques. For many years in most Latin American countries industrial statistics have increasingly suggested that there are number of enterprises exhibiting basically different production methods (Meller 1976). Lately, this situation seems to have worsened and made questionable the frequent assumption that all firms both within a country and in different countries are employing the same neoclassical production function (Merhav 1970). Further, it is usually assumed in the empirical literature that factors are homogeneous and perfectly mobile within an industry, and that factor prices are determined in competitive markets. This implies that within a country productivity differences reflect differences in factor proportions employed by the firms, and that an industry may be viewed as a representative firm (see Salter 1960).

This set of assumptions is not only outmoded but also has been overwhelmingly disproved by the available evidence. Some researchers, confronted with the lack of alternatives, have decided to use Farrell's (1957) efficiency-frontier technique. The implicit concept in this method is that a production technique is technically efficient when using the smallest combination of inputs for a given product level. In other words, this method relies on the idea of minimizing the combination of inputs for a constant production level for the various techniques, in contrast to the method of the production function, which seeks to maximize the product level for a given input level. In practice, the Farrell method consists in obtaining the envelope curve comprising, for different capital-labor ratios, those points which need a minimum combination of inputs to produce a unit of output. This procedure enables the performance of actual establishments to be compared with the best practices observed in reality, instead of taking ideal combinations of inputs as a point of reference. Moreover, as Meller (1976) notes, Farrell's approach has several advantages. First, it is functional form free; second, it can handle establishments using heterogeneous technologies and techniques; and third, it is a useful and simple tool for measuring the relative technical efficiency of different techniques.[10]

As with the other approaches, this method does have several difficulties. Specific problems may be divided into those of a practical nature and those of a conceptual kind better known in previous studies. The most significant of the practical problems are those of cooperation of the enterprises and the availability of data. Cooperation of enterprises represents the first obstacle and is often particularly noticeable in traditional private companies with a less-developed-country setting. It should not be forgotten that in an economy based on private property, total secrecy and control of internal information within a company is a right of the owner of the means of production and is restricted only in a few cases by law.[11]

Data-availability problems arising mainly—though not exclusively—in SMFs arise principally because as with conventional firms, accounting and balance sheet concepts fail to match those that are relevant to theory.[12]

Finally, and perhaps most importantly, the problems posed by non-cooperation of the enterprises and the scant availability of data in most underdeveloped countries can reduce drastically the sample of firms to the extent of divesting it of all representativity.

Concerning conceptual problems, I will refer very briefly only to three issues: product, labor, and capital measuring problems.[13] The empirically measurable product of an enterprise is the value added by an industrial process. But since a factory generally has a variety of products and many different intermediate inputs, in order to estimate efficiency frontiers and production functions one needs to add several items of value added. Each of these individual "value addeds" is determined by adding physical units of products (and inputs) and converting them into homogeneous units using prices. In this sense even though no obstacles might be present in obtaining the value added at the firm level, in order to include in a sample several Latin American and Caribbean countries, one can anticipate a significant problem in knowing which prices to use. To put it differently, in order to obtain internationally comparable value-added units, one must use the same prices to add physical units in the different countries. While this is perfectly feasible in principle, the procedure of using a set of common prices for all products and a set of common prices for all inputs is highly laborious.[14]

When measuring labor, the measure to be used is the total number of worker-hours per time unit. If applied directly, the problem with this measure is that one would be adding the worker-hours of individuals with different rates of productivity when working with production functions. A way around this problem is not to add the different types of labor factor but rather to include them separately. This method enables the importance of each kind of work to be estimated and the different productivities to be assessed. Aggregation is best done not by merely adding the number of worker-hours but rather by converting the various kinds of labor into equivalent units. However, to obtain these equivalent units one needs to use common relative wages. Normally this is done by making the unrealistic assumption that there is a perfect labor market and that consequently relative wages reflect relative marginal productivities.

Even though product as well as labor measurements present certain problems, the case of the capital factor is by far the most difficult. Here, theoretical assumptions are very far from reality. Capital-assessment problems begin when one notes that there is often an enormous disparity between what could be called the market price of a capital good and that good's accounting or tax value (book value). Although similar machinery may be available in different establishments, their different ages represent an additional complicating factor. Moreover, the used-machinery market is quite far from perfect. Therefore, it becomes extremely difficult to obtain reliable prices for such machines and to determine the aggregate value of capital stock.[15] Furthermore, it is usual to find machinery in use that has been rebuilt several times in order to incorporate changes that alter significantly productivity, as compared to the original design equivalents. It is important to recall, likewise, that fixed-asset, depreciation, and revaluation systems differ according to the particular tax schemes governing the enterprises concerned.

In many instances, all the indicated problems imply a volume of obstacles that altogether prevents a reliable study on the relative efficiency of enterprises. A lone positive result in many cases is the actual learning process of the economists who undertake this research, most of whom are usually not very familiar with the industries they wish to study, nor with the techniques through which they intend to obtain itemized information within the factories.

Effects of a Structural Change Directed to Completely Open the Economy to World Trade and Financial Markets

To the problems described in the previous section may be added those difficulties that arise when the economy is reoriented drastically in order to apply the policy prescriptions derived from Western international trade theory. In any underdeveloped country this doctrine is equivalent to putting its economy through a structural change directed at opening it to the world market of goods and capital.

Two or three decades ago the influence of foreign trade and external financing were not considered to be of great importance for the economic policy within any developing country. Although this outlook was changing throughout the sixties, the increasing disarray during the last decade has transformed entirely the traditional role of international institutions, the characteristics of external financing, the international monetary system, and the forms and flows of trade. The old ideas of development and trade in harmony with the philosophy of laissez-faire and economic liberalism have not evolved, and in the scenario today they have been provided with increased power. In fact, the enormous power of transnational companies and international private banks, which most of the time are represented in their dealings with each third-world government by the International Monetary Fund (IMF), has promoted an increasing internationalization of the economy. At the same time this growing internationalization has reinforced the power of the named institutions.

But what is the relationship of this international scene to the problem of measuring the relative efficiency of industrial firms in underdeveloped countries? In fact, the relationship is enormous, and the effects are devastating in terms of employment, distribution of income, freedom, and self-determination. In order to briefly clarify this relationship, in the next few lines the basis of a desirable or "sound" economic policy for an underdeveloped country from the point of view of the IMF will be summarized.[16] The IMF's policies call for the widest possible freedom of play for market forces; many kinds of government intervention (such as price subsidies or protection of domestic industries) are frowned upon as distortions of free-market relations. Whenever a government of an underdeveloped country subscribes to this doctrine, it will receive the public approval of the IMF. On the other hand, whenever a government does not practice these ideas, all the major sources of credit (especially the international private banks) will refuse to lend to a country that persists in defying IMF's "technical" advice. Therefore, every time a country faces a balance-of-payment crisis it must implement a "stand-by" arrangement and an abolition of import controls, an antiinflationary program (controlling government deficits, wage rises, dismantling price controls, etc.), a greater hospitality to foreign investment, and a drastic devaluation of exchange rate to keep later a stable, unitary exchange rate.

The ideal policies that the ultraliberals might like to see adopted are quite often economically or politically out of reach of any civilized government. Consequently a need exists for "strong" governments, as in Chile and Peru in the past few years. In fact the self-imposed "austerity" program of the Chilean government differs with the programs of other countries only in its greater intensity.[17] The results of these programs were predictable: industrial productive activity suffered: high unemployment emerged and a large number of company bankruptcies and close-downs took place. These effects were predictable because, as Vanek (1976) points out, according to the Stolper-Samuelson theorem in an economy that opens to foreign trade the most affected factor will be that which is least available, in this particular case, capital.

Therefore, in a period of recession and change the instability and vulnerability of enterprises (capitalist and self-managed alike) grows enormously, creating great mobility and fluidity in the economy. Consequently, the possibility of studying the relative efficiency of capitalist and SMFs decreases drastically. This situation is commonplace in underdeveloped countries that face more and more frequent crises under the present international financial situation. In such times one of the most serious problems concerning measurement is that of the considerable increase in the pace of changes in the economic field. These changes occur, for instance, when enterprises switch either from one industrial field to another or from an industrial activity to an import trade activity. In addition, both the number of bankruptcies and company dissolutions sharply increase.

As a result, any attempt to measure the relative efficiency between traditional firms and SMFs in a period such as this in fact would not be measuring the efficiency of these two kinds of firms but rather their survival capacity or adaptability in an ultraliberal economic and financial environment.

Consequently, attempting to apply the Farrell technique during such a period of economic change and economic opening might result in severe misrepresentation. This follows because the national enterprises and the multinationals might each be expected to generate their own separate frontiers of relative efficiency having a considerable distance between them. The efficiency frontier of the multinationals would be close to the origin; quite removed from the origin (to the northeast) would lie the efficiency frontier of the national firms. The distance between frontiers would be due principally to the scale economies of the multinationals that result in significantly lower unit costs, to the capacity of these enterprises to produce in industrial free zones where taxation is almost nil and labor cheapest, and to their capacity to obtain financial resources for investment and operating capital needs at a lower cost.[18]

In the case of Chilean national enterprises it must be emphasized that the empirical evidence available does not show a lower relative efficiency in the participatory enterprises and seems to indicate that both the number of bankruptcies as well as the relative efficiency between traditional and SMFs has been similar (Espinosa 1979).

It is also important to consider the implications of the differing objectives of the two kinds of enterprises for the evaluation of performance during a period of structural change. The whole set of objectives of participatory firms contradict the new economic system. To uphold these goals will likely inhibit the cohesion and economic capability of the firm. In these circumstances if the relative efficiency of traditional and SMFs remains similar it would indicate the success of participatory enterprises.

Also, in a period such as this, the traditional profit-maximizing objective of private enterprise is readapted by entrepreneurs to the degree of economic recession; firms seek primarily to survive and by every means endeavor to avoid bankruptcy. To this end, the main accommodating factor is adjustment of the labor force, a method that is adopted in a fundamentally different way by SMFs. The entrepreneur strives for a swift change of activity by eliminating workers whom he considers unfit for the new activity. He seeks to minimize costs (losses) and will, if need be, even close down the plant temporarily. The variable and hence shock-absorbing input are clearly the workers.

By contrast, in SMFs, the survival objective is understood to mean continued employment, even at the expense of wages and internal participation levels in the establishment. A problem arises because wages have a floor, at the level of individual subsistence, that the private entrepreneur does not have. In addition, the workers when faced with adverse market conditions usually try to improve the quality of their goods, and not to change their line of activity. This strategy only prolongs the agony and darkens the road they should have taken in an economy flooded by imports. No matter how much they may improve internal efficiency, reduce costs and wages, and improve the quality of the goods, the lower prices and greater sophistication of the imported goods produced by multinational enterprises in most cases requires the dissolution of the enterprise, with the resulting increase in unemployment.[19]

The New World-Market-Oriented Industry
and Some Final Comments and Conclusions

In most underdeveloped countries there is growing evidence of the emergence of a world-market-oriented industry. This does not, however, represent a more advanced level of development. According to several world-wide studies this process is part of the recent reorganization of industrial production that has been brought about by changed conditions in factors such as technology and communications. One reason for the buildup of plants in some locations in underdeveloped countries is that production in the industrialized countries is no longer as profitable as production in some free-trade zones in the third world. At the same time, not all underdeveloped countries are becoming sites for international manufacturing industries, but only those where conditions such as a stable dictatorship, abundance of cheap labor, and no-tax large-credit conditions make it very profitable to relocate some plants of a company.

This relocation enables advantage to be taken of new technology and allows a growing fragmentation of the production process into a variety of partial operations at different production places (Frobel et al. 1977). At these new production sites within the underdeveloped world production is world-market-oriented, the markets traditionally supplied by the industries of the advanced countries themselves. Therefore, depending on the location selected by transnational firms, there are a few industry-oriented countries and a larger group of still primary-oriented countries within the group of "transitional" countries according to the World Bank terminology (Chenery 1977).

What has been observed, then, as a drastic change in the Chilean economy since 1973 is not an isolated phenomenon. Rather, it is part of a larger process that has been accelerating in the last decade and by which international capitalism is readapting to the most profitable worldwide conditions. The other side of the picture is provided by underdeveloped countries well "trained" in the Western theory of international trade and capital movements, from which export-oriented, free-capital, and free-trade models are adopted.

In any Western country—whether developed or underdeveloped, industry oriented or primary oriented—the obvious manifestation of the process may be observed through the increasing penetration of mass-production goods, which first were only textiles and electronics but which now are continuously expanding to several other industries like metal mechanics and auto production.

Under these new conditions it will be more and more common for the same market to be supplied by transnational production and local enterprises. It will be increasingly difficult to compare the performance of locally-market-oriented enterprises (traditional or self-managed) and world-market-oriented production. These difficulties arise, in part, because export production today is often limited to partial production within the frame of transnationally organized manufacture (Frobel et al. 1977). This means that the whole process of producing one good usually is the result of the production of components in a number of factories at different locations worldwide. The greater the decomposition of a complex production process into elementary units, the more exclusive and noncomparable the capital (and the resulting production function) of those units with another plant in the same industrial branch. Furthemore, the decomposition of the production process may seriously affect any estimate of value added because of transfer-pricing practices within multinational enterprises. Also, multinationals have easier access than domestic firms to modern technology, and an entirely different kind of capital and labor are used by the transnational plant. The higher part of the value of its capital is accumulated knowledge allowing wide ranges for over- or under-valuation depending on the specific conditions faced. The decomposing of productions into elementary operations facilitates the use of unskilled and semiskilled labor with little previous experience at minimum wages.

The previous discussion of the limitations of the comparative analysis of relative efficiency took into account only the production process from within. Consideration has not yet been given to obstacles from the external (demand) side of the enterprise. There is the familiar problem of advertising or the enormous capacity of transnationals to create new wants. Also, multinationals are able to differentiate their products in order to have a situation of pure monopoly or monopolistic competition. For the sake of brevity I will not enter into further details here. A large and well-documented section of literature is available today in this field (United Nations 1973).

Summarizing the previous discussion, it is easy to envisage an increased dismantling and close-down of local enterprises (traditional or self-managed) if a free-trade policy is adopted by most underdeveloped countries. Furthermore, because of the highly different kind of productive units represented by local plants and multinational companies regarding concentration of knowledge, technology, financial and physical capital, markets, and raw materials, it is not possible even to imagine the use of similar production functions for both types of firms. Consequently, if all firms are evaluated by using similar methods of evaluation, it is likely that local or national enterprises, no matter how efficient within a closed economy, apparently will be found to be less efficient than worldwide production firms.

Finally, a number of questions may be raised on the applicability of concepts and techniques to estimate the relative efficiency or the performance of firms within the new economic structure in most "transitional" countries. The new economic structure contains the bulk of employment being provided by the expansion of commerce and the service sector. Industry seems no longer to provide much hope to the large masses of unemployed and underemployed. At least one pertinent question is whether the concepts and techniques available are still valid for these new types of businesses, which have a totally different type of capital and a frequently intangible product.

Notes

1. An example of this kind of analysis can be found in Espinosa and Zimbalist (1978, chapters 5-7).

2. Among studies that deal with the performance of participatory or self-managed enterprises within a global transformation of the economy, see on Peru: Knight et al. (1975), Knight (1976), Sector de Propiedad Social (1980), and Solis (1980); and on Chile: Barrera (1978), Espinosa and Zimbalist (1978), and Ruiz-Tagle (1979).

3. This has been the case, for example, in Chile between 1970 and 1973, Peru between 1974 and 1978, and more recently in Jamaica and Nicaragua (post-Somoza).

4. For good analyses of some cases in Columbia, Ecuador, and Venezuela, see Borda (1976).

5. This is, therefore, a limited-reformist position; when PCs are used within a controlled-change program they can attain only marginal modifications of the prevailing system.

6. Enterprises in rural areas usually begin in the most backward lands, with little or no irrigation, while urban-sector enterprises are of less than efficient scale and in activities with little market and old technology.

7. See for example: Vanek (1970, chapter XV, and 1973).

8. In the preparation of this section the work of Knight (1974) was an important source.

9. For studies using production functions see Svejnar and Jones in this volume. The seminal article for the frontier-type functions is Farrell (1957) and an early application is Timmer (1970).

10. The main problem with the method is that the frontier is established by means of extreme observations in the available data and, therefore, the position of the frontier is highly sensitive to observation errors. Since the

frontier depends only on observations contained in the sample taken, a larger sample can move the frontier closer to the origin.

11. Although some of the necessary data are usually available from tabulations at the National Bureau of Statistics of each country, the need of segregating to four digits or of identifying similar productive units with SMFs on which some information is available requires knowledge of some data at the factory level. Most of this information is considered to be confidential by private companies, and although the responsible officials in each factory are assured that the data obtained will be kept in strict confidence, in most cases the reply is negative. Among the many reasons given for this the most common are doubt that their cooperation would bring possible benefits to the user; high cost involved to the company in order to prepare and provide the information being requested; and certain doubts on the future confidential nature of the data.

12. For example the usual theoretical assumption that presumes one product and two or three inputs is rarely found anywhere in practice. In most cases it is impossible to separate inputs, machinery, and personnel exactly participating in each one of the goods or products manufactured in an establishment. What most enterprises try to do within a market economy is to diversify or differentiate products of their manufacture. An additional complication is found in enterprises operating more than one plant. In these cases, the individuals responsible for the accounts at the plant sometimes are unaware of the cost of inputs or of the final selling price of the products since these are bought and sold by other units in the firm that may be located in other cities.

13. For an extended analysis of other problems met at the microeconomic level in manufacturing industries, see the quite realistic study of Knight (1974).

14. However, it might be possible to find some sufficiently acceptable indirect form like some specific rate of exchange for the industrial branches under analysis.

15. Knight (1974) refers to an indirect form of capital assessment that, although being an imperfect approximation to determine the existence of capital in an enterprise, at least allows an estimate of the physical index of the existing capital. This procedure entails recording the driving force in each enterprise under an age-group classification. Thus, one horsepower of a certain age may be taken to represent a different production factor to that of one new horsepower.

16. For a more formal presentation of these ideas see Fleming (1964), Horsefield (1969), and Rhomberg and Heller (1977).

17. The three main features of this program are strict monetarism, an opening of the economy to foreign markets, and a severe reduction in the degree of participation by the state in productive activities. For a more detailed treatment see Payer (1974).

18. Some econmists object to the comparison of multinational and national enterprises on the basis that these enterprises cater to different markets and that their products are quite different. However, in the case of Argentina, Brazil, Chile, Uruguay, and some other Latin American countries, because of the enormous demonstration effects originated by many of the imported goods and the great expansion of domestic credit made possible through increased external indebtness, the market does not seem to be segmented within the group that maintains its buying capacity. On the new international division of labor see Frobel et al. (1977).

19. However, this apparent rigidity of SMFs compared to capitalist firms may prevail only when participatory firms are isolated (and not numerous and federated), and when they are particularly vulnerable to a rapidly changing context, as in developing countries. Note, for example, that the Mondragon group of PCs seems to be more flexible than capitalist firms in responding to a general crisis (see Thomas and Logan 1981).

Part III
Self-Managed
Economies and Self-
Managed Sectors

5

The Effects of Enterprise Self-Management in Yugoslavia: An Empirical Survey

Saul Estrin and
William Bartlett

This chapter surveys the empirical literature concerning the effects of enterprise self-management on economic behavior in Yugoslavia. The following section describes the empirical analysis of the predictions from static economic theory, and is largely concerned with allocative efficiency in different markets. Issues of dynamic theory, such as the effects of self-management on growth, are considered in the third section. First, however, the main institutional changes in Yugoslavia are briefly reviewed.

There have been three major reforms since the introduction of Soviet-type planning in 1946.[1] The reforms between 1950 and 1952 replaced central planning by a decentralized mechanism denoted the "Visible Hand" (see Neuberger 1970), characterized by investment planning, regulated goods markets, and nominal enterprise self-management. The development strategy remained essentially Soviet, based on a high share of investment in gross domestic product (GDP), which was largely allocated to the industrial sector. Self-management had little impact on resource allocation in the early years of the period, because enterprise decisions were circumscribed by high taxation of net revenue, and trade, price, and wage controls. The system was slowly liberalized during the 1950s and early 1960s, but economic development was directed from the center until investment planning was replaced by a regulated capital market in 1965. The reforms at that date abolished many of the mechanisms for detailed economic control, and significantly increased the autonomy of self-managed firms (SMFs) to take economic decisions in a regulated-market framework. Economic problems after 1965, such as slower growth rates, rising unemployment and inflation, and balance of payments disequilibria, led to the gradual reassertion of central controls. These culminated in the 1974 reforms, which enforced guidelines to ensure that enterprise decisions conformed to a Social Plan.

It should be noted that nominal self-management was introduced into a relatively less developed, and regionally fragmented, economy (see World Bank 1975). Thus, the authorities were primarily concerned with economic development, both for the country as a whole, and especially the more

83

backward regions, and the institutional experimentation with self-management and markets can be viewed as instruments to attain this goal (see
Bartlett 1980b). The evidence on the effects of self-management must be
judged in the context of the Yugoslav environment.

Questions from Static Theory

Predictions

Economic theory[2] shows that a fully competitive system could sustain the
same allocation under either capitalism or self-management (Drèze 1976).
Empirical work is usually based on the assumption that self-management
affects resource allocation, either through a change in the production possibility set, or because the economy has not attained a competitive equilibrium. The former approach leads to studies of enterprise behavior and
productivity; the latter to an investigation of the resource misallocation that
could exist in Yugoslavia if capital and product markets were imperfect,
and if self-management were to prevent labor-market clearing. Thus, the
following subsections survey the empirical literature on enterprise behavior
and resource allocation in Yugoslav product, capital, and labor markets.

Economic theory assumes that worker participation in management
alters the enterprise maximand from profits to average earnings per head
(Ward 1958). In addition, it is widely argued that participative arrangements influence enterprise efficiency (see Vanek 1970; Ireland 1980;
Kleindorfer and Sertel 1978). The following subsection surveys the sociological material on Yugoslav enterprises that attempts to tackle these issues.

A self-managed economy will allocate goods and capital efficiently if
product and financial markets are perfectly competitive.[3] The empirical
literature surveyed in the third and fourth subsections is largely devoted to
establishing that both markets have been severely imperfect in practice.
Research on product markets provides a description of industrial structure,
enterprise entry and exit, and price-setting behavior. The numerous studies
of Yugoslav capital markets move beyond description to examine the implications of market imperfections for the allocation of capital and the
choice of technique, and to test the Furubotn and Pejovich (1970) predictions on enterprise savings.

The theory of self-management is primarily oriented to analyze resource
misallocation in labor markets. In most market systems, competitive forces
should equalize wages, and therefore labor marginal products, for a common labor type, although this may be prevented by market frictions. In a
self-managed economy, wages are the residual surplus, which will vary with
every parametric shift, such as a change in prices, costs, or technology.

For example, if product price were to increase for a particular industry, average earnings for all workers would automatically increase, and the existing membership of each cooperative would be reluctant to recruit more labor, since this would reduce their own incomes. The system relies on enterprise entry and exit to transfer labor to alternative uses, and, in the interim, one predicts the emergence of income differentials in Yugoslavia, as well as relatively low rates of labor turnover and the maintenance of high real wages despite excess labor supply.

The final subsection surveys the literature on resource misallocation in Yugoslav labor markets, and the econometric models that attempt to explain the wide intersectoral dispersion of average earnings. Two approaches exist to modeling income differentials in Yugoslavia. The "capital school" asserts that, due to capital-market imperfections, earnings include an implicit capital rental that can be calculated from the capital-labor ratio (Vanek 1973). The "labor school" attributes the problem to the labor-market imperfections of a self-managed economy. It argues that any factor that causes a dispersion of profits in capitalism, most frequently proxied by productivity and concentration, must generate differences in labor demand in a self-managed economy (Estrin 1979a). Although this debate runs through the entire empirical literature on Yugoslavia, it has developed because each side uses strong assumptions to reduce a single hypothesis from economic theory into two nonnested ones. Since earnings are revenue minus nonlabor costs per head, differences in income can be caused by any factor causing a dispersion in either element. The labor school focuses on the determinants of differences in revenue per head, and the capital school on differences in the costs of funds; each relies on the untenable implicit assumption of equality for the marginal products of the alternative factor in different uses.

Enterprise Behavior

It is argued that enterprise objectives would change if workers undertook the entrepreneurial role. The empirical work approaches this problem indirectly, by attempting to measure the influence of workers on decisions in Yugoslav firms. Legally, authority has been vested in the work force, and manual workers have predominated on self-management bodies. A system of participative management, *upravljanje,* has operated upward from workers to the Director through various self-management agencies, and has determined objectives and policy. These decisions have been administered by a conventional management hierarchy, *rukovodjenje,* operating downward from the Director (see Vanek 1972, World Bank 1975). Manual workers made up approximately 77 percent of the members of various participative bodies in 1960, and 67.5 percent in 1970, while the comparable figures for high-level professionals were 4.1 and 6.0 percent (World Bank 1975).[4]

However, there is sociological evidence from questionnaires, and observation of self-management bodies, that in practice the decision-making process is controlled by management rather than by workers. The studies based on questionnaires (see Kavčić et al. 1971; Rus 1978; Šiber et al. 1978; Rus 1979)[5] indicate that, despite the formal structure, management exerts a greater influence over decision-making than workers, who desire a more equal distribution of power. Workers' Councils, through which workers' preferences are actually channeled, are found to have an intermediate level of influence (Kavčić et al. 1971), but even there the influence of managerial staff is predominant. The distribution of influence is found to be uneven over different policy areas (Rus 1978); the Councils predominate in decisions concerning income distribution, employment, and social policy, while management determines production and sales decisions. Obradović (1978) observes decision-making directly, to deal with the problem that respondents to questionnaires might incorrectly perceive the true distribution of power. In a sample of 24 Zagreb firms between 1966 and 1969,[6] he finds that management put forward 72.5 percent of all market-related proposals, nearly all of which were accepted. Moreover, 75 percent of proposals concerning income distribution, and 86 percent of accepted proposals, were made by managerial staff. This evidence suggests a divergence between the formal self-management arrangements and their actual implementation.

However, one cannot deduce from this material that Yugoslav enterprises do not pursue the interests of their work forces. The questionnaire data suggest that workers predominate over income and employment issues through Workers' Councils. Moreover, Tannenbaum (1974) reports that, although workers do not have as much absolute power as managers in Yugoslavia, they have relatively more influence than their counterparts in capitalist economies. Finally, the interests of Yugoslav workers and management may not be fundamentally different.[7] In this case, the measured distribution of influence, whether formal or actual, is of little interest.

It is also suggested that the introduction of worker self-management increases productive efficiency. This hypothesis is tested on Yugoslav interfirm data, using perceived differences in participation as the dependent variable. Two studies (Kavčić et al. 1971; Rus 1978) report that influence over decisions is perceived to be greater by each group in efficient firms,[8] although the influence of managers is relatively greater than that of workers. Inefficient firms are characterized by a more egalitarian distribution of influence that, Rus (1978) argues, induces inertia in decision-making. A large study by Jerovšek and Možina (1978)[9] confirms that more efficient firms have a higher degree of "total" influence on decisions, but finds that efficient and inefficient producers display similar gradients of influence. However, efficient enterprises are characterized by better information flows and a greater delegation of responsibility. These studies suggest that the degree and type of participation has important effects on economic efficiency in Yugoslavia.

One must interpret these results cautiously, because the enterprise maximand might also be influenced by the degree of participation, which would affect the proxies used for efficiency.[10] Even so, some relationship between the degree of participation and productivity in Yugoslavia is established. Taken together, this research by sociologists reveals that the extent and character of actual worker participation varies significantly among Yugoslav firms, which causes differences in both enterprise objectives and productive efficiency. These differences are generally ignored in the studies undertaken by economists.

Product Markets

The empirical work surveyed below describes Yugoslav industrial structure, enterprise entry and exit, and price-setting behavior.[11] It reveals that Yugoslav product markets contain very few firms, and are highly concentrated (see Sacks 1972, 1973; Dirlam and Plummer 1973, Estrin 1979b). As in many other developing economies, this problem is mainly due to the limitations that a small domestic market places on the number of firms that can simultaneously capture economies of scale.

Enterprises in the Yugoslav manufacturing sector are rather large,[12] and there are very few producers in each market (Sacks 1973; Estrin 1979b). Sacks (1973) reports that, of the 18 industrial sectors in 1963, 12 percent contained fewer than 10 firms, 25 percent fewer than 20 firms, and only 22 percent more than 100 enterprises. The comparable proportions for 103 industrial groupings in 1961 were 22, 67, and 7 percent. Finally, of 509 individual products in 1959, 52 percent were produced by fewer than 5 enterprises, and only 18 percent by more than 20 companies. As a consequence, in 1959 a majority of Yugoslav sectors and industries displayed concentration ratios[13] in excess of 70 percent, compared with only 18 percent of American industries in 1963[14] (Sacks 1973; Estrin 1979b). In a similar vein, Dirlam and Plummer (1973) report that, in 1963, 4 firms or fewer produced the entire output in 28 percent of Yugoslav industries; 12 percent of firms accounted for 45 percent of industrial assets; and 5 percent of firms realized 40 percent of net product.[15]

Changes in industrial structure over time can be caused by new enterprise entry, product diversification by existing firms, differential growth rates, mergers, or bankruptcy. The theory suggests that such movements are essential for the attainment of efficient equilibria, but Yugoslav institutional arrangements have not been conducive to enterprise mobility. There has been virtually no incentive to create new firms, because the founders lose all capital rights after the firm begins to produce. Thus, entry of new firms has been largely in the hands of various government units. Moreover, although enterprises can be legally declared bankrupt, this has rarely occurred in practice (Moore 1980), although there have been some mergers over the period. Evidence on entry, and its effects on concentration, are summarized in table 5-1, which shows that state-sponsored entry added, on average, only 1 percent to the stock of existing firms in each year between 1952 and 1968. This may have been largely offset by mergers between 1960 and 1968, except between 1961 and 1963 (Sacks 1973). However, there have been relatively large changes in firm numbers and industrial concentration has declined significantly,[16] which must reflect diversification by existing producers and differential growth rates within industries.

Economic theory predicts a positive relationship between average earnings and the level of concentration, and a negative one between incomes and changes in concentration. These associations are confirmed by Estrin (1979b), using cross-section data for 18 sectors. The partial correlation coefficient between average earnings per sector and the concentration ratio was 0.52 in 1966. Changes in firm numbers, net of state-sponsored entry, were positively related to the level of earnings ($r = 0.66$), and changes in concentration were inversely related to incomes in the sector ($r = -0.22$). State-sponsored entry was not significantly related to levels of concentration or average earnings. This suggests that, while state-sponsored entry is determined by development plans, product diversification by existing firms is signaled by average earnings, and acts to reduce industrial concentration.

Observers agree that Yugoslav product markets do not allocate resources efficiently, but there are two general explanations of the observed price distortions. Horvat (1971, 1976), Sirc (1979), and Moore (1980) attribute the problems to government regulation, while Dirlam and Plummer (1973) and Estrin (1979b) place the emphasis on underdevelopment and the absence of market competition.

The Yugoslav authorities have systematically intervened in the operation of product markets, regulating prices to direct development and contain inflationary pressures.[17] This has primarily operated through price regulation and fixing, but there were price freezes in 1952 and 1965.[18] The extent of the controls gradually increased after 1955, to cover about 70 percent of the value of industrial output by 1965.[19] It is argued that relative prices have become increasingly distorted because of price regulation and enterprise attempts to avoid it (for example, Horvat 1971; Milenkovitch 1971; Moore 1980). Indeed, one of the objectives of the 1965 reforms was a major realignment of relative prices to conform more closely with those

Table 5-1
Entry and Concentration of Yugoslav Firms

A. *The Minimum and Maximum Number of Firms Created in Various Subperiods, 1952-1968*

	1952-1958	1960-1964	1966-1968
Minimum	8	16	3
Maximum	35	41	12

B. *The Proportion of Industries Showing a Change in Firm Numbers and Concentration Ratios, 1959-1970*

	Firm Numbers			Concentration Ratios	
	1959-1963	1963-1968	1968-1970	1959-1963	1963-1968
Increase	53	31	16	18	36
Decrease	13	33	56	46	32

Sources: Adapted from Sacks (1973); Estrin (1979b).

ruling on world markets. However, the bulk of price controls were retained after the reforms (see Horvat 1976; Moore 1980), so serious distortions had emerged again by the end of that decade.

Dirlam and Plummer (1973) attribute Yugoslav price distortions to the imperfect market environment.[20] They report that Yugoslav enterprises set prices in the same manner as their American counterparts—by marking up the cost of a standard unit of production—which could lead to cost-push inflationary pressure and distorted prices in a self-managed system.[21] In this context, Yugoslav price policies can be regarded as a necessary anti-monopolist device,[22] which may act to suppress inflationary tendencies to some extent.

However, there is also evidence that nonmarket considerations dominate decisionmaking. Rocco and Obraz (1968) report that, in a sample of 745 firms, 63 percent determined production type by production possibilities rather than by market demand. This implies that the role of pricing policies—whether distortive or corrective—is somewhat superfluous for resource allocation.

Therefore, Yugoslav product market structure has been severely imperfect, and there has been relatively little new entry or exit of enterprises since 1952. Even so, firm numbers in each industry have increased, and concentration declined, probably as a result of product diversification. Relative prices have inadequately reflected the relative scarcities of produced commodities, although controversy surrounds the causes of these imperfections. The major implication of the empirical work surveyed in this section is that models of self-management in Yugoslavia should explicitly take account of the imperfect market structure.

Capital Markets

The Yugoslav capital market was gradually created between 1952 and 1965, to replace the Soviet-type investment allocation of the central-planning era. The principle of the new system was that enterprises would determine their own capital requirements, which would be financed internally or borrowed from a banking system that had mobilized private savings.[23] The actual changes were gradual, with enterprises obtaining the authority to generate and finance projects during the 1950s, but supply decisions and state investment funds devolved to the banking system only in 1965. Data from the World Bank (1975) report illustrate these developments. From 1950 to 1963, the proportion of savings supplied by the state declined from 90 to 45 percent, while the enterprise share rose from 10 to 35 percent. The 1965 reforms saw a further decline in the state's share, which was matched by an increase in household savings, based on a rise in the personal savings ratio from 7 to 16 percent.[24] Thus, between 1960 and 1963, the state provided 60 percent of fixed investment finance, compared with 30 percent by enterprises and 3 percent by the banks. The reforms meant that, by 1970, the banks were providing 51 percent of the total, compared with 27 percent by enterprises and 16 percent by the authorities. In practice, however, this new capital market, which operated through the banking system, performed the task of financial intermediation inadequately.

It is important to realize that the capital market has been in disequilibrium throughout the postreform period. The authorities pegged the interest rate on bank credits at 8 percent[25] between 1966 and 1972, although inflation rates varied between 7 and 18 percent over the period. The real interest rate has been kept low or negative, even after the banking reforms in 1972, and this has generated a severe excess demand for investment funds (see Vanek 1973; World Bank 1975; Tyson 1977a).[26] Moreover, the banking system has had an effective monopoly of financial intermediation.[27] Because Yugoslav law has permitted virtually no alternative capital flows (see Horvat 1976), financial investment has been composed almost entirely of the liabilities of the banking system. Thus banks, the only channel between voluntary saving and investment, have operated in the context of investment fund rationing.

A major new instrument of financial intermediation appeared during the 1960s—"direct credits" between enterprises—but they represented a further failure of the financial system. The World Bank (1975) and Tyson (1977b) describe this extension of credit between enterprises as largely involuntary, arising because insolvent firms failed to fulfill their financial obligations during periods of monetary restrictions. Encouraged in the knowledge that the authorities would ultimately underwrite their debts, inefficient producers funded investment, or paid wage increases, by defaulting on trading debts. Thus, the average number of days between credit extension and repayment rose from 39 in 1963 to 193 in 1971, and a large number of enterprises had defaulted on outstanding debts by 1971 (Tyson 1977b). These "direct credits" did not increase the net financial resources available for the enterprise sector, but did influence the distribution of funds between firms. The failure to enforce voluntary contracts permitted inefficient firms to preempt resources from their more productive counterparts, and stimulated the demand for capital by eliminating producer risk.

Furubotn and Pejovich (1970) argue that, because self-managed firms could not own the resulting capital stock, the level of internal financing of investment would be less than in a corresponding capitalist firm, even if external funds were available.[28] In fact, although bank loans were the main source of investment finance between 1966 and 1972 (42 percent), retained earnings were maintained at around 37 percent of the total (World Bank 1975). Tyson (1977a) observes that, even after the reforms, enterprises saved a large proportion of their net income, which declined only slightly from 34 percent in 1965 to 32 percent by 1971. She reports that the savings ratio at the enterprise level ranged between 10 and 56 percent from 1967 to 1970, with the average firm retaining between 27 and 30 percent of its net income. She then considers whether these savings were a long-run equilibirum phenomenon, or represented the gradual adjustment of target to actual incomes. Using a permanent income model with lags, with permanent income denoted y^P_t, and the coefficient of adjustment γ, Tyson estimates $y_t = \gamma \, c y^P_t + (1 - \gamma) y_{t-1}$ to discover c, the desired share of savings in target income. The equation is estimated on annual data from 1965 to 1974 and yields statistically significant results in 11 of the 16 sectors of production. In 9 of these 11 sectors, c is estimated at 0.75 or less, and the hypothesis $c = 1$ is rejected in 8 industries. The adjustment coefficient is less than 0.5 in 7 of the 11 sectors, implying a gradual adjustment of earnings to target levels. Thus, Tyson finds that Yugoslav enterprise income and savings decisions can be explained by a permanent-income hypothesis, and that, contrary to theoretical predictions, the desired savings levels are positive and substantial.

A number of major failings in the Yugoslav economy are attributed to inadequacies in capital formation. In particular, it is widely charged that the methods for allocating investment funds are likely to lead to resource misallocation (Dimitrijević and Mačešić 1973; Sirc 1979); that the banking system fails to mobilize private savings sufficiently (World Bank 1975; Sapir 1980); and that the operation of the capital market encourages the adoption of relatively capital-intensive techniques of production (Estrin 1982; Sapir 1980).

The excess demand for investment funds noted above places a considerable onus on the banks' rationing criteria to provide an efficient allocation of resources. However, 44 percent of bank investment funds in 1970–1971 were "earmarked" contributions, formed from the government deposits after 1963, and directly controlled by the Republican or Communal authorities. Most remaining funds were formed from the pool contributed by founding enterprises, who help to determine the allocation of credits. Many observers are concerned that these arrangements encourage the neglect of economic criteria in favor of political and regional interests, so resource misallocation takes both a sectoral and spatial dimension (Dimitrijević and Mačešić 1973; Sacks 1976; Sapir 1980). In consequence, no consistent project appraisal criteria appear to have been applied from 1965 until at least 1972 (World Bank 1975).

There is evidence that this rationing system has led to considerable dispersion in the marginal products of capital among sectors and firms since 1965. Estimates of the real rate of return in the industrial sector as a whole range between 6 and 12 percent (see Vanek and Jovičić 1975; Miović 1975; Tyson 1977a), but detailed studies reveal large variations in capital productivity. Table 5-2, which is adapted from Miović (1975), summarizes the findings for 6 sectors in 3 studies. Although each author uses different data sources and methods,[29] the capital marginal-product rankings and dispersion among sectors prove to be broadly consistent. Miović also considers the dispersion between 15 subsectors of these industry groupings, and the estimated marginal products of capital range from 3.8 to 75 percent, with a coefficient of variation of 76 percent. Although the estimation procedures are imperfect,[30] this literature indicates that large capital-productivity differences persisted in Yugoslavia between 1963 and 1971. However, to place these findings in perspective, while allocative efficiency requires that capital marginal products be equalized ex ante, risk factors may generate an expost dispersion. Moreover, Yugoslavia was capital scarce and underdeveloped, so one might expect differences in capital productivity until the demand for investment funds had been satisfied in every sector.

Dimitrijević and Mačešić (1973) show that the Yugoslav household sector allocated 70 percent of its savings to real assets, and only 30 percent to financial assets between 1967 and 1970. There has certainly been a decline in the net supply of financial resources since 1965. The World Bank (1975) reports that the ratio of financial savings to gross national savings fell from 46 percent in 1963 to 31 percent in 1970. The movements in the ratio of financial liabilities held by the non-financial sector to Gross National Product (GNP) shows that there was no financial growth after an initial spurt in 1965. The ratio climbed from 0.55 in 1962 to 0.67 in 1967, and stagnated thereafter. It seems likely that low or negative real-interest rates hindered the mobilization of private savings, inducing agents to purchase nonfinancial rather than financial assets.

Finally, the acceleration in the rate of growth of the capital stock, relative

Table 5-2
Estimated Marginal Products of Capital

Sector	Franković (1974)	Rockwell I (1970)	Rockwell II (1970)	Miović (1975)
Industry	.08	.11	.10	.06
Agriculture	.07	.06	.06	−.06
Construction	.16	.62	.33	.40
Transport	.01	.10	.09	.04
Trade and tourism	.17	.37	.35	.23
Crafts	.56	.59	.47	.55
All productive sector	.07	.19	.15	.13

Source: Miović (1975).

to output and employment, is associated with capital-market distortions. Sapir (1980) reports that for the industrial sector the annual rate of growth of the capital-labor ratio more than doubled after 1965.[31] Using the average annual rates of growth for 19 sectors from 1952 to 1965, and 1965 to 1973, Estrin (1982) establishes that an approximate halving in the rate of growth of output was matched by a decline of 66 percent in employment growth, but only 8 percent in the rate of capital-stock growth. The rate of growth of the capital stock actually accelerated in 11, and the capital-labor ratio grew faster in 15, of the 19 sectors after the reforms. It seems likely that these changes in the pattern of growth were caused by both the capital-intensive bias of SMFs (see Ward 1958) and the low or negative real-interest rates.[32]

Labor Markets

Theory suggests that SMFs will misallocate labor and prevent market clearing by restricting labor mobility. The material on income, and labor marginal product, dispersion is discussed below, but the evidence on labor-market clearing is indirect and diffuse. For example, Wiles (1977) reports that labor turnover, measured by leavers as a percentage of the industrial labor force, is relatively low in Yugoslavia by international standards. On average, only 1 percent of the Yugoslav labor force per month left their current employment for any reason from 1974 to 1976, compared with between 5.8 and 7 percent in the United States from 1950 to 1975, and 2.5 percent, on average, in the Soviet Union between 1960 and 1962. Numerous studies refer to the apparent reduction in the rate of growth of employment after 1965, which occurred despite the large excess labor supply. The World Bank (1975) reports that the development strategy became "intensive"[33] after 1961, so employment grew at only 2.2 percent per year from 1961 to 1971, though the excess supply of labor was estimated at 1.5 million in 1971. Sapir

(1980) reports that there was a structural break in Yugoslav manufacturing growth in 1965, an important feature of which was the reduction of employment growth from 6.5 percent per year between 1955 and 1965 to 3.3 percent per year from 1965 to 1975.[34]

A corollary of the bias toward capital-intensive techniques of production in a self-managed economy is the emergence of unemployment (see Meade 1972). Registered unemployment in the Yugoslav self-managed sector increased from 3 percent of the labor force in 1955 to 6.7 percent in 1965 and 10 percent in 1975.[35] There were 735,000 registered job-seekers by 1979, and a large number of industrial workers had migrated to seek employment abroad.[36] However, since approximately 2.6 million people migrated from rural to urban areas between 1946 and 1971,[37] the problem may have been caused by supply-side factors. Bartlett (1980) estimates a structural equation of a model in which migration is a function of the expected rural-urban income differential, and this explains up to 83 percent of the variation. A reduced-form equation indicates that the level of unemployment u is positively related to urban wages wu, and negatively related to the growth of urban employment ΔE.[38] This suggests that, in addition to the effects of self-management, observed unemployment has been associated with the structural unemployment familiar in many developing economies.

Estrin (1982) attempts to isolate the effects of self-management on labor-market clearing by relating the demand and supply of employment to real wages in a dual labor-market framework. He reports that, as one would expect with the large rural-labor surplus, the ratio of rural to urban wages remained approximately constant between 1957 and 1965, despite the relatively fast growth of industrial employment. However, the ratio approximately doubled between 1965 and 1971, as the rate of growth of industrial employment declined, and the excess supply of labor increased, providing evidence for the restrictive behavior of SMFs.

The theory predicts that, in the absence of enterprise entry and exit, parametric shifts would cause a dispersion of average earnings. The existence of wide income differentials among regions, skill types, and sectors during the 1960s is noted in several studies.[39] The first systematic analysis of Yugoslav wage differentials, describing the movements in average earnings for different skill groups, republics, and sectors between 1956 and 1969, is due to Wachtel (1972, 1973). The ratio of the extremes of income[40] between 8 skill groups is shown to have increased from 264 percent in 1956 to 330 percent in 1961, after which it declined to 247 percent in 1967. This pattern was repeated in every individual industry, and similar movements were observed in the dispersion of average wages between the 6 republics from 1956 to 1969. The ratio of the extremes rose from 114 percent in 1956 to 149 percent in 1963, after which it declined to 134 percent in 1969. Average wage dispersion among sectors steadily increased over the entire period, with the ratio rising from 152 to 193 percent. Wachtel cites the gradual nar-rowing of skill and republican differentials as evidence for the increasing ef-fectiveness of labor markets over the period.

Estrin (1981) studies intersectoral and interfirm income differences from 1956 to 1974. He confirms the rise in intersectoral differentials observed by Wachtel, which were shown to have reached relatively high levels by in-ternational standards in 1969. An investigation of intersectoral differences by skill and republican groups suggests that the rapid increases in dispersion after 1965 were not caused by changes in the composition of the labor force. Data on firm-size groups are used to indicate interfirm income differences within each sector. In 1968, about 40 percent of sectors displayed an inter-firm income range in excess of 300 percent, with the largest ratio exceeding 1,000 percent in virtually every year between 1966 and 1972. Finally, the in-terfirm and intersectoral data are combined to provide evidence about average income differences in the entire industrial sector. This reveals that between 10 and 14 percent of firm-size groups paid on average, less than 50 percent or more than 200 percent of the industrial mean.

The bulk of econometric work on Yugoslav data is concerned to explain the intersectoral dispersion of average earnings per head, and there is con-siderable controversy about whether capital or labor market imperfections are the main cause of the problem. Most of the results are provided by the "capital school," whose ideas are developed by Vanek and Miović (1970), Furubotn and Pejovich (1970), and Vanek (1973).[41] The seminal paper by Vanek and Jovičić (1975) seeks to establish the empirical validity of the ap-proach. In the first instance, it assumes that the entire dispersion of average earnings per head (y_i) is caused by differences in capital-labor ratios (k_i). However, it would be inappropriate to estimate the relationship directly, since both are enterprise choice variables. Instead, labor and capital marginal products are estimated via a production function, so observed average earnings can be decomposed into "pure" labor incomes (y = the estimated marginal product of labor), and imputed capital rentals. The sec-ond stage of the argument involves regressing unexplained income disper-sion against variables that proxy labor demand phenomena. The model is estimated on cross-section data for 19 industries in 1969.

Denoting output per worker as q_i,[42] and the error component of the regression as μ_i, the relation;

$$q_i = a + bk_i + \mu_i \qquad (5.1)$$

is used to calculate the components of observed income; y = the pure in-come part, and D_i = the part caused by differences in capital-labor ratios.[43] The computations were derived from the definition of observed incomes:

$$y_i \equiv q_i - k_i. \tag{5.2}$$

Now,

$$y_i = y_i + D_i = a + D_i. \tag{5.3}$$

Substituting (5.1) into (5.2) yields

$$y_i = a + (b - 1)k_i + \mu_i. \tag{5.4}$$

Hence,

$$D_i = (b - 1)k_i + \mu_i. \tag{5.5}$$

Vanek and Jovičić compute the components of y_i in equation 5.4 from the estimate of equation 5.1:[44]

$$q_i = 2.51 + 0.09k_i + \mu_i : R^2 = 0.23$$
$$(2.26)$$

The calculated D_i explain between around 5 and 45 percent of observed earnings in each sector, but the earnings' residuals are also very large, reaching almost 50 percent of measured incomes in one sector, and normally in excess of 25 percent. The residual incomes in each sector are then regressed against labor-demand factors, proxied by relative prices, price controls, concentration, and the "newness" of capital. On the basis of t tests, it is concluded that none of these variables significantly influences income residuals, although the correlation coefficient is 0.50. The authors conclude that distortions in capital pricing are the primary determinant of Yugoslav income differences, although they propose a continued search for additional independent variables.

The assumptions of the model and the estimation techniques cast serious doubts upon the validity of these conclusions. It seems unlikely that Yugoslav technology at the sectoral level can be described by an additively separable production function with constant returns. The poor fit of equation 5.1, and the large residuals in computing equation 5.4, are consistent with this argument. At the level of estimation, the primary problem is bias from the omission of variables. Output depends on factors other than labor and capital, and the omitted materials costs mean that even the accounting identity (equation 5.2) does not hold. Finally, none of the hypotheses are properly tested, so that even if the estimators were unbiased, it is impossible to evaluate the status of the results. This is particularly true of the second estimation stage, where independent variables are used to explain a variation in the labor marginal product, which is assumed constant in the first stage. A properly specified test would either include the labor-demand factors in equation 5.1, or include k_i in the residual earnings equation.[45]

Thus, while the Vanek and Jovičic paper is methodologically and conceptually important, it does not adequately establish their explanation of income dispersion.

Supplementary empirical work accepts the basic hypothesis, and uses different data sets to estimate the direct effects of capital intensity on incomes. For example, Staellerts (1980) uses cross-section data for 19 industries in 1962 and 1975, and annual time-series observations for the industrial sector as a whole from 1958 to 1975, to examine this relationship. In the cross-section equations, the coefficient on capital per unskilled labor equivalent is statistically insignificant, with $\overline{R^2}$ of 0.09 (1962) and 0.04 (1975). The estimated time series equation is:

$$y_i = 7334 + 0.158k_i \quad : \quad \overline{R^2} = 0.93$$
$$(15.6) \qquad\qquad DW = 0.48$$

The autocorrelation in this equation is so serious that a time trend performs as well as the capital-intensity variable.

Miović (1975) uses data from a 1971 sample of Slovene firms to test hypotheses about output and income per head.[46] The study confirms that the direct relationship between capital intensity and income is weak, though statistically significant.[47] This leads him to experiment with additional independent variables, in an attempt to proxy for indirect effects. The inclusion of some technological variables, to catch additional sources of capital productivity dispersion, and a $(k_i)^2$ variable does not improve the fit. However, explanatory power is considerably increased by the inclusion of accounting profits per head π_i and percentage capital costs R_i, which also make some of the technological variables significant. Thus, denoting the 4-firm concentration ratio (employment) by M_i, the percentage increase in the value of capital by ΔK_i, and the percentage expenses for capital upkeep by $1n_i$, the final equation is:[48]

$$y_i = 13,889 + 15.61\ M_i - 20.89\Delta K_i - 23.14\ In_i - 341.00\ R_i$$
$$(1.64) \qquad (2.81) \qquad (2.23) \qquad (3.75)$$

$$+\ 0.13\pi_i + 0.003\ k_i : R^2 = 0.33.$$
$$(10.13) \qquad (1.93)$$

Miović argues that he has successfully isolated the indirect effects, as well as a tiny significant direct impact, of capital intensity on incomes. However, the estimation procedure leads one to suspect the validity of this conclusion. The final equation cannot be derived from an economic model of enterprise behavior, and is established by the ad-hoc addition of variables. As a consequence, the right-hand side contains dependent as well as independent variables (that is, k_i and R_i; π_i and M_i), which suggests that the multicollinearity may be due to simultaneous-equation bias. Insofar as one can interpret it, the equation implies that labor-demand factors (proxied by π_i), as well as capital-market imperfections, are important determinants of Yugoslav income dispersion.

The main proponent of the labor school is Wachtel (1972, 1973), who tests his model on cross-section data for 19 industries in each year from 1956 to 1968. His equations, which relate average earnings to labor productivity and industrial concentration,[49] always fit better than those of the capital school.[50] The R^2 for the equation as a whole increases from 0.35 in 1956 to 0.87 in 1965 and 1968, although the model fails to account for income changes over time.[51] The most important determinant of earnings is labor productivity, which explains 30 percent of the income variance in 1956 and 80 percent in 1965, measured by the partial R^2. The significance of the concentration variable declines over the period; it explains 22 percent of the income variance in 1958, but only 5 percent in 1968. It should be noted that the ratio of output to employment is a dependent variable in the enterprise choice set, and there is certainly an omitted variable in the equation, since the research reported above invalidates the assumption of perfect capital markets. Moreover, the accounting identity linking earnings and average productivity[52] may explain the unusually high R^2 that Wachtel obtains from cross-section data. Even so, Wachtel's study does establish the relevance of labor-demand factors in explaining Yugoslav income dispersion.

Estrin (1979a, b) attempts to estimate a full model of income dispersion, which is derived from microeconomic theory, and which allows for differences in both capital and labor marginal products. The equation is the reduced form of an average earnings-maximization problem in an imperfectly competitive environment, subject to a specific production function. The determinants of long-run equilibrium incomes are technical efficiency A_i, proxied by Farrell efficiency measures, product prices p_i, the scale of production θ_i, capital costs R_i, and market concentration M_i. The equation is specified in log-linear form, with the estimated coefficients additive functions of the production parameters. The equation, estimated on cross-section time series data for 19 industries from 1964 to 1972, is

$$y_i = 4.08 + 0.30p_i + 0.42A_i + 0.50R_i + 0.02\theta_i + 0.002M_i : \overline{R^2} = 0.52$$
$$\quad\quad\quad (3.78)\quad (3.76)\quad (9.83)\quad (0.57)\quad (1.05)$$

The results confirm that Yugoslav income dispersion is caused by differences in both labor and capital marginal products, and reject the independent influence of scale and concentration.[53] However, the estimated coefficient on the cost of capital does not have the predicted sign, which implies that the marginal product of capital is negative. This is explained by collinearity among the independent variables, caused by government regulation and data shortcomings. As a consequence, while the methodology is sound, the estimated model fails to provide a consistent explanation of Yugoslav income differences.

Economic Growth

Economic theory provides few testable propositions about the dynamic behavior of the worker-managed economy. The average income maximization literature is static, although Vanek (1971) suggests that growth could be based on forced savings raised through taxation, and the entry of new firms. The permanent income maximization hypothesis (Furubotn 1976) provides a motive for capital accumulation, but the growth rate depends on worker preferences.[54] The dynamic corollary of the Ward (1958) comparative static result is that the dynamic path of the self-managed economy displays a tendency to relatively greater capital deepening and unemployment over time[55] (Furubotn and Pejovich 1970). However, since Drèze (1976) proves the formal equivalence of self-managed and capitalist equilibria, it is not clear how an economy can sustain this path unless there is persistent disequilibrium over time.

In the absence of testable dynamic predictions, empirical work concentrates on associating the rate and pattern of growth with differing phases of economic organization in Yugoslavia. The initial problem is to distinguish between organizational and resource factors as determinants of growth, which has led to a number of "growth accounting" studies to isolate the rate of disembodied technical progress[56] (see Balassa and Bertrand 1970; Maddison 1970; Horvat 1971; Sapir 1980). The findings are summarized in table 5-3, which shows that gross factor productivity has increased by approximately 4.5 percent per annum. Thus, Balassa and Bertrand[57] find that the annual industrial growth rate of 11.8 percent from 1953 to 1965 can be decomposed into a labor contribution of 3 percent, a capital contribution of 4.1 percent, and disembodied technical progress at a rate of 4.7 percent; a result that receives broad confirmation from the other studies.

However, these results are unsatisfactory because they suggest that the residual accounts for more than 40 percent of Yugoslav growth. Further research has attempted to assign part of this unexplained growth to embodied technical progress, such as improvements in the quality of labor or capital inputs. Balassa and Bertrand use a 9-country sample to regress the residual on total input growth, and estimate a coefficient of 0.54. By adding this 50 percent embodied technical progress to the growth of each factor, the residual, denoted "net factor productivity," is reduced to 1 percent. This can be viewed as an estimate of the upper limit of growth due to the impact of self-management on productivity. Maddison (1970) estimates em-

Table 5-3
Accounting for Growth in the Yugoslav Economy, 1950-1974

Sectors (Years)		Q^*	L^*	K^*	αL^*	βK^*	A^*g	A^*n
					Variables[a]			
1. Industry	(1953-58)	10.3	4.4	7.8	—	—	4.4	—
2. Industry and		11.8	6.7	7.3	3.0[b]	4.1[b]	4.7	—
3. mining	(1955-67)	11.8	10.0[c]	11.2[c]	4.5[b]	6.2[b]	—	1.0
4. All economy	(1950-65)	7.1	3.4[c]	9.7[c]	1.7	4.8	—	0.5
5. Manufacturing	(1955-65)	12.6	6.6	9.5	4.8	2.7	4.8	—
6. industry	(1966-74)	7.6	2.2	8.2	1.9	1.1	4.8	—

Sources: 1. Horvat (1971); 2,3. Balassa and Bertrand (1970); 4. Maddison (1970); 5,6. Sapir (1980).

Note: Forms of production function: 1. Cobb-Douglas; 2,3,4. General form estimated weights; 5,6. CES and general form.

[a]Variables: *denotes annual percentage growth rate; Q^* is growth of output; L^* is the growth of employment (manhours in 5,6); K^* is growth of capital stock; A^*g is growth of gross factor productivity; A^*n is growth of net factor productivity; α is output elasticity of labor; β is output elasticity of capital.

[b]Calculated from data provided in original article.

[c]Measured in efficiency units.

bodied technical progress over the period 1950 to 1965. For the economy as a whole, an assessment of educational effects and the relocation of labor from the rural to urban sectors yields an estimate of the growth rate of efficiency labor of 3.4 percent, while the capital stock is estimated to have grown at 9.7 percent. On the assumption of constant returns and equal factor weights, disembodied technical progress is calculated to be 0.55 percent. This is broadly consistent with the Balassa and Bertrand estimate; that the latter is somewhat higher may reflect differences in organizational efficiency between the industrial (self-managed) sector and the rest of the economy. Maddison also attempts to distinguish between autonomous and policy-induced growth.[58] He finds that 4.3 percent of the 7.1 percent annual GDP growth was due to policy-induced factors; comprising 1.2 percent attributed to the quality of labor inputs, 2.8 percent due to capital-formation policies, and 0.3 percent being the policy-induced rate of disembodied technical progress.

Marschak (1968), Balassa and Bertrand (1970), and Sapir (1980) attempt to compare the changes in growth rates between subperiods. Marschak estimates a Cobb-Douglas production function with Hicks-neutral technical progress (μ) and dummy variables on the shift parameter (μ) to allow for efficiency improvements over the transitional period following the 1950-1953 reforms. The best fitting equation is found for the period 1953-1958, with λ set to zero, and estimates μ to be 4 percent. This suggests that institutional reforms had a major effect on Yugoslav growth, but with λ set to zero, the coefficient μ may actually proxy for the more general effects of disembodied technical progress.[59] Balassa and Bertrand examine the subperiods 1953-1959 and 1959-1965, and find a decrease in both gross and net factor productivity, but the extent of the decrease is not reported. Sapir attempts to contrast the pre- and post-1965 reform industrial growth performance, using a constant elasticity of substitution production function with Hicks-neutral technical progress and dummy variables on the shift parameter.[60] Table 5-3 reports the estimated factor contributions, comprising the input growth rates weighted by the imputed factor shares, and a rate of technical progress of 4.8 percent in each period. This shows that the decline in industrial growth from 12.6 to 7.6 percent between the periods was not caused by a reduction in the rate of disembodied technical progress, but by a fall in the contributions of both factor inputs. The reduction in labor's contribution to growth was due primarily to a decline in the rate of growth of employment after 1965, whereas the decline in capital's contribution can be attributed to a reduction in the marginal product of capital. Sapir argues that his findings are consistent with the prediction of capital deepening from static economic theory. However, the estimated coefficient, μ, is not found to be significantly different from zero, which indicates that organizational changes had no impact on growth rates between the two periods.

Two of the studies attempt to compare the rate of technical progress internationally. Balassa and Bertrand (1970) report that Yugoslavia, along with Romania and Spain, enjoyed higher productivity growth (both total and net) than was observed elsewhere in their sample of 10 European countries. In contrast, Maddison (1970) finds that, after accounting for embodied technical progress, residual productivity growth in Yugoslavia was exceeded in 9 of his sample of 22 developing countries.

Structural changes in the composition of output and employment can also be associated with institutional reforms.[61] Moore (1980) develops a new index of structural change, which is shown to have altered rapidly in periods following major organizational readjustments (that is, 1952-1957 and 1966-1971).[62] He argues that both organizational and structural changes utilize resources in a manner that is only indirectly conducive to growth, so that periods of intense structural change represent necessary "latent growth," which does not appear in production data.[63] A combined structural change-production growth index reveals a gradual decline in the overall pace of industrial development over time, without the sharp dichotomy of growth patterns after 1965 reported in other studies (World Bank 1975; Sapir 1980; Estrin 1982). The recent acceleration in industrial growth to 9.2 percent per year between 1970 and 1977, compared with 6.3 percent from 1960 to 1970 (World Bank 1979), is consistent with this hypothesis of latent growth.

Structural change is a commonly observed feature of growth in developing economies, and normal "patterns" of growth have been estimated on

international cross-section data (Chenery and Syrquin 1975; Vahčić).[64]
These studies reveal that the share of manufacturing output, employment,
and exports in GDP were unusually high in Yugoslavia by 1965. Previous
work by Chenery (1960) indicates that deviations from the normal structure
tend to be eliminated in the long run. This suggests that the Visible Hand
period facilitated relatively early industrialization, and that the retardation
of growth after 1965 may have represented an adjustment to a normal pattern
of development, unrelated to the introduction of market self-management.

Conclusions

In this chapter, a large empirical literature has been surveyed in the hope of
identifying the effects of enterprise self-management on Yugoslav economic
behavior. Sociologists have established that efficiency is related to the
degree of participation. However, it is not clear that economists have isolated
effects of self-management independently from the more general impact of
underdevelopment, market imperfections, and government regulation. They
have shown that Yugoslav factor and product markets are severely imperfect, though the growth performance has been respectable by international standards. These findings are generally consistent with predictions
from self-management theory, but causality cannot be attributed because
they could also support competing hypotheses.

This inconclusiveness arises partly because the empirical work has concentrated on providing a description of the Yugoslav environment, and has
not yet attempted to test the central propositions of self-management
theory. However, it also relates to two weaknesses within the theory itself.
First, the models have been primarily concerned with static resource allocation in the short run. As a consequence, they have generated few distinct
propositions for econometric analysis, and have failed to provide predictions about the most important problems in the Yugoslav context—
dynamics and growth. Second, the stylized facts established in this paper
suggest that competitive market assumptions are inappropriate for modeling the Yugoslav environment. The research surveyed above can therefore
be used in the development of new economic theories, as well as to provide
data for future empirical work.

Notes

1. This brief historical survey is intended only to provide background
material. For a full description, see Horvat (1971) , Bićanić (1973), Dirlam
and Plummer (1973), Milenkovitch (1971), Rusinow (1977) and Sirc (1979).

2. This section merely highlights the hypotheses that have been tested
on Yugoslav data.

3. A body of literature argues that private ownership of capital is an additional necessary condition for an efficient allocation (see Furubotn and Pejovich 1970; Sirc 1979). Yugoslav capital markets are so impefect that this hypothesis cannot be investigated empirically. However, when applied to a self-managed economy, the argument takes the form that cooperatives will make inefficient investment decisions in the absence of external funds. This reduces to the proposition, in a general-equilibrium context, that SMFs will not finance investment internally (see Tyson 1977a), which is tested in the subsection on capital markets.

4. There was an increase in the representation of white-collar workers between 1960 and 1970. Skilled and highly skilled workers had an absolute majority in both years (55 percent in 1960; 51 percent in 1970), while unskilled workers were relatively underrepresented.

5. The sample sizes are 590 (Kavčić et al. 1971); 2,115 (Rus 1978); and 461 (Šiber et al. 1978).

6. The study observes 1,800 people participating in nearly 17,000 decisions.

7. For example, Korać and Vlaškalić (1975), Brus (1975), and Furubotn (1971) dispute the view that managers are concerned with growth, but workers only with short-term income maximization.

8. Efficiency is proxied by several variables, including labor productivity.

9. The Kavčić sample covers 4 firms, the Rus study covers 15, and Jerovšek and Možina sample 20 companies, controlled for differences of technology and size. Efficiency is defined by a set of correlated indexes, such as income, output, and investment per head.

10. Thus, these findings are also consistent with the view that increased participation has led enterprises to act in the interest of the work force, by raising the level and growth of income per head.

11. The chapter by Sacks in this volume considers recent changes in the structure of Yugoslav product markets.

12. Thus, there were only 2,500 firms in the Yugoslav manufacturing sector in 1958, approximately 34 percent of which contained more than 250 workers, with only 5.5 percent employing fewer than 15 people. The comparable proportions for the United States were 3.7 and 68.1 percent, respectively.

13. The measure used is the 4-firm sales concentration ratio, showing the proportion of industry sales realized by the largest 4 companies.

14. The American classification contains 469 industries. Only 12 percent of Yugoslav sectors, and 8 percent of industries, displayed concentration ratios below 30 percent, compared with approximately 60 percent of American industries.

15. In 1972, the largest 200 industrial firms accounted for 53 percent of net output in Yugoslavia, and 43 percent in the United States (Estrin 1979b).

16. Between 1961 and 1963, concentration ratios declined by 6.8 percent in each industry, on average.

17. Tyson (1977) considers the various explanations of Yugoslav inflation.

18. Information on pricing policy can be found in Horvat (1971), Bjelčić et al. (1974), and Maksimović and Pjanić (1968).

19. Price controls were exercised over 31.2 percent of the value of net output in 1958, 67 percent in 1962, and 62 percent between 1962 and 1965 (Horvat 1976).

20. The 1974 reforms, which introduced Self-Management Agreements between firms within and between sectors (see Comisso 1980) may have further encouraged collusive rather than competitive behavior.

21. Especially given the imperfect procedures for pricing capital discussed below.

22. They point out that the 1967 codification of price controls recognized the desirability of free price formation, and placed emphasis on market conditions in the administration of controls.

23. The authorities always intended to retain a residual influence over the allocation of capital, to further their development and regional goals (see Horvat 1976).

24. The state's share of saving fell from 39 percent in 1960-1963 to 18 percent in 1970; the household share rose from 10 to 33 percent; and the enterprise share declined slightly from 42 to 34 percent.

25. Except for 1968, when they rose to 10 percent.

26. Although this is an ex ante concept, supporting evidence is provided by the persistency of inflation, balance of payments deficits, and the increase in the ratio of gross borrowing to investment after 1965, which rose from 99 percent in 1960-1963 to 136 percent in 1967-1971 (World Bank 1975).

27. The banking system was also relatively highly concentrated. The number of banks declined from 220 to 1963 to 64 in 1970, and the 10 largest banks accounted for 60 percent of short-term, and virtually all investment credits in 1968.(Dimitrijević and Mačešić, 1973).

28. This conclusion is disputed in Stephen (1980).

29. Rockwell (1970) refers to data from Yugoslavia in 1963 and 1964, Franković covers Yugoslavia as a whole in 1969, Miović employs a sample of 1,637 Slovene firms in 1971. Franković and Miović estimate linear production functions, but Rockwell uses various estimation procedures on the Cobb-Douglas form.

30. The essential problem is the restrictive form of the estimated production functions.

31. It increased from 2.9 percent per year, on average, between 1955 and 1965 to 6 percent per year between 1965 and 1975.

32. Vanek and Jovičić (1975) and Horvat (1976) emphasize the interest-

rate effect, but the World Bank (1975), Sapir (1980), and Estrin (1982) consider both factors to be important.

33. The emphasis in development shifted from increases in employment to accelerated productivity growth.

34. The decline in man-hours was even more marked; from 6.6 to 2.2 percent per year.

35. Primorac and Della Valle (1974) argue that the figures overstated market slack, because a large proportion of unemployment was structural, matched by vacancies.

36. The number of migrant workers peaked at 850,000 in 1973 (Tanić 1979).

37. Around 1.3 million people migrated between 1946 and 1961 (Tanić 1979), and a similar number from 1961 to 1971 (Hawrylyshyn 1977).

38. The estimated equation from 1957 to 1974 is

$$U = 202.47 - 0.15\Delta E + 0.009 WU : \overline{R}{}^2 = 0.84$$
$$(2.04) (9.23)$$

Note that bracketed figures always denote t-statistics.

39. For example, Horvat (1971) mentions some Yugoslav studies on wage differences such as Popov 1968; Korać 1969; Popov and Jovičić 1971), and some findings are also reported in the Western literature (for example, Dirlam and Plummer 1973). Indeed, Miović (1975) and Rusinow (1977) argue that public disquiet about income inequalities may have led to the 1974 reforms.

40. The ratio of the extremes is the largest observation divided by the smallest, expressed as a percentage.

41. Their interpretation has been widely accepted in the Western literature, and within Yugoslavia (Bajt 1981).

42. The variables were denominated in unskilled labor equivalents.

43. a and b represent the marginal products of labor and capital respectively. Therefore, $a = y$ by assumption, and b is the shadow price of capital that, if charged, would eliminate income differences deriving from dispersion in capital intensities.

44. k_i measured at depreciated value.

45. This point is stressed in a paper by Rivera-Batiz (1980), who argues that labor-demand factors must be included in equation 5-1, on the basis of a dual labor-market model. The Vanek and Jovičić equation is reestimated including average enterprise size and the four-firm concentration ratio, and the R^2 rises to 0.73. The capital coefficient remains significant, but the estimator declines to 0.062. This confirms the suggested misspecification of the Vanek-Jovičić paper, though the included labor demand variables are essentially arbitrary.

46. The results from the output-per-head equations are discussed in the capital-market section, and contradict some of Vanek and Jovičić's contentions. For example, the equations are better specified in quadratic form, and the fit is improved by the inclusion of additional variables, such as the "newness" of capital. However, Miović does not use these equations to compute the implicit capital rental, but examines the effects of capital intensity on incomes directly.

47. The basic equation for the industrial sector as a whole is

$$y_i = 13,402 + 0.0063k_i : R^2 = 0.03$$
$$(3.58)$$

Average incomes in the sample are 13,637 dinars.

48. Three insignificant technical variables are excluded.

49. The equations also control for labor quality and regional concentration.

50. For example, denoting labor quality by QL_i , the estimated equation for 1965 is

$$y_i = 158.3 + 0.056q_i + 0.323M_i + 1.72QL_i : R^2 = 0.87$$
$$(4.87) \quad (1.53) \quad (2.82)$$

51. The equation, in rate of change form, is insignificant in every year tested except 1958.

52. $y_i = q_i - k_i$, so, in the absence of other costs, regressing incomes on average productivity and capital intensity produces an R^2, and coefficients, of unity.

53. In annual cross-sections, the concentration coefficient is significant in the early years.

54. Some authors stress the animal spirits of worker-managers (see Korać 1968; Brus 1975); others argue that workers will be less inclined to forego present consumption than capitalists (see Pejovich 1973; Coyne, Chiplin, and Sirc 1977). Atkinson (1973) argues that growth will be influenced by the division of responsibility between workers and managers.

55. This chapter treats the prediction of a rising degree of capital intensity as a comparative static question.

56. These studies use a neoclassical production function, $Q = f(L,K,t)$, where t denotes time, to assess the relative contribution of productive factors, and technical advance, which includes organizational changes. They estimate $\dot{Q}/Q = \dot{A}/A + \alpha\dot{L}/L + \beta\dot{K}/K$, where $\dot{A}/A$ is the rate of disembodied technical progress, and α, β are the output elasticities of the factor inputs, proxied by respective factor shares in a competitive economy. Since Yugoslavia is not perfectly competitive, they are estimated indirectly or

obtained by fitting a specific production function.

57. They assume constant returns to scale, and a labor-output elasticity of 0.45. The residual is not greatly altered by any assumption about relative input weights, since the factor growth rates are similar, and less than the growth of output.

58. The growth due to autonomous changes in factor inputs, and technical advance, is calculated by isolating that part of factor growth that would have occurred in the absence of government intervention such as education, health, and capital mobilization policies). Autonomous disembodied technical progress is assumed to take place at a rate of 10 percent of the rate of growth of autonomous factor inputs.

59. Viewed in this way, Marschak's estimates are consistent with the other estimates of disembodied technical progress reported in Table 5-3.

60. The production function is

$$Q = \gamma \left[\delta K^{(\sigma - 1)/\sigma} + (1 - \delta)L^{(\sigma - 1)/\sigma} \right]^{\sigma/(\sigma - 1)} \cdot e^{(\lambda + \mu D)t}$$

where σ is the elasticity of substitution, $(\lambda + \mu D)$ the rate of Hicks-neutral technical progress, with the dummy variable D set to 0 for 1955-1965 and to 1 for 1965-1974.

61. See Chenery and Syrquin (1975) for the general argument in a developing economy, and Bartlett (1979, 1980b) for specific predictions in the Yugoslav context.

62. Sapir rejects the hypothesis that structural change accounts for the decline in industrial growth, since the Spearman rank correlation coefficients for the shares of each branch in total manufacturing output between the two periods is 0.93.

63. He shows that the indexes of production and structural change are inversely related, after correcting for trend and cyclical effects.

64. Chenery and Syrquin establish the normal patterns using equations of the structural variables for a range of per-capita incomes estimated on data from 101 countries between 1950 and 1970.

6 Giant Corporations in Yugoslavia

Stephen R. Sacks

[F]orces inherent in labor-management are infinitely less likely to lead to inordinate concentrations of industrial power . . . [and a] labor-managed industrial conglomerate is as likely an occurrence as the apocalyptic beast with seven heads and ten horns.—Jaroslav Vanek[1]

The above quotation is the most dramatic of several statements that Vanek makes to the effect that there "is a far lesser danger of gigantism—and a corresponding far greater likelihood of competitive conditions—in labor-managed market structures than in just about any other economic regime" (Vanek 1970, p. 119). The purpose of this paper is to examine empirical evidence from the Yugoslav economy to determine whether that labor-managed economy does in fact behave according to this prediction.

I begin with a brief review of Vanek's theoretical basis for his assertion that "the equilibrium size of a labor-managed firm (LMF) is considerably smaller than that of a capitalist firm" (Vanek 1970, p. 105). Then there follows a brief discussion of the importance of enterprise size for the functioning of a market economy. The bulk of the paper consists of presentation and discussion of the empirical evidence. That evidence at first appears to be self-contradictory, but the apparent confusion can be explained if I clarify what is meant by the concept of an enterprise or firm.

Theory of Firm Size

Vanek's theoretical analysis is built on the by now well-known principle that a LMF will hire workers up to the point where the marginal revenue product of labor falls just enough to equal the average income per worker.[2] At lower levels of labor input an additional worker would add more to enterprise income than he takes as his share of the total; thus, adding a worker would raise the income of the other workers. Conversely, at higher levels of labor input, reducing the labor force by one worker would reduce total revenue by less than the income share that would have gone to that worker; thus, reduc-

I gratefully acknowledge financial support from the National Council for Soviet and East European Research during the time this chapter was written. The discussion of the theory of firm size and of the significance of large size draws on an earlier article of mine (Sacks 1976). However, that article used different analytical techniques.

ing the labor force would raise the average income of the remaining workers. An important characteristic of this optimum level of labor input is that it corresponds to the bottom of the short-run average-cost curve, or what Vanek calls the point of maximum physical efficiency because it maximizes output per worker for the given fixed amount of capital.

By contrast, a capitalist "twin" with the same amount of capital might choose to hire more workers and produce more output. It will continue to hire until the marginal revenue product of labor falls to the price of labor, which, if there is excess profit being made, is lower than the income share of a worker in the LMF. That is, a declining marginal-revenue product curve will intersect the price of labor curve to the right (that is, at a higher level of labor input and hence of output) of its intersection with the curve that represents total income of a worker who gets profit share as well as wage. That it has gone beyond the bottom of its average-cost curve does not matter to the capitalist firm, which is interested in maximizing not average or marginal profit but total profit.

Vanek expands this analysis of input and output decisions to the case where the amount of capital as well as labor is variable. The concept of maximum physical effiency now corresponds to a locus of capital-labor combinations, correponding to the bottom points of different long-run average-cost curves, representing various factor-price combinations. This locus can be projected as a contour on the production-function surface, where it marks the separation between the region of increasing returns and the region of decreasing returns. Just as in the case where the quantity of capital is assumed fixed, the LMF, being interested in maximizing the value of output *per worker,* will not expand beyond the locus of maximum physical efficiency.[3] The capitalist firm, however, being interested in *total* profit, may choose to produce at an output level beyond that locus; that is, it may go beyond the minimum point on its average-cost curve. In fact, the capitalist firm will operate at the bottom of its average-cost curve only under perfect competition. If the price of the product and the capitalist's cost of labor are such as to allow the capitalist firm to earn excess profit, then it will choose a higher output level than the labor-managed "twin." Venek's conclusion is that "the impetus to grow indefinitely, and thus to control a sizeable portion of the market, in the LMF can be expected to be considerably less than in the case of its capitalist equivalent" (Vanek 1970, p. 34).

Before turning to the empirical evidence concerning the size of Yugoslav firms, I consider briefly some of the reasons for believing that firm size is important to the operation of market socialism. It is true, although perhaps not obvious, that concern with the influence of large corporations on the effectiveness of competition is no less relevant in a socialist than in a capitalist framework. Regardless of who owns the banks and the means of production and regardless of how profits are distributed, if an economy relies on market forces to ensure technical and allocative efficiency, then effective competition is necessary for proper functioning of the system. Whether the socialist firm maximizes total profit, profit per worker, or some Galbraithian maximand like size or stability, if the system is designed to rely on the discipline of competition it will work less well in the presence of large firms if they are free of that discipline. Similarly, regardless of their own optimization rules, if socialist firms learn that relatively large size confers advantages in the competitive process, then they, as well as capitalist firms, may expand beyond the size necessary to exhaust physical economies of scale in production.

While the vigor of competition is not necessarily proportional to the number of competitors, effective operation of any market system does require at least a few firms, and for a given size market the presence of larger firms means there is room for fewer others. This is particularly important in a country where the total size of markets is small. To some extent it is possible to rely on foreign firms to provide the necessary competitive pressure. Indeed, since 1965 official Yugoslav policy has been to reduce tariffs and encourage international trade, in part for this very reason. However, balance-of-payments problems and pressure from special-interest groups have hindered the implementation of this policy, and in many industries effective competition requires that there be a number of domestic firms.

In addition to the obvious effect on the number of competitors, there are other considerations. Hart and Prais (1956) for example, discuss the influence of relatively large firms on the effectiveness of competition, emphasizing certain advantages they have over their smaller competitors, such as easier access to capital and lower per-unit costs of advertising and distribution, as well as economies of scale in direct production costs. These advantages reduce the pressures that, in the microeconomic theory of the market system, drive average cost down toward its minimum and price down toward average cost. As relative size differences decrease, however, these advantages tend to disappear. Hence, effective competition (that is, competition that does in fact reduce the gap between price and average cost) is more likely among firms of approximately equal size. The essence of this argument is that the market mechanism works best when every firm perceives a threat that other firms will lure away customers by selling at a lower price, and that this threat is less credible to firms with cost advantages due to size. There are, of course, many other influences on price-cost margins.

The significance of large firm size for effective competition is clearest in cases where firms are large relative to other firms in a particular market—that is, where their size gives them a large share of a well-defined market. However, size relative to *all* other firms (not just those in the same industry) also has significance for the effectiveness of competition. The two most important ways in which large absolute size interfers with competitiveness involve access to capital and what is called *reciprocity*. In an ideally functioning market system a firm's ability to attract capital suppliers and customers depends entirely upon the price and quality of the product or service it sells. However, banks often are more willing to lend, or to lend at a lower interest rate, to a large conglomerate simply because it is large (perhaps because banks believe that the risk is lower when the borrower is large or diversified). This puts smaller firms or potential entrants at a disadvantage. Reciprocity refers to a situation where a division of a large conglomerate acquires customers, not because of the prices or quality of its products, but because other divisions (or customers or suppliers of other divisions) have been pressured to buy from it. For example, the U.S. Department of Justice accused Ling-Temco-Vought of pressuring General Motors to buy steel from an LTV-owned steel producer under threat that an LTV-owned car-rental agency would buy its cars from Ford or Chrysler.

In a broader sense, large size (which may or may not entail a large share of individual markets) can be said to be important per se, because every firm is a potential entrant to other markets and every product competes for the consumer's dollar.[4] Hart and Prais (1956, p. 152) claim that if "large firms today control a greater part of the resources of the economy in relation to the remaining firms than they used to . . . there is a *prima facie* case for saying that opportunities for monopolistic practices are increasing in individual industries."

In the context of socialism the existence of relatively large firms raises a special problem. When economic systems are compared, certain advantages of a competitive market system over command and traditional economies are often discussed. Among them is the fact that society's output mix is more the result of impersonal forces of supply and demand, reflecting a large number of individual consumption and production decisions, than of the decisions of some relatively small group of people. This characteristic is often considered desirable in itself on political grounds (that is, as a limitation on the concentration of power), as well as for its contribution to the efficiency of resource allocation.[5] One of the advantages claimed for market socialism, over the alternative of centralized (or Soviet-type) socialism, is this broad dispersion of decison-making power. As firms grow, however, they draw into themselves certain economic transactions that would otherwise be handled in a marketplace by negotiation between separate decision makers. In fact, Coase (1937, pp. 388-389) defines firms as "islands of conscious power" distinguished by "the suppression of the price mechanism." Similarly, Arrow (1964, p. 403) defines the firm as an organization bounded by a line across which price-mediated transactions take place. Thus to the extent that growth of giant corporations replaces market forces by a hierarchical command structure, a fundamental principle of decentralized socialism is violated.[6]

One might argue that under the Yugoslav form of socialism the principle of worker self-management so broadens the decision-making process within the firm that the number or relative size of firms is unimportant: each worker has a proportionate voice in the decision making of his firm. However, two problems remain. First, the decisions of some workers will have a relatively greater impact on the economy than the decisions of others if sales or assets per worker are greater in large firms than in small firms. Second, while something like a market mechanism is used to govern transactions among the divisions of a single firm, with respect to other firms workers act in their collective interest—that is, they may collude. The economy's output mix, then, results from the production decisions of workers acting in collusive groups, rather than independently, and the number of independent decision-making teams may be no greater than the number of firms.

Some Empirical Evidence

Empirical data on Yugoslavia's large firms is published annually by *Ekonomska Politika,* a weekly news magazine. This equivalent of the *Fortune* "500" list provides data on sales, assets, and number of employees for the 100 to 200 largest enterprises in the country. The number of firms covered has increased over the years since the list was first published for 1968[7] The analysis and conclusions that follow are based on the lists for 1969 to 1978, and focus primarily on the 100 largest industrial firms and the 50 largest trade enterprises.

Tables 6-1 and 6-2 present some basic data on Yugoslavia's large enterprises that I have calculated using the *Ekonomska Politika* lists. From Table 6-1a one can see that in 1978 there were 50 industrial firms that employed more than 10,000 workers each. Of these firms, 16 employed over 20,000 workers, and 5 of them had over 30,000 workers. In the trade sector (table 1b) that year there were 15 firms with over 5,000 employees, of which 3 firms had over 10,000 workers. Looking across the rows, one can see that in virtually every year the number of firms above each size threshold increases, indicating a steady growth in the size of Yugoslavia's largest firms.

Tables 6-2a and 6-2b show the importance of these large firms relative to the rest of the economy. For example, in 1978 industrial firms with over 10,000 workers employed a total of 940,000 workers, or 32 percent of the total industrial labor force. Exactly half of those workers (470,000 or 16 percent of the industrial labor force) worked in firms with over 20,000 employees. That year 7 percent of the industrial labor force (211,000

Table 6-1
Large Industrial and Trade-Sector Firms

	A. Number of Industrial Firms with More than X Workers									
	1969	1970	1971	1972	1973	1974	1975	1976	1977	1978
X = 10,000	12	20	23	25	27	30	37	43	50	50
X = 20,000	1	2	6	8	8	10	11	12	13	16
X = 30,000	0	0	1	1	1	3	3	5	5	5

	B. Number of Trade-Sector Firms with More than X Workers									
	1969	1970	1971	1972	1973	1974	1975	1976	1977	1978
X = 5,000	0	3	4	5	5	6	10	12	11	15
X = 10,000	0	0	1	1	1	3	3	2	3	3

Source: Calculated from data in *Ekonomska Politika,* various issues.

workers) worked in firms with over 30,000 workers. In the trade sector in 1978, 21 and 8 percent of that sector's labor force worked in firms with over 5,000 workers and 10,000 workers, respectively.

Over the 1969-1978 decade the percentage of the industrial labor force working in firms with over 10,000 employees quadrupled (from 8 to 32 percent) while the percentage in firms with over 20,000 workers increased from 1 to 16 percent. Similar steady increases are evident in table 6-2b for the trade sector.

A similar picture emerges if I look at the *Ekonomska Politika* data in a different way. Figure 6-1a shows the share of total industrial-sector economic activity accounted for by the largest 50 firms (ranked by sales). Two important characteristics are noticeable immediately: these 50 firms account for a substantial share of the industrial sector, and their share of economic activity has been rising steadily over the ten years 1969-1978. In 1969 the 50 largest industrial firms accounted for 16 percent of the sector's workers, 25 percent of its assets, and 26 percent of total industrial sales. By 1978 these figures had risen to 31, 45, and 49 percent, respectively. Figure 6-1b shows the same variables for the entire list of 130 large industrial firms, but covers only 1972-1978, because the list was shorter in the early years. By 1978 the 130 largest firms accounted for 48 percent of industrial workers, 65 percent of all industrial assets, and 70 percent of sector sales.

Figure 6-1c shows the largest 50 firms' share of sales, assets, and employment in the trade sector. In this case there does not appear to be the steady increases over the period that are evident in the industrial sector. While the employment and asset shares are considerably higher in 1978 (31 and 35 percent, respectively) than they were in 1969, their share of sales remains fairly constant, at about 34 percent of the sector total throughout the period.

Table 6-2
Industrial and Trade-Sector Workers in Large Firms

	A. Industrial Workers Employed in Firms with More than X Workers									
	1969	1970	1971	1972	1973	1974	1975	1976	1977	1978
$X = 10{,}000_{\%}^{n}$	171	308	379	436	481	551	680	790	926	940
	8	15	17	19	20	22	27	31	33	32
$X = 20{,}000_{\%}^{n}$	22	46	142	194	217	273	319	358	416	470
	1	2	6	8	9	11	13	14	15	16
$X = 30{,}000_{\%}^{n}$	0	0	33	34	48	113	118	188	216	211
	0	0	1	1	2	5	5	7	8	7

	B. Trade-Sector Workers Employed in Firms with More than X Workers									
	1969	1970	1971	1972	1973	1974	1975	1976	1977	1978
$X = 5{,}000_{\%}^{n}$	0	25	33	42	39	59	85	97	102	148
	0	6	7	9	8	11	14	15	15	21
$X = 10{,}000_{\%}^{n}$	0	0	16	18	15	40	41	27	43	56
	0	0	3	4	3	7	7	4	6	8

Source: Calculated from data in *Ekonomska Politika,* various issues.
Notes: n = number of workers (in thousands)
$\%$ = number of workers as percentage of total industrial or trade-sector labor force.

What stands out clearly in all three parts of figure 6-1 is the fact that the large firms' shares of sales and assets are bigger than their shares of employment. That is, sales per worker and assets per worker are greater for the large firms than for their respective sectors as a whole. Table 6-3 presents some data on the industrial firms that I calculated in order to quantify these differences. For each firm and for each year I calculated output per worker, capital per worker, and the capital-output ratio. Then I calculated the average of each statistic for the 50 and 100 largest firms for each year, and took the ratios of these averages to the corresponding statistic for the entire industrial sector for that year. What is shown in table 6-3 is the average over the decade of these ratios.

For example, table 6-3 tells us that over the period 1970-1978 output per worker averaged 73 percent higher in the 100 largest industrial firms than in the industrial sector as a whole. This is in part explained by the fact that capital per worker was on average 55 percent higher in these firms. But this is not simply a matter of more capital: Their capital-output ratio averages 96 percent of the sector-wide capital-output ratio. Apparently, either these firms use capital more effectively or there is some input not being taken into account here. It is possible that they use technologies that are not practical for smaller firms.

The second row of table 6-3 shows that if I look at only the largest 50 firms the contrast with the whole sector is even sharper. Output per worker averages 87 percent greater than the sector-wide figure, and while the capital-per-worker statistic is even higher than for the 100 largest firms, the

A. Largest 50 Firms' Share of Total Industrial Sector

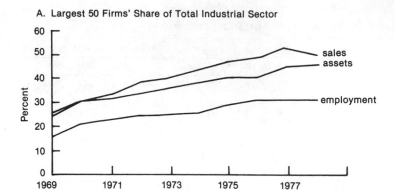

B. Largest 130 Firms' Share of Total Industrial Sector

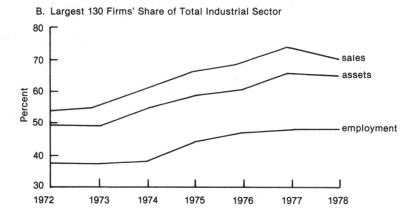

C. Largest 50 Firms' Share of Total Trade Sector

Source: Calculated from data in *Ekonomska Politika*, various issues.

Figure 6-1. Large Firms in the Industrial and Trade Sectors

capital-output ratio is even better: their captial-output ratio is only 93 percent of the sector-wide figure. That is, the 50 largest firms average of 8 percent more output per worker than in the largest 100 firms ((1.87 − 1.73)/1.73 = .08) but have only 3 percent more capital per worker ((1.60 − 1.55)/1.55 = .03) than in those firms.

In order to measure more precisely the relationship among capital, labor, and output, I ran log-linear regressions to fit a Cobb-Douglas production function to the data.[8] The estimated coefficients, which are significant at the 1 percent confidence level, are .35 for capital and .39 for labor. This is a bit surprising, since the sum of the coefficients is less than one, indicating decreasing returns to scale. How can this be reconciled with the implication of table 6-3 that large firms get *more* output from a given amount of capital and labor than the sector-wide ratios would suggest? The answer, I think, is that there are inputs other than capital and labor that are not specified in the regression equation (perhaps land or managerial skill). If other inputs were specified and data were available, quite likely the sum of the coefficients would be higher. Again, it may be that the larger firms use different technologies.

I have already noted that large firms account for a very substantial share of total economic activity in Yugoslavia. In fact, their share is so substantial (the 130 largest industrial firms accounted for 70 percent of total industrial-sector sales in 1978) that if I am interested in changing relative firm sizes I must examine data on subgroups within the *Ekonomska Politika* list. In figure 6-2 I have graphed on the same pair of axes the shares of total industrial-sector activity for the largest 50, 100, and 130 industrial firms. This enables me to think in terms of three subgroups, one consisting of the 50 largest firms, one consisting of firms 51 through 100, and one con-

Table 6-3
Some Basic Statistics on Large Firms Relative to Those Statistics for the Entire Industrial Sector, 1969-1978

	Output per Worker	Capital per Worker	Capital/Output Ratio
Largest 100 firms	1.73	1.55	.96
Largest 50 firms	1.87	1.60	.93

Source: Calculated from data in *Economska Politika,* various issues.
Note: Each element in the table is equal to

$$\left(\sum_{i=2}^{n} \frac{\text{Average statistic over the group of large firms in year } i}{\text{same statistic for the entire industrial sector in year } i} \right) \div n$$

where n is 9 years for the first row of the table and 10 years for the second row. Notice that by calculating a ratio for each year and then averaging, we get pure numbers and hence avoid any need to adjust for price changes.

A. Share of Total Industrial Sales

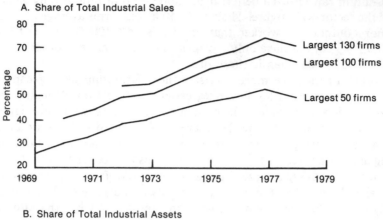

B. Share of Total Industrial Assets

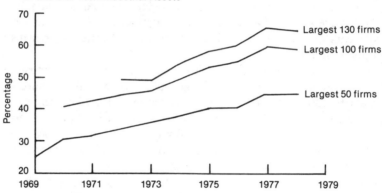

B. Share of Total Industrial Workers

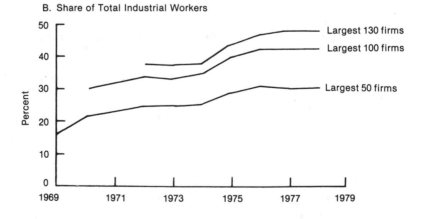

Source: Calculated from data in *Ekonomska Politika*, various issues.

Figure 6-2. Large Firms in the Industrial Sector

sisting of firms 101 throught 130. The fact that the middle and upper lines on the graphs appear nearly parallel to the lower line indicates that the second and third subgroups have retained a fairly constant share of total industrial activity while most of the increase over the decade noted earlier is attributable to the first subgroup.

Actually, while the distance between the top and middle lines on the graphs (the third subgroup's share) has remained at between 5 and 6 percent of industrial sales, assets, and employment, the distance between the middle and lower lines did increase somewhat during the period. In sales and asset terms the share of the second subgroup increased from 10 to 15 percent and from 10 to 14 percent, respectively. In terms of employment, the second subgroup's share increased during the 1970-1978 period from 8.5 to 12 percent. These increases are smaller than the first subgroup's increases over the decade: 23 percent in sales (from 26 to 49 percent of the sector total), 20 percent in assets (from 25 to 45 percent), and 15 percent in employment (from 16 percent of the total to 31 percent). But they are roughly in proportion to the initial relative sizes of the subgroups. Detailed examination of the underlying data shows that the shares of each subgroup relative to the group of giants as a whole have remained quite stable. Furthermore, within each subgroup the increases were fairly uniform.

In the trade sector, changes over this period were less dramatic. The top 50 firms' share of trade-sector sales remained virtually unchanged at 34 percent while their share of total sector assets rose from 27 percent in 1969 to 35 percent in 1978. Only in terms of employment has their relative importance increased substantially, from 12 to 31 percent, with much of this increase occurring in the first and last years of the period. If I divide the large firms into three subgroups (the first 10, the next 20, and the last 20) their relative importance in terms of total growth over the decade is much like that seen in the industrial sector. The third subgroup consistently accounted for about 8 percent of sales and assets and 4 to 6 percent of workers, while the second subgroup showed small increases in its share of sales (from 12 to 14 percent), assets (from 11 to 15 percent), and employment (from 5 to 11 percent). The first subgroup's share of sales was unchanged (at 13 percent) but its share of sector assets increased from 8 to 13 percent. Its increased share of sector employment (from 4 to 14 percent) is the major reason for the 50 firms' substantial increase noted above.

So far I have argued that the firms on the *Ekonomska Politika* list account for a large and increasing share of Yugoslav economic activity. At this point it would be interesting to ask how these firms compare in size and relative importance with large firms in other countries. Since international comparisons of sales and assets encounter numerous problems of appropriate exchange rates, relative prices, and differing procedures for valuing assets, I will restrict the comparisons to employment measures of size.

One way to get some sense of the general magnitude of these firms is to consider the very largest ones and see where they would fall on the *Fortune* ''500'' list of giant American firms. There are 5 Yugoslav firms that in 1978 had over 30,000 workers. The largest employed 66,800, which would make it rank 45th on the U.S. list. The second largest Yugoslav firm (by employment) had 38,800, which would make it rank 111th on the U.S. list. The other three, with 34,000 to 36,000 workers each, would rank on the U.S. list in positions 121, 130, and 131. We can take the same five Yugoslav firms and compare their employemnt size with *Fortune's* list of the 500 largest industrial firms *outside* the United States. In this case they would rank between 69th and 140th. These fairly high rankings for 1978 are quite consistent with some early work done by Rockwell (1968, pp. 12-15) and Pryor (1973, p. 194), both of whom found Yugoslav firms to be large by international standards.

Table 6-4
Aggregate Concentration in Several Industrialized Countries

Number of Firms	Country	Share of Total Industrial Employment (%)
25	United States	18
	France	16
	Yugoslavia	20
33	United States	22
	Germany	23
	Yugoslavia	24
37	United States	23
	Japan	11
	Yugoslavia	26
50	Norway	25
	Yugoslavia	31
50[a]	Sweden	20
	Yugoslavia	20
53	United States	27
	United Kingdom	29
	Yugoslavia	31
100	Germany	17
	United States	25
	Yugoslavia	43

Source: The Yugoslav data are calculated from the *Ekonomska Politika* lists. Data for most other countries are from Scherer (1970), pp. 40, 44, and 45. The figures for Norway, Sweden, and Germany (100 firms) are taken from Pryor (1973) p. 183. Data are for 1978 for Yugoslavia and for 1963 for all other countries except Norway (1948), Sweden (1964), and Germany (100 firms) (1961).

[a]The figure for Sweden is the share of total private-sector employment, which I compare in this case with the Yugoslav figure for share of total social-sector employment.

It is difficult to find comparable data that allow us to make international comparisons of the relative importance of large firms in different countries. In table 6-4 I have gathered together a collection of miscellaneous pieces of information dealing with different numbers of large firms. These allow us to make 7 separate comparisons of Yugoslavia with one or two other countries. In 6 of these comparisons the share of the large firms is higher in Yugoslavia than in the other countries. In the other comparison we see that Yugoslavia's 50 largest firms have the same share of total social-sector employment as Sweden's 50 largest firms have of total private-sector employment.

There is some question about the appropriateness of comparing Yugoslav concentration figures for 1978 with figures for other countries for the early 1960s. Indeed, if I were to use earlier Yugoslav data, I would get quite different results. But Pryor (1973, p. 184) claims that in other countries "the share accounted for by the largest enterprises does not show a general pattern of increase," while in Yugoslavia the increasing trend is unmistakable. The point to be made here is that by 1978 Yugoslavia had exceeded the level of aggregate concentration characteristic of developed capitalist countries in the early 1960s. Whether there have been significant changes in the capitalist countries since then is a matter of some debate, but in any case not of great importance here. Of course, it should be kept in mind that the total size of the Yugoslav economy is smaller than those it is being compared with. If Pryor was correct in suggesting a negative relationship between the size of the domestic market and the degree of concentration, then I might expect the share of the giants to decline as the Yugoslav economy grows. However, these data do not support that hypothesis.

Some Different Empirical Evidence

The empirical evidence presented so far was calculated from the *Ekonomska Politika* lists of large firms. I turn now to a different source of information about the size of economic units in the Yugoslav economy, *Statistički Godišnjak Jugoslavije* (*The Statistical Yearbook*). Table 6-5 shows that during the 6 year period 1971-1977 the total number of economic units doubled. In the industrial sector the number more than tripled, after having held constant between 2,350 and 2,800 since 1960.

This is surprising, given the earlier evidence and an impression from the Yugoslav press that mergers are quite common. I would expect to find that the total number of firms has declined as the larger firms absorbed smaller ones. Nonetheless, the fact of a substantial increase in the number of economic units does not in itself necessarily conflict with the implication of the *Ekonomska Politika* data that large firms are playing an increasingly significant role in the economy. I can imagine that the additional units are

Table 6-5
Total Number of Economic Units

	1969	1970	1971	1972	1973	1974	1975	1976	1977
Total economy[a]	11817	11100	11102	12583	13119	14933	21414	22109	22929
Industrial sector[b]	2435	2374	2398	2773	3217	4100	6495	7320	7731
Trade sector[c]	3132	2901	2968	3683	3689	3881	5423	5150	5269

Source: *Statistički Godišnjak Jugoslavije* for the years 1971 through 1979.
In each yearbook there is a section titled "Opsti pregled privrednih delatnosti" from which these data are taken.
[a]Does not include the private sector.
[b]Includes mining.
[c]Includes catering and tourism.

mostly at the small end of the size distribution and cumulatively do not account for much economic activity. Indeed, in figure 6-3, which shows for selected years size distributions for the economic units in the *Statistical Yearbook* data, it is clear that the largest increases in numbers of units have been in size categories 3 through 6. Because of the way the Statistical Institute defines the size categories, these units are quite small (between 30 and 500 workers) compared to the enterprises on the *Ekonomska Politika* lists.

At the same time there has been some decrease in the number of units in the largest two size categories (those with over 1,000 workers). Again, this is surprising but not logically inconsistent with the increasing relative importance of large firms. We would have expected, on the basis of the *Ekonomska Politika* data, to find an increasing number of firms in the largest size categories, but mergers among the giants could explain the decrease in their number while still allowing them to account for a growing share of total economic activity.

The only thing that could definitely contradict the implications of the *Ekonomska Politika* data is a measure of the aggregate relative weight of the units in the largest size categories. Such data are not available for the trade sector or for the entire social sector, but they are available for the industrial sector. Table 6-6 presents aggregate sales, assets, and employment data for the sum of all firms in size categories 8 and 9 (that is, for all firms with over 1,000 workers). The data are given as percentage of the total industrial sector. Now the conflict with the *Ekonomska Politika* implications is undeniable. Whether I look at sales, assets, or employment, units with over 1,000 workers account for a sharply declining share of total industrial activity. The downturn begins in 1972 or 1973, and by 1977 their share is about one-quarter of what it had been in 1969. By 1976 the figure for employment is lower than the corresponding figure for any of the 9 western countries or 7 eastern countries studied by Pryor (1973, pp. 185, 192) except Portugal.

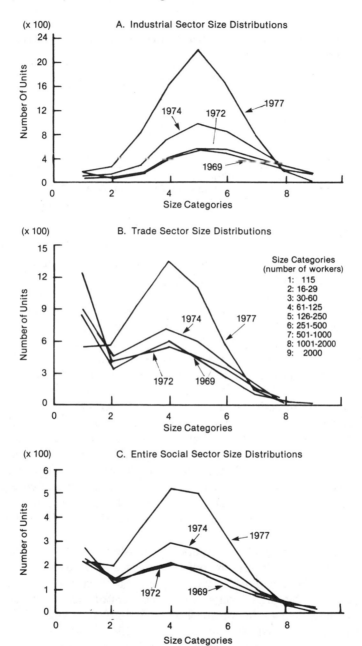

A. Industrial Sector Size Distributions

B. Trade Sector Size Distributions

Size Categories
(number of workers)
1:   115
2: 16-29
3: 30-60
4: 61-125
5: 126-250
6: 251-500
7: 501-1000
8: 1001-2000
9:   2000

C. Entire Social Sector Size Distributions

Source: Statisticki Godisnjak Jugoslavije, 1971-1979.

Figure 6-3. Size Distributions.

Table 6-6
**Relative Significance of Industrial-Sector Economic Units with Over
1,000 Workers**

Percentage	1969	1970	1971	1972	1973	1974	1975	1976	1977
Share of total industrial sales	63	64	65	63	29	50	24	21	17
Share of total industrial assets	64	63	62	57	52	42	24	19	16
Share of total industrial employment	60	61	63	61	57	46	22	19	16

Source: Calculated from data on size distributions in *Statistički Bilten,* nos. 695, 734, 769, 825, 883, 955, 1025 and 1080; and *Statistički Godišnjak Jugoslavije,* 1979, p. 259.

Reconciling the Conflict

How is it that two sources of data lead to such opposite conclusions, one suggesting that large firms are increasingly important and the other suggesting that they are of diminishing significance? The answer is that they are measuring different phenomena. *Ekonomska Politika* has consistently dealt with what is regarded in the business world as an enterprise or firm. This reflects the view common among Yugoslav businessmen that the firm is a meaningful economic unit and is appropriate for statistical analysis, despite the emphasis that the constitutional amendments of 1971, the new constitution of 1974, and the Law on Associated Labor of 1976 have placed on the autonomy of the subunits of enterprises. The Federal Statistical Institute, on the other hand, has shifted its statistical focus onto the subunits of enterprises. Beginning with 1972 it treated as separate statistical units those enterprise divisions that had the status of a legal person, and beginning in 1973 its ''number of units'' refers to Basic Organizations of Associated Labor, or BOALs, which is the official term for the divisions of enterprises. Only in cases where an enterprise is not structured as a collection of BOALs does the Statistical Institute count the entire enterprise as a single statistical unit.

Thus what is seen in table 6-5 is not an explosion in the number of firms, as that word is normally used by both Yugoslav and western businessmen. (In Yugoslavia in term *poduzeca* (enterprise) has been replaced by other terms, usually radna organizacija, but the concept of the firm remains important.) Rather, what is happening is an active implementation the process of divisionalization that was mandated by various legal changes of the 1970s. There is no reason to doubt that this process can occur simultaneously with the increasing relative importance of large firms that is indicated by the *Ekonomska Politika* data. The two trends are logically quite compatible.

Conclusion

The substantiation or refutation of Vanek's predictions depends entirely on which body of data we point to. If I think in terms of the traditional firm, that is, a cohesive body that generally acts as a single unit, or at least as a collection of units that act collusively, then it is the *Ekonomska Politika* data that seem appropriate. In that case the behavior of the Yugoslav economy does not support Vanek's analysis. There have developed what one might reasonably call "inordinate concentrations of industrial power," and conglomerates are considerably easier to find than the apocalyptic beast with seven heads and ten horns. The danger of gigantism is very real, and competitive conditions can be said to be deteriorating as the discrepancy in size between the largest firms and the others increases. An impetus to grow and to control a sizable portion of the market is apparent.

On the other hand, if we think in terms of a different economic unit, the division, which recently has dramatically increased its importance and autonomy,[9] then it is the Statistical Institute's data that should be relied upon. In this case the behavior of the Yugoslav economic system does indeed support Vanek's predictions. There has been a sharp increase in the number of actors and a decrease in the variance of their size distribution. The very strong movement toward economic units of under 500 workers, each with a homogeneous type of activity, is undeniable.

It is impossible to say which of these two is the "correct" way to analyze structural changes in the Yugoslav economy, and hence it is impossible to say whether or not Vanek is correct. But we might consider further the likely implications for the viability of competition in Yugoslavia. Certainly if I focus on the Statistical Institute data on divisions, the prospects for effective competition are promising. But even if I focus my attention on the *Ekonomska Politika* data the prospects are not bad. First of all, it is important to remember that the increasing discrepancy in size is between the group of 100 or 130 giants *taken as a group* and the rest of the economy. *Within* the group of giants (which collectively accounts for 36 percent of total employment in the economy[10]) relative shares have remained fairly stable. Competition *within* this large segment of the economy shows no sign of lessening over time.

Even more important for the effectiveness of competition in the Yugoslav labor-managed economy is the nature of these corporate giants. Mergers are common in Yugoslavia (in 1975 there were 72 mergers in the industrial sector alone). The question is, What is the nature of the relationship among the constituent components of the merged firm? If divisions continue to maintain their identity and autonomy, then competition may not be significantly reduced. Indeed, competition among divisions within a single firm is often quite keen (for example, among the divisions of the Zagreb

Brewery). Whether the merger is vertical, as when a Slovenian food processor merged with a chain of supermarkets to take 29th place on the list of giants, or horizontal, as when three makers of liquor and confections merged to take 42nd place, there is the possibility of continued competition. If these supermarkets are not forced to buy all their vegetables from a sister division, if the divisions making various brands of cognac continue to try to outsell one another, then the economic discipline of competition need not significantly diminish.

There is some evidence that there is at least the possibility of continued competition. Data are available on the number of producers for each of several hundred specific industrial products. Of the 410 items that are identically listed in both 1969 and 1977,[11] 162 had an increase in the number of producers, 141 had a decrease, and for 107 products there was no change in the number of producers. These are figures one would expect from a normally dynamic market economy. Certainly there is no evidence of a decline in the number of potential competitors. That is, mergers have not led to a general dissappearance of competitors. This is consistent with Vanek's assertion (1970, p. 123) that in a labor-managed oligopoly "market structures will tend to be more competitive than in the capitalist situation." But the question of conduct, as opposed to structure, depends on whether the divisions are autonomous decision makers and whether they collude.

I conclude with a few words regarding why these two types of structural changes are occurring. The increase in numbers of divisions (BOALs) is clearly a response to political decisions incorporated into major pieces of legislation adopted during the 1970s. Thus a full explanation requires an analysis of political forces rather than of the logic of the theory of the LMF. The other major change, the increasing relative importance of large firms, is probably to be explained by the economic benefits that accrue to those workers whose firms become large. When a group of divisions merge to form a large enterprise they not only begin to acquire some control over the price of their product, but they also improve their access to capital. Perhaps if the Yugoslav banking system were better able to estimate future profits of borrowers (or if it were replaced by a financing scheme proposed elsewhere by Vanek),[12] then this would not be the case. But at present in Yugoslavia the fact is that large firms do have easier access to capital, and this is likely to be powerful incentive for the growth of large firms.

Notes

1. Vanek (1970, pp. 287-288).
2. This principle was first shown by Ward (1958), and later by Domar (1966). Numerous others have acknowledged and modified it. The follow-

ing summary is based on Vanek's *General Theory,* (1970) especially chapters 2 and 6.

3. If the firm has some monopoly power it will stop expanding before reaching that locus, that is, within the range of increasing returns.

4. See Triffin (1940, pp. 88-89).

5. See, for example, Heilbroner (1972, p. 26).

6. This concern is more prominent in socialism but not unique to it. The famous study by Berle and Means (1968) is an example of concern about concentration of power in a capitalist system.

7. During these years the number of industrial-sector firms listed was 53 in 1969; 100 in 1970 and 1971; 130 for 1972 through 1977; and 140 in 1978. The number of trade-sector firms is 50 for all ten years. The industrial sector is defined very broadly and includes large-scale agriculture, forestry, and construction as well as manufacturing and mining. The trade sector includes tourism and catering (mainly hotels) as well as wholesale, retail, and foreign trade.

8. The standard form of the Cobb-Douglas production function is $Y = A K^{\alpha} L^{\beta}$, where Y is output, K is capital, and L is labor. Taking logs of both sides yields $\ln Y = \ln A + \alpha \ln K + \beta \ln L$, which can be estimated using a standard least-squares regression technique. In order to avoid the need for price adjustments, I ran a separate regression for each of 10 years and averaged the results. Each year except the first had 100 or 130 observations.

9. For a discussion of the extensive autonomy of the divisions of the Yugoslav firm see Sacks (1980).

10. This 36 percent figure is found by dividing the total number of workers in the 130 industrial firms plus the 50 trade firms (1,621,215 in 1978) by the total number of workers in both the social and private economic sectors (4,461,000 in 1978). However, Yugoslav statistics on workers do not include those who are self-employed. In data on industry and trade the difference is negligible, but if we are interested in the total economically active population we should recognize that nearly 3,000,000 private agricultural "workers" are not being counted.

11. *Statisticki Bilten,* nos. 627 (August 1970) and 1086 (June 1978), both titled "Industrija."

12. Vanek (1971) reprinted in Vanek (ed.) (1975).

7 The Performance of the Mondragon Cooperatives in Spain

Henk Thomas

Mondragon is a small town in a densely populated and highly industrial region in the north of Spain. It is also the center of a cooperative group that started in 1943 and that has developed to such an extent that it can be characterized as a labor-managed sector within a mixed—provincial—economy.[1]

In this chapter the emphasis will be on economic questions. First, however, I will give a brief overview of the Mondragon group of cooperatives. Each of the major components—the cooperative factories, the bank, and the educational institutions—are described briefly, and key rules and principles are noted. I then deal with issues of economic performance, particularly the economic performance of cooperative factories during the period 1967-1979. The final section concentrates on the economics of worker self-management. Vanek's work (1975, 1977) on the optimal structure of a labor-managed sector in an economy, and that by Horvat (1976a, 1976b) on issues of distribution under conditions of self-management, will be taken as points of departure in discussing the principal features of the Mondragon cooperatives, and in considering whether Mondragon as a system is indeed more than the sum of the large number of individual cooperatives (more than 130).

An Overview

The key features of contemporary Mondragon are summarized in figure 7-1. Of vital importance for the development of these activities has been a supporting structure made up of a credit cooperative bank and a number of other institutions, mainly in the field of education and training.

This is a condensed account of a larger study, *Mondragon: An Economic Analysis* (Thomas and Logan, 1981), in which the main economic dimensions: employment creation, worker-power planning, finance and planning, and performance and distribution have been analyzed in considerable detail from 1943 as regards education, from 1956 as regards the cooperative factories, and from 1959 as regards the credit cooperative bank. A balanced evaluation of the Mondragon experience has to take its historical background into account; the cooperative history, for instance, cannot be understood without some understanding of the charismatic leadership of Don Jose Maria Arizmendi-Arietta, a Roman Catholic priest, who came to Mondragon in 1941 after the Spanish Civil War. The author gratefully acknowledges editing of the paper by Jean Sanders.

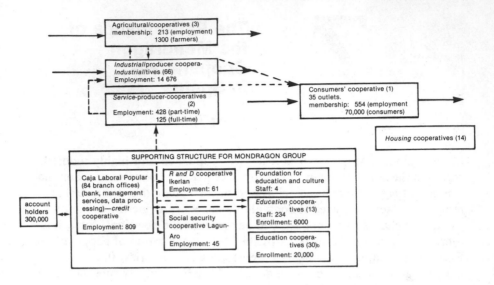

Notes ᵃ _____ purchases from and delivery to markets.
       - - - - -   purchases from and delivery to Mondragon cooperatives.
       All cooperatives are associated with Caja Laboral Popular by way of a contract of association: the cooperatives within the "supporting structure" bloc provide assistance to the entire Mondragon group.
       ᵇ Education cooperatives, associated with Caja Laboral Popular while not being monitored by the foundation for education and culture.

Source: Constructed by the author from data supplied by the Research Department of the Caja Laboral Popular.

Figure 7-1. The Mondragon Group—an Overview (December 1978)ᵃ

In 1979 there were a total of 70 factories with an aggregate employment of 15,672. Most factories are small to medium in size but one is quite large, employing over 3,000 workers. The factories produce a wide range of products, many of which demand high levels of technology and therefore highly skilled workers; products include refrigerators, cookers, automatic washing machines, bicycles, capital equipment, tools, light engineering instruments, and products with electric and electronic parts. The cooperatives produce commodities that are of medium capital intensity. Highly capital-intensive production processes, such as petrochemical complexes, as well as highly labor-intensive products are also found in Mondragon. Some cooperatives produce in part for other cooperatives, such as thermostats and valves for the large factory that produces refrigerators, cookers, and heaters; a cooperative will buy products from other cooperatives, however, only if the products offered are of the desired quality and are cheaper than those of noncooperative enterprises. The first impression is one of hectic industrial activity, of a high degree of technological innovation, and of hard-working people at all levels of the cooperative hierarchy. There is little doubt that the cooperative factories are competently managed and have excellent prospects for the future, the workers' skills being of high level, and the amounts invested in new plants considerable.

Table 7-1 shows some key facts on employment, sales, exports, and investments. During the period from 1960 to 1970, in particular, expansion and structural change were rapid. From 1960 onward, cooperatives increased first to 30 in 1965, and then to 40 in 1970, while average employment jumped from less than 50 in 1960, to over 100 in 1965, and to over 200 in 1970. From then on, expansion has been more moderate, reflecting the economic recession of the seventies, as well as a determined effort by the cooperative group to plan cooperative developments carefully, thereby consolidating the institutional structure that has been created.

The sales figures, even taking inflation into account, clearly show the expansion of production. The dynamic impact of the cooperatives on the economy at large can be seen from the statitstics on exports and investments. In

Table 7-1
Employment, Sales, Exports, and Investment: Selected Facts

	1956	1960	1965	1970	1975	1978	1979
Industrial cooperatives	1	8	30	40	50	66	70
Cooperators	24	395	3395	8570	12543	14676	15672
Sales (all industrial cooperatives) (current prices, million pesetas)	.4	200	1900	7100	17900	38200	50000
Cooperative sales: (Percentage of National Sales in mechanical engineering and consumer durables branches	.004	.7	3.5	8.9	10.3	—	—
Cooperative exports							
as percentage of provincial exports			1	10	12	10	—
as percentage of provincial exports of "own" branches				35	42	48	—
Cooperative gross investments							
as percentage of provincial investments				16	52	62	—
as percentage of investments in "own" branches				19	66	—	—

Source: Assembled from data supplied to the author by the Research Department of the Caja Laboral Popular.

Note: 70 pesetas is equivalent to 1 U.S. dollar.

1978 10 percent of provincial exports originated in cooperatives belonging to the Mondragon group, and almost 50 percent of the exports of their specific branches was accounted for by the cooperative factories; in 1978 cooperative investments represented 62 percent of total provincial investments in industry, which had reached 66 percent of the investments in their own branches in 1975. The cooperatives are thus active in foreign markets and have no difficulty in selling about 20 percent of their annual output to outlets in 40 countries spread all over the world.

From figure 7-1 we see that a few cooperatives have an "agricultural base." Also, there are two service cooperatives, in one of which over 400 women work part-time; the other is a cooperative of experts who offer their expertise in areas such as public relations, marketing, and accounting to various cooperatives. Furthermore, there is a consumers' cooperative with 70,000 members, and a number of cooperatives that finance the purchasing of apartments, for instance, in a building that may, or may not, have been put up by a house-building cooperative.

Figure 7-1 also suggests the crucial importance of the supporting structure for the Mondragon group. Most important is Caja Laboral Popular (CLP), the credit cooperative that in 1978 consisted of a network of 84 branch offices with its main office in Mondragon, and with more than 300,000 account holders. During the first ten years its branches grew to 54 and account holders to 87,000. Between 1975 and 1978, another 20 branch offices were opened, and 110,000 new accounts were added, making 300,000 accounts by the end of 1978—convincing testimony of the still increasing strength of this savings bank. Annual net deposits by then had reached 7,500 million pesetas. The annual surplus in 1979 amounted to more than 1,135 million pesetas, against a sum total of own capital and reserves and of accumulated resources of account holders amounting to 46,100 million pesetas. The financial strength of the Mondragon group can be realized from the fact that the total resources of Caja Laboral Popular equaled 23 percent of aggregate sales value of the associated cooperatives in 1965 and more than 80 percent of the total sales figure in 1978. Through the years the credit cooperative has thus been in an ever improving position to meet the needs of the cooperative factories for working capital and for long-term investments. The bank is called a second-degree cooperative, because its General Assembly consists not only of cooperators—more than eight hundred—who work in the credit cooperative and its branches, but also of institutional members, that is, the producer (industrial) cooperatives (PCs) that are linked to the bank through a contract association, and of representatives of the depositors.

Education is a third important field of activity of the Mondragon cooperative movement. There are numerous educational institutions and it is almost possible to speak of a micro-educational system on cooperative lines in and around Mondragon. Figure 7-2 shows its principal character-

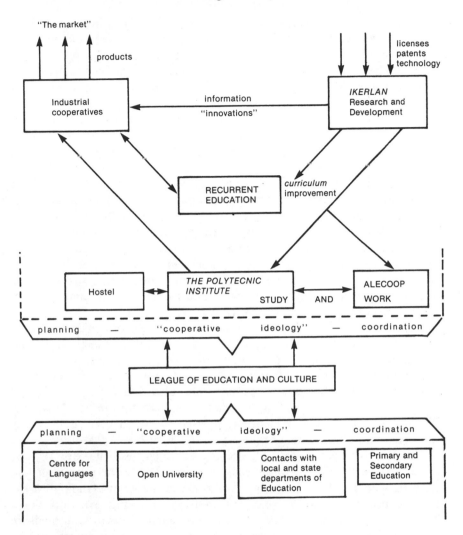

Source: Constructed from data supplied to the author by the Mondragon educational institutions, particularly politecnica.

Figure 7-2. Cooperative Education in Mondragon

istics. First, and most important, is the polytechnic institute, Politecnica, which caters to 1,200 pupils a year at all levels of vocational education, including the engineering-degree level. The courses offered are closely linked to the needs of the factories, and it is thus possible to speak of a complete micropower planning system to ensure that people are prepared for their jobs in the factory.

A second educational institution, Alecoop, of a highly innovative character, is a cooperative factory run by students of the polytechnic institute and where they spend 50 percent of their time during certain periods of their studies. The principle behind Alecoop is that students learn not only in classroom and laboratory sessions, but also by practical work in their own factories. This cooperative factory caters to over 500 pupils at any time. Study and work are fundamental principles of the cooperative movement, and the idea is that by the time students enter the factories they will be familiar with the situation in which they will have to work while still retaining a strong interest in study.

It is in that respect that a third educational activity plays a major role in the Mondragon experience, namely, the cooperative center for recurrent or permanent education, inspired by the 1971 French law on permanent education. For students who come from a great distance, hostel accomodation is available that again is organized in a cooperative manner. Another educational institute which plays an increasingly important role is a center—Ikerlan—for research and development, which previously was merely a department of the polytechnic institute and has recently become an independent research and development (R&D) organization.

In addition to these educational activities that are oriented toward the needs of the industrial cooperatives, there are a number of institutions that are meant primarily for the community at large. For instance, the cooperative group makes funds available to stimulate primary and secondary education in its region. It has set up a language laboratory that caters for the community's need to learn English, French, or German and, in particular, the Basque language. The movement has invested monies in an open university situated 10 kilometers from Mondragon, in which over 1,000 students are enrolled in correspondence courses and evening classes. The core of these educational activities is a braintrust, the Foundation for Education and Culture, with a staff of four experts who are in charge of planning for the future educational needs of the region and of the cooperative organizations. These experts coordinate with state and municipal authorities, and ensure that cooperative ideals become an integral part of provincial educational activities. During the coming decade the cooperative movement will probably have a more outward involvement in public education.

The basic cooperative principles are as follows:[2]

1. an open-door principle that indicates a readiness to extend membership to people who wish to join any of the cooperatives or who wish to establish a new cooperative by associating with the credit cooperative bank;
2. a democratic principle, or general statement about the obligation that the organization be run by elected persons and by democratically approved procedures;

3. guidelines about a limited income for capital and a distribution of surpluses earned in accordance with the work that a person contributes to a cooperative;
4. a community orientation that falls into two parts: first, a readiness to allocate surpluses earned to a fund for social objectives, and second, a policy of creating new jobs to enable more workers to join cooperatives;
5. a philosophical statement about the need to develop a "cooperative spirit."

In addition, more specific guidelines concern the organization of associated cooperatives, the distribution of earnings, and aspects of capital structure and surplus distribution.

Organization

For example, the organization of an associated cooperative falls into two parts: the usual hierarchical structure for the implementation of enterprise policies, and an accountability structure in which the General Assembly, of all workers has highest authority. This General Assembly, in which all workers in a factory have one vote, elects a Supervisory Board, which appoints management for a specified period of time. Management is obliged to report frequently to this Supervisory Board and once a year to the General Assembly.

An innovative body of proved value is the Social Council, which consists of delegates chosen directly from the shop floor, and which provides a two-way channel of communications between workers and the upper echelons of management; it thus serves to keep flows of information going and lines of communication open, while training delegates in details of business operations.

Two other institutions are the Management Council, an advisory body to management and to the Supervisory Board; and the Watchdog Council, which is directly elected by the General Assembly to protect the interest of the entire cooperative and to ensure that the principles of cooperative law are not violated.

An aspect that extends beyond the individual organization is the recent policy of creating groups of cooperatives, which, by pooling specific resources—in particular certain skills—succeed in achieving economies of scale without giving up the relatively small scale of the individual production units. In this way, groups of 6 to 10 cooperatives are obtained, either on a territorial base or on a functional base. It is to be expected that this policy will become an important aspect of the future organizational structure of the Mondragon group.

Distribution of Earnings

With regard to the distribution of earnings and the average level of take-home pay, much emphasis is laid on the concept of "solidarity," which is practiced in three ways.

1. There is a wage policy. To avoid creating a cooperative elite in the community, it was decided that average earnings should be equal to the average earnings level in competitive private enterprises in the immediate environment of Mondragon; in future, the provincial level will become the norm.

2. All cooperatives interlink their average level of earnings as well as their differences; in other words, there is institutional solidarity among the cooperatives. This is important because it gives rise to a certain uniformity in rules and standards that means that in practice some of the largest companies carry out extensive studies on earnings, which are then also implemented by the other cooperatives.

3. There is solidarity within each factory: The maximum earnings differentials are only three to one. This is perhaps the most important incentive in the Mondragon cooperatives, because it ensures that existing differences in earnings are accepted as just and fair by the workers. The implication is that the lowest ranks earn slightly more than those in private enterprises, but that managers and other high ranks earn considerably less than their counterparts.

Factory Ownership

Another fundamental aspect regards the ownership of the factories. Each cooperator upon entering the cooperative has to pay a considerable amount of money as entry fee, of which part is allocated to collective reserves; the greater part is assigned to his or her individual capital account. At the end of the financial year this individual capital account is credited with 6 percent interest and a "dividend"; it is also revalued to take account of inflation. As a result, the capital accounts of individual cooperators have risen quite rapidly. Thus, part of the "own capital" is collective, a form of social ownership. The "individualized" part cannot be paid out to cooperators as long as they work in a cooperative. If a cooperator decides to leave the movement, the accumulated capital reserves therefore suffer a loss. Upon retirement all accumulated individual funds will be made available to the individuals concerned.

Surplus (profit) is distributed as follows: 10 percent is allocated for social purposes, particularly education; at least 20 percent is added to collective reserves; and at most 70 percent is allocated to individual capital accounts, depending on the level of profitability. When profits increase, 10 percent is still allocated to the social fund, but a formula is used that increases the percentage allocated to collective reserves while that allocated to individual accounts, which still accumulate in absolute terms, decreases. Also, no more than 60 percent of the sum total of the computable base—payroll costs and interest payments on resources—can be paid out to individual members' accounts, while at least 30 percent must be made available for allocation to the social fund and collective reserves. Finally, not only are enterprise profits shared by all those who work in the enterprise, but losses are also borne by them, both collectively and individually. When losses occur, part is deduced from collectively accumulated reserves and the remainder from the individual accounts of cooperators.

Economic Performance

It is interesting to study how efficient the cooperatives have been in using the resources at their disposal.[3] I use the ratio-analysis method, but I do not belabor its methodological implications when making comparisons among firms that have different objectives.[4]

Six Ratios

Table 7-2 gives six such ratios for the aggregate group of cooperatives; where possible, ratios for noncooperative enterprises are presented for com-

Table 7-2
Ratio-Analysis of Industrial Cooperatives (1971-1979)

	Sales per Person[a] (1)	Value Added per "Factor"[a] (2)	Value Added per Person[a] (3)	Value Added per Fixed Assets (4)	Pure Surplus per Sales (5)	Pure Surplus per Own Resources (6)	
1971	850	160	245	.64	.04	.08	(.11)
1972	1025 (1250)	225 (210/160)	340 (240)	.88 (.27/.73)	.08 (.05)	.17	(.12)
1973	1175 (1550)	280	410 (335)	1.00	.10 (.04)	.21	
1974	1375 (2025)	365	495	.98	.08 (.04)	.17	(.07)
1975	1425 (2325)	390	540 (475)	.76	.06 (.03)	.11	(.04)
1976	1675 (2800)	505	700	.77	.07 (.02)	.14	(.01)
1977	2000		800 (750)		.06	.12	(−.05)
1978	2600		1000		.025		
1979	3200		1275		.04		

Source: Assembled from data supplied to the author by the Research Department of the Caja Laboral Popular.

[a]thousand pesetas.

Note: Figures within parentheses are values calculated for Spanish industry: in cases (columns 2 and 4) where 2 figures are mentioned the first one belongs to the 500 largest companies and the second one to the remaining companies.

parison. The first four ratios refer to economic performance in terms of productivity; the next two ratios refer to profitability.

Sales per Person. Column 1 indicates the development of labor productivity in a very general sense. Sales per worker doubled between 1971 and 1976. More rapid growth, however, occured in national industry, that is, from 1,250,000 pesetas per employee in 1972 to 2,800,000 pesetas in 1976. Undoubtedly, the rapid creation of employment causes the lower growth rate of cooperative sales per person, as compared to the Spanish economy's overall industrial sector.

Value-Added Divided by Factors of Production. Column 2 is designed by the research department of Caja Laboral Popular to indicate changes in productivity levels. The following formula is used:

$$\text{index of value added} = \frac{S - P \text{ (gross value added)}}{W + \frac{FC}{E} + \frac{WC}{E}}$$

in which S = revenue from sales; P = purchases from third parties; W = number of cooperators; FC = cost of fixed assets per annum; WC = cost of working capital per annum; and E = average annual earnings of cooperators.

The denominator is a composite number (sum) with three elements: number of workers; annual costs of capital divided by the average earnings of cooperators; and the cost of working capital divided by the average earnings of cooperators. The contribution of capital to the production of value added in this way is measured in equivalent "labor units." The result is a practical approximation to a production function; that is, it measures value added as a function of the factors used in production. This indicator has grown from 160,000 pesetas per labor unit in 1971 to 505,000 in 1976. Both the increase in sales per worker and the rapid growth of value added as a percentage of sales have boosted the indicator. Given the doubling of prices during this period, total factor productivity has thus increased considerably. In Spanish industry in 1972 total factor productivity amounted to 210,000 pesetas in the 500 largest enterprises, and 160,000 pesetas in large and medium-sized enterprises. These figures provide an important insight. The cooperative movement occupies a strong position among Spanish industries; the cooperatives' average performance is better than that of the 500 biggest enterprises, and greatly exceeds that of medium and smaller-sized factories.

Value Added per Person. Column 3 rose from 245,000 pesetas per person in 1971 to 1,275,000 in 1979. In 1972, in spite of a downward bias of this ratio due to greater employment creation, the cooperatives performed far better than the small and medium-sized capitalist enterprises: cooperative labor productivity stood at 340,000 pesetas per employee versus private-sector labor productivity of only 240,000. Again in 1973, the cooperative enterprises had higher labor productivity (410,000 pesetas) than the provincial industrial average of 335,000 pesetas; in 1975, cooperative labor productivity of 540,000 compared with a value of 475,000 on Spanish industry, and again in 1977, the cooperatives maintained a slight edge over provincial labor productivity, as evidenced by the figures of 800,000 and 750,000, respectively.

Value Added per Fixed Assets. Column 4 indicates the productivity of capital, a ratio that is commonly used to analyze the "survival potential" of enterprises. Its value—an average of .85—is low by international standards. Value added per total assets during this period averaged .34, which is less than is necessary for a "healthy" enterprise. The industrial sector of Spain has developed underprotective tariffs and it is therefore no surprise that the cooperatives, like Spanish industry in general, show a relatively weak performance in this respect.

Two ratios focus on profitability.

Pure Surplus as a Percentage of Total Sales. Column 5 compares well with net profits in private enterprise. Ulgor, the largest Mondragon PC, had very high net-profit margins in the early 1960s: 18 percent in 1962 and 1963; 12 percent in 1964; and 10 percent in 1965; the average cooperative profitability from 1966 to 1970 was 9, 7.5, 9, and 7 percent. Compared to earlier years this index has fallen considerably, but it still compares favorably with the values obtained for noncooperative enterprises, which reported an average profit margin of 3.6 percent as compared to 7.8 percent for the cooperatives from 1972 to 1976. Surplus in cooperatives may indeed be compared with net profits in private enterprise because the cooperatives link the level of their members' earnings to that of the mechanical engineering sector. Assuming that both categories of enterprises behave similarly with respect to allocating resources for depreciation and interest payments, this is a valid comparison. The figures show clearly that the cooperative movement has recently experienced considerable difficulties; the result for 1978—a surplus margin on aggregate of 2.5 percent—has been the worst in its history. The 1979 results showed an improvement: 4 percent.

Pure Surplus Divided by "Own Resources." Column 6 is high by international norms. In each of the 7 years this index is greater than .07, indicating extremely sound profitability. Wemelsfelder (1978), in a study on Dutch industry, reports that the average yield on own resources for the years 1970, 1974, and 1975 was 4.7, 5.3, and 5.1 percent, respectively. It is also possible to make a comparison with industrial results in Guipuzcoa over a period of

6 years. These stood at 11 percent against a cooperative 8 percent in 1971; at 12 against 17 percent in 1972; and at an average of 3 percent during the years 1974 to 1976 against a cooperative average of 14 percent.

Figure 7-3 shows data on net profits as percentages of gross value added (GVA) and of sales, from 1967 onward; for the years 1972 to 1977 data are also given of net profits for Guipuzcoan industry. This time series shows clearly that 1971 was a difficult year for the Mondragon cooperatives and that 1978 was even worse, following a peak performance in 1973. A small recovery took place in 1979, but it is quite obvious that the entire movement is now experiencing the most difficult time since it began in 1956.

Fortunately, a high percentage of retained profits has created a strong financial situation. In the period 1971 to 1976 the cash flow (total of depreciation and net profits) on average exceeded investments by about 10 percent. The total financial needs of the cooperatives are naturally larger than the amount needed for investment in fixed assets.

Table 7-3 shows the financial strength of the industrial cooperatives. The ratio of own resources to fixed assets slightly exceeds one; there is no risk that outside interests (including CLP) could at any time pressure the

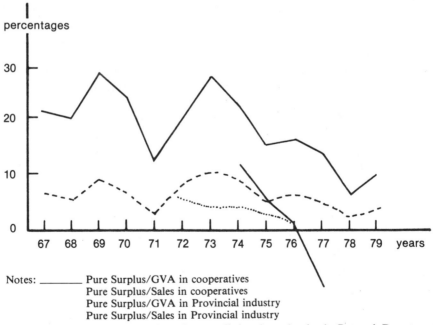

Notes: _____ Pure Surplus/GVA in cooperatives
                     Pure Surplus/Sales in cooperatives
                     Pure Surplus/GVA in Provincial industry
                     Pure Surplus/Sales in Provincial industry

Source: Figures are constructed from data supplied to the author by the Research Department of the Caja Laboral Popular.

Figure 7-3. Cooperative and Provincial Industrial Profitability

Table 7-3
Financial Position of Industrial Cooperatives, 1968-1976

	Own Resources/ Fixed Assets (1)	Own Resources/ Total Assets (2)
1968	1.15	.55
1969	1.18	.51
1970	1.12	.50
1971	1.11	.50
1972	1.24	.48
1973	1.38	.51
1974	1.27	.47
1975	1.11	.48
1976	.99	.46

Source: Ratios are derived from data supplied to the author by the Research Department of the Caja Laboral Popular.

associated cooperatives and force them to part with some of their fixed assets in order to meet financial demands.

Of immediate importance to any company is the relative position of own resources (the second column of table 7-3), and the claims of creditors. This ratio dropped slightly to .46 in 1976. Taking general economic conditions into account, however, and the fact that many new cooperatives had joined, all needing considerable loans, this indicates a strong financial position. In Belgian industry this ratio dropped from about .50 in 1964 to .29 in 1977; in Italy between 1968 and 1977 the average ratio for enterprises fell from .21 to .15.[5] Union Cerrejera, the major noncooperative employer in Mondragon, reported in 1977 that its own resources made up about one-third of total assets (while a ratio of .28 is found for the whole of Basque industry). Furthermore, it makes a difference whether the main creditor is Caja Laboral Popular or "foreign capital" that has penetrated a large number of industries and that supplies a reported 25 percent of their medium-term to long-term capital needs. A huge expansion of total assets of the Mondragon group has been financed for about 50 percent through self-financing, and the remainder by credits granted by Caja Laboral Popular.

Categories of Cooperatives (Branches)

In table 7-4, attention is shifted away from aggregate performance to main industrial branches. The relative weight in terms of sales, employment, and surplus is given for five categories of cooperatives; cooperatives that produce consumer durable goods are the most important in terms of percentage of aggregate sales and aggregate employment. The picture varies with respect

Table 7-4
Distribution of Sales, Employment, and Pure Surplus over Five Categories of Cooperatives, 1967-1979 (percentages)

	Sales					Employment					Surplus (net profits)				
	(1)	(2)	(3)	(4)	(5)	(1)	(2)	(3)	(4)	(5)	(1)	(2)	(3)	(4)	(5)
1967	19	12	13	47	9	24	19	27	20	10	16	5	21	45	13
1968	15	14	17	44	10	21	17	25	26	11	0	9	33	39	19
1969	12	12	15	52	9	17	16	24	34	9	12	9	21	48	10
1970	13	15	16	47	9	15	17	24	35	9	29	10	25	23	13
1971	13	14	15	50	8	14	17	22	38	9	41	10	23	7(-3)	19
1972	11	14	16	51	8	14	16	22	39	9	20	18	18	34(23)	10
1973	12	19	16	43	10	14	19	23	35	9	16	20	20	31(22)	13
1974	14	20	17	38	11	13	20	24	34	9	26	23	16	25(18)	10
1975	13	22	16	37	11	14	20	24	32	10	25	26	9	21(24)	20
1976	14	21	17	37	11	14	20	23	32	11	12	19	3	50(48)	16
1977	—	—	—	—	—	—	—	—	—	—	8	17	24	48	4
1978	14	19	19	39	9	14	21	25	31	9	21	1	18	43(32)	17
1979	14	20	19	38	9	13	21	26	31	9	18	14	24	34	10
Number of Cooperatives															
(1979)	7	22	25	11	5										

Source: Assembled from data supplied to the author by the Research Department of the Caja Laboral Popular.

Note: The figures within parentheses indicate the position of Ulgor. (1) Capital goods; (2) tools and engineering products; (3) intermediate goods; (4) consumer durables; (5) construction activities.

to the creation of surplus. Capital goods-producing factories had a difficult time around 1968, but they moved to the front line in 1971 in terms of contribution to total surplus, while losing out somewhat again from 1976 onward. Tools and engineering products started weak, reached a relatively strong position in 1975, after which losses were barely prevented in 1978. Intermediate goods make a relatively high share of total surplus, except in 1975 and 1976, when they accounted only for 9 and 3 percent. Consumer durables were very weak in the early seventies, when the remaining cooperatives did well, but were strong in years when the capital-intensive cooperatives faced difficulties. Finally, construction, except for 1977, followed its own cycle, making between 10 and 20 percent.

Table 7-5 gives information on value added per factor of production in these five categories of cooperatives during years 1971-1976. It is striking that on the whole the spread of efficiency is narrow, indicating that the cooperative group has been successful in allocating its resources. The only exception is the category of intermediate goods, which in 1975 fell behind considerably; this may have been due to the fact that this category, more than the others, sells its products to other cooperatives and thus enjoys some degree of protection that the other cooperatives do not possess.

This section has analyzed the average behavior of cooperative enterprises in each of five branches, but it goes without saying that individual

Table 7-5
Value Added per Factor in Five Categories of Cooperatives

	(1)	(2)	(3)	(4)	(5)	(6)
1971	160	200	165	155	130	185
1972	225	245	235	205	210	230
1973	280	305	300	260	265	325
1974	365	440	405	325	335	360
1975	390	450	425	325	380	435
1976	505	500	535	415	500	545

Source: Assembled from data supplied to the author by the Research Department of the Caja Laboral Popular.

Note: All figures are in thousands of pesetas.

(1) all industrial cooperatives; (2) capital goods; (3) tools and engineering products; (4) intermediate goods; (5) consumer durables; (6) building materials.

performance may differ widely from average performance. It has always been quite usual for one or more cooperative factories to temporarily experience a loss due to problems of adjustment. This has changed in recent years; in 1977, for instance, 70 percent of all cooperatives made a positive pure surplus, 20 percent reported a loss, and 10 percent just broke even; in 1978 these percentages were 60, 35, and 5 respectively. The speedy reaction of the entire cooperative system to reported losses is indicated by the fact that in 1976 almost all cooperatives that had reported a loss in 1975 greatly improved their results.

Evaluation

Vanek (1975, pp. 34-36 and 1977, pp. 171-198) distinguishes 12 "necessary conditions of an optimal and viable self-managed economy," which we group into four categories: democratic control of the work organization; national ownership of the means of production; a set of conditions that safeguards capital accumulation; and finally, wider aspects of coordination, including the functions of a "sheltering organization" of educational programs and of the need for political democracy. Horvat's arguments on problems of distribution in socialism (1976, pp. 214-242 and 1976, pp. 179-187) are the theoretical inputs for our fifth category on issues of distribution.

On the first category Vanek argues that in any labor-managed situation there should be such an organization of the productive relationships so that ultimate control and authority are vested with those who work in a specific work organization.

It appears that the Mondragon cooperatives satisfy this condition. The highest authority and ultimate control rests with a General Assembly that appoints all members of a Supervisory Board, which in turn keeps close watch on the executive directors. The implication is that ownership of capital does not lead to any formal representation in the organs of these PCs.

Whether in reality the skilled and experienced staff, as well as the managers at higher levels, are not in a position to exercise considerable influence on the entire organization is a problem that requires careful investigation. Even if it would be proved that such influences exist, however, the formal organization of these PCs would still meet the first condition for self-management.

The second condition concerns ownership of the means of production. Vanek has argued in favor of a new concept of "U-ownership" in which capital owners be given a right to a yield that reflects the market scarcity price. So as not to violate the first condition, however, capital owners should not be given representation in the organizational structure of a PC. Both Horvat and Vanek consider the destination of such yields and allow for the possibility that the workers in a specific labor-managed enterprise should have first claim in expressing a preference about the allocation of such financial resources. Mondragon has introduced a form of mixed collective and individual ownership. Each individual cooperator, upon joining a cooperative, needs to pay a considerable amount of money, of which 25 percent is allocated to the reserves and is not refundable; the remainder is entered into an individual capital account on which the cooperator continues to have ownership rights. For the financing of this financial obligation, usual practice is that a small amount is settled as a down payment at the time of joining a cooperative, while the greater part is paid off by monthly wage deductions over a period of maximally two years. The "principle" involved is that each cooperator will thus have funded the costs of his or her own workplace: first by an entry fee as indicated, then by accumulating further amounts at the end of each consecutive year if enterprise surplus allows for such accumulation.

The balance between these two forms of ownership can be changed in two ways. First, a more successful cooperative allocates a greater percentage of surplus to the collective reserves. Second, it can be decided to change the rules under which the surplus gets disbursed. For instance, in one cooperative in 1979, the cooperators decided that they would not draw their individual accumulate accounts at the time of retirement, realizing that such might cause an intolerable strain on the cash flow position in the late 1990s. The Mondragon solution for ownership thus deviates from the necessary conditions spelled out in theory.

A third set of conditions that Vanek emphasizes deals with accumulation of capital and its allocation for future growth. Vanek insists on the necessity of making depreciation allowances available for "the national investment fund," and that yields on capital should be allocated entirely to further growth and development, while the scarcity price levied on the use of capital "should be the same for all users." He then argues for establishing a "shelter organization" that has as its main objective "the promotion of the social good of the participatory sector and of the whole economy." Its main task would need to be the safe-guarding of an adequate flow of financial resources toward the self-managed enterprises, and the further development of the self-managing sector or of the national economy, if the entire country should adopt worker self-management as its strategy for future orientation. Vanek would encourage individual firms to be active in this respect also, namely, by expanding, or by stimulating the establishment of new self-managed enterprises.

The situation in Mondragon makes for easy evaluation. First, there is a very strict regime by which under any circumstances, a sufficient amount of financial resources is set aside to make sure that, over a period of 6 to 10 years, adequate resources will have been accumulated to permit substitution by new equipment. The cooperatives compare favorably to other Spanish enterprises, for which it has been estimated that capital equipment is written off in about twenty years; for the years 1971 to 1976 I have found that the annual cooperative depreciation percentages have been 11, 13, 13, 11, and 9, respectively, of the value of capital assets, annually adjusted to compensate for the inflationary price changes that took place during each of those years.

Cooperatives are also obliged to pay interest at commercial levels on all loans they obtain from CL. The advantage of signing a contract of association with the credit cooperative thus does not consist of securing favorable terms on loans, but of the fact that credit is available to the cooperatives. It is well known that the absence of credit has been an important bottleneck in the long history of cooperatives. In Mondragon this is one of the important reasons why cooperatives have managed to do well over such a long span of time. Rather than cutting of credit lines in times of financial crisis of a particular PC, the cooperative bank engages in active dialogue with the enterprise concerned to investigate the causes of the situation. Various measures may be taken—including bringing in experts, new management, undertaking feasibility studies for new products, and designing new programs of recurrent education—in order to safeguard employment while regaining satisfactory levels of profitability and earnings.

The third flow of financial resources that is available for capital accumulation is the annual surplus. Except for a 10 percent allocation to the funds for social objectives and payments of 6 percent dividend on individual capital accounts, all pure surplus remains available for future development, either in the form of individual capital accounts or as collective cooperative reserves. Thus, of the pure surplus—profits after taxes and this

6 percent have been deducted—90 percent remains available for purposes of self-financing. The objection might be raised that this may lead to inefficiency in total accumulation of funds, since some enterprises have less access to financial means than others. In reality, however, the capital needs for each cooperative are so high that this can create only a minor distortion. The critical factor in this respect is the behavior of the credit cooperative in allocating its resources such that the marginal yield in all alternative lines of production is equalized. The evidence discussed earlier can be taken as an indication that Caja Laboral Popular acts very prudently. In conclusion, it is clear than Mondragon satisfied Vanek's condition regarding the need to raise sufficient resources for growth and capital accumulation.

The fourth set of conditions deals with the need for a sheltering organization, combined with the functions of a market mechanism. Educational programs and political democracy are also deemed to be ingredients or preconditions for a well-functioning system of self-governing social relations in production. In several of his writings, Horvat has emphasized a variety of institutions that are needed to create a solid framework that will permit a proper functioning of worker-managed productive organizations under conditions of societal self-government.

In this regard, the management-services division of CLP can be viewed as having undertaken a monitoring role that supposedly is taken on by the "sheltering organization." Even the fact that the individual cooperatives in Mondragon have a high degree of independence meets the necessary conditions, namely, to prevent the sheltering organization from building up an overwhelming bureaucratic concentration of power. It should be noted that the specific nature of this monitoring role has not been invariant, but has changed as the cooperatives experienced a shifting balance of "plans and markets." During the first fifteen years of existence of these cooperative factories, there was complete dependence on markets in terms of the need to purchase all inputs from other enterprises, as well as to supply products made to local, provincial, national, and even international markets. A fortunate and perhaps determining factor, however, has been that the Mondragon group started at a time when a major boom of long duration, based on new industrialization, got under way in Spain; this boom was to last until the end of the 1960s.

During the seventies, national markets for consumer durables became saturated and the inefficiencies of industrialization under heavy protection were revealed. As a result, the Mondragon group was faced with adverse economic conditions, which became intensified by the world recession. From 1973 onward CLP devoted much energy to developing a management-services department that could undertake planning functions for the entire cooperative group in addition to financial monitoring. Since 1973, CLP has equipped that management services division in such a manner that each year another 10 new cooperatives may sign a contract of association with it; of these, 4 are expected to be private enterprises that wish to transform their organization structure. This is undoubtedly the important reason why the cooperative group continued to expand during the seventies, while elsewhere considerable reductions in employment were recorded.

As for education and political democracy, conditions are satisfied in the following ways. I have noted that during the period 1943-1956, education was the only embryonic cooperative activity in Mondragon, and that since 1956 much emphasis has been given to updating and adjusting educational programs to the needs of the factories. In recent years the Foundation for Education and Culture has directed its energy increasingly toward the wider community: through participation in the planning of primary and secondary education at the provincial level, by being instrumental in establishing an open university with evening courses in a neighboring town, and by advocating the idea that schools should also be set up as cooperative organizations of second degree, with a general assembly consisting of pupils, parents, community representatives, and staff.

In my view a fifth category of conditions should focus on the distribution of earnings. In discussing the "fundamentals of a theory of distribution in self-governing socialism," Horvat distinguishes four major issues.

1. Distribution should be such that it compensates for the work performed by the workers. Earnings typically reflect individual contributions by workers, while surplus-sharing is a reward for collective performance. The workers' income (consisting of paid-out earnings and surplus sharing) must not include elements of rents, which are to be taxed away.

2. The determination of labor incomes is closely related to the manner in which the work is organized. The actual decision making with respect to earnings differentials should be left to the jurisdiction of the General Assembly of a worker-managed organization. This will necessarily involve a process of "social-valuations," and the general effect will be greater egalitarianism. Horvat predicts that differences will be considerably smaller than in nonworker-managed enterprises.

3. Another issue concerns optimum distribution from the perspective of allocational efficiency. Horvat and Vanek reach similar conclusions, by first deriving from neoclassical theory some conclusions about optimality in terms of well-known marginal conditions for each category of workers, and then by underscoring the limited use of such a theory; in particular this is the case under perfectly competitive conditions that hamper interpersonal welfare comparisons. Both authors conclude that a labor-managed economy has greater potential for reaching some optimal distribution of income "because the actors themselves engage in interpersonal welfare comparisons and make the relevant decisions."

4. Last, attention should be given to "distribution according to needs." To the extent that earnings do not cover the needs for "the development of individual capabilities," there should be provision of nonmarket goods by way of collective consumption in six areas: education, medical care, social welfare, culture, physical culture and environmental conservation and creation. Nonmarket arrangements can be provided for such collective consumption.

In the field of distribution, the Mondragon group has performed in an interesting manner. Its contribution toward the community at large has been realized in two directions: first, by following a strategy that aims at the maximum creation of employment; and second, by earmarking 10 percent of the annual pure surplus for collective purposes. Its social-security system has not exclusively served the cooperators and their families; for instance, studies have been undertaken for the entire community of the town and its environment. If the manner is observed in which employment has been created, or has been maintained by associating enterprises that otherwise might have gone bankrupt, one may see the way in which the cooperative educational experience is gradually put at the disposal of the wider community; the manner in which the cooperative social-security system is developing an interest in community health problems also permits the conclusion that in its distribution of income the Mondragon group has given adequate attention to collective needs.

A novel problem is encountered with regard to the level of earnings and their distribution, in the sense that the workings of the labor market have been immobilized due to a very strict earnings policy. As we have indicated earlier, the level of earning of all associated cooperatives is linked, via the level of earnings of CLP, to that of representative firms in the area. Gradually it has been found that the standards set by these firms are not sufficiently stable for a long-term earnings strategy, the consequence being that the benchmark is now set more carefully by an annual study of a large sample of enterprises in the entire province.

Thus the phenomenon of inter-industry or inter-branch earnings differentials does *not* occur in the Mondragon group. The group now even aims at linking the level of earnings of teachers in primary and secondary schools to that of the bank and the factories, so that the average level of earnings, irrespective of the kind of activity, will be identical. Cooperators would then no longer be drawn to other cooperative activities because of a more attractive level of earnings. The monitoring and planning functions of the management services divisions therefore play a crucial role, since all financial obligations such as earmarking funds for depreciation and paying interest to the bank, need to be complied with precisely. The only difference in distribution that remains is the degree to which individual capital accounts grow—a cooperator in a successful firm accumulates larger amounts on own account than a counterpart in a weaker firm.

A final aspect, closely connected with social valuation, concerns the distribution of earnings within a single organization of work; here the three-to-one differentials between highest and lowest earnings before deduction of tax and of social security appear to be quite modest, and are far narrower than the range of earnings differentials found in noncooperative factories.

In Mondragon, principles of solidarity have been successfully translated into real practice. In a sample of 2,500 cooperators, the ratios of the top 1, 5, and 10 percent relate to the median values as 2.1, 1.8, and 1.6.

With regard to the set of necessary conditions, it appears that in Mondragon the total is indeed more than the sum of a number of isolated PCs. The close linkage with a credit cooperative and its management-services division, and the supporting role played by a variety of eduational programs, have given rise to a system of relationships. This system has adjusted quite readily to new circumstances and new challenges, and in recent years there has been a rather greater institutional development than was the case during the early period, when the foundations were being laid. Whether, in another ten years' time, this system of cooperative relationships will further develop as a self-managed sector within a mixed economy, will be one of the most fascinating aspects to watch.

Conclusion

Several indicators were applied in order to investigate aspects of efficiency and to discover how successful the Mondragon group has been in using its resources to create "value added"; furthermore, I have made an evaluation with respect to the economic theory of self-management. Productivity and profitability are higher for cooperatives than for capitalist firms. It makes little difference whether the Mondragon group is compared with the largest 500 companies, or with small- and medium-scale industries; in both comparisons the Mondragon group is more productive and more profitable.

A fair evaluation of "efficiency" must take the objectives of cooperatives, such as the creation of jobs, into account. Job creation in the Mondragon case is an important policy instrument; this underscores the theoretical work of Vanek, who has argued that under conditions of self-management, policy instruments quite different from those applying in situations of "profit-maximization" need to be designed.

Fluctuations of ratio indicators have been considerable, particularly during the 1970s. Domestic and international sales of products have been critical factors in the development of the Mondragon group. It is therefore understandable that Caja Laboral Popular has begun to invest in more stable "markets" such as housing cooperatives, health programs, and education, which will reduce vulnerability to business cycles. The internal strength of the movement is evidenced by the narrow spread of productivity when individual cooperatives are divided into five main categories. This indicates that collective investment policies have been such that resources are reallocated in order to reach a high total yield on financial resources.

Cooperatives that face difficulties can receive a wide range of support, including financial resources perhaps leading to drastic changes in management; a search for new products; new programs of training; and ultimately large new investments with the objective of safeguarding employment. Even if the cash-flow position of the enterprise in question may not permit new financial obligations, this enterprise will benefit from the strong cash-flow position of the entire Mondragon group.

Has the community been subsidizing CLP by permitting it to accumulate high amounts of pure surplus? The critical point here is the use that CLP has made of its excellent financial results. CLP pays "out" 10 percent of the pure surplus to the fund for social projects; of the remaining 90 percent, 70 percent is put aside as "social capital" that can never be monetized and allocated to individuals, while the remaining 20 percent is entered into individual accounts of own employees, of associated cooperatives, and of those who have joined as individual cooperators. These latter individual amounts can be monetized only at the time of retirement or when withdrawing the account in the case of account holding.

The strong performance of the Mondragon cooperatives appears to be due to the fact that the system has been structured in such a way as to satisfy the conditions for an efficient labor-managed sector enumerated by Horvat and Vanek. In the process, the Mondragon group has overcome weaknesses traditionally associated with the PC. Vanek argues that "entry" of new firms is the only mechanism with which to prevent major inefficiencies that are likely to weaken a self-managed economy. The CLP objective of an annual enlistment of at least 10 cooperatives—6 by own promotion and 4 by transformation of existing factories—if successful, will become one of the most important lessons to be learned form Mondragon.

Jones (1980), in a survey of PCs, has used more than a dozen indicators to design a typology of producer cooperatives and to compare their economic and social performance. In that comparison Mondragon scores very favorably. The empirical findings of my research, as well as the evaluation of the model in the light of the theoretical work of Vanek and Horvat, strongly support Jones's conclusion.

Notes

1. Mondragon is a small town of 30,000 people, located in one of the four Basque provinces, which together have a total population of 4 million.

2. These principles, as well as the specific guidelines discussed in this paragraph, are contained in the so-called Contract of Association. This document is signed by CLP and each individual cooperative that wishes to associate with CLP; it also serves as a "constitution" for the entire group of cooperatives.

3. The quality of available data in highly uneven. Statistical information on the Spanish, and thus also of the provincial, economy is very weak; my analysis of the economic performance of private enterprises is therefore restricted. Cooperative data, on the other hand, are of excellent quality; a minute record of all financial operations is kept by CLP's research department, which has a monitoring function.

4. If it is remembered that the average level of cooperative earnings is linked to that of private enterprise, the pure surplus of cooperatives can be compared with net profits of private enterprise. Cooperatives, however, aim at high employment growth; and therefore, any ratio that has employment in its denominator has a downward bias. For further discussions on methodological issues, see the chapters by Levin and Espinosa in this volume.

5. See Medio-banca (1978; pp. 34-35); Bilderbeek (1977); and Slot and Vecht (1975; pp. 52-53).

8

The Mondragon Cooperatives: Guidelines for a Cooperative Economy?

Keith Bradley and
Alan Gelb

Any assessment of worker cooperatives must address two sets of issues: (a) the effect of cooperative organization on industrial relations and efficiency, and (b) the replicability of cooperative experiments and the sustainability of cooperative forms in general. This chapter addresses these issues, emphasizing the second set, with specific reference to the Mondragon group of cooperatives. The Mondragon experiment must have a special place in cooperative studies since it represents the largest, possibly most successful, example of a manufacturing cooperative group, and is perhaps the only major endeavor to meet most of the conditions suggested by Vanek (1975) to define a true cooperative.

The history and organization of Mondragon are documented in other studies and described in the chapter by Thomas in this book. The organization of the present chapter is as follows. The first section describes our surveys of the cooperatives and of two conventional Basque firms, which are used as controls. The second section briefly outlines possible relationships between cooperative organization and efficiency, and discusses the survey results as they bear on these issues. A generally favorable picture of the Mondragon experiment emerges. The third section analyzes three barriers of possible importance in inhibiting the widespread replication of Mondragon; the following two sections present empirical evidence. Conclusions are in the final section.

The Surveys of Mondragon

Basque reserve and political suspicion and the isolation of the region combine with logistical difficulties to inhibit data collection despite the willingness of management.[1] It is difficult to elicit responses on a sufficiently broad basis to provide an adequate perception of cooperateurs.

This research was supported by the Nuffield Foundation. Views expressed are those of the authors and do not necessarily reflect those of the World Bank or the institutional affiliations of the authors.

153

Either of two options for collecting subjective data—open-ended in-depth interviewing and more tightly formatted questions in multiple-choice form—present problems of execution and interpretation. Data collection on a large scale proceeded using the second method, and was complemented by in-depth interviewing of a number of key personnel.[2] Statistical material relating to profitability, sales, and similar variables was not collected because of its availability in publications and our a priori decision, based on previous studies, to regard the cooperatives as successful business enterprises. Two questionnaires were distributed, the second including the possibility of postal return to reduce bias caused by the inclusion of potentially sensitive questions. The surveys were not identical but contained many questions in common. Responses were obtained from a diverse range of cooperatives to reflect variations within the group over size, age, product, technology, and location. Overall, some 1,200 replies were achieved, a response rate of 30 percent. Seven lengthy interviews were conducted, one with a founding member of Mondragon, the rest with high officials of the Caja Laboral Popular. These emphasized personnel and other policies of the manufacturing cooperatives, firm-community relations, and the operations of the Caja.

The first survey covered 11 cooperatives, concentrating on Ulgor and Arrasate. Newer, smaller enterprises were also surveyed. The second survey covered 4 cooperatives, 2 located in the town of Mondragon and 2 outside it. Considering obvious characteristics, the data appear to be representative. Of the respondents to the first survey, 13 percent were female. Of the sample, 32 percent were below 30 years of age; 37 percent, between 30 and 40 years; 21 percent, between 40 and 50 years; and 10 percent over 50 years. (The average age of Mondragon workers was known to be 34 years.) Dates of joining the group spread over the last 22 years, with slight clustering over 1967 to 1971. Of respondents, 34 percent were unskilled; semiskilled and skilled cooperateurs accounted for 27 and 15 percent, respectively; and administrative and managerial staff for 13 and 11 percent. Profiles of respondents to the second survey were rather similar, although the sample was slightly younger.

Mondragon's product diversity and spatial distribution pose some problems for the selection of an appropriate control group. We decided to also use the control to obtain perceptions of Mondragon through the eyes of other workers in the Basque country. Some familiarity with the cooperatives, even by reputation, was essential. Two firms were chosen: Union Carrejera in Mondragon is long established and comparable to Ulgor; Mayc, in Vitoria, is located in a large industrial area and in product and technology is comparable with local cooperatives. Overall 280 responses were achieved, a response rate of 42 percent. In the tables below, the enterprises of the control group are designated as "firms," and those of the subject group as "cooperatives."

Profiles of the control and of the subject groups are in most respects quite similar. There are somewhat more women (24 percent) in the control group, slightly more unskilled workers and a more pyramidal wage structure. While age profiles are similar, greater proportions of workers joined the control firms before 1956 and over 1972-1976. The former difference reflects Mondragon's rapid growth; the latter, higher staff turnover in conventional firms. The selection of the control firms proved to be successful in obtaining respondents possessing some familiarity with Mondragon. Workers claimed, on the whole, considerable knowledge of the cooperatives; in fact 91 percent indicated that they had friends or relatives working in a cooperative in the Mondragon group.

Cooperative Organization and Industrial Efficiency

How, and to what extent, can Mondragon's commercial success be attributed to its cooperative organization, rather than to more commonplace factors such as good conventional management, innovative process and product development, easy access to loan capital, and so forth? By "cooperative organization" is here meant the constellation of ownership patterns, rules, and community relations so distinctively part of Mondragon.

Theoretically, cooperativism can enhance the efficiency of an enterprise in at least three ways.[3] First, if it succeeds in promoting high trust relationships between workers and managers and inhibits the alienation of workers from owners of the means of production, the cooperative form may reduce resistance toward traditional forms of hierarchical or "vertical" control. Industrial relations, even in a conventional form, will therefore proceed more smoothly. Second, profit-sharing by the entire work force generates pressure for "horizontal" control. Peer pressure among workers thus may support, rather than frustrate, vertical management. Third, at the individual level, stronger monetary incentives, if coupled with an appreciation of the role of discipline and work effort in the success of the enterprise, might be expected to encourage self-discipline—the voluntary individualistic alignment of priorities and goals with those of the enterprise.

Survey results and interviews suggest that Mondragon's cooperative organization is, indeed, significantly associated with its success through such relationships. As described in the fourth section, both the subject and the control groups rank Mondragon's "cooperativism"—worker involvement in their enterprises—as its most dominant characteristic. To assess differences between cooperative and firm working conditions, subject and control groups were asked comparable questions focusing on environmental receptivity: for example, whether they sometimes felt prevented from voicing grievances and opinions, the gulf perceived between management and workers, and the potential role for trade unions within their enterprises. The last is taken as an indicator of perceived capital-labor interest conflict. To cross-check results, the control group was asked to rate aspects of Mondragon's work environment relative to that of their own firms. Responses indicate a more favorable industrial environment for the cooperatives, which is plausibly associated with improved X-efficiency.[4]

As further described below, the cooperatives appear to maintain unusually high trust relationships between managerial and nonmanagerial members. Conflict typically accompanying hierarchical control appears correspondingly low, with little disagreement over the necessity for disciplinary codes assessed both by Mondragon members, and by the control group, as strict.

Significant horizontal reinforcement appears to be evoked as a result of worker shareholding combined with an appreciation of the role of effort in the success of the enterprise. Although formal supervisory responsibilities of the subject and the control groups are similar in profile, and both groups accept the importance of effort in success, mutual encouragement by workers appears to be far more prevalent in the cooepratives than in the control firms. Survey results do not suggest that Mondragon is perfect—disenchanted individuals and factions clearly exist—but a generally favorable relationship among cooperative organization, working environment, and efficiency is strongly indicated.

Obstacles to a Cooperative Economy

Mondragon thus appears rather successful when judged by the first set of questions. Is it, then, a widely replicable experiment? Here we investigate three potential barriers to a cooperative economy: ethnicity, employee mobility, and the role of screening in the selection of cooperateurs.

Ethnicity

The "Basqueness" of Mondragon has been held to be of great importance to its success. Cultural and political factors are highlighted by other studies as providing a foundation receptive to ideas of self-management. Significant cultural features include a high Basque propensity to save relative to that of other working people. High trust relations among workers are said to have been generated through working men's drinking clubs.[5] The political factors have been dominated by substantial repression of Basque cultural activity and expression, which may have provided a binding force and created consensus among the Basque people. It has been suggested that in the absence of such unusual circumstances successful cooperatives are much less likely. "Basqueness" is, it should be noted, a subjective rather than an objective concept. Historically, the Basque country has always drawn and assimilated immigrants, and there is no formal distinction between Basque and non-Basque.

In the cooperatives the real distinction is between those who have integrated themselves with the local community and those who have not done so.

Mobility

The following results argue against ethnicity as the determining factor of Mondragon's success. However, we contend that a more significant obstacle to the widespread establishment of Mondragon-style cooperatives is the difficulty of reconciling them with labor mobility. A high proportion of cooperatives appears to be established in areas where mobility is low for geographical or occupational reasons.[6] It is significant that Mondragon emphasizes the degree of integration into local communities—the "morality" of workers—in hiring decisions, strengthening its community links by developing social and welfare services and by preferentially hiring children of cooperateurs.

The community-cooperative link might be important for several reasons. Obviously cooperative solidarity can be cemented through social, nonwork contact, generating familiarity and high trust relationships among cooperateurs.[7] Additionally, strong community ties can lower labor mobility and reduce the desire of members to withdraw capital while working for the enterprise. Labor and capital mobility are both important, for they bear on the equity constraint facing cooperatives. The total capital stock of an enterprise may be considered as being composed of loan capital and equity or own resources. Equity must remain in the hands of cooperateurs for them to be capable of taking autonomous decisions.[8] Gearing limits restrict available assets per worker to a multiple of equity per worker, even with good access to loan capital.[9] In the long run the problem is to maintain sufficient equity to accommodate technical change and sustain growth.[10]

Regionalized populations of low mobility are plausibly less inclined to desire to withdraw capital from their enterprises, to remit to other geographic areas. Withdrawals by existing cooperateurs may be limited by regulation only if consensus on the desirability of limitations is maintained, but individual equity shares *must* be withdrawn by departing cooperateurs if control is to be maintained within the enterprise.[11] If new cooperateurs are unable (or unwilling) to replace equity withdrawn by retiring members, equity-worker ratios decline. Reliance upon communal or "socially owned" equity is, on the other hand, likely to reduce incentives especially to reinvestment of cooperative surplus.[12]

In Mondragon, equity is accumulated by members in the course of their employment span through retentions of corporate surplus in individual accounts. Clearly, the higher is the proportion of long-serving cooperateurs, the higher will be the average equity-worker ratio for the enterprise as a whole. The relationship between labor turnover, growth and equity is examined in the next section.

Screening

The third issue we focus on is the possible role of screening of cooperateur applicants in Mondragon's success. Two types of screening may be distinguished—"social" and "monetary." To the extent that these barriers reduce the entry of workers with a history of unemployment and job change or with "noncooperative" value systems, Mondragon's success may not be duplicated merely be transplanting its organizational rules.

In all firms screening on entry takes into account variables not strictly related to the task at hand. Blackburn and Mann (1979) emphasize selection of workers in conventional firms by criteria of obedience and regularity. Mondragon selection also emphasizes "attitudinal" variables, but these are specific to cooperatives. In drawing up short lists of applicants the most important of such variables is integration: both into the local community, and, potentially, into the cooperative. This carries high weight in assessing candidates.[13] Following acceptance, a worker undergoes a trial period of about six months during which time foreman's reports again stress heavily his social acceptability. Promotion too, takes "social" variables into account.

Monetary screening is induced by requiring a down payment, and the potential freezing of a part of this by cooperative management should the member intend to depart. While the exact contribution and method of payment varies according to circumstances, the average contribution roughly equals one year's pay at the lowest grade. A proportion must be paid in cash on entry. If, for the average Basque worker, the down payment is perceived as a significant amount, monetary screening might result in a work force with characteristics different from those of the rest of the population. Unless funds are easily borrowed, for example, past employment plays a large role in permitting a worker to join. At the same time cooperative success is likely to increase the pool of potential applicants: cooperative employment may not be for all, especially for those most in need of jobs.

Ethnicity, Community, and Capital Withdrawal

Basque nationalism is indeed strong in Mondragon. Within the cooperatives the official language is Basque, there is some pressure on non-Basque speakers to learn the language, and Basque political parties are supported overwhelmingly. However, Basqueness is not seen as an overridingly significant feature of Mondragon either by its workers or by those at other local firms. Table 8-1 indicates the rankings of four characteristics of Mondragon as seen by its own workers and by workers in the control group.

Rankings are very similar for subject and control groups. The most distinctive feature of Mondragon is perceived to be its cooperative nature.[14]

Table 8-1
Mondragon and Its Workers

A. *Rankings of Mondragon Characteristics by Subject and Control*

Mondragon Characteristic	Enterprise of Respondent							
	Cooperatives				Firms			
	1	*2*	*3*	*4*	*1*	*2*	*3*	*4*
Cooperativism, Involvement in firm	59	33	11	4	42	31	14	8
Security of employment	31	35	23	3	34	32	19	11
"Basqueness"	8	28	33	35	9	15	22	60
Payments	3	11	34	57	15	22	45	22
Total	100	100	100	100	100	100	100	100

B. *Cooperateurs' Identification with Certain Groups*

Group	Ranking			
	1	*2*	*3*	*4*
Cooperative management	45	23	12	21
Cooperative workers	34	50	8	2
Basque workers generally	16	18	35	26
Spanish workers generally	5	8	46	50
Total	100	100	100	100

Source: Calculated from the survey data.

Security of employment is generally ranked second. Far behind come the ethnic nature of the cooperatives and their level of payments.

While from outside of the Basque provinces the Basque dimension is accredited strong causal significance, from inside, against the backdrop of general Basqueness, this characteristic is far less important. Although 80 percent of cooperateur respondents describe themselves as Basque, so do 72 percent of the control group. The gulf between Mondragon workers, as perceived by themselves, and Basque workers appears in some sense to be sharper than that perceived between Basque and Spanish workers. Respondents were asked to rank groups whose behavior they identified most closely with their own interests. The results are shown in table 8-1B.

Mondragon's cooperateurs' identification with each other appears to be much stronger than with outside workers. Further decomposition of responses in table 8-1B shows that Mondragon managers identify their interest most closely with those of nonmanagerial cooperateurs. The latter identify most closely with their own management.[15] Unusually high trust relationships exist on Mondragon, both laterally among members and vertically through the control hierarchy. This vertical high trust relationship is thought to be important in maintaining consensus on the cooperatives, and inhibiting the emergence of worker alienation.

Integration into a tight, close-knit community was argued in the third section to be a potentially important factor in preserving the equity capital of a cooperative. Mondragon provides strong support for this hypothesis, interpreting respondents claiming to be non-Basque as those not integrated into their communities; see table 8-2. It is clear that the close balance between those desiring to withdraw capital and those content with the status quo is maintained only by the high proportion of cooperateurs integrated into the Basque communites.

The location of individual cooperatives would also be expected to affect the desire to withdraw capital. Subsamples within the cooperative group support this hypothesis. Only 44 percent of Mondragon-based respondents to the second questionnaire indicated a desire to withdraw accumulated profits, but 67 percent of the cooperateurs situated in larger industrial centers outside the town of Mondragon desired to do so. Basque and non-Basque proportions were similar in these two groups, but responses suggest that the latter group feels less well integrated into their cooperatives than does the former. Of the sample based in the town of Mondragon, 83 percent had many friends and relatives working in their enterprise, compared to only 47 percent of the group based outside the town. Cooperateurs in large urban centers generally seem to have been more prepared to consider employment in other firms in response to hypothetical offers of higher pay, and were strongly attracted to the cooperative by the prospect of work. In their attitudes to management and the Caja Laboral Popular, they appear to be less imbued with the cooperative ethic. Lack of a close link between cooperative enterprises and local communities may therefore render equity accumulation more difficult by expanding the horizons of cooperateurs.

Reallocation of cooperateurs within the Mondragon group is not infrequent. Our data suggest that potential mobility from the cooperatives to other firms is low. Mondragon's promise of job security (a distinctive feature as seen by the control: see table 8-1) appears more important than its level of payments. Respondents were asked whether they would be willing

Table 8-2
Desire to Withdraw Accumulated Profits while Working

| Integration | Desire for Withdrawal | | | | |
	Yes	Percentage	No	Percentage	Total
Basque	342	75	376	85	718
Non-Basque	113	25	66	15	179
Total	455	100	442	100	897

Source: Calculated from the survey data.

Note: $\chi^2_1 = 13.8$: significant at 0.005.

to transfer to other hypothetical enterprises for specified wage premiums.[16] Responses are shown in table 8-3. Column headings classify respondents by their own enterprise—cooperative or control firm—and by a hypothetical destination. Numbers indicate those expressing a desire to transfer, or unwilling to change. Cooperateurs and workers differ very significantly in their willingness to leave their respective enterprises. Cooperateurs are slightly more ready to transfer to a hypothetical local "Spanish" cooperative, but they generally are far less potentially mobile than workers in the control firms.

The smaller turnover in the Mondragon group leads to a different pattern of joining dates than that which would be expected in a conventional firm. Joining profiles differ into two important respects. Firstly, Mondragon's sustained, rapid expansion implies relatively few joiners before 1960. Second, the joining-date distribution of the control group is bimodal, indicating a large number of recent joiners despite the general economic slowdown after 1972; the firms contain a larger proportion of transients than do the cooperatives.

Lower intrinsic mobility of cooperateurs may be advantageous in that it blunts the conflict between compressed cooperative wage differentials and labor-market forces. In its absence, maintaining managerial and specialist skills could prove a more severe problem for the cooperatives. [17] However, emphasis on job security raises potential difficulties for the coexistence of cooperatives with conventional capitalist enterprises. To cope with possible shifts in demand, the diverse product mix of Mondragon is essential to facilitate the transfer of labor among enterprises experiencing different

Table 8-3
Potential Labor Mobility

	Enterprise of Worker					
	Cooperative		Cooperative		Local Firm	
Destination	(A) Spanish Cooperative	Percentage	(B) Local Firm	Percentage	(C) Local Firm	Percentage
Incentive to leave						
No monetary incentive	18	3	8	1	11	4
10-50% salary increase	167	31	155	27	144	54
Would not change	353	66	398	72	113	42
Total	538	100	561	100	268	100

Source: Calculated from the survey data.

Notes: A-B $\times \frac{2}{2} = 6.5$ significant 0.05.

B-C $\times \frac{2}{2} = 64.3$ significant at 0.005.

fortunes. This is seen as a major safety valve by cooperative management, but provides only limited flexibility even to so well-developed a group as Mondragon, where marketing and technology changes are currently forcing consideration of redundancy.[18]

Redundancy and labor turnover affect equity availability considerably if, as in Mondragon, retained surplus credited to individual accounts is the main form of equity accumulation. Mondragon's history allows the computation of equity accumulated over a 22-year period by an average cooperateur, assuming Mondragon rules of sharing surplus and taking conditions over the past 22 years as reasonably representative.[19] Starting from an index of 100, an equity account doubles in about 5 years, then increases steadily to reach about 800 after 22 years. The longer serving is the cooperative work force on average, the higher, therefore, will be the average equity per worker E. Rapid growth, by raising the proportion of new to old cooperateurs, lowers E. So does labor turnover, as the proportion of old cooperateurs falls.

E has been computed for four scenarios. With no growth and no labor attrition through turnover, $E = 430$. Introducing steady growth at 3 percent per annum lowers E to 388, a fall of 10 percent. With the employment profile of our first sample, $E = 385$. This indicates that, assuming low labor turnover and continuing profitability, Mondragon equity per worker is capable of increasing during a transition to steady growth. Retirement of older cooperateurs should pose little problem for Mondragon, even if retirees may withdraw accumulated profits. In contrast, labor turnover is a potentially serious problem. With a 3 percent rate of attrition, E for the sample profile falls by 9 percent from its previous value. If 10 percent of the work force quit every year, E falls by almost one-third.

In balanced growth with labor attrition at some constant percentage rate, the vintage profile of cooperateurs depends approximately on the sum of the growth and the attrition rates; a rise in either puts equal downward pressure on E.[20] A 3 percent rise in attrition thus needs to be offset by a similar fall in growth to maintain the cooperative's capital stock. It is difficult to grow without locking in a cooperative work force for very substantial periods.

One apparent way out of this dilemma is to rely upon "socially owned" equity held by the collective rather than in individual accounts. This might, however, lead to a reduction in efficiency, due to a fall in individual incentives. At Mondragon, it appears that those who have been longest with the group (and who hence have accumulated most equity)[21] are far more inclined to cite their investments as a factor motivating concern that they and their fellows work well: see table 8-4. While this result could be attributed to other factors (such as age differences) it is nonetheless suggestive.

In summary, a number of obstacles limit the replicability of Mondragon-style cooperatives in the broader industrial society. To maintain incentives and encourage reinvestment of surplus it is necessary for a significant portion of

Table 8-4
Capital Holdings and Desired Work Intensity

Years at Mondragon	(a) Strong	(b) Weak	Ratio a/b	Total (%)
18+	56	6	9.33	11
8–17	241	77	3.13	57
Up to 7	127	54	2.35	32
Total	424	137	3.17	100

Source: Calculated from the survey data.
Note: $\chi_2^2 = 10.2$ significant at 0.01.

the capital of a cooperative to be owned by its individual cooperateurs. Changing conditions and technology probably render labor mobility generally desirable, although Brown and Medoff (1978) provide some evidence to the contrary. Perhaps more important is the preservation of in-dividual choice in changing firms, location, or occupation. Yet, within a Mondragon-type system, a conflict appears between the three objectives: (a) high mobility, (b) equity accumulation, and (c) appropriately structured in-centives for reinvestment of surplus. For locational—and perhaps ethnic—reasons, naturally low mobility of Mondragon cooperatives has diminished the potential conflict between these objectives, permitting rapid growth and accumulation.

Screening and Cooperative Success

Almost all our cooperative respondents considered their initial contribution as a fairly large sum to invest. In the eyes of the control group, the contribu-tion is perceived as the prime barrier to joining, followed closely by the fear of being "locked in" and unable to withdraw capital. The capital require-ment plausibly screens out a substantial number of lower-income appli-cants, just as potential "locking in" would be expected to reduce applica-tions by workers not seriously intending to stay.[22] Table 8-5 compares the employment experience of cooperateurs and control group workers im-mediately prior to their current status. The higher proportion of previously unemployed in the control is probably associated, at least to some extent, with the capital requirement of Mondragon. In addition, a past history of unemployment or job instability may act as another qualitative screen to cooperative entrants.

Further evidence of screening is provided by table 8-6. Cooperateurs tended to see the cooperatives as one of a range of alternative opportunities. Correspondingly, relative to the control, they declared themselves to have

Table 8-5
Prior Employment Status

	Enterprise of Respondent				
Status	Cooperative	Percentage	Firm	Percentage	Total
Employed before joining	687	67	122	44	809
Unemployed before joining	341	33	151	56	492
Total	1,028	100	273	100	1,301

Source: Calculated from the survey data.
Note: $\chi^2 = 45.0$ significant at 0.005.

been less motivated to join merely because of a desire for work. This impression is reinforced by the observation that 65 percent of cooperatuers indicated that they would have refused a similar job at a local conventional firm, had one been offered, in favor of joining their cooperative, in spite of the deterent posed by the capital contribution. In a sense, and relative to conventional firms, Mondragon has provided jobs to those *not* needing them.[23] Job creation is thus substantially indirect—through siphoning workers off other firms—partly because of the ability of the cooperative to select desirable members.

Table 8-6
Alternative Employment for and Motivations of Workers

A. Alternative Employment Opportunities

	Enterprise of Respondent				
Opportunity	Cooperatives	Percentage	Firms	Percentage	Total
No	332	33	139	50	471
Yes	675	67	137	50	812
Total	1,007	100	276	100	1,283

Source: Calculated from the survey data.
Note: $X_1^2 = 28.2$ significant at 0.005.

B. Main Motivation for Joining Enterprise

	Enterprise of Respondent				
Motivation	Cooperatives	Percentage	Firms	Percentage	Total
Cooperative/Working Conditions	628	68	61	25	689
Employment	298	31	183	75	481
Total	926	99	244	100	1,170

Source: Calculated from the survey data.
Note: $\chi_2^2 = 146.1$: significant at 0.005.

What evidence exists that screening might contribute to a diminution of industrial conflict on the cooperatives by maintaining consensus? Rigorous formulation and testing of any such relationship must be approached with caution for several reasons. How can we measure "cooperative attitudes" or the circumstances under which individuals joined? Both dependent and independent variables are multifaceted, subjective amalgams. Additionally, the sample of cooperateurs is necessarily limited to those selected—we cannot sample those failing to enter—and even were this possible, such a group could not be expected to comment credibly on an unexperienced work situation. As described below, the nonrandom distribution of cooperateurs over characteristics biases estimated relationships rather severely.

For each composite variable several responses were selected to represent various facets, and multiple regressions performed between each facet of the dependent variable—attitudes—each facet of the independent explanatory variable—circumstances of joining—and a set of "standardizing" variables to take into account the possible influences of third variables correlated with dependent and independent variables. Let

$$Y_i = \text{facet } i \text{ of "cooperative attitudes" where } i = 1, 2, \ldots, 7;$$
$$X_j = \text{facet } j \text{ of "joining condition" where } j = 1, 2, 3, 4;$$
$$S_k = \text{standardizing variable } k \text{ where } k = 1, \ldots, 7.$$

Each of the 28 regressions takes the form

$$Y_i = a_{ij} X_j + \sum_{k=1}^{7} b_{ik} S_k$$

assuming linear relationships. Facets of "cooperative attitudes" and "joining conditions" are[24]

$$Y_1 = \text{perception of greater job control;}$$

$$Y_2 = \text{perceived degree of participation in important decisions;}$$

$$Y_3 = \text{ability to voice opinions or complaints;}$$

$$Y_4 = \text{perceived "distance" between cooperative workers and management;}$$

$$Y_5 = \text{view of the Caja Laboral as acting in workers' interests;}$$

$$Y_6 = \text{desire to withdraw shareholding from cooperative;}$$

$$X_1 = \text{willingness to have taken similar job outside cooperative;}$$

$$X_2 = \text{perception of cooperative on joining as only employment opportunity;}$$

X_3 =   declared principal motive for joining cooperative;

X_4 =   whether in employment before joining cooperative.

Standardizing variables included are age, sex, "Basqueness," joining date, wage, occupation and "ideology." The last variable is proxied by perceptions of the role of management on conventional Basque firms.

Empirical results are affected by worker-selection biases. Selection is heavily influenced by social and attitudinal assessments as well as by skill, functional, and educational considerations. Mondragon interviewers are probably influenced in their selection by a set of variables that includes our variables X_1-X_4. Perfect screening over these variables would be expected to result in not merely orthogonal, but compensating variations between the X_i and between the Y_i. For example, to be acceptable, a prospective worker, if currently unemployed, might be required to demonstrate greater "cooperative" motivation than one employed, since the latter is, prima facie, more likely to be joining out of an acceptable cooperative impulse. Similarly, attitudes favorable and unfavorable to cooperativism would tend to offset rather than reinforce each other. The estimated a_{ij} would then be expected to be nonsignificant and of random sign. A full test of perfect screening is therefore the dominance of compensating variations between the "entry" variables and the "attitude" variables, as well as the absence of any significant relationship between the two types.[25]

Correlation matrixes between the independent and dependent variable facets are shown in table 8-7. Correlations are low, yet generally statistically significant. More importantly, all signs for the X_i are as would be predicted in the absence of screening, and only two nonsignificant correlations between the Y_j differ from the pattern. The X_i and Y_j components do indeed exhibit some common "directionality," although dispersion about their common directions is large.

Table 8-8 shows the matrix of regression coefficients a_{ij} as obtained from the 28 regressions. Coefficients are small, yet 16 out of 28 are significant at the 5 percent level; and the signs of 23 coefficients (including all 16 significant ones) are consistent with the hypothesis that attitudes toward the cooperative relate systematically to the circumstances under which individuals join. Broadly speaking, individuals who see the cooperative as one of a range of employment possibilities, and hence who are less dependent on for a job, exhibit more "cooperative" attitudes. The coefficients can be interpreted as probabilities. Then if 100 workers were to join the cooperatives as a last resort, compared to 100 workers joining with alternative options of employment, about 16 extra would perceive a serious division between management and workers.[26] The potential growth of division within enterprises is considerable.

It is not possible to form unbiased estimates of the relationship between characteristics and attitudes that would prevail with a less rigorous selection

Table 8-7
Correlation Matrixes

A. X_i Correlation Matrix

	X_1	X_2	X_3	X_4
X_1	1			
X_2	.24*	1		
X_3	−.46*	−.24*	1	
X_4	−.35*	−.10*	.30*	1

B. Y_j Correlation Matrix

	Y_1	Y_2	Y_3	Y_4	Y_5	Y_6	Y_7
Y_1	1						
Y_2	.16*	1					
Y_3	−.13*	−.26*	1				
Y_4	.10*	−.06[a]	.30*	1			
Y_5	.19*	.19*	−.14*	−.25*	1		
Y_6	−.07	.02[a]	.11*	.11*	−.02	1	
Y_7	−.06	−.10*	.14*	.19*	−.13*	.07	1

Source: Calculated from the survey data.
*Significant at 1% level.
[a]Sign inconsistent with common directionality.

policy. However, selection, as noted above, biases the regression coefficients toward zero probably very significantly, so that they understate true values, providing lower bounds. Attempts to expand the cooperatives unduly rapidly, or to emphasize the objective of direct job creation (that is, the offering of employment to individuals less able to find work in conventional firms) would probably result in a considerable weakening of these cooperatives' present ideological solidarity.

Table 8-8
Regression Coefficients a_{ij}

Index $_j$	Index i			
	1	2	3	4
1	−.13*	.04[a]	.13*	.09*
2	−.05	−.12	.24*	.24
3	.05	.11*	−.07	−.10*
4	.13*	.16*	−.13*	.04[a]
5	−.06*	.05[a]	.07*	.10*
6	.06	.10*	−.10*	.07[a]
7	.03	.13*	−.06	.05[a]

Source: Calculated from the survey data.
*Significant at 5% level.
[a]Inconsistent sign.

Conclusion

In many respects, the remarkable cooperative experiment of Mondragon demonstrates advantages of a cooperative economy. The consensus-building and efficiency-inducing potential of the cooperatives is suggested by the survey results described in the third section of this chapter. The present chapter has sought also to analyze barriers to replication of Mondragon in a wider industrial setting. We conclude that these barriers are quite substantial—but different in nature to those frequently cited.

Basque ethnicity per se does not appear to be so major a factor as to prevent the replication of Mondragon. More problematical are linkages with local communities and limited labor mobility: first, these two factors appear to contribute to the maintenance of consensus; second, they partially insulate the cooperatives from competitive pressures of the external labor market, permitting a more compressed payments scale; third, limitation of cooperateur horizons helps to retain capital by reducing the desire to remit savings to distant areas while working. Fourth, low labor turnover is vital for the maintenance of cooperative equity capital. Cooperative survival may not be easy in a fluid labor market with general labor mobility and technology changes.

Communal, rather than individual, capital holdings may reconcile the maintenance of equity with labor mobility—but at a high cost. Individual shareholdings appear to play an important motivating role at Mondragon—76 percent of our sample saw their investments as a major factor in their belief that other workers and themselves should work especially well. Divorcing rewards from returns to cooperative capital provides a strong incentive for decapitalization.

In certain respects—notably prior unemployment experience—Mondragon cooperateurs differ from control workers. Screening may provide Mondragon with a distinctive pool of workers more likely to identify with the cooperative ethic and to maintain solidarity with fellow cooperateurs. As alternative opportunities decrease, the pool of potential cooperateurs increases to include more individuals viewing the cooperatives primarily as a job opportunity. Unless screening is perfect, greater pressure is placed on socialization processes after entry to maintain consensus.

What then are the prospects for Mondragon-type cooperatives in a modern industrialized economy? From a "static" viewpoint, probably rather good, because of the efficiency-raising potential of the cooperative form. U.S. experience also suggests this potential, albeit in less truly cooperative circumstances than those of Mondragon (see University of Michigan 1979).

A dynamic analysis over the lifetime of an enterprise suggests a less favorable outlook because of the generally high mobility and relative absence of community attachment common in major industrial regions. There are, of course, exceptions to this rule—two notable examples would appear to be Switzerland and Japan. In fact Mondragon seems not too dissimilar to the large Japanese cartels in a number of respects—internal mobility but limited internal-external movement, community links, job tenure, and responsibility for social security. In the more fluid environment characteristic of other developed economies there are, however, quite sizable pockets of relative immobility and community attachment in which Mondragon-type enterprises might flourish with appropriate access to loan capital. It is interesting to note the tendencies toward cooperate establish-ment in such regions in the Northeastern United States, where they might stabilize local communities.

Stabilization is not, however, achieved without a cost. The locking in of labor and capital tends to inhibit quantity and quality adjustment in cooperative labor markets, which must then adjust through implicit prices. Nonprice adjustment is forced onto the remaining labor market, which bears the brunt of fluctuations in employment levels. A clear example of this is the dual functioning of the Japanese labor market over the 1970s.

Notes

1. For example, very low reponse rates to early surveys were attributed by management to a combination of personal and political questions that might allow respondents to be identified. Elimination of these questions in later surveys improved response rates.

2. The logistic difficulties presented by large-scale interviewing together with Basque reluctance to discuss sensitive points with outsiders biased us toward surveys, which, in addition, are able to take advantage of the high level of literacy achieved in the Basque country.

3. For a formal model underlying this description and more extensive empirical results, see Bradley and Gelb (1981).

4. X-efficiency is defined and distinguished from allocative efficiency by Leibenstein (1966).

5. See, for example, Oakeshott (1978), pp. 168-169. Thomas and Logan (1980) too emphasize the distinctive history and cultural features of the Basque region.

6. A number of examples in Canada, the United States, Australia, France, and the United Kingdom may be cited to support this observation; see Bradley and Gelb (1980a).

7. See Bradley and Gelb (1981) for description of the role of trust rela-tionships in Mondragon. The role of the community in attempts to establish employee-owned firms in the United States has been significant; see, for ex-ample, Zwerdling (1978).

170   Participatory and Self-Managed Firms

8. In fact, one of the difficulties faced by many cooperative experiments is the small share of equity held by many workers.

9. Difficulties of cooperatives in the United States and United Kingdom have partly been ascribed to the reluctance of bankers to lend to cooperatives; see, for example, Thornley (1981); Rothschild-Whitt (1979). Mondragon, through the establishment of the Caja Laboral Popular, has relaxed this total capital constraint—but a potential equity constraint remains. Debt-equity ratios have risen slightly in Mondragon, but at about 1:1 they are considerably lower than in many conventional firms.

10. Distinction between small family firms and cooperatives is not easy from this point of view—both may, at a certain stage of development, be constrained by equity shortage. Firms, however, have the option of making public equity offerings; cooperatives may be compromised by doing so.

11. Various ways of overcoming this problem have been mooted by Caja Laboral Popular officials but none seems to fully solve the problem. For example, providing retirees with pensions in lieu of payouts reduces their security because the pension becomes the residual bearer of risk.

12. It is understood that Yugoslav cooperatives, whose capital is socially owned, currently face this problem for there is no incentive for older workers, some of whom occupy managerial positions, to generate a surplus for reinvestment. For an analysis of this and related issues, see Jensen and Meckling (1979).

13. The importance of the integration criterion was highlighted in all interviews with cooperative management.

14. As noted in Bradley and Gelb (1981) this may not be easy to distinguish from other characteristics such as job security.

15. See Bradley and Gelb (1981).

16. Cooperateurs were, in addition, told to assume the possibility of complete capital withdrawal without penalty.

17. The cooperatives have been able to recruit managers through their own ranks and to keep them through a variety of nonmonetary incentives. Recruitment of specialists from outside is more difficult. Tension between labor market and cooperative forces is indicated by the decision in 1979 to formally widen differentials on Urssa in the large industrial city of Vitoria. Our survey indicates a strong desire for greater equalization of payments in Urssa, especially among the lower paid. It is interesting to speculate on whether the internal labor market will provide continuing upward mobility as technology levels of the cooperatives rise.

18. Lagun Aro (the cooperatives' social service) is studying the possibility of introducing unemployment insurance. The extension of the central agency to shoulder redundancy expense is seen as necessary to shift the burden from industrial cooperatives (interview with Antonio Calleja, Director, Caja Laboral Popular, July 1979).

19. Nominal assets of an average cooperateur over 1956-1977 are estimated by Thomas and Logan (1980). Real asset profiles may be computed by deflating nominal profiles by revaluation coefficients.

20. Let $L_0 = 1$; then $L_i = (1 - g)^i/(1 + q)^i$ where g and q represent growth and attrition rates, respectively, and L_i represents the number of cooperateurs of vintage i.

21. As described by Thomas (1981), despite the fact that cooperatives may accumulate at slightly different rates, capital holdings are well proxied by length of service.

22. Further evidence of the role of the screening effect of cooperative entry requirements is provided (in a different context) in Bradley and Gelb (1980b).

23. Possible variation in third variables between sample and control that contribute to the different profiles in Tables 8-4, 8-5, and 8-6 do not undermine the screening argument since such variations are themselves probably the result of screening. For example, Mondragon may employ fewer females because females are more likely to want temporary employment or have less access to funds. Neither is the different pattern of joining dates between the cooperative and control groups responsible.

24. These are regarded as separate facets rather than as constituting a set of variables scalable according to some criterion such as that of Guttman. There is no reason, for example, to believe that a positive answer to X_1 should imply a similar response X_2 but that positive X_2 should not necessarily imply positive X_1, etc. Estimation should ideally be in a logit form and joint, as seemingly unrelated regressions. All coefficients here are obtained by single-equation OLS.

25. Individuals may be considered to possess a characteristic vector $z = (X_1, X_2, X_3)$ where X_1 and X_2 provide indications of ideological commitment, and X_3 denotes other attributes such as skills. The x_i are distributed over the population of potential cooperative workers, and selection involves choosing workers for whom $f(X_3, X_2, X_3) > k$ where k is some cut-off score. Positive correlation between X_1 and X_2 in the population will be biased toward negative values by selection, the bias being stronger the higher is k and the more weight is placed on X_1 and X_2 relative to other variables. For an indication of possible bias, let X_1 and X_2 each take value 1 and 0 with probability 0.5, and be positively correlated with coefficient 0.6. Omit the influence of X_3. If 40 percent are rejected by screening, correlations between X_1 and X_2 for the *selected* workers is -0.2. Screening changes the sign of ex post observed correlation from its value in the population of all workers.

26. Interpretation of regression coefficients as probabilities is appropriate in the case of dichotomous dependent variables. To avoid the problems of probabilities fully outside the (0, 1) range, logit or similar

transformations may be used. Two of the seven dependent variables are trichotomous variables: for these, simple linear scaling (constant interval) has been adopted.

**Part IV
Participation in
Industrialized Western
Economies**

9 British Producer Cooperatives, 1948–1968: Productivity and Organizational Structure

Derek C. Jones

Widely differing theoretical expectations exist concerning the economic performance of participatory firms and labor-managed firms (LMFs). While some good empirical studies of these firms by economists have been undertaken, there remain considerable gaps in the empirical record. In general, theoretical controversies have not yet been tempered by enough careful empirical analysis.

A specific case in point is the producer (industrial-worker) cooperative (PC). While Vanek (1971, in Vanek (ed.) 1975) expects good performance from well-structured PCs, others are much less sanguine (Jensen and Meckling 1979). Many disagree regarding the critical features accounting for variation in performance among PCs. In particular, the relationship between aspects of internal organizational structure and economic performance is much debated. In this chapter I provide evidence that bears on this relationship. By estimating production fuctions I evaluate the separate effects on productivity of worker participation in control, in ownership, and in surplus.

First, the theoretical literature in this area is reviewed. Next, the salient characteristics of the specific group of firms under study, namely, long-established British PCs in the printing, footwear, and clothing industries, are described. After outlining the econometric specifications used, the results are presented, and the findings are compared with those of other researchers. In a concluding section the implications of this and other studies for the relationship between organizational structure and economic performance in general, and the nature of the optimal PC in particular, are discussed.

Theoretical Considerations

Most economic theory in the area of participation and labor management is concerned with the case of the pure labor-managed economy—essentially one in which all control in all firms is vested in work forces and on an equal

The research for this paper was partially supported by a grant from the Leverhulme Trust. The paper has benefited by comments from Dave Backus, Jan Svejnar, and, above all, Don Schneider.

175

basis among workers. The relevance of many of these models for real-world "participatory" forms, in which partial and often unequal control accrues to workers, and which often exist as pockets within industrial capitalist economies, is not clear. The scarcity of pertinent theoretical literature is particularly apparent when attention is focused on the relationship between important aspects of organizational structures in participatory firms—such as participation by workers in control, ownership, and the surplus (profit)—and measures of economic performance, such as productivity. Nevertheless there have been some important attempts to theorize about relevant aspects of specific participatory types.

For the case of the PC important work has been done by Vanek (1975, introduction), who outlines various rules for efficiency in LMFs from the standpoint of the relationship between organizational structure and economic performance. Most important are those which provide that (a) all control should be vested in the work force and on an equal basis; (b) investments should be financed other than through collective retained earnings; (c) capital should be remunerated at its scarcity price; and (d) an apex organization (supporting structure) should be established to shelter, fund, and promote LMFs. Vanek argues that firms that come closest to satisfying these conditions will perform best.

Several of the featues stressed by Vanek have a long history in the economics literature. Seldom, however, have other authorities stressed the same complete list of aspects emphasized by Vanek. Even when there is apparent agreement among authors on the general contribution of a particular factor to economic performance, often there is marked disagreement as to underlying causal mechanisms. Sometimes both cause and effect are in dispute. These points can be illustrated by focusing on some of these questions explored by Vanek.

Concerning the relationship between participation in decision making and productivity, Vanek and many other contemporary economists expect a positive association. Cable and Fitzroy (1980a,b) view worker participation as a way of replacing the traditional antipathetic relationship between workers (and their representatives) and owners (and their representatives) with cooperation. Furthermore, cooperation will enlarge the available economic pie.

Some bygone orthodox economists made similar claims. Marshall (in Pigou 1925, p. 347) states that substantial gains would follow from having worker representatives on boards. However, often the supposed advantages of worker participation are offset by other factors. Thus, Marshall states that managers of PCs would be unable to undertake decision making quickly and, because of opposition from worker-members, might end up making the wrong decisions.[1] Other orthodox economists also appear to suggest that positive relationships exist between participation and performance, but that these relationships hold only when partial participatory forms are considered.[2]

At the other end of the spectrum are those economists who always expect a negative relationship between participation and performance. The Webbs (1920) argue that great difficulties follow from the relationship between managers and worker-members in an industrially democratic firm. More recently, Jensen and Meckling (1979) criticize the claim that LMFs, including PCs, are efficient. The authors stress the problem of preference formation when worker preferences are not identical. Control problems allegedly will result; these will be particularly troublesome in larger firms.

A similar range of views is apparent when the expected relationship between productivity and participation in the surplus is examined. Cable and Fitzroy (1980a,b), develop a theory based on group, not individual, incentives. They argue that profit sharing with workers is required in order for workers to agree to work together with owners. In predicting a positive relationship between productivity and profit sharing, Cable and Fitzroy are joined by other contemporaries including Vanek (1975) and Bernstein (1976).

Economic theorists of yesteryear held similar views. Both Marshall and Mill see various economic advantages flowing from the incentive mechanisms at work in firms practicing profit sharing. These advantages include a lowering of unit labor costs, an improvement in discipline, and an elimination of restrictive labor practices (Jones 1976, p. 11).

Anticipating a strand in the contemporary counterargument, however, Mill is not completely convinced that sharing the economic surplus with workers is a good thing to do. He posits that the consequence of worker participation in the surplus would be that managers might not receive monetary rewards as large as they would have otherwise. Alchian and Demsetz (1972) develop these arguments most forcefully. Introducing the concept of team production, they argue that it is difficult to determine the productivity of individual team members. Difficulties of monitoring the performance of other team members means that incentives are created for individual team members to shirk. To minimize the potential for shirking by team members, a team monitor (manager) is needed. Efficient monitoring in turn requires that a bundle of property rights be vested in the central monitor, and of these rights the ability to keep the residual reward is deemed to be essential to efficiency—in other words, the sharing of the residual with workers will reduce the efficiency both of the monitor and of the enterprise. The expectation of an inverse relationship between profit sharing and performance is shared by Samuelson (1977). Jensen and Meckling (1979, p. 485) extend the monitoring argument. They argue that as the labor force grows each individual will have a stronger incentive to shirk;

consequently shirking will become more difficult and more expensive to detect. Profit sharing will be particularly dysfunctional in larger firms.

A third and related issue is that of the relationship between worker ownership and performance. For Vanek (1975) and Cable and Fitzroy (1980a,b), individual worker ownership is not crucial to providing for high productivity in the firm. For Vanek, individual ownership is irrelevant if the bundle of property rights normally associated with ownership of capital is split so that the right to control and the right to receive all net income accrue to workers as workers rather than as capital suppliers. In situations where laws do not permit such separation—and in most Western industrialized countries even cooperative laws require capital ownership for member-ship—a certain level of individual worker ownership may be expected to be positively associated with performance. In such cases, however, control rights should not be proportional to ownership.

Other authors identify substantial individual worker ownership as the principal factor eliciting high levels of performance. For Oakeshott (1978, p. 243) a large individually owned capital stake is viewed as essential for producing a motivated and committed work force. In contrast, Jensen and Meckling (1979, pp. 494-495) implicitly indicate the importance of having rights proportional to capital ownership in all organizations. They see the absence of this characteristic in LMFs as a principal reason for the emergence of control problems within such firms.

When the way in which different authors view interaction of these various elements affecting performance is examined, more differences are revealed. For example Cable and Fitzroy (1980, p. 166) hypothesize that there will be an interaction between the effects of worker participation in decision making and the effects of profit sharing on performance. Vanek and Bernstein also expect such a relationship, though both admit that this relationship may be clouded by the failure to fulfill other conditions necessary for good performance.

In sum, this brief survey reveals widely differing expectations concern-ing the nature and the complexity of the relationships between performance and, respectively, participation in decision making, in the surplus, and in ownership. Even when there is some shared view among authors the agree-ment may be confined to certain size classes of firms or for certain ranges of values. For example, some suggest that a positive relationship between per-formance and participation in decision making may be expected to operate only up to a critical level of worker power.

Clearly there remains much to be done on a theoretical level in sketching out the rationale for and the details of the relationship between aspects of or-ganization and performance. To prompt informed discussion, this chapter tests some simple competing hypotheses. As a preparatory step, in the next sec-tion I briefly review salient features of the group of firms under investigation.

Characteristics

The oldest surviving form of worker cooperative in Britain is the long-established PC. Many of these PCs have been established for more than 70 years; the oldest, Walsall Lock, was formed in 1874. While most belong to the official organ of the British cooperative movement, the Cooperative Union, only about seven are presently members of the Cooperative Productive Federation (CPF), a body founded in 1882 to help promote and defend the interests of PCs.

PCs began for one of two principal reasons. Many were formed by retail cooperatives (sometimes with the assistance of a trade union, sometimes by only the trade union) to provide a particular service or product for the retailers. This was often the case in the printing industry, and sometimes in clothing. In footwear, however, many PCs were formed at the initiative of workers in times in economic distress. Some PCs were formed following the lockout of 1895 in the boot and shoe trade. In other cases the impetus for foundation came during or following a strike.

Long-established PCs are registered as industrial and provident societies. For membership in a PC, ownership of a certain (and ordinarily a nominal) number of shares is legally required. Typically there are three classes of members: workers, other individuals (particularly former workers), and other societies (particularly retail cooperatives, other PCs, and trade unions). Only in exceptional cases do current workers own a majority of the share capital. In many cases, though, the vast majority of workers are members, and often a majority of members are workers. Most importantly, adherence to the cooperative principle of "one member, one vote" means that in many cases, particularly in the footwear industry, a majority of the committee of management are workers. In some cases all the members of this single-tier policy-making board are workers. However, in certain PCs, especially in printing and clothing, there are few (perhaps no) worker representatives on the management board. In nearly all cases provision exists for direct worker participation in nondirective decisions through work committees of various kinds.

Financial characteristics of long-established British PCs differ substantially from those of comparable capitalist firms. A PC is constrained by law to paying a limited interest on share capital. Since shares remain at their nominal or par value, substantial collective ownership of assets exists. There are legal restrictions inhibiting a PC's ability to raise outside financing; for example, preference shares cannot be issued. Relatively little use is made of permissible external capital sources such as bank overdrafts. In practice most PCs rely on internal financing from retained earnings that cannot be recovered by individual workers except upon dissolution of the society.

Regarding earnings, most PCs distribute part of their net income (surplus) to workers as an annual bonus. Usually workers receive bonuses in proportion to their income from work. Other shares often go to customers as a form of rebate and to capital owners. Frequently a union shop exists in PCs; consequently rates of earnings normally at least equal prevailing union rates. PCs generally do not have specific egalitarian policies concerning relative earnings of their members.

The period under study in this paper, 1948-1968, was not a good one for long-established PCs. The number of PCs fell from a postwar high of 48 in 1948 to 30 in 1968; by 1975 only 17 remained. Moreover, no new PCs that are members of the Cooperative Union and that are registered under the Industrial and Provident Societies Act were formed after 1950. No new PCs were formed after the 1930s in the industries that are the focus of this paper.

In table 9-1 basic statistical information on important characteristics of the firms being studied is provided. Table 9-1A reveals that most PCs continue to be in printing and that during the period under study many footwear PCs perished. With respect to both sales and labor force, on average, clothing PCs are the largest and printing PCs the smallest. There is also considerable variation in the size distribution of PCs. Though many PCs in printing provide employment for only about 20 workers, one firm has a labor force in excess of 600. In clothing the size spread is even greater, ranging from 10 to 1,300.

Table 9-1B shows that with respect to worker representation on the board of management, footwear PCs on average provide for much more worker participation than do printing and clothing PCs. Also, a higher proportion of workers in footwear PCs elect to join the society than workers in either clothing or printing PCs. Both the value of an individual worker's share in the surplus and of that worker's individual stake in the firm, on average, are higher in footwear than in the two other industries. Also, some printing and clothing PCs do not permit individual worker ownership and seldom distribute surplus to workers. In real terms, both the value of the bonus distributed to workers and of individual stock ownership became less significant over time during the period 1948-1968.

The fact that levels of participation, income sharing, and worker ownership are highest in footwear suggest that an examination of the performance of footwear PCs in relation to printing and clothing PCs is likely to offer insights into the merits of the competing theoretical views discussed earlier. However, the disappearance of many footwear PCs during 1948-1968 may complicate the interpretation of results derived from a changing population of firms.

Econometric Specification and a Review of Earlier Related Empirical Work

In principle there are a number of different ways of approaching the problem of evaluating performance empirically.[a] Production functions can be

---

[a]For a list of abbreviations and definitions of variables, see the appendix.

Table 9-1
British PCs, 1948–1968

A. Numbers, Work Forces, and Sales[a]

	All PCs			Printing			Footwear			Clothing		
	N	Workers	Sales	N	Workers	Sales	N	Workers	Sales	N	Workers	Sales
1948	46	6640	5.50	17	1268	0.96	15	1830	2.12	8	2850	1.98
1958	41	4898	6.46	13	1206	1.67	12	1358	1.91	8	1775	2.28
1968	30	3375	6.18	13	1061	2.07	7	686	1.46	6	1267	2.10

B. Participation, Income Sharing, and Ownership[b]

	Printing				Footwear				Clothing			
	(1)	(2)	(3)	(4)	(1)	(2)	(3)	(4)	(1)	(2)	(3)	(4)
1948	.33	.59	15	20	.91	.75	40	56	.36	.53	28	33
1958	.36	.50	20	14	.80	.80	12	46	.40	.37	9	33
1968	.37	.43	8	11	.84	.66	19	38	.29	.40	8	12

Source: Data taken from *Cooperative Statistics*, various editions, and the annual reports that PCs submit to the Registrar of Friendly Societies.

[a]Sales figures are in £ millions at current prices.

[b]All entries are *averages* for PCs in that industry. Entries are as follows:

(1) Proportion of the board of management that are workers;

(2) Proportion of the labor force that are members;

(3) Value of a worker's share in the surplus (£ 1958 constant price).

(4) Value of a worker's individual ownership of capital (£ 1958 constant price).

estimated to include variables representing worker participation, worker ownership, and worker participation in the surplus. Alternatively, efficiency frontiers can be estimated for different sets of firms classified according to important features of organizational structure, such as variation in participation. Total factor productivity of PCs can be estimated and then regressed against variables capturing key aspects of organizational structure. Instead of total factor productivity, diverse ratios—especially accounting ratios including several measures of profitability—might be estimated and regressed against worker participation in control, in ownership, and in surplus.

The approach adopted here is to estimate production functions. This is done in part because of space limitations. More importantly, the approach extends the work reported in an earlier paper (Jones and Backus 1977). Also, an opportunity is afforded for comparison of the results with those of other researchers who have used similar methods, most notably Cable and Fitzroy.

In an earlier paper Jones and Backus (1977) tested hypotheses derived from Vanek's (1971) theory of financing for long-established British PCs in footwear. Data were a combination of time series and cross-sections for footwear PCs existing between 1948 and 1968. In one set of exercises (Jones and Backus 1977, pp. 503-506) production functions were estimated that included a separate and additional variable representing worker participation in decision making (P_j).[3] Several measures of participation were used, such as $P1$, the proportion of the board of management that are workers. Both Cobb-Douglas (CD) and constant elasticity of substitution (CES) production functions were estimated in log-linear form with the dependent variable the log of valued added per worker. Support was found for the proposition that participation improves productivity, although—as with capital and labor coefficients—participation coefficients varied much between classes and with functional form.

Cable and Fitzroy (1980a,b) also proceed by estimating augmented production functions. An index of participation (P_i) is constructed from subjective evaluations provided by firms responding to a questionnaire on the degree of worker participation in various facets of decision making. In addition to P_i the authors include three incentive variables that capture the effects of the distribution of a bonus to labor (TOL), individually owned worker capital (WO), and total worker earnings in the form of incentive pay (I). Separate measures of white- and blue-collar labor input were employed. Cable and Fitzroy begin by testing for the disembodied view (they include these augmenting variables as separate and additional factors). In addition, to test the claim that P_i acts *within* the production function (the embodied view) they divide the sample into "high-participation" and "low-participation'' subsamples and estimate separate equations for each set of firms. CD production functions were estimated in log-log form with the dependent variable being the log of total value added. The study covers 42 firms practicing ''industrial partnership'' in West Germany; none is viewed as an example of a firm controlled entirely by workers. Represented are 18 industries, and cross-sectional observations for 1974-1976 are pooled to produce a single sample of 126 observations with time dummies added for 1975 and 1976.

In the disembodied estimate Cable and Fitzroy find that participation, though measured in various ways, always is significantly and positively correlated with ouput. Apart from the labor-input coefficients, however, all other variables are statistically insignificant or of the wrong sign. The regression results for the embodied view again suggest a positive relationship between participation and output. Productivity effects are particularly striking in the set of high-participation firms, where all three incentive variables exert a positive influence on output; but in low-participation firms all three coefficients are negative. Also, when an index of participation that focuses on strategic, rather than all, issues is used, the results are less clear cut. In fact, results for both high- and low-participation sets of firms are very similar to the results discussed above for the low-participation firms. The authors do not examine whether participation effects are different in large and small firms.

This brief review of previous work suggests that of the hypotheses discussed earlier, the only one for which there is consistent empirical support is the proposition that a positive relationship between participation in decision making and output or productivity exists. This result holds despite a wide variety of methods, including subjective indexes and indicators of aspects of formal structure, having been used to measure participation in decision making. It also holds when different techniques are used to include it in production functions, particularly for embodied and disembodied estimates. However, available evidence on the relationship between incentives and performances is less clear cut, as is the way in which participation and incentives interact. The work of Jones and Backus (1977) on size and participation effects suggests that incentive effects too may be affected by size. The sensitivity of estimates to different ways of measuring key variables indicates the need for more experimentation to resolve these theoretical and empirical controversies.

With these considerations in mind I proceed to estimate production functions for British PCs in the footwear, printing, and clothing industries during the post-World War II period. The data are a combination of cross-sections and time series—the observations represent all existing PCs from 1948 to 1968 at five-year intervals for which values for all variables are available. The CD functional form of the próduction function is used. When the production function is augmented to include variables representing P_i, (TOL), and (WO), the logarithms of these variables are used in estimation, and the dependent variable is total value added (V), the CD form becomes

$$\ln V = a_1 + a_2t + a_3\ln K + a_4\ln L + a_5\ln P_i + a_6\ln (TOL) + \qquad (9.1)$$
$$a_7\ln (WO) + e_t$$

This is the form used by Cable and Fitzroy, and I designate it CD1. When the dependent variable is per-worker value added, incentive variables are included on a per worker-member basis, and a log-linear form is used, the CD form becomes

$$\ln V/L = a_1 + a_2t + a_3\ln K/L + a_4\ln L + a_5P_i + a_6(TOL)/L_m + \qquad (9.2)$$
$$a_7(WO)/L_m + e_t$$

This is the form used by Jones and Backus (1977), and it is designed CD2.[4]

The available data permit estimates of these forms to be made for the following sets of PCs:[5] (a) undivided industry and pooled industry samples; (b) industry and pooled industry samples divided according to size; (c) industry and pooled industry samples divided according to levels of participation; and (d) pooled industry samples divided according to both participation and size. For each of these sets two estimates of the CD1 form, differing in the ways in which participation is measured, are reported. Only one estimate of the CD2 form is reported for all sets, that where participation is measured as the proportion of the board of management that are workers $(P1)$.

Results

Undivided Samples

In table 9-2 estimates are reported for footwear, clothing, printing, and for all industries combined. For each of these undivided samples the two equations reported are of the CD1 form: log-log with total value added as the dependent variable. Expressions 3, 6, 9, and 12 in the table are log-linear with per-worker value added as the dependent variable, and incentive variables are on a per worker-member basis. For all industries, all estimates show that participation in decision making when measured as the proportion of the board of management that are worker members (ln $P1$ or $P1$) is positively associated with total value added or output per worker. But the relationship is not always significant, and when significant it is only once at a 5 percent level. Furthermore, when participation is measured by the proportion of the labor force that are members (ln $P2$ or $P2$) a negative, though never significant, relationship with total value added or output per worker exists.

In the CD1 form, the incentive variable (ln TOL) is statistically insignificant for footwear PCs. However, for printing, clothing, and all industries combined, (ln TOL) is positively associated with total value added and at a 5 percent level of significance. When the CD2 form is estimated, and the incentive variable $(TOL)/Lm$ included in a per worker-member (rather than a total logarithm) way, for all industries there is strong evidence that surplus sharing aids productivity. For the other incentive variable, worker ownership, at this level of aggregation the evidence points firmly in the other direction. Usually worker ownership is negatively, though insignificantly, correlated with productivity, but in two cases (expressions 6 and 10) the negative relation is significant.

Industry Sample Divided according to Size

Earlier I discussed how and why different authorities expect the effect of P, (TOL), and (WO) to vary according to firm size. In order to test these differing views, here separate regressions for "large" and "small" PCs in different industries are estimated.[6] The results are reported in tables 9-3 and 9-4. For comparative purposes the expressions that are estimated for all divided samples are identical to those estimated for undivided samples.

For all large samples, worker representation on the board tends to be positively associated with productivity. This is always true for CD2 estimates, significantly for clothing and printing. For CD1 estimates the evidence is mixed, though for large footwear PCs there is a significant and positive relationship between $P1$ and V. With $P2$, the evidence is inconclusive. While with large clothing PCs there is a significant and positive relationship, for footwear and all firms taken together the evidence shows that raising the fraction of the membership that are members detracts from productivity.

A much clearer picture emerges concerning the effects of surplus sharing in large British PCs. For all PCs in printing, and clothing, (ln TOL) is positively and significantly related to output. Except for clothing, the result holds irrespective of functional form. For footwear, however, no such relationship exists and, indeed, there is a suggestion that sharing of the surplus with workers may be dysfunctional. The estimates show no obvious effects of individual worker ownership on productivity for any sample or for any particular form of estimation.

For small PCs in footwear there is evidence that worker representation on the board promotes higher productivity. This effect is consistent with the result for large footwear PCs. Regarding clothing PCs, there is some

Table 9-2
Production Functions for Undivided Samples

Form	$\ln K$ $(\ln K/L)$	$\ln L$	$\ln P_1 (P_1)$	$\ln P_2 (P_2)$	$\ln TOL (TOL/Lm)$	$\ln WO (WO/Lm)$	Constant	R^2 Adj.
A. Footwear ($n = 55$)								
(1) CD1	0.337 (2.832)*	0.623 (5.974)*	0.098 (0.946)†		0.005 (0.343)ns	-0.017 (-0.311)ns	-0.291 (-0.654)ns	.79
(2) CD1	0.329 (2.722)*	0.617 (5.873)*			0.003 (0.224)ns	0.011 (0.167)ns	-0.113 (-0.262)ns	.79
(3) CD2	0.371 (4.167)*	-0.032 (-0.447)ns	0.004 (1.199)‡	-0.004 (-0.040)ns	0.154 (0.927)‡	-0.068 (-0.757)ns	3.030 (7.941)*	.34
B. Printing ($n = 55$)								
(4) CD1	0.144 (1.717)*	0.862 (9.292)*	0.004 (0.113)‡		0.034 (2.985)*	-0.012 (-0.442)ns	-0.293 (-1.377)†	.97
(5) CD1	0.141 (1.766)*	0.858 (9.079)*			0.035 (2.965)*	-0.004 (-0.149)ns	-0.262 (-1.253)‡	.97
(6) CD2	0.223 (2.720)*	0.050 (1.392)†	0.001 (1.973)*	-0.009 (-0.227)ns	0.007 (1.415)†	-0.033 (-1.815)*	2.831 (14.634)*	.48
C. Clothing ($n = 36$)								
(7) CD1	0.157 (.830)ns	0.677 (4.267)*	0.029 (0.476)ns		0.097 (3.860)*	-0.012 (-0.193)ns	.142 (.339)ns	.85
(8) CD1	0.043 (0.230)ns	0.812 (4.049)*			0.108 (3.972)*	0.031 (0.749)ns	0.102 (0.243)ns	.89
(9) CD2	-0.027 (-0.163)ns	-0.019 (-0.205)ns	0.001 (0.723)ns	-0.109 (-0.722)ns	0.201 (2.077)*	0.005 (0.150)ns	2.66 (5.187)*	.03
D. All Industries ($n = 146$)								
(10) CD1	0.161 (2.169)*	0.803 (11.487)*	0.027 (0.851)‡		0.035 (3.790)*	-0.020 (-1.118)‡	-0.173 (-0.976)‡	.90
(11) CD1	0.117 (1.638)†	0.829 (12.204)*			0.038 (3.831)*	0.001 (0.042)ns	-0.117 (-0.025)ns	.90
(12) CD2	0.222 (3.395)*	-0.008 (-0.221)ns	0.001 (1.199)‡	-0.022 (-0.557)ns	0.013 (1.812)†	-0.007 (-0.430)ns	2.979 (15.206)*	.18

Source: Data derived from information supplied to the author by the Research Department of the Cooperative Union, Manchester.

Notes: Numbers in parentheses are t statistics for the estimated coefficients.
*coefficient is significantly nonzero at the .05 level (one-tail test).
†coefficient is significantly nonzero at the .10 level (one-tail test).
‡coefficient is significantly nonzero at the .20 level (one-tail test).
ns coefficient is not significant at the 0.20 level (one-tail test).

Table 9-3
Production Functions for Large PCs

Form	$\ln K$ (lnK/L)	$\ln L$	$\ln P_1$ (P_1)	$\ln P_2$ (P_2)	$\ln$ TOL (TOL/Lm)	$\ln$ WO (WO/Lm)	Constant	R^2 Adj.
A. Footwear (n = 24)								
(1) CD1	0.583 (3.414)*	0.488 (2.954)*	0.356 (1.444)†		−0.005 (−0.208)ns	−0.066 (−0.589)ns	−1.099 (−1.308)†	.80
(2) CD1	0.448 (2.876)*	0.673 (5.274)*		−0.335 (−2.163)*	0.018 (0.759)ns	0.167 (1.545)†	−0.913 (−1.155)‡	.83
(3) CD2	0.565 (5.568)*	0.180 (1.043)‡	0.001 (0.827)ns		−0.026 (−0.091)ns	0.220 (0.683)ns	1.802 (1.989)*	.67
B. Printing (n = 23)								
(4) CD1	0.289 (1.312)‡	0.625 (1.366)†	−0.003 (−0.021)ns		0.061 (2.574)*	−0.033 (−0.677)ns	0.235 (0.134)ns	.96
(5) CD1	0.267 (1.350)*	0.518 (1.401)†		−0.119 (−0.470)ns	0.062 (3.042)*	−0.017 (0.151)ns	0.995 (0.540)ns	.96
(6) CD2	0.184 (0.909)‡	0.082 (0.576)ns	0.001 (0.994)‡		0.009 (1.199)‡	0.164 (0.405)ns	2.578 (2.999)*	.16
C. Clothing (n = 18)								
(7) CD1	−0.024 (−0.657)ns	1.125 (2.605)*	0.129 (0.544)ns		0.086 (1.935)*	0.104 (0.560)ns	−1.145 (−0.999)‡	.81
(8) CD1	−0.185 (−0.474)ns	0.960 (2.189)*		0.418 (1.179)‡	0.043 (0.769)ns	0.122 (3.700)ns	−1.221 (−1.434)†	.83
(9) CD2	−0.24 (−0.622)ns	−0.003 (−0.002)ns	0.001 (1.015)‡		−1.208 (−0.587)ns	−1.585 (−2.070)*	2.423 (2.780)*	.33
D. All Industries (n = 65)								
(10) CD1	0.055 (0.462)ns	0.794 (6.800)*	−0.111 (−1.300)‡		0.062 (4.024)*	0.036 (3.676)ns	0.209 (0.445)ns	.84
(11) CD1	0.068 (0.562)ns	0.799 (6.796)*		−0.111 (−1.012)‡	0.066 (3.839)	0.037 (0.551)ns	0.169 (0.347)ns	.84
(12) CD2	0.307 (2.570)*	−0.019 (−0.226)ns	0.000 (0.232)ns		0.008 (0.931)‡	−0.270 (−0.951)‡	3.047 (6.330)*	.21

Source: Data derived from information supplied to the author by the Research Department of the Cooperative Union, Manchester.

Notes: Large PCs in Footwear and Clothing are those where there are more than 100 workers; in large printing PCs L > 50.

Numbers in parentheses are t statistics for the estimated coefficients.

*coefficient is significantly nonzero at the .05 level (one-tail test).

†coefficient is significantly nonzero at the .10 level (one-tail test).

‡coefficient is significantly nonzero at the .20 level (one-tail test).

nscoefficient is not significant at the 0.20 level (one-tail test).

Table 9-4
Production Functions for Small PCs

Form	ln K (lnK/L)	ln L	ln P_1 (P_1)	ln P_2 (P_2)	ln TOL (TOL/Lm)	ln WO (WO/Lm)	Constant	R² Adj.
A. Footwear (n = 31)								
(1) CD1	-0.079	1.560	0.261		0.028	-0.061	-3.346	.68
	(-0.426)ns	(6.528)*	(1.804)*		(1.594)†	(-0.951)‡	(-3.329)*	
(2) CD1	0.032	1.359		0.001	0.001	0.013	-2.514	.64
	(0.174)ns	(5.485)*		(0.006)ns	(0.733)ns	(0.169)ns	(-2.490)*	
(3) CD2	0.052	0.597	0.001		0.404	-0.027	-0.339	.18
	(0.344)ns	(3.030)*	(1.141)‡		(2.070)*	(-0.328)ns	(-0.329)ns	
B. Printing (n = 32)								
(4) CD1	0.146	0.973	-0.021		0.017	0.016	-0.786	.76
	(1.093)‡	(5.356)*	(-0.399)ns		(0.924)‡	(0.327)ns	(-1.070)‡	
(5) CD1	0.166	0.973		-0.022	0.018	0.014	-0.871	.71
	(1.184)‡	(5.358)*		(-0.414)ns	(0.975)‡	(0.325)ns	(-1.143)‡	
(6) CD2	0.201	0.025	0.001		0.419	-0.066	2.924	.57
	(1.993)*	(0.190)ns	(0.929)‡		(1.973)*	(-2.514)*	(4.796)*	
C. Clothing (n = 18)								
(7) CD1	0.057	0.616	-0.055		0.079	0.054	1.186	.79
	(0.263)ns	(2.190)	(-0.777)ns		(2.703)*	(0.788)ns	(1.219)‡	
(8) CD1	0.073	0.807		-0.221	0.077	0.038	0.443	.81
	(0.414)	(2.419)*		(-1.223)‡	(2.769)*	(0.955)‡	(0.430)ns	
(9) CD2	0.147	-0.165	-0.000		0.063	0.009	0.265	.27
	(0.911)‡	(-0.284)ns	(-0.116)ns		(0.668)ns	(0.126)ns	(0.541)ns	
D. All Industries (n = 81)								
(10) CD1	0.124	0.996	0.015		0.018	-0.008	-0.910	.82
	(1.277)‡	(7.054)*	(0.391)ns		(1.536)†	(-0.272)ns	(-1.590)†	
(11) CD1	0.088	1.041		-0.032	0.021	0.014	-0.959	.82
	(0.940)‡	(7.077)*		(-0.715)ns	(1.707)*	(0.616)ns	(-1.664)*	
(12) CD2	0.117	0.129	0.000		0.120	0.007	2.278	.24
	(1.412)†	(0.997)†	(0.488)ns		(2.202)*	(0.351)ns	(3.423)*	

Source: Data derived from information supplied to the author by the Research Department of the Cooperative Union, Manchester.

Notes: Small PCs in Footwear and Clothing are those where there are less than 100 workers; in small printing PCs L <50.

Numbers in parentheses are t statistics for the estimated coefficients.

* coefficient is significantly nonzero at the .05 level (one-tail test).
† coefficient is significantly nonzero at the .10 level (one-tail test).
‡ coefficient is significantly nonzero at the .20 level (one-tail test).
ns coefficient is not significant at the 0.20 level (one-tail test).

evidence of a statistically significant relationship between ln $P1$ (or $P1$) and productivity for large PCs, but for small clothing PCs there is some evidence of a negative and significant relationship between these variables. For printing PCs the evidence does not point firmly one way or the other, though the only significant estimates show a positive relationship between $P1$ and productivity. Interestingly, however, for small clothing PCs there is a negative and significant relationship—the reverse of the situation in large clothing PCs. All other cases are statistically insignificant.

As with large PCs, in small PCs in clothing, printing, and all firms together, surplus sharing is always positively related to productivity. This is the case for both CD1 and CD2 forms and the relationship is nearly always statistically significant, often at the 5 percent level. Most strikingly, the phenomenon applies to footwear too, where for larger PCs there is some slight evidence that surplus sharing harms productivity.

As with large PCs, worker ownership does not seem to matter much for any group of firms or for any method of estimation.

Sample Divided according to
Levels of Participation

To test the claim that incentive variables act within the production function (the embodied view), in this section industry samples are divided, where possible, into "high" and "low" participation subsamples. I experimented with different methods to divide the sample. The procedure followed was to designate "high" participation PCs as those in which $P1 \geq 0.5$ and $P2 \geq 0.5$. Adoping this procedure meant that there were sufficient observations for estimation for only high-participation footwear, and for only low-participation clothing and printing PCs. That is, no industry was able to be split into both high- and low-participation subsamples. Such a division could be made only when all industries were merged. Accordingly, separate equations were estimated only for these pooled industry subsamples using calculations similar to those reported earlier. Results are reported in table 9-5.

In both cases it is clear that a disembodied effect of participation does remain—usually the constant term is statistically different from zero. Moreover, the direction of the effect is different for the two sub-samples—negative for high-participation PCs but positive for low-participation PCs. Interestingly, when $LP3$, the proportion of the membership that is workers, is included in the estimates, the effect varies according to participatory class—positive for high and negative for low—participation PCs.

Surplus sharing exerts a positive and statistically significant influence in both high- and low-participation PCs. Marked differences, however, are evident concerning the way in which worker ownership affects output

Table 9-5
Production Functions for High and Low Participation PCs

Form	$\ln K$ ($\ln K/L$)	$\ln L$	$\ln P_3$	$\ln TOL$ (TOL/Lm)	$\ln WO$ (WO/Lm)	Constant	R^2 Adj.
A. All High ($n = 66$)							
(1) CD1	0.033 (0.251)ns	0.889 (6.753)*		0.019 (1.564)†	0.066 (1.431)†	− 0.366 (− 1.114)‡	.90
(2) CD1	0.031 (0.234)ns	0.890 (6.703)*	0.027 (0.272)ns	0.018 (1.420)†	0.061 (1.206)‡	− 0.399 (− 1.120)‡	.90
(3) CD2	0.016 (1.346)‡	0.028 (3.393)ns		0.248 (1.662)†	0.003. (0.116)ns	2.695 (8.550)*	.16
B. All Low ($n = 80$)							
(4) CD1	0.173 (2.145)*	0.741 (8.693)*		0.059 (4.470)*	− 0.018 (− 1.272)‡	0.171 (0.736)ns	.92
(5) CD1	0.124 (1.379)‡	0.769 (8.725)*	− 0.057 (− 1.194)‡	0.067 (4.543)*	0.010 (0.370)ns	0.269 (1.095)‡	.92
(6) CD2	0.219 (2.528)*	− 0.004 (− 0.086)ns		0.010 (1.259)‡	− 0.002 (− 0.067)ns	3.053 (11.7337)*	.22

Source: Data derived from information supplied to the author by the Research Department of the Cooperative Union, Manchester.

Notes: Numbers in parentheses are t statistics for the estimated coefficients.
    *coefficient is significantly nonzero at the .05 level (one-tail test).
    †coefficient is significantly nonzero at the .10 level (one-tail test).
    ‡coefficient is significantly nonzero at the .20 level (one-tail test).
    nscoefficient is not significant at the 0.20 level (one-tail test).

between the two groups. Whereas in high-participation firms worker ownership causes higher output levels, with low-participation PCs the relationship usually runs in the other direction, sometimes significantly so.

Samples Divided by Size and Participation

The estimates reported in table 9-3 indicate that the estimates reported in
table 9-2 have been obscured to the extent that different parameters pertain
to PCs of different sizes (different levels of participation). In this subsection
to test the claim that incentive variables act within the production function
and that size matters too, the all-industry samples are divided by both size
and level of participation. Separate calculations were estimated for the four
subsamples using expressions similar to those reported earlier. Results are
reported in table 9-6.

As with the estimates for samples divided only by levels of participation,
reported regressions suggest that a disembodied effect of participation does
remain—the constant term usually is statistically significantly nonzero.
Again, the effect varies with level of participation, being negative for high-
and positive for low-participation PCs. As in table 9-5, when ln $P3$ is
included in the estimates, the direction of the effect exerted changes according
to participatory class, though only one estimate is statistically significant.

Worker participation in the surplus always enhances output and, with
the exception of high-participation small PCs, results are statistically
significant. When the effects of worker ownership are examined, it seems
that cross-classifying PCs by participation and size does not produce results
materially different from partitioning based upon level of participation
alone. As before, whereas in high-participation firms—whether large or
small—worker ownership causes higher levels of output, in low-
participation PCs worker ownership detracts from productivity.

Conclusions

By estimating production functions, the effects on productivity of worker
participation in decision making, ownership, and the surplus are evaluated
for long-established British PCs in footwear, clothing, and printing. To perform different tests the production functions are augmented in various
ways, and estimates were made for subsamples of PCs according to size
and/or level of participation. While some relationships are consistent for all
industries and subsamples, more often important differences between
industries and within industries, including the all-industry sample, for different subsamples of PCs are evident.

In the footwear industry where worker representation on the board

Table 9-6
Production Functions for All Producer Cooperatives Divided according to Both Participation and Size

Form	$\ln K$ ($\ln K/L$)	$\ln L$	$\ln P_3$	$\ln$ TOL (TOL/Lm)	$\ln$ WO (WO/Lm)	Constant	R^2 Adj.
A. Large and High Participation (n = 28)							
(1) CD1	0.071 (0.416)ns	0.925 (5.861)*		0.028 (1.507)†	0.103 (1.142)‡	−1.038 (−2.307)*	.89
(2) CD1	0.064 (0.367)ns	0.937 (5.353)*	0.037 (0.179)ns	0.025 (1.115)‡	0.091 (0.792)ns	−1.110 (−1.811)*	.88
(3) CD2	0.243 (1.600)†	0.117 (1.331)†		0.033 (0.103)ns	0.047 (0.150)ns	2.136 (4.059)*	.39
B. Large and Low Participation (n = 27)							
(4) CD1	0.072 (0.380)ns	0.737 (4.119)*		0.105 (3.376)*	−0.046 (−1.380)†	0.432 (0.525)ns	.81
(5) CD1	0.013 (0.049)ns	0.752 (3.980)*	−0.080 (−0.321)ns	0.112 (2.860)*	−0.003 (−0.018)ns	0.643 (0.605)*	.80
(6) CD2	0.322 (1.409)†	−0.226 (−1.336)†		0.008 (0.586)ns	−0.950 (−1.592)†	4.262 (4.512)*	.25
C. Small and High Participation (n = 38)							
(7) CD1	0.038 (0.178)ns	1.014 (4.710)*		0.009 (0.489)ns	0.054 (0.953)‡	−0.878 (−1.182)‡	.78
(8) CD1	0.027 (.125)ns	0.979 (4.141)*	0.066 (0.426)ns	0.007 (0.366)ns	0.044 (0.689)ns	−0.763 (−0.952)‡	.77
D. Small and Low Participation (n = 53)							
(9) CD1	0.145 (1.689)*	0.722 (5.167)*		0.053 (8.847)*	−0.011 (−0.801)ns	0.563 (1.094)‡	.85
(10) CD1	0.091 (0.968)‡	0.807 (5.307)*	−0.061 (−1.354)†	0.059 (4.112)*	0.012 (0.554)ns	0.420 (0.806)ns	.85

Source: Data derived from information supplied to the author by the Research Department of the Cooperative Union, Manchester.

Notes: Numbers in parentheses are t statistics for the estimated coefficients.
*coefficient is significantly nonzero at the .05 level (one-tail test).
†coefficient is significantly nonzero at the .10 level (one-tail test).
‡coefficient is significantly nonzero at the .20 level (one-tail test).
nscoefficient is not significant at the 0.20 level (one-tail test).

(P1) is high, disembodied estimates for both large and small subsamples support the proposition that participation (P1) enhances productivity. A similar relationship, though seldom statistically significant, exists for the undivided footwear sample. With printing PCs, no consistent and statistically significant relationship exists between P1 and productivity, and the direction of the relationship is sensitive to partitioning of the industry by size. Similar sign switching is particularly apparent for clothing PCs; whereas there is a positive relationship between P1 and productivity for large clothing PCs, for small clothing PCs participation tends to lower output. The inclusion of P2 (the proportion of the labor force that are workers) as a different proxy for participation in disembodied estimates suggests that in printing and footwear, for both undivided and samples divided by size, there is no material effect. With clothing PCs, size does matter; whereas in large PCs measuring the proportion of worker members enhances productivity, in smaller PCs the effect is the opposite.

Disembodied estimates also show the incentive variable working differently among industries, particularly when PCs are classified by size. In footwear, income-sharing aids productivity in small PCs, but for large PCs partial sharing of the surplus is dysfunctional. Alternatively, in printing and clothing, productivity is always improved by sharing the surplus with workers, particularly in large firms. Worker ownership is seldom found to affect productivity one way or the other, in all industries and in all size classes.

To test the embodied view of participation, similar production functions are estimated for two divisions of the all-industry sample, where the basis for partitioning is a critical level of participation. The samples are further divided on the basis of size and additional estimates made. For high- and low-participation samples, however, a disembodied effect of participation remains. Moreover, this effect is positive for low-participation PCs and negative for high-participation PCs.

Surplus sharing evinces higher productivity in both high- and low-participation PCs, irrespective of size. More importantly, classifying by level of participation produces evidence that a positive worker-ownership effect exists. A capital stake by workers seems to enhance productivity when accompanied by high levels of formal participation (P1) and a high fraction of the labor force electing to be members (P2). This is the case even in large PCs. But when participation is low, worker ownership is seen to reduce productivity, even in small PCs.

There is some evidence that the way in which participation is measured influences the estimated effects of participation on productivity. When participation (P1) is measured as a simple ratio, and estimated in the CD2 form, then nearly always participation tends to envince higher levels of productivity. No such consistent effect was noted when the logarithm of P1 was used and CD1 estimates were made. However, for the two incentive variables worker ownership and surplus-sharing, it matters little whether they are measured on a total logarithmic basis or on a per worker-member basis.

Overall, these results offer partial support for particular conclusions of other recent empirical studies, notably those of Cable and Fitzroy (1980a, b). The embodied estimates show that for the incentive effects of worker ownership to operate, a high level of participation is needed. However, in the estimates for British PCs (and unlike those of German participatory firms), a disembodied effect of participation remains. Furthermore, some disembodied estimates for British PCs (and unlike those reported by Cable and Fitzroy), show statistically significant participation and incentive effects. Disembodied effects of participation are particularly apparent in PCs characterized by high levels of participation (footwear) and incentive effects in particular size classes (small).[7] Consequently, at this stage it seems unreasonable to conclude that neither the embodied nor the disembodied approach is the most fruitful. Perhaps different approaches will be found to work best in participatory situations with substantially different levels of participation? The evidence suggests that simple formal indicators of participation (such as $P1$) have a useful role to play in empirical analysis. That is, until the construction of participation indexes assumes a more scientific nature, their subjectivity will continue to remain a troublesome matter and will suggest a role for more straightforward formal indicators. Finally, the sensitivity of some parameters to both functional form and to particular measures indicates a need for further experimentation in these areas.

In general, the results reported here support those theorists, such as Vanek, who expect beneficial effects to flow from worker participation in decision making and in surplus. Equally, they refute the most pessimistic predictions of others, such as Alchian and Demsetz, and Jensen and Meckling. There is some evidence that incentive effects of profit sharing with workers are lessened in large firms, even when there is substantial formal worker participation in decision making. The evidence also supports the assertion that capital stakes in enterprises by workers will promote productivity.

The more general implication of these findings is that viable structures for PCs will include features that provide for substantial participation by workers in surplus and in decision making at all levels in the organization. An additional requirement may be an initial capital stake. As such, the findings support those of other studies, including Jones (1980) and the chapter by Thomas in this book.

Given these results, future research in this area must be extended in various ways. The production-function approach can be usefully extended to different subsamples such as individual industries classified by both level of participation and size. For periods before and after 1948–1968 data may be available to allow not only additional estimates for the three industries studied here, but also for other industries, such as building. Also, individual-firm time-series estimates might usefully be undertaken. Finally, techniques other than production functions need to be used.[8] There is still an urgent need for extension and comparison of differing empirical approaches to evaluating theories of the performance of participatory firms.

Notes

1. See Marshall (in Pigou 1925, p. 243), and Marshall (1919, p. 294). Also the authority of management might be undermined (see Marshall 1964, p. 255).

2. See for example the views of Robertson, Mill, and Pigou as discussed in Jones (1976, pp. 7-14).

3. Worker collective ownership also was included to test the Vanek hypothesis of the deleterious effects of collective funding and nonpayment of capital rents to capital owners. Since these issues are not the focus of this paper, those results are not reviewed here.

4. Various other forms of the CD function can be estimated. Some of these would involve no difference in substance from those reported here. For example the CD function could be estimated by

$$\ln V/L = a_1 + a_2 t + a_3 \ln K/L + a_4 \ln L + a_5 \ln P_i + \qquad (9.3)$$
$$a_6 \ln (TOL)/L + a_7 \ln (WO)/L$$

The resulting estimate of the coefficients would be identical to those found with equation 9.1 above but the multiple correlation coefficient would be much higher. However, if equation 9.1 were amended by P_i replacing $\ln P$ in equation 9.2 and by $\ln(TOL)/Lm$ replacing $(TOL/Lm$, then meaningful differences would emerge.

5. When estimates are made to test the embodied view of the effects of participation, critical values of $P1$ and $P2$ are used to separate groups of PCs. Then those measures of participation are not included in the estimates, but sometimes another measure of participation, $P3$, is included.

6. Various methods were experimented with to divide the samples. For clothing and footwear, dividing according to whether or not the PC provides employment for more than 100 is the adopted procedure. For printing pragmatism required that a different procedure be followed, namely, whether or not $L \geq 50$.

7. The effects of particular industries may have been obscured in the Cable and Fitzroy analysis because of the multiple-industry nature of the data. Also in their estimation procedure no attempt was made to test for the effects of size.

8. Earlier (Jones 1974) I used various approaches including efficiency frontiers and ratio analysis. In general the evidence presented there is consistent with the results flowing from the augmented production approach adopted here. For example, the estimation of separate efficiency frontiers for high- and low-productivity PCs in the textile industry showed that high-participatory PCs undertook technical change at a faster rate than did PCs with low levels of participation.

Appendix 9A: Variables and Data Sources

A. Definitions of Variables

$V =$ Value added = Sales/P_r − Purchases of intermediary inputs/P_w + change in stocks/P_w where P_r is the retail price index and P_w is the wholesale price index for the appropriate industry

$L =$ Worker — equivalent hours = $[N_m H_m + N_w H_w (F_w / F_m) + N_y H_y (E_y / E_m)]$ where N_m, N_w, N_y are the number of men, women, and youths employed by a given PC; $H_m (H_w, H_y)$ is the industry average number of hours worked by men (women, youths); $E_m E_w, E_y$ is the industry average earnings rate for men (women, youths).

$K_1 =$ Net assets = long-term finance = total assets (liabilities) − (bank overdrafts + share interest and balance disposable + sundry liabilities).

$K_2 = K_1/C$, where C is a capital-goods price index.

Participation (P_1)

$P_1 =$ Proportion of the board of management that are worker-members
$P_2 =$ Proportion of the labor force that are members
$P_3 =$ Proportion of the total membership that are worker-members

Incentives

$(TOL) =$ Total surplus distributed to workers/P_r
$(WO) =$ Total share capital owned by workers/P_r
$(TOL)/Lm =$ Surplus distributed on average to each worker-member
$(WO)/Lm =$ Share capital owned on average by each worker-member

Time

$t = 1$ for 1948, 2 for 1953, 3 for 1958, 4 for 1963, 5 for 1968

Data Sources

Data on PCs are usually taken from two sources:

1. Measures of value added, capital, labor and incentives are derived from data on individual PCs held by the Research Department of the Cooperative Union, Manchester. (These data are abstracted from annual returns that societies make to the Cooperative Union.)

2. Measures of participation are derived directly, either from annual returns made by individual PCs to the Cooperative Union, or from a similar report that, because of registration under the Industrial and Provident Societies Acts, societies are required to make on an annual basis to the Registrar of Friendly Societies.

Indexes

Capital Goods: for 1948-1963, table E of London and Cambridge Economic Service (1971); for 1968, 1969 Blue Book.
Wholesale Prices: table E of London and Cambridge Economic Service (1971).
Retail Prices: table 90, Department of Employment and Productivity (1971).

Hours and Earnings

Hours: tables 44, 45, Department of Employment and Productivity (1971).
Earnings: tables 41, 42, Department of Employment and Productivity (1971).

10 Codetermination and Productivity: Empirical Evidence from the Federal Republic of Germany

Jan Svejnar

The system of employee participation in management, as it was established in the Federal Republic of Germany by the Codetermination Laws of 1951 and 1976 as well as by the Works Constitution Acts of 1952 and 1972, is widely considered to be the most advanced, economy-wide form of industrial democracy outside of Yugoslavia. The establishment of German codetermination coincided temporally with a period of rapid economic growth, relatively peaceful industrial and labor relations, and political stability. As a result, the idea that the performance of the German economy may have been stimulated by the codetermination system has been the subject of never-ending polemics both within and outside of Germany. Moreover, many countries have examined the German system for possible adoption in their own environments.[1] Accordingly, numerous studies, including the famous Biedenkopf Committee Report (1970) and the Bullock (1977) Committee Report, have inter alia attempted to ascertain the economic impact of the codetermination system. Unfortunately, no study has yet provided a satisfactory estimate of the impact of codetermination on productivity. Very few of the existing studies are analytical in nature, and those that do employ an analytical approach do not deal with the nationwide system of codetermination.

In this chapter, I use the available data to estimate the productivity effects of the participatory systems established by the 1951, 1952, and 1972 laws in Germany. In the following two sections I discuss the participatory institutions established by these laws and review the methodologies and findings of the existing studies. The fourth section contains the analytical model and the econometric estimates of the present study. The summary and conclusions are in the final section.

I would like to thank Peter Lyman for excellent computational assistance.

Institutional Framework

The end of World War II witnessed the spontaneous emergence of works councils in many German plants.[2] The allied occupation authorities legalized the existence of the works councils through Control Council Law no. 22 of April 1946, but at the same time the authorities granted the councils only limited and advisory powers. As a result, the councils did not officially obtain real participatory functions until the passage of the Works Constitution Act in October 1952.

In a parallel development, the allied authorities in 1947 permitted the tentative establishment of the so-called codetermination (Mitbestimmung) system in several iron and steel companies. This system of joint labor-management-shareholder decision making was further elaborated and legally extended to all firms in the iron-steel and coal-mining industries by the Codetermination Law of May 1951. This law gave employee representatives considerable participatory roles in the higher echelons of the company hierarchy. Unlike the single-board Anglo-American system of company organization, the German system is based on two boards: the Board of Directors (Aufsichtsrat) and the Management Board (Vorstand). The 1951 law provided for equal representation of shareholders and workers on the Boards of Directors. The two equally represented parties jointly co-opt a neutral member who is supposed to represent the public interest on the board and to cast the decisive vote in the case of an impasse. The Board of Directors usually meets four or five times a year, appoints the Management Board, approves all major policy decisions such as takeovers, mergers, and manpower planning, and it also scrutinizes the company accounts. Hence, the 1951 law gave workers and shareholders in iron-steel and coal mining equal decision-making powers with respect to medium- and long-term policy decisions. In addition, the law established the position of a "labor director" (Arbeitsdirektor) on the Management Boards of the iron-steel and coal-mining companies. The labor director has equal rights and responsibilities with the other directors (technical and commercial) on the Management Board, but generally he is in charge of industrial relations and labor affairs of the company. The 1951 law ensures that the labor director can be appointed and dismissed only with the approval of the worker representatives to the Board of Directors. As a result, the labor director is uniformly a prolabor person. Since the Management Board performs all the daily managerial tasks and the labor director communicates closely with the worker representatives to both the Board of Directors and the Works Council, any participation-induced productivity effects can easily be made operational by the Management Board. It is often hypothesized that increased worker participation in management will indeed lead to greater economic efficiency. If this hypothesis is correct, the 1951 law should have an observable productivity effect.

The Works Constitution Act of 1952 gave worker representatives one-third of the seats on the Boards of Directors in firms with 500 employees or more. This minority worker representation was applied to all the remaining industries with the exception of air transport and shipping. Not only did the workers covered by the 1952 act gain only a minority representation on the Boards of Directors, they did not obtain any direct or indirect representation at the level of the Management Board. Hence, with respect to board representation, the 1952 law is generally regarded as having generated less participation than its 1951 counterpart.

An important provision of the 1952 Works Constitution Act relates to the establishment and jurisdiction of the works councils. The act stipulates that a works council is to be elected in every plant employing at least five people. The council is to represent all employees, not merely the unionized ones, and it is to be elected by a secret ballot every two years. The act gives the works council the rights to (1) handle grievances, administer the social-welfare agencies of the plant, and supervise the enforcement of the applicable labor laws, (2) negotiate with the management about wages and working conditions (as a supplement to the industry-wide collective agreement between the trade union and the employers' association), hiring and firing, discrimination, work rules (including on-the-job training), and changes in the plant (such as technical changes, mergers, transfers, introduction of new work methods), and (3) be informed on other relevant matters. It has often been asserted that the numerous works council provisions of the 1952 act could lead to greater productivity of the plants due to increased worker motivation, better internal resolution of conflicts, greater firm-specific on-the-job training, and more efficient organization of the workplace. At the same time, proponents of the traditional view that trade unions exert a negative effect on productivity can a priori expect the works-council provisions to allow for similarly negative effects.[3] The provisions for the enforcement of labor laws and negotiations about the working conditions, work rules, and plant changes could lead to featherbedding or make-work rules, which could directly decrease productivity and slow down the rate of technological innovation. Since both views are compatible with the legal provisions of the 1952 act, the actual effect of participation on productivity is a matter of empirical inquiry.

Before proceeding to the empirical investigation it is worth noting that the 1972 Works Constitution Act further extended some of the works council rights granted by the 1952 Act. The works council now has the right of full codetermination (equal say with the management) on matters such as job evaluation, employment policies, training, layoffs and working hours,[4] accident prevention, and wage structure.

Finally, the German participatory system was significantly influenced by the Codetermination Law of 1976, which went into effect in 1978. In several years it will be of interest to examine the economic effects of this law as well.

Existing Studies

Studies on the economic effects of codetermination can be divided into the earlier ones, which are primarily institutional in nature, and the more recent ones, which tend to be more analytical. The best study in the first category was performed by Blumenthal (1956), who tried to examine the impact of codetermination on labor cost and productivity in the steel industry. Blumenthal's conclusions are based on interviews and the examination of earnings, price, production, and labor productivity indexes. He reports (1956, p. 84) that "taking quantitative and qualitative findings together, it appears that under codetermination strong upward pressure on wages and salaries existed, at least in the initial period, and that there is fairly sound presumptive evidence that a cause and effect relationship may have been operative here." In two recent econometric studies I have examined this proposition in a more systematic manner (Svejnar 1977, 1981) and found that the estimated long-term effect of codetermination on earnings has been about 5 to 7 percent in iron and steel. With respect to productivity Blumenthal (1956, p. 79) found that "on the basis of the available, though somewhat less than satisfactory data, postwar improvements in labor productivity were neither much greater nor much smaller in iron and steel than in most of the other industries." In examining the index of industrial production Blumenthal (1956, p. 82) noticed that "after 1949 the iron and steel industry actually increased its output less than did the other industries." It was only in the area of growth of producer prices that Blumenthal found iron and steel leading the other industries. While Blumenthal's findings have certainly been provocative, to the best of my knowledge there has been no systematic analysis performed in this area to date.

An analytical productivity study based on German data has been recently performed in a related area by Cable and Fitzroy (1980a,b). Using a sample of 42 firms belonging to the industrial partnership category, the authors analyzed the effects of participation, P, incentive pay I, profit sharing π_e, and workers' capital M on total productivity Y. On the basis of questionnaire responses the authors constructed an index measure of participation P. Since there is no universally acceptable weighting scheme that would enable one to classify various participatory forms into a single index, the authors experimented with numerous weighting schemes. Like Espinosa and Zimbalist (1978), they fortunately found that the analytical results were "generally insensitive to the choice of weights over a fairly wide range" (Cable and Fitzroy 1980a, p. 168 and 1980b, p. 107). Entering P, I, π_e, and

M into a Cobb-Douglas production function, Cable and Fitzroy found the disembodied productivity effect of participation to be strongly positive and statistically significant. The corresponding sample-wide effects of π_e and M were not significantly different from zero while the effect of I was negative.[5]

The Cable and Fitzroy (1980a,b) study is important because it suggests that productivity is positively related to the degree of participation, at least in a specific class of firms. At the same time, the Blumenthal (1956) study, while analytically less sophisticated, raised important questions about the productivity effects of the industry-wide and nationwide codetermination systems introduced in the Federal Republic since World War II. The next section addresses these questions more formally.

The Econometric Model and Empirical Results

The empirical strategy of this chapter is guided by the availability of data. Since no individual data exist on a large number of firms operating under the various participatory schemes, the estimates of this paper are based on industry-level data. In order to capture the introduction and existence of different participatory systems, the cross-sectional (cross-industry) data are pooled with time series for the 1950-1976 period. Assuming that the possible effect of participation on productivity takes the form of a disembodied change, it is possible to postulate the following Cobb-Douglas (CD) production function:

$$Q_{ti} = \alpha_{oi} \ (e^{\alpha_1 t}) \ (e^{\alpha_2 B_{ti}}) \ (e^{\alpha_3 C_{ti}}) \ (e^{\alpha_4 D_{ti}}) \\ L_{ti}^{\alpha_5} K_{ti}^{\alpha_6} \ e^{V_t} ,$$

(10.1)

which in a logarithmic form becomes:

$$\ln Q_{ti} = \ln \alpha_{oi} + \alpha_{1i} t + \alpha_2 B_{ti} + \alpha_3 C_{ti} + \alpha_4 D_{ti} + \alpha_5 \ln L_{ti} + \\ \alpha_6 \ln K_{ti} + V_t .$$

The terms are defined as follows:

t = time in years;

i = industry i;

Q_{ti} = an index of value of net product (value added) in industry i at time t, evaluated at 1962 prices;

α_{0i} = the intercept in industry i;

α_{1i} = the annual rate of disembodied technological progress in industry i;

B_{ti} = a dummy variable coded 1.0 from 1952 on in industries covered by the 1951 Codetermination Law, and coded 0.0 otherwise;

C_{ti} = a dummy variable coded 1.0 in the remaining industries from 1953 on and 0.0 otherwise;

D_{ti} = a dummy variable coded 1.0 in all industries from 1973 on and 0.0 otherwise;

L_{ti} = the number of hours worked by production workers in industry i in year t;

K_{ti} = gross capital stock of industry i in year t evaluated at 1962 prices;

V_t = an error term

The production function in equation 10.1 thus allows individual industries to have specific intercepts, α_{0i}, and rates of technological progress, α_{1i}. The effects of the various codetermination laws on productivity are captured as constant disembodied impacts (shifts in intercepts) given by α_2, α_3, and α_4.

For purposes of econometric estimation it is useful to rewrite equation (10.1) as

$$\ln (Q_{ti}/L_{ti}) = \ln \alpha_{0i} + \alpha_{1i} t + \alpha_2 B_{ti} + \alpha_3 C_{ti} + \alpha_4 D_{ti} + \qquad (10.2)$$
$$(\alpha_5 + \alpha_6 - 1) \ln L_{ti} + \alpha_6 \ln (K_{ti}/L_{ti}) + V_t$$

or

$$\ln (Q_{ti}/L_{ti}) = a_{0i} + a_{1i} t + a_2 B_{ti} + a_3 C_{ti} + a_4 D_{ti} +$$
$$a_5 \ln L_{ti} + a_6 \ln (K_{ti}/L_{ti}) + V_t .$$

The advantage of this formulation is that the coefficient a_5 directly measures the returns to scale. If $a_5 < 0$ the production function displays decreasing returns; $a_5 > 0$ implies increasing returns. Moreover, Kmenta's (1967) approximation to the constant elasticity of substitution (CES) production function can be expressed in a similar form:

$$\ln (Q_{ti}/L_{ti}) = a_{oi} + a_1t + a_2B_{ti} + a_3C_{ti} + a_4D_{ti} + \qquad (10.3)$$
$$a_5\ln L_{ti} + a_6\ln (K_{ti}/L_{ti}) + a_7 (\ln (K_{ti}/L_{ti}))^2 + V_t .$$

Should $\alpha_7 \neq 0$, the CES form of the production function may be regarded as superior to the CD form. In this case the estimated coefficients $a_0, \ldots ,$ a_7 from equation (10.3) can be used as starting values for a nonlinear estimation of the unapproximated CES production function.

The empirical results, which will be examined presently, are estimated on the basis of equations (10.2) and (10.3). Before presenting the results it is desirable to discuss briefly the data and the relative limitations of the present approach.

The data on value added Q_{ti}, and the number of hours worked by production workers L_{ti}, were collected from the *Statistical Yearbook of the Federal Republic of Germany*. The industry-specific values of the gross capital stock K_{ti} were calculated by Professors Krengel, Baumgart, Boness, Pischner, and Droege (Krengel et al. 1973, 1975, 1977).

The possible limitations of the present approach are those that are usually associated with time-series and aggregate production-function studies. The output measure should ideally consist of homogeneous physical units. Since in practice this unit is impossible to obtain, the second-best alternative is to use deflated measures of net product (value added). Fortunately, the latter variable is available for this study. The labor input should ideally be measured in terms of a standardized unit, such as the "equivalent worker hour." In this study it is possible to use the "hours worked by an average production worker in a given industry." This measure is clearly superior to other variables commonly used in aggregate and time-series studies, such as average number of persons employed.[6] At the same time, it is not possible to aggregate different types of labor according to skill, sex, and experience, or to allow for changes in these variables over time. The most difficult task in production-function research is of course the construction of a satisfactory measure of capital. The volume of capital services is the ideal measure, but it is never available. Yet, knowing what the ideal measure is tells us that net capital is not a very appropriate measure because it reflects the age of the equipment. Gross capital stock is therefore a better measure, and it is used in this study.[7] There are many other general problems that are reviewed elsewhere.[8] As can be seen, however, the present study is able to mitigate many, though clearly not all, of the shortcomings associated with aggregate and time-series studies.

The results in columns 1 and 2 of table 10-1 correspond to the CD and the approximated CES functions, respectively. They are based on 374 observations from 14 industries in the period 1950-1976. The estimated annual rates of industry-specific (disembodied) technological progress range in the CD specification from 3.3 percent in iron and steel foundries to 9.1 percent in the chemical industry, while the corresponding range in the CES formulation is 3.4 to 9.4 percent.

The estimated (once-and-for-all) effects of the codetermination laws are reported in rows B_{ti}, C_{ti}, and D_{ti} of table 10-1. The estimates are not significantly different from zero for the 1951 Codetermination Law and the 1952 Works Constitution Act. The introduction of the 1972 Works Constitution Act seems to have been associated with a 3 percent decrease in productivity. While this productivity decrease is statistically significant, its magnitude is too small to allow a clear interpretation given the data and techniques at our disposal. The results in table 10-1 therefore seem to suggest that the establishment of codetermination through the 1951, 1952, and 1972 laws had no perceptible effect on productivity.

Table 10-1
OLS Estimates of Selected Production Function Parameters Based on Equations 10.2 and 10.3: All Industries from 1950 to 1976

	1. Cobb-Douglas (10.2)		*2. CES (10.3)*	
Industry time trend (t)				
Coal mining	0.037	(0.0026)	0.036	(0.0026)
Iron ore mining	0.049	(0.0048)	0.051	(0.0053)
Potash and rock salt mining	0.070	(0.0027)	0.073	(0.0037)
Other mining	0.057	(0.0034)	0.056	(0.0036)
Iron-making industry	0.050	(0.0032)	0.052	(0.0041)
Iron and steel foundries	0.033	(0.0026)	0.034	(0.0026)
Steel drawing and cold rolling mills	0.061	(0.0028)	0.062	(0.0032)
Industry of nonferrous metals	0.058	(0.0025)	0.060	(0.0032)
Chemicals	0.091	(0.0027)	0.094	(0.0041)
Saw mills and timber processing	0.067	(0.0034)	0.068	(0.0036)
Paper industry	0.068	(0.0034)	0.071	(0.0044)
Industry of investment goods	0.057	(0.0034)	0.059	(0.0040)
Industry of consumption goods	0.065	(0.0034)	0.066	(0.0035)
Food, tobacco, and beverages	0.058	(0.0030)	0.060	(0.0041)
Other Coefficients				
B_{ti}	−0.011	(0.0249)	−0.005	(0.0258)
C_{ti}	−0.004	(0.0152)	−0.007	(0.0157)
D_{ti}	−0.034	(0.0124)	−0.032	(0.0126)
$\ln L_{ti}$	−0.244	(0.0382)	−0.281	(0.0553)
$\ln (K_{ti}/L_{ti})$	−0.032	(0.0397)	0.007	(0.0576)
$[\ln (K_{ti}/L_{ti})]^2$			−0.011	(0.0122)
R^2	0.999		0.999	
N	374		374	

Source: *Statistical Yearbook of the Federal Republic of Germany*; Krengel et al (1973, 1975, 1977).

Note: The dependent variable is $\ln (Q_{ti}/L_{ti})$. Values in parentheses are the estimated standard errors.

The estimated labor coefficient a_5 is negative in both functional forms and hence suggests that the production function displays decreasing returns to scale. The negative CD coefficient estimated on ln (K_{ti}/L_{ti}) is counterintuitive, as it signifies a negative marginal product and output elasticity of capital ($\alpha_6 < 0$). This unexpected result is usually associated with the measurement of capital as a stock rather than as actual capital (capacity) utilization. While the measures of output and labor input fluctuate with economic cycles, capital stock usually changes only gradually over time as new investment takes place. As a result, during economic downturns production data often display a decrease in Q and L together with an increase in K. The problem is not limited to our data. For instance, in their firm-level study Cable and Fitzroy (1980a,b) obtained a CD coefficient on capital that was not significantly different from zero ($\alpha_6 = 0.0008$, $t = 0.015$). These findings may arise from a particular measurement of capital in Germany.[9] Irrespective of the reasons for these findings, the question remains as to whether the estimated effects of codetermination (coefficients on B_{ti}, C_{ti}, and D_{ti}) are affected by the sign/value of the capital coefficient.

In dealing with this question, it must be noted that, while the coefficient on ln (K_{ti}/L_{ti}) is negative in the CD form of table 10-1, it is not significantly different from zero at convential significance-test levels. Moreover, the corresponding coefficient in the CES form is positive, although it is also insignificant. While this more detailed examination of the results mitigates the counterintuitive finding of $\alpha_6 < 0$ in the CD form, it also highlights the fact that the CES coefficient on $(\ln (K_{ti}/L_{ti}))^2$ is not statistically significant. This in turn supports the CD function as the appropriate estimating form.

In order to check the reliability (robustness) of the estimated effects of codetermination, I have used two alternative approaches to generate additional estimates. The first approach amounts to reestimating equation 10.2 with economic constraints imposed on its coefficients. The second approach disaggregates the data so as to increase their institutional and technological homogeneity.

Since the existence of a negative marginal product (output elasticity) of capital is hardly credible from the point of view of economic theory, it may be argued that, if necessary, the theoretically predicted (positive) sign ought to be imposed on the data. This may be done directly by imposing a positive lower bound on the estimated coefficient of ln (K_{ti}/L_{ti}) in equation 10.2 and estimating the CD function by nonlinear least squares. Alternatively, one may impose the frequently invoked assumption of constant returns to scale, which is known to have often generated positive input coefficients in circumstances where an unrestricted CD form would not do so. Since constant returns are easier to justify than an arbitrary lower-bound restriction on α_6, I have decided to reestimate equation 10.2 under the assumption of constant returns to scale ($a_5 = 0$).

Table 10-2 contains the relevant estimates of a constant returns-to-scale CD function based on equation 10.2. The equation displays the theoretically predicted positive and significant coefficient on $\ln (K_{ti}/L_{ti})$. Moreover, the estimated effects of the three codetermination laws are all very small (though of differing signs), thus indicating that the constant-returns restriction does not alter significantly the earlier conclusion of a limited impact of codetermination on productivity.

Estimates in tables 10-1 and 10-2 are derived from a procedure that, except for intercepts and rates of disembodied technical change, constrains all the industries to display an identical production function. In view of the possible institutional and technological differences among the 14 industry groups,[10] this constraint may not be warranted. In order to increase the homogeneity in the institutional and perhaps technological characteristics of the data, the tests were replicated for selected groups of industries. Estimates in table 10-3 are based on data from the following industries: coal mining, iron-ore mining, potash and rock-salt mining, and other mining. These industries use workers who are represented by the same trade union and who have similar skills and sex composition (mostly male miners). The industries are also expected to use relatively more homogeneous capital services. All are covered by the 1952 law, but only coal mining operates also under the 1951 law. The other group of industries on which additional tests were performed (tables 10-4 and 10-5) is composed of the iron-making industry, iron and steel foundries, steel-drawing and cold-rolling mills, and the nonferrous-metals industry. The workers in these industries are also represented by a single trade union, and the production-function characteristics are again expected to be more homogeneous than for the

Table 10-2
OLS Estimates of Selected CD Production Function Parameters Based on Equation 10.2 under Constant Returns to Scale: All Industries from 1950 to 1976

B_{ti}	-0.063	(0.0249)
C_{ti}	-0.039	(0.0149)
D_{ti}	0.006	(0.0113)
$\ln L_{ti}$	0.0	—
$\ln (K_{ti}/L_{ti})$	0.139	(0.0310)
R^2	0.999	
N	374	

Source: *Statistical Yearbook of the Federal Republic of Germany*; Krengel et al (1973, 1975, 1977).

Note: The dependent variable is $\ln (Q_{ti}/L_{ti})$. Values in parentheses are the estimated standard errors. The coefficient on $\ln L_{ti}$ is constrained to 0.0.

Table 10-3

OLS Estimates of Selected Production Function Parameters Based on Equations 10.2 and 10.3: Selected Industries—Coal Mining, Iron Ore Mining, Potash and Rock Salt Mining, and Other Mining—from 1950 to 1976

	1. Cobb-Douglas (10.2)		2. CES (10.3)	
B_{ti}	−0.041	(0.0558)	−0.004	(0.0581)
C_{ti}	−0.063	(0.0350)	−0.073	(0.0348)
D_{ti}	−0.089	(0.0273)	−0.081	(0.0271)
ln L_{ti}	−0.181	(0.0673)	0.351	(0.1081)
ln (K_{ti}/L_{ti})	0.075	(0.0669)	0.181	(0.0846)
$[\ln (K_{ti}/L_{ti})]^2$			−0.039	(0.0197)
R^2	0.999		0.999	
N	108		108	

Source: *Statistical Yearbook of the Federal Republic of Germany*; Krengel et al. (1973, 1975, 1977).

Note: The dependent variable is ln (Q_{ti}/L_{ti}). Values in parentheses are the estimated standard errors.

overall sample. The first three industries are covered by both the 1951 and 1952 laws, while the last one is subject to the 1952 law only.

The mining results in table 10-3 suggest that the 1951 law did not have a significant productivity effect. The 1952 law is associated with an almost significant negative impact of 6 to 7 percent, and the 1972 law is found to have coincided with a significant 8 to 9 percent decrease in productivity. The findings with respect to the 1951 and 1952 laws are generally in harmony with the estimates in tables 10-1 and 10-2. The results for the 1972 law are somewhat more extreme. In all other respects the results are satisfactory, for both production functions display mild decreasing returns-to-scale and positive-input coefficients.

Estimates of the codetermination effects in the iron-steel and metals industries (table 10-4) suggest that none of the three laws had a significant productivity effect. As in table 10-1, however, the CD form generates a negative estimated coefficient on ln (K_{ti}/L_{ti}). In this case imposing constant returns to scale merely mitigates the negative coefficient but does not reverse its sign. As a result, I have used nonlinear least squares to reestimate the CD function for the iron-steel and metals industries with constant returns and a lower bound of 0.1 on the coefficient of ln (K_{ti}/L_{ti}). The results, presented in table 10-5, indicate that the lower-bound constraint of 0.1 is indeed binding and that, with the exception of the 1952 law, the estimated impact of codetermination is not significantly different from zero. The positive 12.6 percent effect of the 1952 law is significant. However, given that the estimate is more than twice as large as its counter-

Table 10-4
OLS Estimates of Selected Production Function Parameters Based on Equations 10.2 and 10.3: Selected Industries—Iron-Making Industry, Iron and Steel Foundries, Steel-Drawing and Cold-Rolling Mills, and Industry of Nonferrous Metals—from 1950 to 1976

	Cobb-Douglas (10.2)		CES (10.3)	
B_{ti}	−0.045	(0.0315)	−0.037	(0.0318)
C_{ti}	0.054	(0.0442)	0.038	(0.0454)
D_{ti}	−0.005	(0.0218)	0.0132	(0.0251)
$\ln L_{ti}$	−0.233	(0.0690)	−0.321	(0.0920)
$\ln (K_{ti}/L_{ti})$	−0.263	(0.0815)	0.090	(0.2592)
$[\ln (K_{ti}/L_{ti})]^2$			−0.069	(0.0480)
R^2	0.995		0.995	
N	106		106	

Source: *Statistical Yearbook of the Federal Republic of Germany*; Krengel et al. (1973, 1975, 1977).

Note: The dependent variable is $\ln (Q_{ti}/L_{ti})$. Values in parentheses are the estimated standard errors.

part in table 10-4, it appears that the result is due to the input-coefficient constraints and ought to be interpreted with caution.

Conclusions

The present study uses the best available industry-level data to estimate the impact of codetermination on productivity. At the same time, since the data are rather aggregated and contain only a limited number of pre-1952 and post-1972 observations, the results must be treated as tentative. Overall, they suggest that the introduction of employee participation through the 1951 Codetermination Law and the 1952 Works Constitution Act had no significant effect on productivity. These findings are fairly robust to differences in sample selection and contradict some of the negative-effect hypotheses advanced by Blumenthal (1956). Yet, the findings do not support the assertion that the German postwar economic prosperity was due primarily to codetermination. The data may not be sufficiently adequate to eliminate this possibility, but they do not lend it support.

The productivity effect of the 1972 Act is found to be either insignificant or mildly negative. The reliability of the negative estimate is hard to assess, and more analytical work, based on superior data sets, is clearly needed before more conclusive results can be obtained.

The methodology of this paper is more advanced than that used by Blumenthal (1956). At the same time the present study examines the same

Codetermination and Productivity

Table 10-5
Nonlinear Least-Squares Estimates of Selected CD Production Function Parameters Based on Equation 10.2 under Constant Returns to Scale and the Constraint $a_6 = \alpha_6 \geq 0.1$: Selected Industries—Iron-Making Industry, Iron and Steel Foundries, Steel-Drawing and Cold-Rolling Mills, and Industry of Nonferrous Metals—from 1950 to 1976

B_{ti}	−0.058	(0.0308)
C_{ti}	0.126	(0.0487)
D_{ti}	0.031	(0.0206)
$\ln L_{ti}$	0.0	—
$\ln (K_{ti}/L_{ti})$	0.100	(0.0773)
R^2	0.994	
N	106	

Source: *Statistical Yearbook of the Federal Republic of Germany*; Krengel et al. (1973, 1975, 1977).

Note: The dependent variable is $\ln (Q_{ti}/L_{ti})$. Values in parentheses are the estimated asymptotic standard errors. The coefficient on L_{ti} is constrained to 0.0 while a lowerbound of 0.1 is imposed on the coefficient of $\ln (K_{ti}/L_{ti})$ during iterations. The Gauss-Newton method was used and convergence was achieved.

forms of participation, and the results are thus comparable. The methodology of this study is similar to that employed by Cable and Fitzroy (1980a, b). However, the two studies use different data sets as well as a different measurement of participation. They also examine diverse participatory institutions. Consequently, it is rather difficult to compare the present results to those obtained by Cable and Fitzroy. The findings of the two studies are not mutually exclusive; rather they may be regarded as complementary.

Notes

1. Similar participatory systems have since been legally established in Austria, Denmark, Luxemburg, Netherlands, Norway, and Sweden.

2. For detailed discussions of the German participatory institutions, see for instance Blumenthal (1956), Fürstenberg (1969, 1977), Sturmthal (1964), Vollmer (1976, 1979), and Thimm (1980).

3. A concise summary of the possible positive and negative effects of unions on productivity can be found in a recent empirical study by Brown and Medoff (1978).

4. It is now a relatively well-established custom in Germany to vary hours of work before resorting to layoffs.

5. For results of additional tests see Cable and Fitzroy (1980a, b).

6. Using the number of persons employed would be especially inappropriate in the German context, where firms vary hours of work before resorting to layoffs.

7. For exact derivation of the gross capital stock see Krengel et al. (1973, 1975, 1977).

8. See for instance Walters (1963), Griliches and Ringstad (1971), and Levin in this volume.

9. The problem is of course not limited to Germany. For a recent encounter of this phenomenon in Turkey, see Krueger and Tuncer (1980).

10. Some of these groups, such as the industry of investment goods; the industry of consumption goods; and the industry of food, tobacco, and beverage goods are in fact considerable aggregates.

11 Participation and Performance in U.S. Labor-Managed Firms

Michael Conte

The purpose of this chapter is to present and to review the principal evidence on the productivity of labor-managed firms (LMFs) in the United States. A firm is regarded here as labor managed if the most important decisions of the firm are made by individuals who represent the work force in the company. Not all deciders must be nonmanagerial workers, and not all workers must have formal voice in the company. Though this definition is loose, firms that fall into the category are easily recognized. In the United States, the only firms that meet these criteria are owned by their workers, either fully or in substantial part. Many nonemployee-owned firms have plans for participation in decision making. The view adopted here is that the differences between partially participative firms and true LMFs are so great as to merit separate study for the two types. As there are several good reviews of the effects of partial participation on organizational efficiency already in print (see in particular Lowin 1968, Blumberg 1968, and Meyer 1970), this chapter concentrates on efficiency in the case of full participation, that is, labor management.

There are two basic types of LMF in the United States: classical producer cooperatives (PCs) and companies with employee stock ownership plans (ESOPs). In a PC, all the shares are owned by workers, although all workers may not own shares. Voting rights are equal for all members of the cooperative irrespective of the number of shares they may own. On the other hand, the ESOP form prescribes no particular structure of ownership or control. Employees may own a very small interest in the company, or as much as 100 percent of the equity. Voting rights may be apportioned on any principle (usually the number of shares owned). The PC and ESOP forms are described further in connection with the studies.

The statistical studies break down into two main groups. Studies that make comparisons of performance averages for labor-managed vs. conventional company groups are reviewed together in the third section of this chapter. Studies devoted to correlation and regression (hypothesis-testing) analyses are reviewed individually in the fourth section. It is clear from the brief description given here that the structure of the two forms is so distinct as to raise questions about the generalizability of conclusions across forms.

The author would like to dedicate this chapter to William F. Whyte in honor of his pioneering contributions to the field of employee-ownership and participation.

Theoretical Underpinnings

The research reviewed in the third and fourth sections is based, either explicitly or implicitly, on a psychological model of perception, motivation, and communication within work organizations. The purpose of this section is to specify the basic outline of such a model that might command some agreement. This model is developed and presented here to provide a theoretical basis on which to evaluate the empirical results of the papers reviewed below.

The model is presented schematically in figure 11-1. Boxes enclose the basic independent and/or dependent variables. Solid arrows indicate what are hypothesized to be causal relationships. Broken circles represent moderating variables, and broken arrows indicate which relationships are being moderated.

A basic characteristic of the model is that all objective, or structural, features of the work organization operate on the behavior of individuals in the firm via their perceptions. For example, worker ownership, a structural feature, operates on attitudinal motivators via its influence over worker perceptions of ownership (arrows 2 and 11).[1]

Worker ownership and perceptions thereof are proposed to influence the degree of actual worker participation in organizations (arrows 3 and 4). Therefore, perceptions of worker ownership affect individual motivation both directly and indirectly via their influence on actual participation. The direct link between perceptions of worker ownership and worker attitudes is moderated by at least three variables (arrow 14): perceptions of performance-reward contingency in the firm, perceptions of pay equity and perceptions of levels of pay. Performance-reward contingency refers to the actual connection between levels of effort in the firm and financial rewards.[2]

Perceptions of worker ownership and participation are hypothesized to affect pay rules and pay levels in the firm (arrows 8 and 10), and may also moderate perceptions of pay levels in the firm as satisfactory or equitable (arrows 9 and 13). Worker perceptions of performance-reward contingency, pay equity, and pay levels are hypothesized to interact with ownership and perceived participation in their respective influence on the attitudinal motivators (arrows 14 and 15).

Participation is the principal independent variable of interest. The definition of participation is generally agreed upon in the literature. According to Lowin (1968, p. 69): "By participative decision making we mean a mode of organizational operations in which decisions as to activities are arrived at by the very persons who are to execute those decisions. Participative decision making is contrasted with the conventional hierarchical mode of operations in which decision and action functions are segregated in the authority structure."

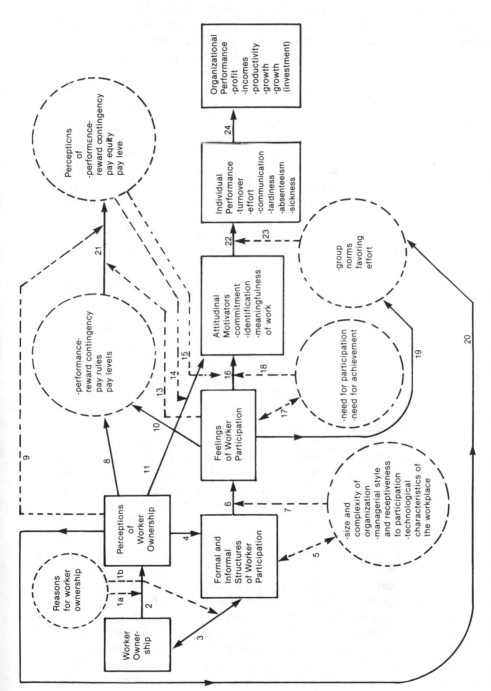

Figure 11-1. Psychological Model of Perception, Motivation, and Communication within Work Organizations

As usual, defining and measuring a concept are two different functions. It is assumed in the model under discussion that participation is measurable (that is, that one can refer to "more" and "less" participation). The problems with this are addressed elsewhere in this volume. The degree of participation in the firm may be affected by the ownership structure in the firm and by worker perceptions of ownership. It is not assumed here that workers who own the firm actually participate in all decisions that affect them. This is impossible in practical terms, and it appears to be very far from the case in some firms where workers own all the equity in the company. Worker ownership does not guarantee participativeness in decision making.[3] The hypothesis here is that it raises the likelihood, or probability, of worker participation, so that, in a large enough sample, one would observe a positive connection between the extent of worker ownership and the extent of worker participation.

The immediate effect of participation in decision making is to impart a feeling of participation to workers. According to the model, workers' perceptions of their influence in the firm are moderated (arrow 7) by the size and complexity of the organization, by managerial style and receptiveness to participation, and by technological characteristics of the workplace. The latter two of these variables may also directly affect and be directly affected by the informal structures of participation in the firm, accounting for the double-headed arrow 5. Complexity and size of the organization may have a powerful influence on the perceived degree of participation. Bureaucracy and an individual sense of power may be incompatible. Relations with unions, and union approval and support of worker participation programs may also have an impact on felt participation, and may feed back into the formal participation system.

The model postulates that perceptions of ownership and participation act to heighten attitudes that motivate workers. The psychological literature has developed a taxonomy for these motivators, the most important being commitment, identification with the firm, and meaningfulness of work. Commitment usually refers to a worker's intention to remain with the firm, and would therefore be directly linked to the rate of turnover in the firm. Identification refers to the sense that there is a commonness of purpose between the worker and the firm. Meaningfulness of work is a sense of involvement of the worker with his or her job, per se. The latter two have direct hypothetical links to effort, communication, tardiness, absenteeism, and sickness. The basic hypothesis, then, is that increased levels of perceived participation will result in cost-reducing behaviors.

The relation between attitudinal motivators and individual performances, or behaviors (arrow 22), is moderated by "group work norms." The model suggests that group norms favoring effort will be strengthened by perceptions of ownership and/or participation (arrows 19 and 20), and that the existence of these norms interacts with individual motivators to produce higher levels of individual performance than would exist in their absence.[4]

The final link in the model is between individual and organizational performance. The basic hypothesis here is that if individuals in the firm work harder, communicate better, stay longer with the firm, and are on the job for more of their regular hours, then the organization will be better able to meet its goals.

The goals of an organization clearly depend upon its structure. The rightmost box in figure 11-1 lists several of the likely goals of an organization. Profit and high income levels for some or all employees are ultimate goals. High productivity, innovation, and growth (investment) may be goals in themselves, or they may be viewed as intermediate in affecting levels of profit and/or income. It would be ideal to assess the performance of U.S. LMFs on all these possible goals simultaneously. However, none of the studies have done this. All five goals listed above except one (innovation) have been assessed in at least one of the studies reviewed below.

Comparisons of Performance Averages

Derek Jones (1977, 1979) has done the most extensive work to date in collecting and analyzing basic performance data for U.S. PCs. He analyzed the cooperatives by type, or "cluster." Four of these clusters represent industry groups (foundry, barrel making or cooperage, shingle, and plywood). A fifth cluster consists of cooperatives in a variety of industries initially financed by the Knights of Labor. In addition to these five clusters, Jones grouped miscellaneous PCs into an early general (1860-1889) group and a late general (1896-1937) group. Of the seven clusters, the only one with extant firms is the plywood group.

In an attempt to assess the "viability" of the PCs in the United States, Jones made estimates of the average life span of firms in each cluster. The results were inconclusive, with average life spans varying from less than 5 years for the Knights of Labor cluster to 21 years for the plywood cluster. According to Jones, no conclusion can be drawn regarding the comparative longevity of cooperative and conventional firms for lack of data. Nonetheless, PCs can clearly survive for substantial periods of time. The longest life span he recorded was 53 years for a barrel-making company.[5]

In addition to his analysis of longevity, Jones gathered data on labor productivity and profitability for individual cooperatives, and compared these to country, state and/or national averages for conventional firms in the same industry. For three cooperative foundries, he found that output per capita was greater than the all-firms county average for conventionally owned foundries by 42, 5, and 21 percent, and that their productivity exceeded the national average as well. On the other hand, labor productivity for two barrel-making cooperatives was below both the local town/county and state averages for barrel makers. The latter finding is tempered by the fact that the data on barrel-making PCs were not for the same year as the town/state averages. This may be a significant consideration on account of product market volatility.

In addition to looking at labor productivity, Jones analyzed profit data for selected firms in the foundry, plywood, and early general clusters in Massachusetts. His general conclusion from this analysis was that PCs can make profits, some over long periods of time (10 years or more). Jones did not compare cooperative profit performance with the performance of conventional firms. One reason for this is that profits in the two groups are not quite comparable because the cooperative wage bill is not fixed in the labor market. The profit and wage claimants substantially overlap in the PC, which clouds the separability of the two flows. Profit data are particularly unreliable when there is a tax on profit but not on wages. In such a case, the cooperative is naturally led to raise the wage bill, which lowers the recorded level of profit but leaves unaffected the pretax total (wage and profit) income of cooperative members.

While Jones's results are not conclusive, it is fair to say that they leave room for the hypothesis that cooperative performance can be equal or superior to that of conventional firms. The main piece of evidence that is missing concerns the capitalization of the firms that were studied. Jones presents no information on the capitalization of the cooperatives he analyzed (most probably because none was available), so it is impossible to judge whether the superiority of the foundry cooperative or the possible inferiority of the cooperage cooperatives represents superiority or inferiority in the allocation of all resources.

Further evidence on the plywood cooperative cluster is available from several cases where the Internal Revenue Service challenged the right of cooperatives to pay high advances (the term used for labor income) on the grounds that this constituted tax evasion rather than legal avoidance. The question hinged on whether the surplus of cooperative advances over average wages for plywood workers in the area represented a simple return to capital (taxable under corporate profit laws) or a return to greater efficiency of cooperative labor.

The cooperatives were required to show that the higher pay received by members reflected greater productivity on their part. They did so, to the satisfaction of the Internal Revenue Service, by using some traditional and some nontraditional measures of productivity, including square-foot output per labor hour, grade of output, and grade of input. The overall results indicated that workers in the cooperatives under study produced a greater volume of higher quality output from lower quality inputs than that in the average conventional plywood company.

The tax-court reports available to the author do not supply any of the specific statistics used in making the courts' determinations. Katrina Berman (1976), who served as a consultant to several of the plywood cooperatives in these tax cases, reports that PCs have performed very well relative to the rest of the industry, in several cases showing a 20-50 percent higher average performance for the PCs. According to Berman, the tax audits indicate that many cooperatives achieve productivity of 30 percent or more above the productivity levels in conventional plants.

While indicative of good productivity performance, the findings that Berman presents raise a number of questions. Not all cooperatives were audited because not all cooperatives pay such high wages. Some cooperatives routinely pay wages that are low relative to the (labor) market, and most cooperatives have paid less than the market rate at some time in their histories. The tax studies that Berman refers to, therefore, describe the most successful of the plywood cooperatives, and so are not representative of the cooperatives as a group. One can conclude from these data only that some plywood cooperatives are very efficient indeed.

A related and important issue is that it is not clear from the court evidence why these select cooperatives are productive; it may be due to the participative environment that Berman describes and attributes high productivity to, but to know this one would need evidence that the less successful coops were less participative on the average. Evidence from the Bellas study, reviewed below, indicates that this is actually the case.

Another type of evidence that one would like to have and that is not supplied by other studies relates to the dispersion of performance levels in conventional plywood companies. Perhaps there are some noncooperative plywood companies that are 20-50 percent more efficient than the industry norm. If this is the case, the high performance levels for the most successful cooperatives can be interpreted as a "normal" reflection of performance dispersion: to be expected, and without which plywood cooperatives should be adjudged as inferior.

For these and other reasons, the tax-case evidence must be viewed as suggestive, but far from conclusive, that worker-owned plywood cooperatives function better than conventional plywood mills. The studies indicate that some cooperatives function considerably better than the average conventional firm in terms of short-run productivity (output per worker). This knowledge suggests three questions: (1) What accounts for the high labor productivity in some of the cooperatives (and conversely, why is it not observed in others)? (2) Does this partial productivity measure imply that some plywood cooperatives use economic resources (land, labor, and capital) more efficiently than the average cooperative or conventional firm?

And (3), what does this imply for the viability of cooperatives in the U.S. economy (does good overall economic performance imply sustained existence)? Each of these questions is important from both the theoretical and the policy perspectives.

While the tax-case evidence does not supply any direct clues as to the reasons for higher labor productivity in several of the coops, Berman (1967, 1976) and Dahl (1957) have interpreted the evidence in terms that bear a strong resemblance to the model sketched in figure 11-1. Dahl places emphasis upon ownership as the cause of greater efficiency, though his evidence is impressionistic, based upon informal interviews with cooperative members and managers. The causal model implicit in Dahl's explanation involves arrows 11, 22, and 24 from figure 11-1.[6] There are variations in the percent of workers who are owners, but not in the percent of worker ownership. One must conclude, therefore, that Dahl believes that owners work better than employees. Berman (1976, p. 5), on the other hand, stresses the participation-productivity relationship and takes institutional features such as autonomous work groups, elimination of status symbols, a single job classification for all, selection of own leaders, and dissemination of economic information to be the principal determinants of the PC's superior economic performance.

The Dahl and Berman explanations represent competing hypotheses of productivity determination in U.S. LMFs. While no solid evidence is adduced to support one hypothesis over the other, the tax-case literature serves the purpose of drawing the theoretical lines of battle. Is it ownership, per se, or worker participation that causes high performance levels in some coops? Dahl (1957, p. 43) provides an interesting and important twist on this question by suggesting that "excessive" participation may in fact have a negative influence on overall performance in the cooperatives.

Dahl clearly sees ownership as the dominant motivator. Berman rejects this explanation, almost completely dismissing ownership per se as a motivator. The studies reviewed below shed some light on these issues.

Correlation and Regression

Bellas

Carl J. Bellas (1972) has done a study of the plywood cooperatives using economic, behavioral, and attitudinal measures. His analysis has three objectives: (1) to determine the extent of the difference in performance among the cooperatives; (2) to examine the observed relationship between worker-owner participation and mill performance for the purpose of determining if there is a true relationship between these two variables; and (3) to examine, individually, the operating and organizational variables and their observed relationship with mill performance for the purpose of determining if there is a true relationship between performance and any of these variables.

This is clearly a broad mandate. Bellas's results support Berman's findings of higher performance levels in some cooperatives—but not in all—as compared to industry norms, and go some distance in explaining the origin of these performance differences.

Bellas defines plywood cooperative performance in relation to the objectives of the cooperatives themselves, as he interprets these objectives. The goals of cooperative members, according to Bellas, are to achieve high levels of income and job security. This leads immediately to an aggregation problem with an accompanying trade-off. As current income levels rise, holding all else constant, job security may decline due to a lack of capital replenishment or contingency funds. Bellas therefore adopts both short-and long-run performance measures: immediate returns, as measured by current income, and deferred returns, measured by changes in share value.[7]

In addition to defining and operationalizing measures of performance, Bellas offers an objective measure of participation. The definition of participation is similar to that of the first section of this chapter. Bellas operationalizes the concept by means of an index comprising (1) the percentage of worker-owners who served on the board of directors during the period 1963-1967, (2) the percentage of worker-owners serving on committees in 1967,[8] (3) the number of board meetings normally held during a year, (4) the number of general meetings normally held during a year, and (5) the effectiveness of methods used to communicate minutes of board meetings to the worker-owners.

Feelings of participation, according to Bellas, stem from involvement in decision-making processes in the firm.[9] Bellas's index of participation, presented above, is an attempt at measuring the extent of employees' involvement in decisions. Bellas makes no attempt here to capture employees' perceptions directly through an attitudinal survey. This may have been due to considerations of cost or time. Needless to say, the absence of attitudinal information makes validation of the central hypothesis concerning employees' feelings impossible. It is not clear, for instance, that the types of participation included in Bellas's index are those that would stimulate feelings of participation among the operating workers. Some of the specific participation practices that are measured affect only a small number of workers who once were involved in the types of decision making measured in the index.[10] In spite of these shortcomings, Bellas's participation variable is probably correlated with members' sense of participation and so may serve as a proxy for the latter. Bellas tests his model by means of simple correlations (multiple regression was performed but the results were not reported). Rather than running two sets of correlations, one for short-run performance and another for long-run, Bellas combines these two into an index of performance by adding the average per-member financial distributions over a 5-year period to the change in the book value of a working share over the same period.[11] This index is then correlated with three categories of variables: (1) his index of participation (Pt), (2) variables related to the composition of the organization, and (3) variables related to operations.

As part of his analysis, Bellas compares the hourly wage of two groups of cooperatives with that of the conventional companies. Six "high-performance coops" had an average hourly income 25 to 35 percent higher than those in the conventional mills in the years 1963-1967. The remaining "low-performance coops" averaged slightly above to slightly below the hourly income rates of the conventional mills in the same period. These results indicate that there is substantial variation in performance levels within the cooperative group. Bellas's correlation results also indicate that these differences are highly correlated with (1) differences in participativeness within the cooperative group; (2) the ratio of worker-owners to all owners; (3) average total capital; and (4) the ratio of worker-owners to the total work force. These are the only tested variables with a significant relation to cooperative performance. *The correlation of participation with performance was .661, the highest of all the tested variables*, and was significant at the .005 level of confidence.

While Bellas does not interpret all these findings in connection with his central hypothesis, there are a number of interesting conclusions to be drawn, and some that may not be drawn. The principal conclusion of the analysis is that the degree of participativeness explains more of the difference in performance among the cooperatives than any other variable taken alone. This is a strong case for the effect of participation on performance.

The second highest correlation, that between performance and the ratio of worker-owners to all owners, may be interpreted as follows: either having a greater fraction of owners working in the plant leads to higher performance levels, or vice versa. The latter interpretation is plausible, for members do often seek work outside the cooperative when cooperative earnings are down. In the absence of a hypothesis supporting the former interpretation, the latter appears to be the more plausible interpretation of this coefficient.

The third highest correlation, namely, between performance and average total capital, is quite straightforward. One would expect the productivity of labor to vary directly with the capital endowment of the firm, and it does.

The fourth highest correlation is with the ratio of worker-owners to the total work force. The fraction of workers who are owners is significantly related to mill performance at the 5 percent level of confidence. While this result is to be expected from the model in the first section of this chapter, it is not easy to interpret. One hypothesis is that variation in ownership, per se, leads to performance differences; that is, that arrows 2, 11, 22, and 24 are the important ones. Another possible conclusion is that the ownership pattern is correlated with another variable, like participation, which influences cooperative performance. In this case, the r value of .49 for this variable (worker-owners/total work force), would reflect the importance of arrows 3, 6, etc. It is not possible to tell from Bellas's results whether ownership is directly related to performance or not because each of the correlations was run on a zero-order basis. The analysis does not settle the issue of whether the pattern of ownership has an independent effect on performance or, rather, works through its effect on participation. Multiple regression would be necessary to clarify this issue, but these results were not reported.

The fifth highest correlation is the negative correlation between performance and the percentage of production from purchased veneer. This correlation is almost high enough to be significant at the 5 percent level. While this may seem to be a rather uninspiring finding at first blush, it takes on some interest when one takes the plywood-production process into consideration. Plywood is formed by gluing together layers of veneer that, in turn, are stripped from logs. The stripping process may be the most crucial stage of plywood production from the cost point of view. A conscientious operator can strip significantly more veneer from a log than will a half-hearted operator. The negative coefficient implies that cooperatives that do their own stripping save on cost. Perhaps this implies that cooperatives that do not do their own stripping cannot take advantage of one of the principal cost benefits of participation. This is, of course, only one of several possible inferences, but Berman's emphasis upon the care taken to reduce waste in the cooperatives as a major source of efficiency appears to support this interpretation.

Bellas clearly sees participation as a key ingredient in a cooperative's success, and the analysis leaves no doubt that participation and performance are indeed highly correlated. Another point clear from the analysis is that worker-ownership is not sufficient to guarantee high levels of performance in a private-market economy such as the United States.

Rhodes

Susan Rhodes's study (1978) of motivation in one conventional plywood mill and one cooperative plywood mill does not measure ultimate organizational performance. The Rhodes study is included in this review, nonetheless, because it sheds light on the Dahl, Berman, and Bellas findings.

Rhodes analyzes the psychological and behavioral concomitants of worker-ownership and worker participation. The study goes beyond Dahl, Berman, and Bellas in that there is an attempt to quantify some of the intermediate variables and relationships that determine company performance. While this approach is standard in the organizational behavior literature, the Rhodes study is the only one to apply these methods to a plywood cooperative.

Rhodes does not seek to define an index of performance for the company. Rather she concerns herself with a subset of intermediate behavioral outcomes that, at least in theory, are related to cost performance. These are absenteeism, tardiness, accidents, turnover, and grievances.

Rhodes's overall model is a variation of the model outlined in the first section of this chapter and is presented in figure 11-2. It is possible, without elaborating the details of the model, to indicate differences from and similarities to the basic model of the first section. Ownership and participation are given as ultimate determinants of performance as in the earlier model in figure 11-1. In contrast to the earlier model, performance-reward contingency is posited as a completely independent variable, in spite of the fact that contingency of rewards on performance is usually thought to be enhanced by worker ownership. Note also that there is no arrow in figure 11-2 from ownership to participation. This appears to the writer to be a serious theoretical omission in light of the fact that ownership is normally thought to convey certain powers of decision with it.

The three "independent" variables in the left-hand box are hypothesized to have their effect on worker behavior through their effect on two sets of intermediate variables. Worker-ownership, performance-reward contingency systems, and opportunities for participation in decision making lead to a number of psychological sets, including group norms favoring productivity, performance-reward contingencies (or perceptions thereof, as the body of the report clarifies), and perceived participation in decision making. These psychological sets, taken together, create a second psychological set, organizational commitment, which is posited to be more proximate to the behavioral outcomes. Organizational commitment, in turn, leads to cost-related behaviors. The relation of the first group of psychological variables to the second is moderated by yet another psychological variable, (perceptions of) pay equity.

There is no attempt here to evaluate Rhodes's model in the context of the psychological literature except to say that the model appears to oversimplify several causal and interactive relationships. Irrespective of the validity of the overall model, several of the results of testing are interesting.

Rhodes administered questionnaires to a sample of workers in one conventional plywood mill and one cooperative. All respondents in the cooperative were worker-owners, even though there were 65 out of a total of

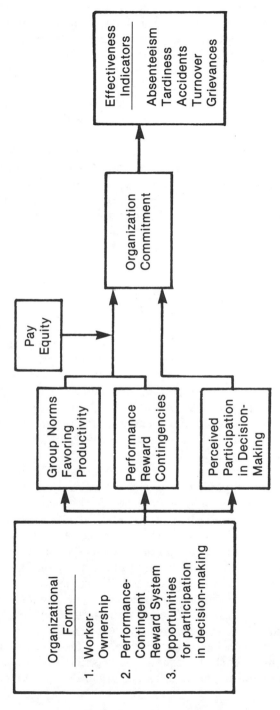

Source: S. Rhodes, *The Relationship Between Worker Ownership and Control of Organizations and Work Attitudes and Behaviors.* Report, U.S. Department of Labor, Employment, and Training Administration, Office of Research and Development, September 1978, p. 000.

Figure 11-2. Rhodes's Schematic Model

160 workers who were nonowners at the time of administration.[12] The questionnaires elicited a wide variety of demographic, attitudinal, and behavioral information, used for purposes of either hypothesis testing or statistical control. (Classical scientific control was invoked to the extent possible by selecting the conventional firm to match the cooperative on a number of characteristics.) The results of Rhodes's hypothesis testing are summarized in table 11-1. In addition, Rhodes provided a table of regression coefficients (not reported here) from estimating the determinants of organizational commitment.[13] Her results shed considerable light on the economic and psychological dynamics of participation. Note that none of the relations between ownership and other variables in the model can be estimated using Rhodes's experimental design. This is because there is no variance on the ownership variable within firms. Presumably, none of the workers in the conventional mill owned shares in the company, while all of the respondents in the cooperative were shareowners.

For the purpose of this review, Rhodes's principal results concern her hypotheses regarding participation, hypotheses numbers 3, 6 and 9. Hypothesis 9, that commitment will be greater in a cooperative than in a conventional firm, was supported. Mean commitment in the cooperative was measured as 5.3 on a 7-point scale, while the mean for the conventional firm was 4.8. The difference between the means was found to be significant.[14]

In an analysis not reported here, Rhodes confirms hypothesis 3, that perceived participation is greater for worker-owners in the cooperative than for workers in the conventional firm. Moreover, regression analysis indicates strong support for hypothesis 6, that perceived participation is positively related to organizational commitment. This relation is significant at a higher level of confidence in the cooperative than in the conventional mill, and the effect of participation on commitment is greater in magnitude in the former than in the latter.

At first glance, these results appear to solve most of the issues of this paper. Commitment and participation are shown to be higher (among members) in cooperatives than among employees in conventional firms, and they are also shown to be positively related to each other. As commitment is hypothesized to bear a positive relationship to performance, so should participation. Unfortunately the interpretation of Rhodes's results are not clear cut. In the first place, there is no indication in the study that the plywood cooperative under study is any more "successful" than the comparison conventional mill. The only performance-related data that Rhodes reports for both companies is wage levels, which were almost exactly equal over the years examined by the study. The conventional mill was actually chosen with this equality in mind for control purposes. Hence, the fact that participation levels in the cooperative were higher over the study period is no indication of a positive relationship between participation and organizational performance.

**Table 11-1
Major Hypotheses and Outcomes in Rhodes's Study**

Number	Hypothesis	Outcome
1.	Worker-owners in a cooperative perceive that the reward system is contingent upon performance to a greater extent than do workers in a conventional organization.	Supported
2.	Group norms favoring productivity are present in the cooperative to a greater extent than in the conventional organization.	Not supported
3.	Perceived participation in decision making is greater for worker-owners in a cooperative than for workers in a conventional firm.	Supported
4.	The perception of performance-reward contingencies is positively related to organizational commitment.	Not supported
5.	Group norms favoring productivity are positively related to organizational commitment.	Supported
6.	Perceived participation in decision making is positively related to organizational commitment.	Supported
7.	Pay equity moderates the relationship between performance-reward contingencies and commitment, such that there is a stronger positive relationship between the perception of performance-reward contingencies and organizational commitment for those who perceive high pay equity than for those who perceive low pay equity.	Not supported
8.	Pay equity moderates the relationship between group norms and commitment, such that there is a stronger positive relationship between group norms favoring productivity and organizational commitment for those who perceive high pay equity than for those who perceive low pay equity.	Not supported
9.	Organizational commitment is greater among cooperative owners than among workers in a conventional organization, other things being equal.	Supported
10.	Organizational commitment is negatively related to absenteeism, tardiness, and accidents.	Not supported
11.	The mean responses of employees in a conventional firm are greater than those of worker-owners in a cooperative for the following measures: (1) absenteeism; (2) tardiness; and (3) accidents.	Not supported
12.	Turnover and grievance rates are greater in the conventional firm than in the cooperative.	Supported

Source: S. Rhodes, *The Relationship Between Worker Ownership and Control of Organizations and Work Attitudes and Behaviors.* Report, U.S. Department of Labor, Employment, and Training Administration, Office of Research and Development, September 1978.

Rhodes's results pertaining to relationships contained in her motivational model are no more supportive of the underlying participation-productivity hypothesis. In particular, the rejection of hypotheses 2, 4, 7, 10, and 11 call significant parts of the model into question. Whether these results are serious blows to the model depends upon the interpretation accorded them and, of course, upon replication in other sites.

A few brief comments on the rejected hypotheses may be helpful. Those hypotheses most closely related to economic cost show mixed results. The individual behavior variables affected in Rhodes's theory by commitment are turnover and grievance rates, absenteeism, tardiness, and accidents. Rhodes finds no empirical support for a relation between commitment and the latter three variables. Commitment affects turnover and grievance rates in the predicted fashion, but not absenteeism, tardiness, and accidents. This result appears quite plausible to the writer, because commitment (as defined and measured in the study) is a willingness, or desire, to remain with the firm. It appears that the relation between commitment and anything except turnover is not a priori defensible. It would seem that the model places too much emphasis on a narrowly defined variable.

In this connection, it would appear that the model does not include some behavioral variables that may be of some significance in determining organizational effectiveness: effort and communication. These are both relatively difficult to measure as compared with the other behaviors measured in Rhodes's study. Rhodes's conclusions, therefore, do not rule out the possibility that the basic individual motivation-based model of organizational outcomes acts through its effects upon individual behaviors.

How can one understand the difference in mean responses of employees on absenteeism, tardiness, and accidents? In reality, there is not enough data to draw any conclusions from these results. Two data points are not sufficient to provide a test.

The conclusion that stands out in the Rhodes study is that participation is indeed a powerful predictor of individual attitudinal responses (like commitment and group work norms) in highly participative work organizations. M. eover, there is sufficient variation in perceived participation among worker-owners to establish this correlation. The participative organization does not instill equal perceptions of participation throughout its membership. This result draws attention to the need for study of the moderating variables in translating participative structures into perceptions of participation in LMFs.

Long

Richard Long (1977, 1978a,b) conducted the most extensive applications of work-organization motivation theory that have been attempted in a North

American LMF. In spite of several clear limitations, this study provides very strong evidence for the participation-productivity relationship in LMFs and goes a long way to answering many of the ancillary questions that surround the issue.

Long (1977, p. 3-A) addresses five specific research questions: "At the organizational level of analysis three questions are addressed: (1) the immediate and longer term effects of employee ownership on patterns of organizational influence and participation; (2) the effects on job attitudes of organization members; and (3) the effects on certain characteristics and attributes of the organization, such as patterns of cooperation and group work norms."

Question (1) above appears to correspond to arrow 3 in figure 11-1, question (2) to arrows 2 and 11, and question (3) to arrow 20.

"At the individual level of analysis two main questions are addressed: (1) the effects of individual share ownership in individual job attitudes; and (2) the relative effects of individual share ownership and individual participation in individual job attitudes, and whether interaction effects between individual share ownership and individual participation may exist."

Question (1) in this paragraph corresponds to arrows 2 and 11 in figure 11-1, while question (2) corresponds to a comparison of arrows 2 and 11 to arrows 6 and 16. The model in figure 11-1 does not allow for interaction effects between share ownership and participation. Long's implicit model is more complex than that of figure 11-1 in this respect. Long's study was based upon data collected in a single employee-owned company. The company, Byers Transport Limited, was the second largest freight carrier in the province of Alberta, Canada in 1975. The company was established in 1934 and was wholly purchased by a major air carrier in western Canada, Pacific Western Airlines (PWA), in January, 1969. A series of events, described in detail by Long, led to an employee purchase of the company in 1975. These events involved temporary poor performance, but the company was on the road to profitability before the employees purchased it.

Long's analysis of Byers is based upon financial, attitudinal, and behavioral data collected at two points in time: December 1975, about 7 months after the employee takeover, and again one year later, in December 1976. The principal financial data that were collected were gross-revenue and net-profit figures collected on a yearly basis from 1970, and on a monthly basis from June 1974, one year before the ownership change. Long also collected figures on the amount of claims made by customers for freight damage or loss and on pounds loaded per worker-hour by freight handlers and drivers.

Two behavioral measures of employee satisfaction and commitment were collected: grievance rates and monthly separation rates. Attitudinal data were collected from a sample of 87 employees at Byers in December

1975 and 82 employees in December 1976. This was out of a total of approximately 190 employees. The questionnaires elicited a wide variety of attitudinal information including information on (1) attitudes on organizational integration, involvement, commitment, general satisfaction, and motivation to work; (2) aspects of satisfaction such as for compensation, social satisfaction, the work itself, promotion, supervisor; (3) other perceptions and attitudes, including performance contingencies, concern for other's performance, perceived task interdependency, job security, attitudes toward change; (4) organizational attributes such as cooperation, communication, group work norms, organizational trust, worker commitment to goals; (5) perceived changes in the organization, and (6) felt participation. Long used these variables to test relationships in his model of motivation and effectiveness in work organizations. His model places considerable emphasis upon individual motivation and job effort, while Rhodes leaves these variables out altogether. Long also adds for consideration two new variables that are well established in the literature: propensity for organizational change (Coch and French 1948; Seashore and Bowers 1970) and quality of organization decisions (Maier and Hoffman 1960; Maier 1963).

Long's description of the structure for employee participation at Byers makes it clear that not much of emphasis was placed upon employee participation via the Board of Directors, and no other formal mechanisms were developed for promoting employee input into decision making.

Regarding employee shareholdings, about 73 percent of the employees had initially purchased stock. Whereas 100 percent of the managers had purchased stock, the proportion for nonmanagers was 65 percent. By December 1976, the proportion of employees who were shareholders dropped from 73 to 52 percent. Long does not indicate how many managers sold their shares, but a significant number of nonmanagers sold their shares, so that by December 1976 only 42.2 percent of nonmanagers owned shares in the company; only a minority of nonmanagers were shareholders.

Long's assessment of the effect of employee-ownership at Byers consists of comparing the gross financial and production data from before the employee takeover with measures of the same variables at two points in time after the takeover, and of analyzing questionnaire data in a hypothesis-testing framework. While the gross financial and production performance data cannot provide conclusive evidence for any hypothesis, they do suggest that overall organizational performance at Byers significantly improved after the employee takeover.

To draw conclusions on the relationships among employee ownership and participation and performance, Long conducted extensive analyses of the questionnaire data. Those findings related to the main theme of this chapter are presented here, along with a small number of other findings that are briefly summarized in the following paragraphs.

According to the employee survey, overall satisfaction increased dramatically in the first year of employee ownership, as did the feeling of job security (even though management clearly announced that policies on penalties and terminations would not change as a result of the change of ownership). Neither of these variables has any proved relationship to productivity, but these results indicate an important change in the work climate.

Concerning those variables with a hypothesized relationship to productivity, 45.3 percent of managerial employees reported that their personal job effort had "increased considerably or greatly." Moreover, 42.9 percent said the same thing about their "productive work," 27.5 percent about "others' job effort," and 40.5 percent about "communication between management and employees." For all the variables mentioned here, very few individuals reported decreases.

Both workers and managers were asked about current amounts of participation and changes in those amounts over the previous year at three levels: job decisions, departmental decisions, and organizational policies. For each of these levels, both workers and managers were asked about "workers' influence," and their own "personal influence." About 50 percent of nonmanagers reported that their participation in decisions at all levels had either not changed or decreased over the previous year, with about one-quarter or fewer of the nonmangers reporting that their participation had increased "considerably or greatly." The situation was perceived quite differently by managers. No managers reported any decline in workers' influence or their own influence over the previous year. Of managers, 48.8 percent indicated that workers' influence over organizational policies had increased "considerably or greatly" over the previous year. This compares with 23.8 percent of nonmanagers who felt the same way, and about 50 percent of nonmanagers who felt that their influence over organizational policies had decreased or not changed.

In addition to changes in their perceived levels of influence, Long asked workers and managers to indicate how much influence workers in general and the respondent himself or herself had over job decisions, departmental decisions, and organizational policy at the time of the interview. The median worker responded that he or she had "some say" over job decisions and departmental decisions, and "little or no say" over organizational policy. Managers tended to feel that they had a "great deal of say" over job decisions and departmental decisions, and "some say" over organizational policy. These results are interesting in comparison with the amount of influence that both groups felt they should have at each of the three levels. In general, workers felt deprived of influence at each of the three levels. (This conclusion is based upon subtraction of the measured amount of influence that workers said they actually had from the amount they said they felt they should have at each level.) Managers felt less decisional deprivation than workers, except perhaps in regard to organizational policy.

In spite of the perceived deprivation on participation reported by nonmanagers, the nonmanagerial respondents reported quite high levels of integration, involvement, commitment, and motivation at the time of the first interview. Long's data also indicates that employees felt the presence of performance-reward contingencies and concern for the performance of others (group work norms).

One observation based on the results from Long's second questionnaire administration is of interest. Nonmanagerial workers indicated in most cases that each of the attitudes they were asked about had improved during the second year, typically by a small amount. Managers also indicated that each of the variables asked about had increased; in some cases by a large amount. At the same time, the reported *levels* of these variables for both managers and nonmanagers declined over the intervening year. This is an interesting finding, with many possible interpretations. No interpretation is provided here, but there is clear need for further assessment of the longitudinal changes in attitudes in LMFs as labor management becomes embedded in the corporate structure.

Given the wealth of information reported by employees at Byers, Long has a good basis to assess the absolute and relative importance of ownership and participation upon attitudes of employees in an LMF. In correlational analyses of ownership and participation with the other variables under study, it is found that both ownership and participation are significantly correlated with a number of job attitudes, performance-reward contingencies, and concern for others' performance (group work norms). On the whole, participation is significantly related to more of these variables than is ownership.

The real tests of interest lie in the results of the regressional analysis, which are reported in table 11-2. A clear distinction is shown here in the ways that ownership and participation affect individuals in a work organization. While both ownership and participation have independent effects upon integration and involvement, the variables of commitment, satisfaction, and motivation are clearly related to only one of the two. *Commitment appears to be a function of ownership, while satisfaction and motivation are determined by feelings of participation* in decision making. *These results represent the only test in the literature of the independent effects of ownership and participation*, and are very clear in their interpretation: commitment appears to be *un*related to participation, while motivation and satisfaction are *un*related to share ownership per se.

Long did not collect any survey data on individual behaviors, and so it was impossible to test the behavioral implications of the above findings. Nonetheless, the simple definitions of the variables analyzed would suggest that ownership most strongly affects levels of absenteeism and turnover, while participation most strongly affects levels of effort in the firm. The former of these hypotheses has already been borne out, as discussed in the

Table 11-2

Combined and Independent Effects of Share Ownership and Participation, Controlling for Length of Service (Nonmanagers)

		Beta Weights	
	$R^2(\%)$	Share Ownership	Participation
Integration	14.7[†]	.24[*]	.30[†]
Involvement	42.5[‡]	.34[‡]	.56[‡]
Commitment	12.3[†]	.36[‡]	.08
Satisfaction	23.2[‡]	.20[*]	.44[↓]
Motivation	13.4[†]	.00	.37[‡]

Source: R.J. Long, *The Effects of Employee Ownership on Job Attitudes and Organizational Performance: An Exploratory Study.* Ph.D. dissertation, Cornell University, 1977, p. 162. Reprinted with permission.

Notes: $N = 59$.

[*] $P < .10$, one-tailed.

[†] $p < .05$, one-tailed.

[‡] $p < .01$, one-tailed.

section on Rhodes's study. The latter of these hypotheses has not been tested in the context of an LMF.

Conte And Tannenbaum

Michael Conte and Arnold Tannenbaum's 1978 study contained analyses of two types: a case study of financial and other performance data at one worker-owned company where the employee purchase was financed by a federal government loan, and a survey of wholly or partially worker-owned companies in the United States. The case study is not reviewed here.

The survey analysis by Conte and Tannenbaum involved 98 companies. Of these, 68 had ESOPs and 30 had direct ownership, though not all of these were traditional producer cooperatives. About 50 percent of the ESOPs were wholly owned by their employees, while only 19 percent of the directly owned firms were wholly owned by employees. Of the directly owned companies, 78 percent had at least a majority employee interest. Overall, the majority of the firms in the sample had a very substantial amount of employee ownership.

Conte and Tannenbaum conducted 15 to 20-minute interviews with the president of each of the companies in the sample, or with his designee. The principal data collected included percent of employee ownership; percent of nonmanagerial employee ownership; percent of employees participating in ownership; whether worker representatives sat on the board of directors of the company; whether employee-owners had a vote associated with their stock ownership; and the level of profit in the firm in the previous year. Profit levels were provided in only 23 cases.

Each of these variables was entered into a regression for these 23 cases, with profit as a dependent variable. Profit was expressed as a ratio of two ratios: the numerator was the ratio of profit to sales in the responding firm, and the denominator was the ratio of profit to sales for comparable-sized firms in the same industry. Profit was adjusted in cases where employees made considerably more than employees in conventional firms in the same industry. The adjustment consisted of adding to the profit figure the total of wages paid to employees over and above what they would have received if they had worked the same number of hours in a conventional firm in their industry and in their area. This adjustment was made only in the case of the plywood cooperatives, as the wage test appeared to apply only to them.

"Percent equity owned by workers" was the only independent variable that proved significant in the regression, and this only in the regression that used the adjusted-profit variable. The interpretation of this (rather large) coefficient is straightforward: the greater is worker ownership as a *percent* of total ownership in the company, the greater is profit performance in relation to the industry average. It is statistically conceivable that the correlation of ownership and performance may reflect a reverse causation; that is, the goal of profit performance may encourage workers to purchase shares. However, casual observation of share purchase and ownership practices in a number of employee-owned companies suggests that this is probably not the case.

Of the remaining results from the regression, most interesting is the finding that participation through voting and employee representation on the company's board of directors has no effect upon profit performance. This appears to contradict the findings in the studies reviewed above that participation does have a clear relationship with motivation, which should, in theory, have an effect upon productivity and profitability. There are two possible conclusions that one can draw from this result: either the results of the previous analyses are to be doubted, or the participation variable used by Conte and Tannenbaum did not tap the degree of felt participation in each firm. There is good reason to believe the second of these conclusions, particularly given the results from the Rhodes and Long studies. Recall that each of these studies was conducted in only one participative firm. Yet great dispersion in participation levels was observed within each firm. This implies that the amount of felt participation within a company may depend substantially upon the presence of other moderating factors that Conte and Tannenbaum were unable to measure.

In spite of the various possibilities for interpretation, the fact remains that the Conte-Tannenbaum regression supports the hypothesis that it is ownership, and not participation, that has the greatest effect upon profit-related performance in worker-owned companies. In light of the findings that would indicate the contrary from the studies reviewed above, the question must be regarded as unresolved at the present time. Further cross-sectional analysis is needed, wherein data on both financial and attitudinal variables is available from a wide variety of firms in several industries.

Conclusions

Research to date has generated a model of motivation in participative firms with testable hypotheses. Several of these hypotheses have been tested in the context of LMFs in the United States, and these analyses are reported in this chapter.

The central question of this chapter concerns the effect of participation on performance in firms that are highly participative. While the psychological theory lying behind the model of motivation in the labor-managed firm was developed in the context of organizations with limited degrees of participation, the theory is applicable in firms that are highly participative. Because there is a possibility for considerably more interactions when the model is applied to the entire organization than to a shop, division, or other relatively small part of an organization, the results of the analysis are likely to be more complex. This is certainly the case in the analyses reviewed in this chapter.

As a result of these analyses, there is no question that participation is highly related to individual motivation. The outstanding questions that remain unanswered are not whether or not there is a relation between participation and motivation in U.S. LMFs, but rather (1) under what conditions will this relation be more or less pronounced, and (2) does individual motivation lead to organizational efficiency? These are the research questions for the future. It is hoped that development of the psychological model of motivation in the first section and the discussion of the analyses to date presented in the second section will aid in answering these questions.

Notes

1. This may appear to carry the emphasis upon subjectivity too far. Yet it has been found (Hammer and Stern 1980) that workers who actually own shares in a worker-owned company may not have strong feelings of ownership, and that the feelings of ownership may not vary significantly with number of shares owned.

2. The theory of performance-reward contingencies is grounded in the expectancy-valence theory of motivation developed by Vroom (1960) and Lawler (1973). Individual motivation stems from the belief that (1) a person's

work will result in successful performance, (2) a certain outcome (high levels of pay in this case) will follow from this performance, and (3) the outcome is desirable (that is, has a positive valence).

3. Two cases where worker-owners apparently have not been afforded satisfactory opportunities for participation come to mind. In the Vermont Asbestos Group (VAG), a 100-percent employee-owned ESOP company, Zwerdling (1978) reports that meetings of the board of directors were actually closed to workers in the plant, and that a number of important decisions were made by "management" that ran counter to the expressed wishes of the workers. Another 100-percent employee-owned ESOP is out on strike at the time of this writing (*Business Week*, September 22, 1980, p. 39). While the basic issue apparently concerns a benefit agreement originally made with the previous parent company, it is difficult to imagine that workers would strike a plant if they felt that they actually make the decisions at the plant.

4. This may be regarded as the opposite of "soldiering," a group norm favoring low effort levels often referred to in connection with fear on the part of workers that high levels of performance will serve, in the long run, to increase not pay but only demands for performance.

5. The fact that none of these firms is extant at this time does not imply that the producer cooperatives failed in the financial sense. Some, in fact, were so financially successful that they were sold to an entrepreneur or group of entrepreneurs for large capital gains, while others gradually lost their cooperative character as a result of the hiring of wage-earning employees.

6. An important issue in connection with this hypothesis of Dahl's is that all the cooperatives are worker-owned to the same degree (100 percent). There are variations in the percent of workers who are owners, but not in the percent of worker-ownership. Dahl apparently believes that owners work better than hired employees, irrespective of their participation in decision making.

7. Bellas's short-run performance measure is clearly a proxy for labor productivity. Holding retained earnings constant, income per worker will vary directly with net output per unit of labor. The long-run performance measure, growth in the value of the firm (synonymous with increases in share values, because the number of shares is typically fixed), is well suited to its task. The better the performance of the firm in meeting its objectives, the more valuable is membership in the firm. This should, in theory, be reflected in a premium on share ownership, as more individuals will bid for purchase of shares in companies that promise long-term success than in one that is likely to falter.

8. No data were available to Bellas on this variable for the years 1963-1966.

9. Bellas addresses two issues in connection with this hypothesis: (1) the importance of actual vs. "felt" participation, and (2) structural obstacles to conveying a feeling of participation. In theory, the ownership of the cooperative conveys the power of decision to its members. Nonetheless, "some of the mills are able to establish a sense of meaningful involvement among their owners, but others have 'failed' in this regard" (Bellas 1972, p. 39). As most of the plywood cooperatives have the same organizational structure, including structures for participation, Bellas appears to be placing emphasis upon the moderating influence indicated by arrow 7 in figure 11-1. Ownership and formal participative structures may not transmit felt influence in the absence of suitable moderating influences. While Bellas indicates that "any program designed to include the worker requires more than an impressive purpose to achieve the desired result" (Bellas 1972, p. 41), Bellas does not indicate the factors that he belives to be important moderators.

10. Recall that the index measures the number of members on the board of directors and various committees, the number of board and general meetings, and the "effectiveness" of methods used to communicate the minutes of board meetings to members. Board and committee meetings involve a relatively small number of members at any one time. Regarding general meetings, it is not clear that a sense of participation will be developed through attendance at such gatherings. Bellas notes that there is even some resistance to attendance at general meetings, such that a penalty system is invoked for nonattendance at some of the cooperatives.

11. This pooling of the two performance measures is unfortunate. It is not clear what this sum actually measures. If Bellas had combined each year's performance with each year's growth in share values, he might have argued that the resulting sum is a measure of the firm's net income, which is, in turn, a reflection of the total return to factors employed in the firm: labor and capital. Members' annual income itself would not measure this because it ignores retained earnings. Efficient market theory would suggest that retained earnings will be reflected in share values. Hence, the sum of annual income and changes in share values should reflect the net income of the firm per worker.

12. There is no reason given in the Rhodes study for the exclusion of nonowners in the survey.

13. See Rhodes (1978, p. 114). Note that the statistical methodology employed here does not follow directly from the model sketched in figure 11-2, which implies an interactive role for pay equity, but this variable appears to have been inserted linearly in the regression equation.

14. Jan Svejnar has pointed out that it is possible to divide this difference into components associated with the independent variables and an autonomous component. Rhodes does not report doing this, and does not provide the necessary statistics from her sample and regression analysis to do it.

12 The Performance of Italian Producer Cooperatives

Alberto Zevi

Little attention has been paid to the analysis of Italian producer (industrial-worker) cooperatives (PCs). This oversight is particularly important since not only do PCs have a long history in Italy, but also Italy is the Western European country where this particular form of worker participation in management has had its broadest development.

In this chapter, I first look at the history of Italian PCs; particular attention is paid to the period since 1945. A discussion of the organization and structure of PCs follows, and the relationships that have grown up among them are stressed. Most attention, however, is given to an examination of large manufacturing and construction PCs that belong to the largest federation serving Italian PCs. Survey data during 1975-1978 are used to examine diverse aspects of PCs in these two industrial groups, whose behavior is often compared to that of conventional firms as reported in published studies. In a concluding section, I compare my results with those drawn from studies of other PCs, and interpret the Italian experience from the standpoint of recent developments in the economic theory of labor management.

History and a Statistical Overview

The first Italian PCs arose, as did other Italian cooperatives, during the second half of the nineteenth century.[1] Many early PCs began as artisans' cooperatives and were most successful in northern Italian cities, where "trade" traditions were strongest. However, the same period witnessed cooperative initiatives, as promoted and encouraged by industrialists, as well as those that had developed from worker initiative. The latter frequently followed business crises. Though cooperatives were established in many fields, they were more frequent among construction and public-works sectors, which are characterized by high numbers of members and workers.

Contemporary with the earliest cooperatives, the first centralized organizations for mutual assistance and coordination were formed. In 1865 the Associazione Industriale Italiana was set us as a result of Luigi Luzzati's efforts to spread the idea of cooperatives throughout the country. In 1887 the First Congress of Italian Cooperators was held, in which over 200 societies, representing diverse sectors (consumers, agriculture, and labor), participated. By far the most important result of the congress was the creation of the Federazione delle Societa Cooperatire Italiane, which, in 1893, changed its title to Lega Nazionale delle Cooperative e Mutue (LNCM), still in use. Representatives of all groups, including liberals, socialists, and Roman Catholics, were members. Until 1919, and the establishment of the Confederazione Cooperative Italiane (CCI) the Lega was the single national association of Italian cooperatives.[2] During this period there was a steady increase of PCs from 167 societies registered in 1887 to 600 in 1900; the peak was reached in 1922 at 8,830 societies. There was an abrupt reversal of this trend, however, during the fascist years: in 1927 the number of PCs dropped to 1,306, and by 1940 it dropped even further to 1,247.

Not until the end of World War II did the cooperative movement again gather impetus. Table 12-1 shows data since 1951 on the number of PCs in existence, the number of new PCs created during particular years, and the number of PCs belonging to the three associations. Apparently only about one-third of PCs belong to federations. Most authorities, however, believe that the official figures include many "independent" PCs that do not engage in productive activity. Consequently, the scope, extent, and nature of the Italian PC movement is probably best illustrated by focusing on federated PCs.

These data enable two distinct periods to be identified. The first, 1951-1972, shows a standstill in the cooperative phenomenon while the sec-

Table 12-1
Italian Producer Cooperatives, 1951-1979

Year	All PCs				Federated PCs		
	PCs[a]	PCs[a]	New PCs	Total	LNCM	CCI	AGCI
1951	—	4,572	—	—	—	—	—
1961	—	4,684	374	—	—	—	—
1971	6,679	4,626	419	—	—	—	—
1972	6,428	4,139	477	2,719	1,279	1,131	309
1973	6,572	4,420	549	—	—	—	—
1974	7,314	4,860	699	—	—	—	—
1975	7,995	5,377	861	—	—	—	—
1976	8,572	5,893	1,076	—	—	—	—
1977	12,040	6,696	1,396	—	—	—	—
1978	14,207	7,854	1,826	—	—	—	—
1979	16,126	9,055	2,047	5,204	2,611	1,935	658

Source: Statistiche della Cooperazione, Ministero del Lavoro e della Previdenta Sociale, Dirazione Generale della Cooperazione, Divisione IV, Schedario Generale, Bollettino Statistiche, Roma, various years.

[a]The first column includes PCs that do not have mutual-aid provisions in their statutes. The second one considers only those that have mutual aid provisions in their statutes.

ond, 1972-1979, reveals a remarkable and steady increase in the number of PCs. Table 12-2 shows the number of workers employed in PCs by major industry.[3] The figures indicate the importance of construction both for number of PCs as well as for total employment.

Cooperative legislation in Italy is guided by the universally recognized principles of cooperatives adhering to the International Cooperative Association: one man, one vote; free and voluntary membership; limited remuneration of the underwritten capital. In PCs there is no upper limit on the number of members, but there must be no fewer than 9.[4] Generally, the members must be workers and must practice the trade specified in the cooperative's charter. If the charter allows it, outside or honorary members can be admitted. Technical and administrative workers can account for no more than 12 percent of the total membership.[5]

Membership, which must be approved by the cooperative's elected board of directors, implies underwriting a share of the capital. The new member may also be required to pay an admission fee as well as a sum determined by the board of directors by considering the latest balance sheet and calculating the cooperative's accumulated reserves. Capital underwriting by workers is limited since they cannot hold a share greater than 10 million lire.[6] Underwritten capital cannot be remunerated at a rate of interest higher than 5 percent. A member who withdraws is repaid only the paid-up value of his share.

Sometimes members can share in financing the PC with loans. In this case, if the sums deposited with the cooperative do not exceed a set amount, and if the interest paid by the cooperative to the member is not higher than

Table 12-2
Italian PCs 1951-1971, by Industry

	1951		1961		1971	
	a	b	a	b	a	b
Extraction	103	4,706	145	3,463	93	1,882
Manufacturing[c]	496	12,013	604	17,373	486	13,175
Manufact. nonmetal						
mineral prod.	84	3,888	112	6,673	95	4,067
Mechanic	113	2,522	87	2,500	95	3,376
Textile	64	1,925	63	1,265	59	766
Timber	122	1,628	94	1,709	76	1,381
Other	113	2,050	248	5,226	161	3,585
Building	1,482	38,496	884	40,163	784	32,630
Total	2,081	55,215	1,633	60,999	1,363	47,687

Source: Census, 1951, 1961, 1971.

Notes: a = number of PCs: b = employment: c. cooperatives operating in Food and Tobacco industries are not considered. In fact, the vast majority of these are not PCs but agricultural cooperatives.

that defined by government authorities, then the remuneration of loan capital benefits from various tax reductions.[7]

Cooperatives must allocate no less than 20 percent of the current year's profits to a legal reserve fund. According to the statute of individual cooperatives, the remainder can be used to (a) remunerate capital under-written by the members within legal limits; (b) increase the reserve fund; (c) finance social and service activities; and (d) be distributed among the working members in proportion to the work done in the cooperative.[8]

Depending on the relative size of total salaries and wages compared to all other costs (excepting costs of raw and secondary materials), retained profits may be either exempt from or subjected to reduced rates of cor-porate and local income taxes. In addition, profits allocated to funds not apportionable among members—such as collectively owned reserves—are now exempt from corporate income tax.

The main organ of the PCs is the members' (general) assembly, which approves the budget and decides the profit distribution. It is possible, in the case of cooperatives comprising more than 500 members, to organize separate assemblies, each of which elects delegates to the general assembly. This assembly appoints the board of directors, which, in turn, must be com-posed of cooperative members or have a mandate from them.

One characteristic of the Italian cooperative movement is the promotion of close ties among cooperatives. Mention has already been made of the na-tional organizations of cooperatives formed since the end of the last century. Beyond these connections, other, more strictly economic forms developed during the early part of this century, known as cooperative consortia. Con-sortia are second-stage cooperatives; individual cooperatives make up a con-sortium. Early consortia were formed almost exclusively to participate in public contracting commissions. Subsequently, they were set up to carry out more complex and specific functions such as the common acquisition of machinery and raw materials, product research, exports, and procuring and use of financial resources. Consortia are similar to cooperatives in both struc-ture and regulations, except that the minimum number of members needed to set up a consortium is 5 instead of 9. Besides this, the underwritten capital cannot be less than a certain amount, presently not less than one million lire. With consortia eligible for public contracts, residual profits must be divided among a consortium's member cooperatives in proportion to the labor force of each (calculated either on wages or on workdays).

The Italian cooperative movement is unitary. All forms of cooperatives belong to the appropriate national organization or the "national associa-tion of representation, assistance and protection"—LNCM, CCI, or Associazione Generale delle Co-operative Italiane (AGCI). These associa-tions are recognized by the state under certain conditions. The main require-ment is to oversee the member cooperatives, and the control is performed by an inspection committee of the associations; member cooperatives are audited at least once every two years.

The national associations do not perform economic functions. They collect a contribution from the cooperatives, generally proportionate to their turnover, to be used exclusively to pay for representative and protectional activities. Nonetheless, the role played by these associations has never been reduced to the activities prescribed by the law. They have always tended toward promoting new cooperatives as well as "directing" and coordinating their growth, particularly through the political activity of setting up consortia.

Since 1947 a special credit institute for Italian cooperatives has existed, when the Banca Nazionale del Lavoro set up a special section for cooperative loans. But since this bank cannot collect savings from the public, this arrangement has severe limitations. Within the LNCM two associations organize PCs: the national association of PCs (ANCPL) includes PCs in construction and manufacturing. The national association of service cooperatives (ANCS) includes PCs mainly in transportation, cleaning, and maintenance.[9] Various consortia and companies also belong to the LNCM, which supplies services to all the member cooperatives. From the point of view of PCs, the most important of these are (a) Fincooper, a financial consortium; (b) Unipol, an insurance company; (c) The Agency for Technical Assistance; and (d) Intercoop, a consortium that works for all the cooperatives on an international commerce level, specializing in intercooperative trade.

Performance

In this section, I draw on research undertaken by the LNCM that examined social and economic aspects of large PCs that were members of the LNCM during 1975-1978.[10] Examined were 143 PCs, which sold goods and services valued at 915 billion lire in 1978 and employed 34, 246 workers. The 79 construction PCs represented 55.2 percent of all PCs, and accounted for 74.3 percent of the total turnover, 73.3 percent of the employed workers, and 76.4 percent of the membership. The distinction between cooperatives in the building and the manufacturing industries is useful apart from industrial-sectoral differences. There are considerable differences, in terms of formation patterns, size, and features of the markets each type of enterprise is directed toward; all these factors suggest separate industry analyses of the phenomena.

With regard to formation, in large part in the construction sector, PCs originated from independent initiatives on the part of groups of workers. Manufacturing PCs, however, nearly always were the result of the failure of private enterprises. On average, construction PCs are larger than those operating in private industry. The former had an average of 339 workers and sales of 6,696 billion lire in 1978, while the latter had sales of 3,676 billion lire and provided employment for 116 workers. Construction-sector cooperatives make much use of consortia and work mostly on orders, whereas manufacturing cooperatives are present on the market individually and in sectors that are generally characterized by heavy competition. Construction PCs usually are older than manufacturing PCs. Of the former, 75 percent were founded before 1950; only 50 percent of manufacturing PCs were founded before then.

Examining construction PCs more closely, in 1978, as a group, their sales turnover was a little more than 680 billion lire, and 26,807 people were employed, of whom 18,492 were members. As for their size distribution, 24.1 percent had fewer than 100 workers, 69.6 percent employed from 100 to 1,000, and 6.3 percent provided jobs for more than 1,000 workers.

During the four-year period studied, the number of construction PCs dropped from 104 to 79. This was the result of a merger policy promoted by the consortia and by the representative associations during the seventies. Its purpose was to adjust the cooperative structures to new market demands and competition.

Turnover, value added, and employment all increased during the four-year period at respective annual rates of 32.9, 31.8, and 7.0 percent. Since for construction as a whole costs rose 17.5 percent, valued added rose 18.6 percent and employment fell by 0.5 percent, these are very significant trends. In the same period, PCs' fixed assets increased annually by 37.4 percent. On average, from 1975 to 1978 members of PCs comprised 70.6 percent of the jobholders. However, this average conceals a trend toward diminishing membership, dropping from 72.4 percent in 1975 to 69.0 percent in 1978. An analysis of the balance sheet and of the profit-and-loss accounts shows that the contribution made by members to cooperatives' financing, in terms of share capital, is very low. However, this was compensated by polices aimed at limiting the distribution of profits to members (or of favoring reinvestment in collectively owned assets) and boosting the utilization of members' resources through loans. In 1978, reserves that came from allocations of nondistributed profits were 9 times higher, and members' loans were 3.4 times higher, in absolute value, than the value of underwritten capital.[11]

Available data on capitalist firms and PCs operating in the same sectors are not completely uniform, and must therefore be evaluated cautiously when comparing performance. Nevertheless, they do give us some elements that are worth noting. I first compared PCs with the total of all active construction companies in Italy having more than 50 employees.[12] I then concentrated attention on the results given by surveys of the largest non-cooperative enterprises in construction (see Mediobanca 1979). Of all construction companies with more than 50 employees, PCs turned out to be by far the most dynamic. Table 12-3A shows comparative growth rates. Table 12-4A records evidence on various indicators of economic performance. Though value added per worker typically is higher in capitalist firms (in 1978 by about 14 percent), since capital-labor ratios are much lower in PCs than in capitalist firms (in 1978 by about 39 percent), it seems that in terms of total factor productivity PCs in fact perform better than do capitalist firms. Also there is a slight but increasing difference in the labor cost per worker.[13] PCs also experienced much higher rates of profit than did capitalist firms, both with respect to sales (turnover) and expressed as a fraction of own funds. Considerable differences also exist regarding financial charges. For PCs, in fact, charges are a little over half of what they are for capitalist firms in the same industry.

Surveyed were 64 manufacturing PCs, the sales of which amounted to 235 billion lire, employment 7,439 persons, and membership 5,717. On average, manufacturing PCs are much smaller than construction PCs. In 1978, 64.1 percent of the companies had fewer than 100 workers, 29.7 percent from 100 to 300 workers, and only 6.2 percent gave jobs to more than 300 people. The sectors involved were also varied: 30.5 percent operated in metal working; 18.8 percent in the wood and furnishing industry; 14.1 percent in sectors connected to building; 6.3 percent in glass, and 28.1 percent in various others.

The survey results, details from which are reported in tables 12-3B and 12-4B, show that manufacturing PCs have enjoyed rapid growth, although at a slower rate than the construction PCs. Sales, value added, and employment have increased during the period examined at annual rates of 27.9, 24.4, and 3.4 percent, respectively. During the same period, the prices of industrial products and finished products in Italian industry have increased annually by 15.8 and 15.2 percent, whereas employment decreased annually by 4.6 percent. Contrary to what has taken place among building PCs, the phenomenon of combinations of PCs was not particularly prevalent during this period. In fact, only one case occurred of two metal-working PCs merging. Manufacturing PCs have a slightly higher percentage of working members than do building-sector PCs. From 70.1 percent worker membership in 1975 there was an increase to 73.3 percent in 1978. It must be pointed out that the number of members out of the total number of workers varies considerably from sector to sector. In 1978, the highest ratio was 96.6 percent in the glass sector and the lowest 64.7 percent in building materials. The employment increase registered in 1975-1978 was accompanied by strong investment activity. Fixed assets increased at an annual rate of 25.6 percent.

An analysis of the balance sheet structure and profit-and-loss accounts of manufacturing PCs allows one to identify features similar to those of

Table 12-3

Growth of Capitalist Firms and Producer Cooperatives in Construction and Manufacturing, 1975-1978

	1976/1975			1977/1976			1978/1977		
	PC	C	LC	PC	C	LC	PC	C	LC
A. Construction									
Turnover	39.4	11.8	14.6	39.7	21.1	22.3	20.8	11.6	7.4
Employment	13.6	−9.6	3.1	4.2	−2.8	−3.3	4.9	−7.0	−4.4
Value added	40.5	14.1	16.6	35.0	20.8	22.4	20.6	12.5	9.0
Fixed assets	48.2	—	16.0	28.8	—	16.7	35.8	—	9.5

	1976/1975			1977/1976			1978/1977		
	PC	SC	MC	PC	SC	MC	PC	SC	MC
B. Manufacture									
Turnover	37.8	34.0	27.2	28.6	21.0	19.9	17.9	12.1	12.2
Employment	5.2	−1.3	−0.7	4.1	−0.5	−2.2	0.9	−2.2	−3.4
Value added	33.9	28.7	24.0	28.1	19.8	18.1	12.6	11.6	12.6
Fixed assets	25.0	—	15.3	31.0	—	12.1	21.0	—	11.9

Source: Data on cooperatives from Lega survey. Data for capitalist firms calculated from Mediobanca (1979) and ISTAT (various editions).

Notes: PC = producer cooperatives; C = capitalist firms with more than 50 employees; LC = large capitalist firms (share capital of more than 10 billion lire), SC = capitalist firms with 50–500 employees; MC = capitalist firms with share capital of less than 1 billion lire.

All entries are growth rates.

building PCs. Share capital is seen to always play a limited role, even though it constitutes a higher share of financial activity than in construction PCs. Capital underwritten per member was 105.4 percent higher in 1978 than in building PCs. Reserves and members' loans, even though of considerable size, are in absolute value, respectively, 4.1 and 1.4 times greater than share capital. These cooperatives carry sizable debts, higher than in either the building sector or private enterprises. The composition of debt is more similar to that of capitalist enterprises (with elevated short-, medium-, and long-term agreements with banks) than it is to PCs active in the construction sector. Charges are consequently high with respect to turnover, and higher than those of construction PCs.

The data for PCs were then compared with data for other Italian enterprises employing from 50 to 500 persons and with the data available from surveys of medium-size firms,[14] (see table 12-3B). In this case, as with building, sales and employment in PCs grew much faster than in capitalist firms between 1975 and 1978. Furthermore, compared to large capitalist manufacturing firms (MC), while value added per worker in PCs was about 16 percent lower, fixed assets per worker were 30 percent lower. That is, manufacturing PCs may be more productive once allowance is made for

Table 12-4

Comparative Productivity of Capitalist Firms and Producer Cooperatives in Construction and Manufacturing, 1975–1978

		1975	1976	1977	1978
A. Construction					
v.a./employee					
	PC	—	8,157	10,133	11,778
	C	7,059	8,905	11,065	13,386
	LC	8,539	9,649	12,206	13,921
l.c./employee					
	PC	—	6,428	7,840	9,236
	C	5,115	6,458	7,980	9,600
	LC	6,203	7,444	9,235	10,659
f.a./employee					
	PC	—	5,184	6,148	8,045
	LC	8,499	9,441	11,348	13,036
f.ch./turnover (%)					
	PC	2.4	2.6	3.2	3.7
	C	4.5	5.0	6.0	6.0
	LC	9.4	9.1	9.5	9.3
profit/turnover (%)					
	PC	3.9	3.5	4.5	3.7
	LC	−0.2	—	0.3	0.2
profit/own funds (%)					
	PC	18.7	18.9	24.1	20.3
	LC	−0.9	0.1	1.4	0.9
B. Manufacturing					
v.a./employee					
	PC	—	9,174	11,233	12,348
	SC	7,113	9,272	11,165	12,745
	MC	8,403	10,499	12,681	14,768
l.c./employee					
	PC	—	6,656	7,951	8,888
	SC	5,283	6,561	7,847	8,979
	MC	6,547	7,791	9,244	10,729
f.a./employee					
	PC	—	8,196	10,262	12,120
	MC	11,257	13,078	15,000	17,354
f.ch./turnover (%)					
	PC	4.7	4.9	6.0	5.3
	MC	4.8	4.8	4.8	4.4
profit/turnover (%)					
	PC	1.9	2.0	3.4	4.5
	MC	−0.8	0.5	0.2	0.6
profit/own funds (%)					
	PC	7.7	10.7	21.0	28.1
	MC	−3.9	2.4	1.2	3.4

Source: Data on cooperatives are taken from the LNCM survey. Data for capitalist firms taken from Mediobanca (1979) and ISTAT, various editions.

Notes: PC = producer cooperatives; C = capitalist firms with more than 50 workers; LC = large capitalist firms (share capital of more than 10 billion lire); SC = capitalist firm with 50–500 employees; MC = capitalist firms with share capital of less than 1 billion lire. v.a. = value added; l.c. = labor cost; f.a. = fixed assets; f.ch. = financial charges.

All entries, except percentages, are in thousands of lire and are in current prices.

variation in capital endowments. Rates of profit are also considerably higher in PCs than in other enterprises.

Summary and Interpretation

Three conclusions follow from the preceeding discussion. First, LNCM PCs have shown high growth rates during the period 1975-1978. Related to this, growth of PCs seems to be concentrated during the 1970s, after a lengthy period of standstill. Second, during 1975-1978 PCs were more dynamic than capitalist firms, enjoying faster rates of sales and employment growth. PCs also recorded better rates of profit and maybe higher levels of productivity. Last, considerable differences exist between PCs in construction and those in manufacturing.

Given the general level at which I have analyzed the available data, it is not possible to comprehensively discuss the reasons behind PCs' behavior. The circumstances that influenced the trends described are undoubtedly many and varied; a deeper and more detailed treatment is needed before undertaking a thorough discussion. The following tentative remarks are offered primarily as a means of indicating some possible future research topics.

In explaining the recent growth in the number of Italian PCs it is perhaps noteworthy that the 1970s were characterized in Italy by a broad and constantly increasing participation by citizens and workers in every aspect of the economic, social, and political life of the country. This suggests that there is a close link between the broadening of the basis of democracy and thus participation on the one hand, and the spreading of cooperative initiatives (in all forms, including PCs) on the other. This same phenomenon occurred at the turn of the century and in the periods immediately following both World Wars. It is difficult to specify the ways in which the growing "demand" for cooperative organization ("demand" that is reflected in the growth in the number of cooperatives during the indicated periods), can reflect upon the performance of PCs already in existence. There does seem to be, however, a relationship between broadening of the democratic base and success levels reached by PCs.

In accounting for the better performance of PCs compared to capitalist firms, it does not seem that this can be explained in terms of the lower cost of various factors. In fact, when there are discernible differences in the two enterprise systems between the incomes of labor and/or the cost of capital, they can be attributed to differences in capital-labor ratios and to dissimilar composition and utilization of both these factors. Remuneration differentials are important. White-collar workers in PCs typically receive lower incomes than do their capitalist counterparts. In some areas there are limits placed on remuneration differentials within single PCs.[15] In this situation it is essential to evaluate whether the lower remuneration has been compensated by structures identifiable with the enterprise that cannot be found in capitalist companies, and to what degree the differences with respect to the capitalist enterprises can be maintained over a long period.

Most PCs examined are located in areas that typically enjoy high activity rates and relatively high wage levels. This is true not only of the years included in the study, but also at least from the middle of the sixties. Therefore, while the PCs studied have shown that they are capable of maintaining and even increasing job levels, it must be remembered that they accomplished this in a situation of almost full employment.

At the same time, with regard to labor, it should be noted that the labor market during the seventies was especially difficult for Italian enterprises. This was expressed in lower variability of employment, which began to take on the features of a fixed cost. In many ways, this fact put private businesses in the same conditions as PCs.

Concerning capital, there were developments that might have brought operating conditions of capitalist firms closer to those of PCs. During recent years in Italy, it has been increasingly difficult for all businesses (but particularly the larger enterprises) to obtain venture capital and to secure medium- and long-term credit. In this circumstance, one of the greatest problems of PCs in a capitalist economy (difficulties involved in securing external capital) was probably partially camouflaged by the fact that all other enterprises found themselves in a similar situation.

Also, the ability of PCs to obtain capital recently has benefited from the special relationship between worker members and PCs. Attracted by high yields and low risks, members have greatly increased loans made to PCs. Furthermore, despite the inability to individually recuperate investments allocated out of surplus to collective funds, the 1970s witnessed increasing internal reinvestment. This apparent contradiction with the prediction of Vanek's theory of financing (Vanek 1971 in Vanek (ed.) 1975) is perhaps explained by individual members being interested in long-term job security rather than in maximizing immediate income per worker.

In accounting for differences among PCs, in part this reflects exogenous differences among the sectors within which PCs operate. But there are also important endogenous differences that deserve more careful analysis. These factors include the role of the consortia, the relationships between the PCs and the market, and the ways in which PCs are created. To recapitulate, substantial use is made of the consortia structure by building PCs. While the consortia act principally to secure contracts, they also carry out financing activities, backing the member cooperatives mostly through advance payments. Manufacturing PCs have developed this same instrument only partially. The positive role of the consortia clearly can be interpreted as being consistent with those who argue that viable PC sectors require shelter organizations (Vanek 1975, introduction). A thorough analysis of the relationship binding consortia and PCs seems therefore to be both useful and necessary.

Building PCs approach the market differently than do other PCs. The problem is to estimate the degree to which building PCs' capacity for rapid growth depends on this factor. Not to be overlooked are the various origins of the PCs themselves. The question to be considered here is: To what degree does having been established subsequent to the failure of a capitalist enterprise (and this is the most prevalent factor common to the manufacturing PCs) compromise or at least obstruct potential growth?

Finally, when tackling these and other research topics, it is likely that behavioral investigations will need, as points of departure, models of PCs that assume objective functions that are far more complex than those usually adopted in much of the formal economic theory of labor management. For example, in many Italian PCs job security for the membership seems to be an important objective, even if it is at odds with maximizing per-worker income of existing members.

Notes

1. For more detailed accounts see Basevi (1953), Dal Pane (1966), Fabbri (1979), and Sapelli (ed.) (1981).

2. In 1952 a small number of cooperatives seceded from the Lega and a third federation, the Associazione Generale delle Co-operative Italiane was established.

3. Note that, since different sources are used in constructing tables 12-1 and 12-2, the two tables are not directly comparable.

4. The minimum membership for PCs that participate in public contracts is 25. A further condition in this case is that the number of nonmember workers cannot be greater than the number of worker-members.

5. Until 1971, technical and administrative members could not constitute more than 4 percent of the worker-membership. Until 1947 members of PCs participating in public contracting could be only workers.

6. This figure is the result of a provision of December 30, 1980. Previously the maximum was 6 million lire.

7. Currently, the most a member can lend to his or her cooperative is 17 million lire. The maximum interest that the cooperative can pay is 13.5 percent. The member must pay a 10 percent tax on this, instead of the 20 percent tax to be paid on interest derived from other uses of capital (stocks and bonds, saving deposits, etc.). These provisions, although subject to

much modification, were introduced in the cooperative law ratified in 1971. Even though members' loans were frequent previous to this, they underwent remarkable growth thereafter.

8. Individual cooperatives may have bylaws providing for the distribution of profits among nonmember employees. In many cooperatives belonging to the Lega, the "auxilliaries" (the name commonly given to nonmember workers) benefit to the same degree as the members in the profit distribution.

9. The ANCS began in 1975. Previously all PCs belonged to a single organization.

10. Since 1979, the Lega has made annual surveys of the largest member cooperatives in each sector (see LNCM 1979, 1980). The comparisons drawn in the following pages are based on the fundamental data from these surveys.

11. The per-worker loan, share capital, and reserve figures were, respectively, 2297, 667, and 5975 thousands of lire in 1978.

12. See ISTAT, *Supplemento al Bollettino mensile di Statistica,* various years.

13. Regarding this, it must be noted that PCs show varying employment make-up. The ratio of white- to blue-collar workers for PCs in 1978 equaled 12.0 percent as opposed to 15.4 percent for all industries in this sector with over 50 employees.

14. The comparison with medium-size enterprises must be made very carefully. On average, capitalist firms employ about double the number of workers compared to PCs. Also, the fields of activity of the two groups of manufacturing firms are rather different. See ISTAT, various years, and Mediobanca (1979).

15. In the province of Ravenna, in PCs belonging to the LNCM, the highest pay level can be no more than 2.7 times more than the lowest. Market conditions, however, are urging that these limits be changed.

Part V
Participation Elsewhere

(in D.C. Jones and Jan Svejnar ed.)
Participatory and self managed firms
Lexington Books 1983
Bubien D.C. Lexington Book
D.C Heath and company
Lexington Books

13

Changing Values and Preferences in Communal Organizations: Econometric Evidence from the Experience of the Israeli Kibbutz

Avner Ben-Ner

The presence of communes has been recorded throughout human history. In modern times, communes have appeared and disappeared like comets. Their disappearance has often been taken as a demonstration of their inability to survive and as a proof of their failure, and of the failure of the communal ideas upon which they were founded.

In the first section of this chapter, I argue that the generally inevitable economic and social interaction between communes and a larger and dominant noncommunal environment brings about a gradual decommunalization in the values and objectives of communes' members. To accommodate the transformed values, the economic structure and system of communes will be transformed up to the point of their demise qua communes and their transformation into private for-profit organizations. This transformation is likely to occur regardless of the probable superiority of communes over private for-profit firms in terms of economic efficiency.

From this theoretical proposition a testable hypothesis is formulated, suggesting that preferences over collective versus private consumption have changed in a direction that indicates decommunalization of values in the Israeli kibbutz movement. A simple economic model of the kibbutz is constructed that is employed to estimate revealed preferences in the kibbutz movement from cross-sectional data in 1955 and 1965, using a "seemingly

I have greatly benefited from comments by, and conversations with, Edward Ames and Egon Neuberger. Most helpful comments were also received from many individuals, including Michael Burawoy, Michael Hurd, Estelle James, John Michael Montias, Richard Nelson, Charles Perrow, Louis Putterman, John Winn, the editors of this book, and from participants at the Symposium on the Economic Performance of Participatory and Labor-Managed Firms, and seminars at Yale University, University of Pennsylvania, and Harvard University. Haim Barkai was helpful in several ways: making the data, including several computed variables, available to me; encouraging this research; and, in general, setting the stage for empirical study of communes. It is my fault, and that of the space limitations, that I have not used all comments received; I maintain responsibility for errors of any kind. William Bidwell's assistance in editing the English and Beth Summers' skillful typing are acknowledged with gratitude. The paper was compiled while I was a research associate at the Program on Non-Profit Organizations at the Institution for the Social and Policy Studies and lecturer in economics, Yale University.

unrelated nonlinear regression equations" technique. Changes in the preferences between these years are assessed using a "counterfactual" method. Given the fact that the methods employed are novel and yet unrefined, and because of the difficulties posed by availability of data, the empirical results—which confirm the hypothesis—should be considered as suggestive rather than conclusive.

While concluding from a review of empirical literature that the kibbutz is at least as economically efficient as other types of economic organizations in the Israeli economy the essay suggests that it is likely that communal organizations such as the kibbutz, operating in private-market economies, will converge to the most prevalent, the private for-profit type of organization. The final section summarizes and concludes the chapter.

Communes, Environment, and Decommunalization of Values and Economic Structure

A commune may be defined as follows: a voluntary association of "free individuals carrying on their work with the means of production in common, in which the labour-power of all different individuals is consciously applied as the combined labour-power of the community"[1]; an organization where economic decision making encompasses simultaneously the spheres of production, investment, and consumption. Consumption is distributed in an egalitarian fashion, mostly in the form of collective consumption, severing most connections between individual contribution to production and remuneration in the form of consumption. A commune is also an economic, social, and very often religious and political entity with well-defined boundaries, with generally highly democratic organization (relative to other contemporary institutions), striving toward "harmony, brotherhood, mutual support, and value expression."[2]

In general, it is useful to define *demise* of organizations as the disappearance of specific organizations either via bankruptcy (being unable to meet financial responsibilities), by simple extinction as members leave the organization, or by transformation into a different type of organization.[3] In the literature on communes (and cooperatives, to which communes are closely related) several reasons for their demise have been suggested.[4] An additional cause that seems to account for a large number of cases of demise of communes via organizational transformation is related to the interaction between communes and their environment.

Communes, as organizations marginal (in terms of their size) to the larger society and economy, tend, over the long run, through necessary incessant interactions with this society, to adopt that society's values and norms. This change in the values of a commune's membership will then be reflected in a restructuring of the organization and its economic structure and system to reflect less communal values; ultimately, the nature of the organization itself will be changed.

Interactions between communes and their noncommunal environment occur at various levels and cannot be totally avoided even by the most isolationist of communes. This is all the more true of integrated economies in which various units are interconnected on the market. Because of their small size, communes cannot rely on a strictly autarkic economy; they have strong economic incentives to participate in market transactions in order to take advantage of benefits from trade. Trade opens channels of impact or routes by which the noncommunal environment influences the activities, opportunities, and, eventually, the values of commune members: production, marketing, and consumption.

In order to participate in trade a commune has to produce tradeables. In most cases this implies competition with other economic enterprises, which, in turn, requires communes to be able to produce in a competitive way. This necessitates adoption of the best available technologies for production.[5] In a competitive market economy, the "menu" of such technologies will be rather limited. If the available technologies carry with them social attributes such as the necessity for a minute division of labor and separation between planning and execution (see, for example, Braverman 1974), this opens an avenue for the introduction of inegalitarian practices, and, eventually, inegalitarian attitudes, at the workplace. Furthermore, these technologies are said to be alienating, deskilling, and uninvolving for those working with them. Thus this process is likely to have a negative impact on communal values.

Profitable use of many types of capital equipment demands more than one daily shift. This, of course, is quite antithetical to communal life, which involves on-the-job and after-work interaction among members; such interaction is substantially impaired by shift work. In order to avoid underutilization of capital, communes may also resort to "outside help"—hired wage laborers. In addition to the dangers to the existence of communes as communes stemming from the incentive to hire workers that are cheaper than members (Ben-Ner 1981), the presence of hired wage laborers on the commune has several aspects that are antagonistic to communalism. Since their work incentives are different from, and possibly opposite to, those of the commune members-owners, hired wage laborers have to be supervised for the "proper" fulfillment of their jobs. Thus, members become supervisors and engage in "payment to workers according to observed results"—practices not to be tolerated among members. Moreover, paying wages to some of the workers on the commune introduces a cash nexus that most communes try, for good reasons, to avoid.

Goods produced on the commune have to marketed. Commune members have to engage, on behalf of the commune, in capitalist competition—something not very compatible with communal norms and values. Commune representatives have to adopt business attitudes acceptable to the noncommunal majority of their business associates. In addition, they may require special amenities as simple instruments of their own labor: special clothes for representation, cars, telephones, per-diem expenses, and so on and so forth. Since these items are not available to the majority of commune members, their assignment to some introduces another inegalitarian aspect to the commune's life. And, in view of the professionalization of many such jobs, this inequality is not easily remediable through the venerable communal solution of job rotation.[6]

Communes sell in order to buy. The purchasing of goods and services is another activity that increases the contacts of the commune with the environment in a specific way: according to the rules of competition and to individualistic consumerism. To be sure, I am not suggesting here that the mere exposure to goods of a private nature, coupled with an increased income derived from sales on the market, necessitates an increased purchase of those goods. (This represents an income effect; as argued below, changes in preferences have an independent but complementary impact on consumption patterns). All that is argued at this stage is that exposure to noncommunal categories of consumption goods leaves a noncommunal imprint on the values of those who are exposed to them.

Clearly, there are other more direct means whereby the values and norms of the noncommunal environment are offered to, and impressed upon, communes' members. Mass media fulfill an important role in this respect. The compulsory educational system designed by the (noncommunal) state is another important channel for the transmission of the environment's values.[7]

Communes do not stand helpless in the face of this "destined" decommunalization of values. The phenomena mentioned in the previous paragraphs have been well known to commune members everywhere and in all times, and various attempts have been made to moderate their impact. These range from attempts to prohibit all unnecessary mingling with hired wage laborers or, conversely, trying to bring them as near as possible to the status of members through participation in decision-making and sharing in profits, through attempts to prohibit the introduction of outside mass-media instruments or to supplant those with commune (or communal movement) instruments, to attempts to prohibit all member-travel outside the commune except for that for necessary business affairs. Importantly, communes attempt to transfer their values to their new generations through educational means and through day-to-day socialization in communal living. In general, a picture of a struggle between sets of values emerges from the experience of communes, regardless of time or location. The larger the number of communes in the environment of any given commune, and the greater the interaction among the communes, the smaller the net impact of the noncommunal environment's values on the commune members.

There are additional countervailing factors in the process described above. A noncommunal environment does not produce a uniform set of values, all noncommunal. After all, it also producers the very conditions for the establishment of communes. It is necessary, however, to distinguish between the factors that bring members of the environment to join or establish communes, and the factors that influence the values of commune members in the direction of decommunalization. While the birth of some communes may occur simultaneously with the demise of others, the two events may be considered separately for analytical purposes.

Capitalist economic development in general brings about the weakening or even the severance of various group ties, exchange orientation, and a shifting of the commitment of individuals from larger groups (for example, extended families) to more limited groups (for example, nuclear families). Values and relations characteristics of Gemeinschaft are replaced with values and relations characteristic of Gesellschaft.[8] During the same process of capitalist economic development communes become more integrated in the economy and society, their physical isolation is threatened, and their permeability increases. Accordingly, communes are likely to adapt their values to those of a developing capitalist society that are antagonistic to communal values. Collective-public orientation of members is weakened and is gradually replaced by individual-private orientation. Members reorient themselves so that smaller groups such as their natural families replace the commune as the primary reference group.

However, the economic and social organization of a commune is geared to satisfy needs of a collective rather than a private character. Thus, in the course of time, the communal form of organization no longer suits the new values and objectives of members and is replaced by a more privately oriented type of organization,[9] culminating with a transformation into a private for-profit organization.[10]

The Kibbutz in Context

During the first two decades after the establishment of the State of Israel, its economy and society went through major transformations. The economy expanded rapidly; for example, during the period 1950-1965 the real gross national product (in 1955 prices) increased more than five times (and more than 2.5 times per capita), and private consumption grew more than 4 times (more than twice per capita), and public consumption, including military expenditure, over 3.5 times (more than 1.7 times per capita). Over the same period (1950-1965) the population grew from 1.266 million to 2.566 million.

These developments were accompanied—and probably facilitated—by the fast development of an economic infrastructure and institutions characteristic of developed economies. More and more economic units started to produce for the national and international markets rather than for local or regional ones. Domestic and international flow of capital expanded very fast and was encouraged by the government, which also gave massive support to private capital accumulation. The concentration of private capital increased considerably, and the distribution of income became increasingly unequal, along the patterns of developed countries and unlike those of the Jewish prestate society. The society also grew more differentiated, and classes became more distinct compared to the relatively homogeneous prestate period. Thus, compared to most other countries, Israel has gone through a very rapid economic and social capitalist development.[11]

The kibbutz movement reached maturity long ago. By 1936, 27 years after the establishment of the first kibbutz, 47 kibbutzim were in existence with a population of 10,575; in 1951 there were 189 kibbutzim with a population of 64,523; and in 1972 the number of kibbutzim was 235 with a population of 101,103 (Barkai 1977, p. 249). The findings of the few studies that have attempted to study the kibbutz's internal organization, economic efficiency, and contribution to the country's welfare in a comparative manner indicate fairly strongly that on these grounds at least, the kibbutz is a successful form of organization.

Matching, according to the type of product they produced, 6 kibbutz factories with 6 privately-owned factories in Israel, Seymour Melman (in Horvat et al. 1975) found that in terms of productivity of labor, productivity of capital, efficiency of management (net profit per production worker), and cost of enterprise administration (administrative staff per 100 production workers) the kibbutz factory appears to be superior to the privately owned factory.[12]

On the basis of a very comprehensive empirical study of the Israeli kibbutzim, Haim Barkai concludes: "The empirical study of production and income distribution . . . shows that . . . the kibbutz as a collective unit has shown that it has performed no worse, to say the least, than its market counterparts both as regards efficiency and saving rates" (1977, p. viii). Barkai (1978) found that in the 12 years between 1954 and 1965 the (value of) marginal product of labor (in constant Israeli lira) grew about 3.5 times. And this growth was not due to excessive capital (or land) intensities. The rate of return to capital in agriculture had been high and rising (with fluctuations, from 6.6 percent in 1954 to 14.1 percent in 1965), coupled with more than a doubling of the capital-labor ratio. Similarly, in manufacturing, "very high gross real rates of return were maintained in the very period in which capital-labor ratios in manufacturing almost doubled. This means

that in manufacturing, as in agriculture, the rapidly rising marginal productivity of labor cannot be explained in terms of 'excessive' capital intensity''
(ibid., p. 110).[13]

In manufacturing, the nominal rates of return on capital in the kibbutzim were much higher than the marginal rates paid by kibbutzim for commercial credits, and the net real rates of return (of 10 percent and more)
were higher than the real rates of interest that the Israeli government and
financial institutions had to pay for foreign credit. Similar results apply
with regard to agriculture (Barkai 1978, pp. 11-12). The real net rates of
return were higher in manufacturing than in agriculture; consequently, in
the period under consideration (as well as in later years), kibbutzim invested
considerably more in the former than in the latter. Barkai concludes that,
given the findings regarding the rates of return on capital, the (value of)
marginal product of labor was consistently and considerably higher than
comparable market wages, and given the pattern of kibbutz investment,
kibbutz economic behavior must be considered as economically efficient.

From an analysis of the kibbutz economic system in terms of the
decision-making, motivation and information structures, the features of a
highly efficient system emerge. Additionally, the study of an economic
model of the kibbutz (of which a simplified version is presented below)
reveals that the kibbutz method of allocation of resources is compatible
with rational economic calculation (Ben-Ner 1981, chapters III and VI).[14]

The kibbutz movement has been participating in the country's
economic, social, political, and cultural life ever since the establishment of
the first kibbutz in 1909. The decreasing portion of Israel's Jewish population—a better yardstick than the entire population—involved in the kibbutz
movement (from about 8 percent in 1948 to slightly over 3 percent twenty
years later), the intensification of the market economy and the movement's
greater reliance on it, and the general developments outlined above brought
about a qualitative change in the nature of the kibbutzim's involvement in
the Israeli economy and society and an increase in the degree of their
permeability.

The developments in the Israeli economy were followed by changes in
the values of the Israeli society. The clear trend was from Gemeinschaft
values to Gesselschaft values, from collective-public to individual-private
orientation.[15] Social scientists have noted that the change in the values of
kibbutz members followed the trend in the values of the general Israeli
society.[16] This was put very succinctly by Yehuda Don, quoting Menachem
Rosner: "Fast economic growth, which induced materialistic thinking 'was
saturated with disintegrating elements for both solidarity and collectivism,
for society in general as well as for the kibbutz itself' " (Don 1977, p. 59).

Against the background of the picture of the kibbutz as an apparently
efficient and successful economic organization, I turn now to the assess-

ment of changes in the values of kibbutz members over the period from 1955 to 1965.

Changing Values in the Kibbutz Movement

Values and Preferences

Most attempts of social scientists to measure norms, values, and attitudes of people employ a questionnaire technique, and sometimes historical case studies.[17] I adopt a different strategy for the evaluation of changes in communal values. This strategy is based on replacing values by preferences over economic variables, and substituting the analysis of respondents' answers with an analysis of their actual behavior.

Let me first give a somewhat simplistic and circular—but nonetheless useful—definition of communal values: these are values held by people who view the communal type of organization as superior to other types of microorganization. I would argue that communal values have counterparts in terms of preferences over economic variables.

It is possible to classify kibbutz consumption in three ways:

1. Mode of distribution: *free distribution* (goods and services that are free and available to the individual member in unlimited quantities; for example, food, electricity, water, medical aid, children's education, child rearing, on-the-kibbutz cultural events, laundry services); *quota, or rationed, distribution* (goods and services that are allocated to members in equal amounts determined by kibbutz decision-making organs, for example, housing, furniture, clothing, durables, vacation trips abroad); *personal monetary allowance* (equal small money allowance to be spent at the individual member's discretion, equivalent to "pocket money"); and *satisfaction of special needs* (items not included in the consumption menu of the kibbutz, or extra allocation of rationed items, for example, higher education, some musical instruments, medical care, financial help to relatives living off the kibbutz);

2. Mode of consumption: *collective consumption* (goods and services that are consumed collectively by many members, including all local public goods; for example, meals in the communal dining hall, child rearing, child education, on-the-kibbutz cultural and social events, laundry, tailoring, and similar services), and *private consumption;*

3. Locus of production: *on the kibbutz,* and *outside the kibbutz* (purchased by the kibbutz on the market).

The three categories of (a) free goods and services, (b) collective consumption, and (c) consumption goods and services produced on the kibbutz for its own consumption, all cover to a large extent the same set of goods and services. For convenience, I will call these *collective consumption* goods and services,[18] and the rest *private consumption* goods and services. In light of the earlier discussion of this chapter, it can be seen without further elaboration that the intensity of preferences over collective versus private consumption is highly positively correlated with the intensity of communal values.

In sum, I intend to measure the change in the intensity of preferences over collective consumption versus private consumption as an indication of a change in the same direction in the degree of communalism of values. A simple consideration of the trend in the relative levels of the two categories of consumption is probably what comes first to mind for measuring such changes. However, this measures the communalism of the economic structure and system[19] but not necessarily the communalism of preferences. Income, technology, prices, and other effects may be responsible for relative changes in the consumption basket without any accompanying changes in preferences (or even with contradictory changes in preferences). Consequently, it is necessary to look directly at the preferences of kibbutzim, and compare them over time.

Several methods for the estimation of preferences have been suggested in the literature.[20] In this section I follow common practices by attempting to learn about kibbutzim's preferences as these preferences are revealed by their actual economic behavior, which I assume to be derived from optimization principles. Changes in preferences will be assessed using "counterfactual" methods.

An Economic Model of the Kibbutz

The model of the kibbutz specified below in functional form is a simplified version of that discussed in detail in Ben-Ner (1981, chapter VI) and adapted to data limitations and computational complexities. The unit of observation was chosen to be the individual kibbutz and not the individual member.[21]

The first two arguments in the kibbutz objective function are collective consumption, which is produced on the kibbutz; and private consumption, which is purchased on the market. The remaining three arguments are related to work in various production branches (three, in this model: industry, agriculture, and production of collective consumption). They indicate kibbutz preferences over various attributes associated with work (for example, member involvement in decision-making and nonhierarchical organization, job rotation, work environment, possibility for personal fulfillment, social relations at work, and so on), which vary with the technologies and other features of various kibbutz branches. From this point of view, the kibbutz is not indifferent with regard to the branches in which members work.

This kibbutz objective function is assumed to be maximized subject to labor and income constraints.[22] The labor constraint assumes a fixed amount of members' labor-days available to the kibbutz. The income constraint asserts that the total revenues from proceeds from sales of agricultural and industrial goods on the market, which are produced solely for that purpose, minus the monetary cost of using capital (either paying for rental or replacing worn-out capital) in all production branches, minus the costs of purchasing private consumption on the market, plus the net exogenous income of the kibbutz, has to be equal to zero:

$$\max W = u_1 H_3 + u_2 X + u_3 H_1 A_{11} + u_4 H_2 A_{12} + u_5 H_3 A_{13} \qquad (13.1)$$

$$- \tfrac{1}{2}(M_1 H_3^2 + M_2 X^2 + 2N H_3 X)$$

$$- \lambda_1 (H_1 A_{11} + H_2 A_{12} + H_3 A_{13} - L)$$

$$- \lambda_2 (H_1(1 - r_1 A_{21}) + H_2(1 - r_2 A_{22}) - H_3 r_3 A_{23} - X + D)$$

Decision variables: H_1, H_2, H_3, X.
[Comments in squared parentheses in the definitions below refer to issues of direct empirical relevance for the estimation of preferences].

u_1, u_2, u_3, u_4, u_5, M_1, M_2, and N: parameters of kibbutz objective function;

λ_1, λ_2: Lagrangean multipliers associated with the two constraints;

H_1: the value added of industrial output (revenue minus material and services costs);

H_2: the value added of agricultural output (revenue minus material and services costs);

H_3: the value of collective consumption goods and services [(calculated by Barkai and included in the data set). Since H_3 is produced on the kibbutz, and does not have clear counterparts on the market, its value was estimated using market wages for imputation of labor input plus the market value of services of consumer capital, including services of housing and communal structures (see also Barkai 1977, pp. 125, 148)];

X: the value of private consumption goods and services (bought on the market);

L: members' total labor-days in production branches (H_1 = industry, H_2 = agriculture, H_3 = collective consumption). [Unfortunately, only total kibbutz payments to hired wage laborers were available in the data set, but not their input in labor-days (or according to branch breakdown). Consequently, hired wage laborers were treated as a constant neutral factor in production and included in the kibbutz's net exogenous income, D];

D: net exogenous income [includes kibbutz income from assets, personal reparations from Germany, transfer payments, wages of members who work outside the kibbutz, governmental contributions to the kibbutz as a municipal entity, branches that are not classified as either H_1, H_2, or H_3 (mostly having zero or very small values), plus costs of capital depreciation in the three production branches, that is, $H_1 r_1 A_{21} + H_2 r_2 A_{22} + H_3 r_3 A_{23}$ (in order to avoid double counting of these costs in the second constraint in equation 13.1, once as depreciation and again as investment); *minus:* municipal costs, costs in non-H_1, H_2 or H_3 branches, all taxes (it was not possible to specify precisely the variable tax rates scheme; these taxes are, however, very small), payments to hired wage laborers, transportation costs (which in the data set are given for the entire kibbutz without further specification), net investment (since this is a static model), net change in debts with respect to the previous year];

A_{11}: labor coefficient in industrial production [members' labor-days in industrial production divided by H_1];

A_{12}: labor coefficient in agricultural production [members' labor-days in agricultural production divided by H_2];

A_{13}: labor coefficient in production of collective consumption [members' labor-days in production of collective consumption divided by H_3];

A_{21}: capital coefficient in industrial production [capital stock in industry divided by H_1];

A_{22}: capital coefficient in agricultural production [capital stock in agriculture divided by H_2];

A_{23}: capital coefficient in production of collective consumption [capital stock in production of collective consumption divided by H_3];

r_1 = annual depreciation rate of capital in industrial production [was set equal to .07];

r_2 = annual depreciation rate of capital in production of collective consumption [was set equal to .13];

r_3 = annual depreciation rate of capital in production of collective consumption [was set equal to .1].

[The annual depreciation rates of capital were set arbitrarily, but in accordance with accepted rates (for such rates in the 1950s, see Kanovsky 1966, pp. 89-91)].

This model consists of a truncated quadratic objective function, and two linear equality constraints. Quadratic objective functions have been popular for some time, in particular with studies of decision making. A quadratic function is attractive since it provides a second-order approximation to a large class of functions (Lau 1974, pp. 183-185). I have truncated the quadratic objective function in the sense that the three arguments representing work were entered only at the first power and without interaction among themselves, or between them and consumption arguments. The inclusion of additional terms in the objective function would complicate the computational problem tremendously because of the presence of the technological coefficients. In any given year, the technological coefficients are assumed fixed, and the production functions to be linear. A kibbutz's technologies are either determined by the federation that established the kibbutz, or are chosen later by the members. In any event, the technologies, as expressed by the coefficients A_{ij}, differ across kibbutzim and change over time for any given kibbutz.[23]

The size of kibbutz membership is not a short-run decision variable for the kibbutz, since members cannot be expelled (almost for any reason), and the supply of potential members is very inelastic. The number of members' labor-days available to the kibbutz is assumed to be determined institutionally and fixed, and the labor constraint is assumed to be binding (see also definition of L above). Capital equipment, on the other hand, is not a binding constraint but the kibbutz is assumed to constantly replace worn-out capital (or build equivalent monetary reserves).[24]

It was not possible to incorporate constraints on consumption limiting inequality among kibbutzim (see Ben-Ner and Neuberger, forthcoming) without rendering the model impossible to estimate. Inspection of the data shows that while the per-capita consumption inequality among kibbutzim is small, there are no clear-cut upper constraints and lower constraints, along which "poorer" and "richer" kibbutzim would line up. Of course, such constraints may still exist but be perceived with some variation by different kibbutzim. Two key theoretical concepts, collective consumption and private consumption, are only roughly approximated by the variables H_3 and X; a full identity between goods and services produced on the kibbutz and collective consumption was imposed, and X includes expenditures on food of which the majority should be included in collective consumption.[25]

The kibbutz chooses the level of industrial production, agricultural production, production of collective consumption, and purchase of private consumption. Since the technologies are given to the kibbutz, with fixed coefficients, the above choices imply also the level of employment of capital, and the allocation of the fixed amount of labor. Since data are given in constant (1958) prices, the model cannot allow for choices over physical quantities for given prices, but only over expenditures in constant prices. Consequently, the preferences estimated from this model include the prices of 1958. While for intrayear comparisons the bias is inconsequential, for interyear comparisons the bias is of unknown direction and magnitude. Attempts to remedy the problem by introduction of explicit prices that are allowed to change between years (1955 and 1965) render the present model intractable; moreover, such attempts are frustrated by the unavailability of data.

Estimation of Preferences

Equation 13.1 cannot serve for purposes of estimation, since W is not observed. However, from first-order conditions for maximum one can derive a set of reaction functions representing desired levels of the decision variables of the kibbutz. The reaction functions for H_2, H_3, and X, including an additive error term, are as follows (the reaction function for H_1 was dropped since in the econometric estimation only three equations will be retained; see below):

$$H_2 = B_1X_1 + B_2X_2 + B_3X_3 + B_4X_4 + B_5X_5 + B_6X_6 - \frac{B_3}{B_5}B_4X_7 + B_8X_8 + e_1 \tag{13.2}$$

$$H_3 = -B_2 + B_4y_1 - B_3y_2 - B_5y_3 + e_2 \tag{13.3}$$

$$X = B_8 + \frac{B_3}{B_5}B_4y_1 - B_3y_3 + B_6y_2 + e_3, \tag{13.4}$$

where

$B_1 = 1$

$B_2 = \dfrac{u_1M_2 - u_2N}{N^2 - M_1M_2}$

$B_3 = \dfrac{(u_3 - u_4)N}{N^2 - M_1M_2}$

$B_4 = \dfrac{u_5M_2}{N^2 - M_1M_2}$

$B_5 = \dfrac{(u_4 - u_3)M_2}{N^2 - M_1M_2}$

$B_6 = \dfrac{(u_3 - u_4)M_1}{N_2 - M_1M_2}$

$B_8 = \dfrac{u_1N - u_2M_1}{N^2 - M_1M_2}$

$$X_1 = \frac{yL - DA_{11}}{Z} \qquad\qquad X_5 = \frac{wA_{11}A_{12}A_{13}y - A_{11}{}^2A_{12}w^2}{Z^2}$$

$$X_2 = \frac{yA_{13} - wA_{12}}{Z} \qquad\qquad X_6 = \frac{A_{11}{}^2A_{12}}{Z^2}$$

$$X_3 = \frac{A_{11}A_{12}A_{13}y - 2A_{11}{}^2A_{12}w}{Z^2} \qquad\qquad X_7 = \frac{A_{11}A_{13}}{Z}$$

$$X_4 = \frac{A_{13}{}^2y - A_{11}A_{13}w}{Z} \qquad\qquad X_8 = \frac{A_{11}}{Z}$$

$$y_1 = -A_{13} \qquad\qquad y = (1 - r_1A_{21})$$

$$y_2 = \frac{A_{11}A_{12}}{Z} \qquad\qquad Z = A_{11}(1 - r_2A_{22}) - A_{12}(1 - r_1A_{21})$$

$$y_3 = \frac{A_{11}A_{12}w}{Z} \qquad\qquad w = r_3A_{23}$$

B_2, B_3, B_4, B_5, B_6, B_8 (the parameter associated with X_7 in equation (13.2) was expressed as $(-B_3/B_5)$ B_4 are terms composed of the underlying parameters of the objective function (that is, they reflect the preferences of kibbutzim); X_1, X_2, . . . , X_8, y_1, y_2, y_3 are terms composed of technological coefficients, labor and net income availabilities, and capital replacement costs per unit; and H_2, H_3, and X are functions of these terms.

In order to obtain estimates of B_2, . . . , B_6, B_8, H_2, H_3, and X are regressed on X_1, . . . , X_8, y_1, y_2, y_3; they, and e_1, e_2, and e_3 are $T \times 1$ vectors, T being the number of observations (for example, $e'_i = (e_{i1}, e_{i2}, . . . , e_{iT})$, $t = 1, . . . , T$).

The following assumptions are made:

$$E(e_i) = 0 \qquad\qquad (i = 1, 2, 3)$$

and

$$E(e_ie'_j) = \sigma_{ij} I \qquad\qquad (i, j = 1, 2, 3)$$

where I is a unit matrix of order $T \times T$ and σ_{ij} is the constant variance in each equation. These assumptions imply that the error term in each equation is homoscedastic and nonautocorrelated (for $i = j$), and the correlation between contemporaneous disturbances in different equations is non-zero, but is zero between all lagged error terms (for $i \neq j$). The contemporaneous variance-covariance matrix is assumed to be positive semidefinite.

The income constraint in equation 13.1 (associated with the Lagrangean λ_2) indicates that the four dependent variables (each multiplied by a constant) sum up to a constant. Just as in the case of budget shares in the typical consumer-theory case, one reaction function is redundant and has to be eliminated in estimation. I have chosen to drop the reaction function for H_1.[26]

The Estimation Procedure

The error terms in the various regression equations are most likely correlated. This is so because for each kibbutz, common, immediate factors affect decisions regarding industrial production, agricultural production, collective consumption, and private consumption, apart from the independent variables specified in the regression equations. Seriatim estimation of the three regression equations yields inefficient estimates for the parameters (Zellner 1962). Moreover, the need to take into account relationships among the parameters within and across equations introduces into the system nonlinearity in these unknown parameters.[27]

In order to take these considerations into account, I used a "seemingly unrelated nonlinear regression equations" estimation procedure suggested by Gallant (1975) and Malinvaud (1966, chapter 9), which is an extension of Zellner's (1962) estimation technique.[28]

The estimators derived in this fashion are, in general, strongly consistent, asymptotically normally distributed, and asymptotically more efficient than the seriatim, single-equation, least-squares estimators (see Gallant 1975; Malinvaud 1966 and 1970).

Data

Data pertaining to a large number of economic variables in 1958 prices were available for virtually all Israeli kibbutzim for the years 1954-1965, according to year of establishment and federation affiliation. The three major federations, HaKibbutz HaMeuhad (United Kibbutz)—KM; Ihud HaKvutzot VehaKibbutzim (Union of Kvutzot and Kibbutzim)—IKK, and HaKibbutz HaArtzi (National Kibbutz)—KA, are differentiated according to organizational, ideological, political, and other aspects. In particular, the degree of communalism seems to vary across federations much more than within federations.[29] Accordingly, the three federations were treated separately as distinct samples, under the assumption that all kibbutzim that belong to a given federation have the same objective function.

For purposes of assessment of changes in preferences the two available extreme years were considered, 1955 and 1965 (1954 could not be used because the variable "net exogenous income" required some information from the previous year). Thus, 6 samples obtain: KM in 1955 and in 1965, IKK in 1955 and in 1965, KA in 1955 and in 1965. As seen in the Appendix to this chapter, the sample size T is smaller than the actual number of kibbutzim in these years. The reasons for that are as follows: kibbutzim established in 1954 and 1964 or 1955 and 1965 were eliminated from the samples of 1955 and of 1965 on the grounds that they were in too "fluid" a situation and not near their optimum; kibbutzim for which no data were available (2 such kibbutzim, in 1965); kibbutzim for which some data were missing or the data were of very poor quality (mostly kibbutzim established just two years before 1955 or 1965). In all, the sample sizes are smaller than the actual number of kibbutzim by 6 to 18 percent.

Computation

Malinvaud suggested the use of the Gauss-Newton method for the estimation procedure outlined above. The Time Series Processor (University of Wisconsin TSP computer program package) contains this method. Using this package to implement the estimation procedure, estimates of the parameters of the system (13.2) to (13.4) were obtained for the 6 samples mentioned above.[30]

Results: Changes in Communal Preferences and Differences Among Federations

The estimates of $B_2, \ldots, B_6, B_8$ for each of the 6 data sets are tabulated in table 13-1. Means and standard deviations of variables can be found in the Appendix to this chapter.

How can one determine whether a shift in preferences has taken place between 1955 and 1965 in any of the federations, and what was the direction of such possible shift? Several indicators, such as the rate of substitution between collective and private consumption, are excluded because they require knowledge of the underlying parameters of the objective function. Since there are 8 such underlying parameters (u_1, u_2, u_3, u_4, u_5, M_1, M_2, and N) and only 6 estimated parameters (B_2, B_3, B_4, B_5, B_6, and B_8), it is impossible to recover the former from the latter (for some general conditions for recoverability, see Friedlaender 1972; Hughes Hallet 1979).[31]

For a given federation in a specific year, preferences are reflected by the set of estimated parameters, $B_2, \ldots, B_6, B_8$. For the three federations in each of two years I obtain 6 such sets of parameters. In view of the problems raised in the previous paragraph, it is necessary to assess a possible shift in the preferences of various federations using "counterfactual" methods. Considering federation KM, for example, one may ask the following

Table 13-1

Estimates of the Objective Function Parameters—$B_2, \ldots, B_6, B_8$

	KM 1955	KM 1965	IKK 1955	IKK 1965	KA 1955	KA 1965
B_2 St. error	−1.69465 (.180814)	−3.68435 (.313612)	−1.53666 (.151395)	−1.96141 (.18246)	−1.81874 (.294771)	−4.39226 (.509403)
B_3 St. error	−.014199 (.0384436)	3.55615 (3.23654)	−.102351 (.0648784)	−.678595 (1.09709)	.45073 (.0721298)	22.3093 (4.92310)
B_4 St. error	−1.1529 (.701792)	9.16868 (6.06968)	5.22935 (1.35999)	4.21403 (1.89024)	.532845 (2.62963)	11.1764 (9.13296)
B_5 St. error	−.0521602 (.0452623)	−1.54925 (.639905)	.0795677 (.0268431)	−.53765 (.160301)	−.222175 (.0288831)	−1.40978 (1.02393)
B_6 St. error	.122076 (.481510)	1.01687 (4.06217)	−3.26046 (.330595)	−15.5504 (3.70241)	.652804 (.231384)	44.0409 (10.9935)
B_8 St. error	.224713 (.243441)	2.69629 (.603961)	−.0649089 (.30819)	3.99288 (.823293)	.142495 (.609216)	−5.77865 (3.06466)
T	47	46	64	67	63	61

Source: Calculated from the survey data.

Note: The estimates correspond to the definitions of the parameters $B_2, \ldots, B_6, B_8$. The values in parentheses are asymptotic standard errors.

question: What would be the difference in the ratio of collective consumption to private consumption in the event that kibbutzim had the resources and technologies of 1955 and the preferences of that year (that is,. $\{B_{i_{KM}}{}^{55}\}$), as compared to the event that they had the same resources and technologies (of 1955) but the preferences of 1965, $\{B_{i_{KM}}{}^{65}\}$?[32] According to the hypothesis of this chapter, that some decommunalization of values took place, one would expect the former ratio to be greater that the latter. In general, if some decommunalization of values occurred between 1955 and 1965, the ratio of fitted collective consumption to fitted private consumption in 1955 would be greater than the ratio of predicted collective consumption to predicted private consumption in 1955 (that is, apply parameters estimated in 1965 to values of independent variables—resources and technologies—in 1955):

$H_3{}^{55}$ fitted$/X^{55}$ fitted $> H_3{}^{55}$ predicted$/X^{55}$ predicted, for every federation.

In order to ameliorate problems connected to prediction outside the range of estimation, and since the point predictors may be biased, the test was applied also in the opposite direction. The following hypothesis was formulated:

$$H_3{}^{65} \text{ fitted}/X^{65} \text{ fitted} < H_3{}^{65} \text{ predicted}/X^{65} \text{ predicted},$$

in addition, differences in the preferences of the three federations were assessed. The widespread opinion is that the KA federation is the most communal, and IKK the least. The formulation of the hypotheses is similar to the case of shift in preferences: would a federation with its own preferences have a higher (or lower) ratio of collective-to-private consumption than with the preferences of another federation? (It can be shown that this test is equivalent to a test on the marginal rate of substitution between collective and private consumption).

In sum, the ratios of fitted and predicted values of collective consumption and private consumption were computed for all federations. Since the distribution of these ratios is unknown, the hypotheses were tested using the distribution-free positive signed rank test (Wilcoxon test). The hypotheses and the tests are summarized in table 13-2.

In general, the findings in table 13-2 indicate that the null hypotheses are rejected, at various levels, in favor of the alternative hypotheses, except for the three cases where the test statistic assumes a negative value. In the latter cases, the null hypotheses are rejected (when rejection is warranted) in favor of the opposite to the alternative hypotheses.

The hypothesis that preferences have decommunalized over time is supported by the findings. First, by applying the estimated parameters of each federation in 1955 to its own independent variables in 1965, I obtain the case whereby this "counterfactual" ratio of predicted collective consumption to predicted private consumption is higher than the ratio that results from using the 1965 parameters and independent variables—the ratio of fitted values (see boxes (II, I), (IV, III), and (VI, V) in table 13-2). The same results hold true if the estimated parameters of each federation in 1965 are applied to its independent variables in 1955 (boxes (I,II), (III, IV), and (V, VI)).

Second, by applying parameters estimated in 1955 for federation i to independent variables of federation j in 1965, the same picture emerges, perhaps somewhat more strongly. All federations' preferences were less communal in 1965 than in 1955; thus if I compare the most communal federation in 1965 with the least communal in 1955 I find that the former has a lower collective-private consumption ratio (boxes (IV, I), (VI, I), (II, III), (VI, III), (II, V), and (IV, V) in table 13-2 for estimated parameters in 1955 applied to 1965's independent variables, and boxes (III, II), (V, II), (I, IV), (V, IV), (I, VI), and (III, VI) for the opposite).

Regarding the differences in the degree of communalism in the preferences of the three federations in 1955 and 1965, some interesting results obtain. The general opinion within and without the kibbutz movement is that the "ideologically" most communal of the three federations is the KA federation (which is also politically the most left oriented), while the least communal is the IKK federation, and the KM federation in between, possibly closer to KA (see also Ben-Ner and Neuberger, forthcoming).

The findings in table 13-2 confirm only partly this opinion with respect to the *preferences* over collective and private consumption. IKK certainly

Table 13-2
Decommunalization Hypotheses and the Corresponding Wilcoxon Test Statistics

	Applied to Independent Variables of:	I KM 1955	II KM 1965	III IKK 1955	IV IKK 1965	V KA 1955	VI KA 1965
				Estimated Parameters of:			
I	KM 1955		RF>RP 5.96	RF>RP 5.45	RF>RP 5.95	RF<RP −.5	RF>RP 5.96
II	KM 1965	RF<RP 5.91		RF<RP 4.98	RF>RP 4.66	RF<RP 5.91	RF<RP 1.619
III	IKK 1955	RF<RP 6.93	RF>RP 4.31		RF>RP 5.81	RF<RP 5.62	RF>RP 4.89
IV	IKK 1965	RP<RP 7.12	RF<RP 6.92	RF<RP 5.67		RF<RP 7.12	RF<RP 6.14
V	KA 1955	RF>RP −2.12	RF>RP 6.25	RF>RP 5.73	RF>RP 5.99		RF>RP 6.01
VI	KA 1965	RF<RP 5.72	RF>RP −2.57	RF<RP 3.70	RF>RP 4.11	RF<RP 5.91	

Source: Calculated from the survey data.

Note: RF = ratio of fitted value of collective consumption to fitted value of private consumption.

RP = ratio of predicted value of collective consumption to predicted value of private consumption.

$RP \lessgtr RP$ = represents the alternative hypothesis regarding the difference in preferences (over time, between federations, or both), the null hypothesis being "no difference in preferences", i.e., RF = RP. The numbers are values of the Wilcoxon positive signed rank test statistic which has an asymptotic $N(0, 1)$ distribution. The alternative hypotheses $(RF \lessgtr RP)$ were formulated so that rejection of the null hypothesis in favor of the alternative hypothesis will be expressed by a *positive* number greater than Z_α.

Values of Z corresponding to a few special value of α are given below, for reference:

Z	1.282	1.645	1.960	2.326	2.576	3.090	3.291	3.891	4.417
α	.90	.95	.975	.99	.995	.999	.9995	.99995	.999995

emerges as the least communal in preferences in both 1955 and 1965, with the difference much more noticeable in 1965 (see boxes (I,III) (V, III), (III, I), and (III, V) for 1955 and boxes (II, IV), (VI, IV), (IV, II), and (IV, VI) for 1965). The findings, however, seem to lend support to the proposition that KA is not more communal in preferences than KM, and even raise the possibility that the opposite might be true (see boxes (V, I), (VI, II), (I, V), and (II, VI).

The ratio of actual collective consumption to actual private consumption may be taken as a rough indicator of the degree of communalism of the kibbutz economic structure and system.[33] There is no statistically significant difference between the means of these ratios between KM and IKK, and KM and KA in 1955; for KA and IKK in 1955, however, the difference is significant at the .15 level. There is no statistically significant difference between the means of KM and KA in 1965 (except at the .25 level); the means of KA and IKK in 1965 are different at the .1 level; the difference between the means of KA and IKK is statistically highly significant in 1965 (at .05, one tail) (see table 13-3).

A decommunalization in the economic structure has taken place in all three federations; the means of the ratios of actual collective consumption to actual private consumption are significantly different, at the .005 level, in 1955 as compared to 1965, for all federations.[34]

Summary and Conclusions

Communes that form a small minority within societies based on radically different, individualistic values and principles are subject to pressures that may ultimately bring about their demise. The larger society—the environment of a commune—although possibly subject to contradictions, has usually the ability to control the economic, social, political, and cultural life in order to ensure its own stability and to further its own development. It does so

Table 13-3
The Economic Structure: Ratios of Actual Collective Consumption to Actual Private Consumption

	KM	IKK	KAA
1955	.994597	.979392	1.01882
St. dev.	(.240582)	(.223425)	(.187822)
1965	.867042	.785644	.900283
St. dev.	(.227168)	(.423928)	(.232113)

Source: Calculated from the survey data.
Note: The values in parentheses are standard deviations.

through certain economic institutions and relations (for example, markets, unequal remuneration, cash nexus), technologies (for example, those that promote hierarchical decision making and minute division of labor), patterns of conduct in business (for example, those that differentiate executives' work style and environment from those of other workers), mass media and culture (for example, such that create a favorable atmosphere for the aforementioned spheres). These institutions, relations, patterns of conduct, and attitudes are clearly antithetical to communal values and principles of organization.

Communes are linked to their environment in numerous ways because of the practical impossibility of communal autarky and because the larger society does not permit the development of entirely autonomous entities within it. The links between communes and their environment strengthen and multiply as the latter grows and its institutions become more firmly established. Communes, in their relations with the larger society, must participate in its economic institutions, be technology takers (because they are unlikely to be able to develop technologies of their own or find alternative ones to those available from the environment), be conduct takers in business relations (in order to be accepted as business associates), and the like. Clearly, communes will try to minimize the impact of the environment; they may seek geographical seclusion, or try to find niches on the market that will permit them to behave differently from the environment or to participate on the market while minimizing the contacts with noncommunal participants.[35] They may limit the amount of contact of individual members with the environment that might occur through mass media or by direct communication. And they may reinforce communal values through education, socialization, cultural activities produced by communal organizations, and, more generally, by attempting to fulfill most human needs on the commune and under its control.

The long-run process can be described as a progressive one in which communes give up part of their communal values, thereby weakening their mechanisms for resisting further impact of the environment, which in turn leads to a further decline of communal values. The economic structure and system are adapted to the transformed values. This gradual and possibly prolonged process ends with a thorough reorganization of the commune and its transformation into a private for-profit organization. Thus, communes are both value takers and type of organization takers (just as they are price takers). Importantly, their demise as communes is not necessarily due to their internal organization, but to their unavoidable interaction with their noncommunal environment.

From the theoretical proposition spelled out above I hypothesized that the values of members of existing successful communes—Israeli kibbutzim—are likely to decommunalize over time; a decommunalization of the economic structure and system of kibbutzim was expected to follow. In order to test this hypothesis, I argued that a correspondence can be established between communal values and preferences over collective versus private consumption in the weak sense that changes in the intensity of preferences indicate changes in the same direction in the intensity of values. Using a "revealed preference approach," and with the aid of an economic model of the kibbutz as a communal organization, preferences were estimated from cross-sectional data on individual kibbutzim in 1955 and 1965. Changes in preferences were assessed using a "counterfactual method." The following "counterfactual" question was asked: Given the conditions (that is, the independent variables) of 1955, which year's preferences would conduce to a higher ratio of collective to private consumption—those of 1955 or those of 1965?

The empirical findings indicate that between 1955 and 1965 a change in preferences did indeed take place in all three major Israeli kibbutz federations. More specifically, I found that, for the same independent variables, preferences extracted from data from 1955 would lead to higher ratios of collective consumption to private consumption than preferences extracted from data from 1965. The difference in these ratios, statistically highly significant, represents a decommunalization in preferences. As claimed earlier, preferences over economic variables correspond to communal values. Therefore, decommunalization in the former implies decommunalization of values in the kibbutz movement.

The economic structure and system of the kibbutzim (as approximated by the ratio of actual collective consumption to actual private consumption) has also decommunalized between 1955 and 1965.

While the results of the econometric study clearly support the hypotheses of this chapter, a qualifying comment is in order. The econometric study had to cope with two kinds of constraints: econometric tractability and availability of data. For these reasons, for example, it was assumed that all kibbutzim that belong to the same federation have the same objective function. Variations in observations on the dependent variables were said to stem from variations in exogenous factors (technologies and resources, the independent variables) outside the control of the individual kibbutz. While this is very likely to be true in a static model in the short run, a dynamic multiperiod model of the kibbutz would have been a more correct approach to the problem at hand. Other problems were encountered in identifying precise empirical counterparts to theoretical variables (especially in the case of consumption and hired labor), and in incorporating prices into the model. Clearly, these constraints, as well as some other issues raised earlier in this chapter, while not uncommon in econometric studies, detract from the reliability of the results.[36]

Obviously it is impossible to prove statements regarding the demise of communes with evidence drawn from existing ones. I hope, however, that I have provided a methodology for determining whether existing organizations experience changing preferences and thereby become candidates for transformation into different types of organizations. Although characterized by very rapid social and economic changes, the period under consideration in this chapter was very short, and one would expect few, if any, fundamental changes just for that reason. Moreover, the communes studied here belong to a successful movement and are situated within an environment not altogether hostile to their values and principles. And yet, while keeping in mind the limitations of the empirical work, the findings show that a process of decommunalization was already set in motion during the period studied.

The proposition put forward in this essay may possibly appear as an obvious one. However, social reformers,[37] commune members,[38] and researchers[39] have asserted that communes are viable even if situated in a very different environment. Moreover, some view the changes in communes—both at the level of values and at the level of the economic structure and system—as adaptations to the environment that assure their survival.[40] I have suggested that these adaptations are just as likely to form part of the process that leads to the demise of communes.[41]

I end nevertheless with the hopeful words of a "practitioner," a kibbutz member sympathetic to my analysis: "No matter how dim the prospects of communes' survival are, I am *living today* in a society that many dream to establish and *live in tomorrow*."

Notes

1. Marx (1906, p. 90); he does not discuss communes explicitly.

2. Kanter (1972, p. 2). This definition of communes applies to what contemporary writers term as "intentional" communities or communes.

3. By types of organizations I mean private for-profit organizations, cooperatives, communes, nonprofit organizations, or state-owned organizations.

4. See, for example, Vanek (ed.) (1975, pp. 11-38, 445-455); Kanter (1972); Jones (1979); Shirom (1972); Berman (forthcoming); Bellas (1972); Ben-Ner (1981); Ben-Ner and Neuberger (forthcoming).

5. In the long run in a highly competitive economy, communes will be able to maintain their members only if they provide them at least their reservation—pecuniary and nonpecuniary—incomes. Unless members have a preference for the communal type of organizations, or certain technologies, this can be assured only by employing the best available technologies. It is precisely the argument of this section, that these preferences will be grad-

ually eroded, and therefore the best technology adopted.

6. By appealing to cognitive dissonance theories, one would expect that unavoidable inegalitarian practices will induce inegalitarian attitudes and values.

7. In general, modern states do not tolerate the existence of entirely autonomous entities in their midsts, but attempt to affect the conduct of these entities to conform with "accepted" norms through various laws and regulations.

8. In Gemeinschaft relations people interact as whole personalities affectively and expressively; in Gessellschaft relations people interact only for specific purposes, contractually and instrumentally. (See Kanter 1972 for a detailed discussion of these concepts; also E. Fischoff, Introduction in Buber 1958).

9. For instance, collective consumption goods and services (such as communal dining or child rearing) are produced and consumed quite differently from private consumption goods and services. A major shift from collective to private consumption requires a restructuring of the commune's economy. Elwood Mead, in a document submitted to the Joint Palestine Survey Commission, stated that "the almost universal failure of such experiments elsewhere emphasized the wisdom of so designing houses and farm buildings [to be built for kibbutzim] as to make them suitable for use by the cultivators of individual farms" (quoted by Barkai 1978, p. 4). Visibly enough, communal architecture differs from individual farm architecture. See also footnote 19.

10. The discussion of the process of decommunalization of values of commune members through their interaction with a noncommunal environment has been influenced by the works of Rosabeth Kanter (1972) and Diane Barthel (1979) on communes. See also broader theoretical works by Lane (forthcoming) and Steward (1955). The exposition of this process has been inspired by the "transmission and response" framework developed by Tyson and Kenen (1980).

11. See, for example, Halevi and Klinov-Malul (1968) and Pack (1971) and various articles in Eisenstadt et al. (1970).

12. These conclusions are derived from a very small sample, and the definitions of the economic variables as well as the statistical practices are somewhat deficient.

13. The results by Barkai discussed here were obtained from the direct estimation of Cobb-Douglas production functions for agriculture and manufacturing based on cross-sectional data for each of the approximately 200 kibbutzim. In agriculture, the production function was defined over labor, capital, and land; in manufacturing, only over labor and capital.

14. See also Tannenbaum et al. (1974) for an empirical analysis of kibbutz factory motivation structure in comparison to that of factories in Austria, Italy, the United States, and Yugoslavia.

15. See, for example, Antonovsky and Arian (1972), Eisenstadt (1970), and Lissak (1970). See also changes in the pattern of voting (Lucas 1977). These authors, as well as those cited in the next footnote, do not discuss explicitly the changing values in terms of collective-public orientation versus individual-private orientation.

16. See, for instance, Niv (1978-1979), Rosner and Avnat (1978-1979) (and their references), Eisenstadt (1978-1979), Talmon and Stup (1970), and Gazit (1972). While there is considerable disagreement among various authors (and between myself and most of them), the evaluation of the direction of change, if not its depth, is uniform. Niv (1978-1979) presents a very good discussion of the kibbutz-environment relationship.

17. Menachem Rosner and associates (1978-1979) have made a major study comparing the values and attitudes of kibbutz members born on the kibbutz to those held by their parents' generation in the kibbutz. While their study was not aimed directly at changes in communal values, its results can be interpreted as confirming the hypothesis of this section. An excellent historical case study of the Amana Colonies was done by Barthel (1979).

18. Notice that the term "collective consumption" is used here in a somewhat different sense than in much of the economic literature; it resembles, however, the usage in Burton Weisbrod's writings (for example, 1980).

19. The smaller ratio of collective to private consumption reflects a less communal economic structure and system since it is associated with comparatively fewer collectively consumed goods and services, fewer goods and services distributed freely, and fewer goods and services produced in the kibbutz.

Bennett (1977) suggests a classification of the socioeconomic systems of several organizations on a continuum from communalism to cooperation (from Hutterian Colony, through a left kibbutz, moshav shitufi, moshav ovdim, to Matador cooperative farm in Saskatchewan). While there is no explicit reference to the criteria for that ordering, the chart on p. 69 presented by Bennett can clearly accommodate my criterion for communalism in economic structure, and, by extension, for communalism of values. Putterman (1980) measures the degree of collectivity in production in Tanzanian villages according to the proportion of peasants' time allocated to private versus collective plots. Israelsen (1980) distinguishes between communes and collectives according to the mode of distribution of income; in the former it is unrelated to contribution to production, in the latter it is. See also footnote 9.

20. For a survey of the literature on estimation of preferences, see Ben-Ner (1981), where a justification of the assumption of the optimizing behavior on the part of the kibbutz is given, too. On the matter of changes in preferences, the literature is much scarcer. The reason is that most neoclassical economists view individual and group preferences as exogenous

to the economic sphere. Moreover, leading theorists consider the fixity of preferences as a methodological necessity (Peleg and Yaari 1973, p. 391). Others view the fixity of preferences as a superior assumption to the contrary assumption (Becker 1976, p. 5). (Further discussion of this issue can be found in Ben-Ner 1981). Clearly, the position of this essay is diametrically opposed to these opinions. But see also Pollack (1978), Felix (1979), and Kapteyn, Wansbeek, and Buyze (1980).

21. First, the members of a kibbutz can be considered a team, given the high degree of homogeneity in their preferences defined over broad categories of economic activity. Second, the individual member is not a decision-making unit; there are virtually no actions captured by this model that a member can take independently of the kibbutz decision-making organs. Third, to the extent that differences in the preferences of individual members do exist, this would be of concern for a different type of research (for example, one dealing with collective decision-making processes), with little effect on our subject matter.

22. Since the size of the membership is assumed to be fixed, specification of the objective function in-toto or per-member yields identical optimal values for the decision variables.

23. While it is probably true that an economy faces a relatively "malleable" capital, this seems not to be so of an individual production unit, in most economic activities. The capital equipment under the control of an economic unit is of a putty-clay type, requiring a unique labor-capital ratio; that is, a fixed coefficient linear production function (see Johansen 1972). Even if one would like to estimate fixed-coefficient nonlinear production functions, this would not be feasible. The reason is that many kibbutzim are rather young at the first period of observation, or have added and abandoned some production activities. Thus, econometric estimation from longitudinal data would be impossible or very unreliable for most kibbutzim because of too few (if any) degrees of freedom in estimation.

24. The land is, of course, a factor in production. However, in addition to being an almost trivially binding constraint, land has not been included in the model because (1) the added computational difficulties would have been extraordinary, and (2) it would have reduced (being an additional constraint) the degrees of freedom for the solution of the parameters of the objective function.

25. Collective consumption has not been corrected for the percentage of children in the kibbutz population. Children, an exogenous factor in this model, have an almost fixed claim on collective consumption, other things being equal. It turns out, however, that the percentage of children increased only slightly between 1955 and 1965; moreover, the effect of such an increase would have increased the corrected collective consumption in 1965. This may only strengthen the results of this paper.

26. Assuming an additive error term for each of the four reaction func-

tions (industrial production, agricultural production, collective consumption, and private consumption), the following general system of regression equations can be specified:

$$v_{it} = \sum_{j=1}^{N} \beta_{ij} q_{ijt} + \epsilon_{it}$$

$i = 1, \ldots, 4$ (number of equations)

$j = 1, \ldots, N$ (number of independent variables)

$t = 1, \ldots, T$ (number of observations)

where v_{it} represents the ith dependent variable and q_{ijt} the jth independent variable in the ith regression equation, and β_{ij} its associated parameter.

However, the income constraint indicates that the four dependent variables, each multiplied by a constant, sum up to a constant. It follows that if ϵ_{it} is a zero-mean random error,

$$\sum_{t=1}^{T} \epsilon_{it} = 0 \ (i = 1, \ldots, 4)$$ and the resultant contemporaneous variance-

covariance matrix of the ϵ_{it} is singular (Powell 1974, p. 48). Now, if I were to estimate the four regression equations seriatim, the singularity of the contemporaneous covariance matrix would be of no consequence. However, such estimation would yield inefficient estimates for the parameters, since the error terms in the various regression equations are most likely correlated. This implies an estimation procedure that involves the inverse of (the estimate of) the contemporaneous covariance matrix, which is zero (see text, below). If the independent variables were identical across equations, seriatim least-squares estimation would yield efficient estimates (Zellner 1962, p. 351). However, as equations (13.2) to (13.4) indicate, this is not the case. The solution to this problem is to drop one of the equations of the system. The resultant system has a contemporaneous covariant matrix of full rank. The estimates obtained from "Zellner estimation" (or maximum likelihood estimation) are invariant under the choice of which equation is deleted. See Powell (1974, p. 48) and his references (ibid., footnote 17); also Theil (1972, pp. 335-336).

27. The independent variables $X_1, \ldots, X_8, y_1, y_2$, and y_3 are defined in terms of technological coefficients A_{ij} ($i = 1, 2; j = 1, 2, 3$), the labor availability L and the exogenous income D (the underlying independent variables that vary across kibbutzim), and the fixed annual depreciation rates r_1, r_2, and r_3. The use of the redefined variables causes the system to be linear in the independent variables.

28. The first step is to obtain least squares estimators $\hat{B}_2 \ (H_2), \ldots,$

$\hat{B}_6\,(H_2),\ \hat{B}_8\,(H_2),\ \hat{B}_2(H_3),\hat{B}_3\,(H_3),\ \hat{B}_4\,(H_3),\ \hat{B}_5\,(H_3),\ \hat{B}_3\,(X),\ \left(\dfrac{\hat{B}_4}{B_5}\right)(X),\ \hat{B}_6(X),$

by minimizing (in equations 13.2-13.4) $\displaystyle\sum_{t=1}^{T}e^2{}_{1t}$, $\displaystyle\sum_{t=1}^{T}e^2{}_{2t}$, and $\displaystyle\sum_{t=1}^{T}e^2{}_{3t}$ seriatim.

Thus, equality between certain parameters across equations is not yet imposed and, consequently, $\hat{B}_3\,(H_2)\ =\ \ddot{B}_3\,(H_3),\ =\ \ddot{B}_3\,(X)$ will *not* generally hold. ($\hat{B}_2(H_2)$ denotes the least squares estimate of B_2 in equation 13.2, and so forth).

The second step is to compute the residual vectors from each equation, $(\hat{e}_{1\prime},\ \ldots,\hat{e}_{1T}),\ (\hat{e}_{2\prime},\ \ldots,\hat{e}_{2T}),$ and $(\hat{e}_{3\prime},\ \ldots,\hat{e}_{3T})$, and estimate the elements $\hat{\sigma}_{ij}$ *of $\hat{\Omega}_c$ to obtain* $\sigma_{ij}\ =\ \frac{1}{T}\hat{e}_i\hat{e}_j^!$

$$\hat{\Omega}_c\ =\ \begin{bmatrix} \hat{\sigma}_{11} & \hat{\sigma}_{12} & \hat{\sigma}_{13} \\ \hat{\sigma}_{21} & \hat{\sigma}_{22} & \hat{\sigma}_{23} \\ \hat{\sigma}_{31} & \hat{\sigma}_{32} & \hat{\sigma}_{33} \end{bmatrix}$$

Now the three regression equations can be "stacked" into one superequation:

$y\ =\ f(\Theta^0)\ +\ e$

where

$y\ =\ (H_2^!,H_3^!,X^!\,),\quad H_2^!\ =\ (H_{21}\ ,\ H_{22}\ ,\ \ldots\ ,H_{2T}\,)$

$H_3^!\ =\ (H_{31}\ ,\ H_{32}\ ,\ \ldots\ ,\ H_{3T}\,)$

$X^!\ =\ (X_1\ ,\ X_2\ ,\ \ldots\ ,\ X_{T1}\,)$

y being of order $3T\ \times\ 1;$

$f(\Theta)\ =\ (f_1\,(\Theta_1\,),\ f_2\,(\Theta_2\,),\ f_3\,(\Theta_3\,)\,)$

$f\,(\Theta)$ being of order $3T\ \times\ 1,$

$f_1\,(\Theta_1\,)\ =$ right-hand side (RHS) expressions for $H_2^!$,

$f_2\,(\Theta_2\,)\ =\quad$ RHS expressions for $H_3^!$,

$f_3\,(\Theta_3\,)\ =\quad$ RHS expressions for $X^!$,

all defined by equations (13.2) to 13.4).

$$\Theta = (\Theta'_1, \Theta'_2, \Theta'_3)$$

$$\Theta'_1 = (1, B_2, B_3, B_4, B_5, B_6, B_8)$$

$$\Theta'_2 = (B_2, B_4, B_3, B_5)$$

$$\Theta'_3 = (B_3, B_4, B_5, B_6, B_8)$$

$$e = (e'_1, e'_2, e'_3)$$

Thus, this stage includes the imposition of the restrictions regarding the relationships among the unknown parameters across the regression equations.

The third step is to obtain generalized least-squares estimators $\hat{\Theta}$ by minimizing

$$Q(\Theta) = \frac{1}{T} [y - f(\Theta)]' (\hat{\Omega}_c^{-1} \times I) [y - f(\Theta)]$$

29. A discussion of differences between federations is provided in Ben-Ner and Neuberger (forthcoming).

30. Because of the nonlinearity in the parameters of the system of regression equations, it is possible to obtain multiple minima of the sum of squared residuals (see footnote 28.) In order to ensure that a global minimum was reached, I have experimented with various sets of initial values for the parameters. In all cases but one there are fairly firm grounds to believe that a global minimum was reached. In the case of KA 1955, convergence was not achieved in spite of experimentation with various starting values for parameters, criteria for convergence, or increasing the number of iterations. The high computational costs of such experimentation led me to retain the set of estimates that were associated with what seemed to be a sum of squared residuals very close to the global minimum.

31. The irrecoverability of the underlying parameters of the objective function has also precluded an analysis of fulfillment of second-order conditions for maximum (which require, besides diminishing marginal utilities, that the denominator of $B_2, \ldots, B_6, B_8, N^2 - M_1M_2$, be negative). All that can be said in this respect is too speculative and has too little bearing on the subject of this chapter to be presented.

32. Peltzman (1975) attempts to measure the impact of safety devices in automobiles on variables such as death rates and injuries. He compares actual with predicted values, whereas I used fitted versus predicted values. It seems more appropriate to compare statistically derived values among themselves, rather than observed (actual) values with statistically derived ones.

33. See footnote 19 and associated text.

34. To test differences in means I used the t-test. It is interesting to note that while it does not seem that the differences among the several federations with regard to preferences were any greater in 1965 than in 1955 (though no explicit attempt was made to measure the magnitude of the difference), their differences with regard to the communalism of the economic structure were much greater in 1965 than in 1955. Thus it seems that the economic structure and system grew more dissimilar during the period under discussion. Also, the more communal the structure was in 1955, the slower the decommunalization in values occurred.

35. Communes may attempt to concentrate on labor-intensive or craftsmanlike production (producing such items as wooden toys and hammocks) or to sell their products by mail, or to like-minded groups, or through cooperative marketing organizations.

36. Allowing for a distribution of preferences across the kibbutzim would yield the present model intractable. For a discussion of such problems, see Yatchew (1980). Regarding the possibility of a dynamic model, the nearer one gets to a general-equilibrium formulation, the analytical treatment becomes formidable, and the econometric problem insolvable. Prices could not be incorporated because of their unavailability. Moreover, their inclusion would have rendered the model used in this chapter unestimable. Comparable works have faced the same problem of separating prices from estimated preferences (see, for example, Friedlaender 1973). I have reestimated the model, after making various adjustments in variables that might remedy some of the problems mentioned in the text, and have not obtained results that contradict the findings presented in this essay.

37. Nineteenth-century "utopian" social reformers (Buchez, Fourier, Proudhon, Owen, and others) believed not only that communes can survive in a capitalist economy, but also that they may serve as vehicles for economic and social transformation of the society in a communal direction.

38. Most commune members with whom I have spoken believe that communes are here to stay.

39. Barkin and Bennett (1972) argue that, in spite of certain changes precipitated primarily by their relative exposed economic position, the kibbutz and the Hutterite colony succeeded in "retaining the essential and basic institutions of communal property, living, and decision-making" (p. 458). Therefore, the authors suggest, "communal economics and social oganization can survive in an individualistic, capitalistic world, and accept much of the instrumental frame of that world with minimal compromise of basic tenets and practices—at least up to a point" (p. 458).

40. This is the position of Barkin and Bennett (1972). Niv (1980) is more careful in allowing that to be one possibility, the other being demise (or, in his language, "disintegration").

41. Showing that a process of decommunalization of values takes place

over time does not, of course, prove that the explanation of the process suggested in this chapter is correct. It can lend support to alternative explanations as well. For example, one could argue that communal values are distributed normally in any population, and those who establish communes come from one tail of this distribution. As a second generation is born, "drawing" its values from the entire distribution, the average values must shift toward the mean of the distribution; thus, by necessity, a commune will grow less communal over time. However, this explanation requires strong assumptions about human characteristics that do not seem to be supported by our knowledge of human beings. Another possible explanation for the change in the economic structure and system of the kibbutz in favor of private consumption argues that individual preferences become more important at higher levels of income, and they find their expression in private consumption. However, this explanation does not imply or account for changes in preferences, which is the aspect I have discussed in this chapter. I plan to deal elsewhere in more detail with alternative explanations for changes in preferences and changes in patterns of consumption.

Appendix
Means and Standard Deviations of Variables

	KM 1955		KM 1965		IKK 1955		IKK 1965		KA 1955		KA 1965	
	Mean	*SD*	*Mean*	*SD*	*Mean*	*SD*	*Mean*	*SD*	*Mean*	*SD*	*Mean*	*SD*
H_1^a	75.7234	147.654	159.217	252.804	53.2656	193.684	100.940	235.276	40.5556	67.1706	290.459	489.224
H_2^a	302.340	161.906	1218.00	496.407	332.672	221.700	1253.15	492.601	313.206	171.061	1211.49	425.556
H_3^a	213.915	129.342	428.370	193.440	185.672	109.811	372.851	211.396	191.317	82.7117	458.049	162.232
X^a	228.149	153.176	543.500	321.067	190.922	110.432	481.970	239.995	185.175	73.8203	550.623	252.444
A_{11}	.0959728	.157497	.0425845	.123105	.0971761	.160672	.0247879	.0431882	.139563	.515209	.021099	.029697
A_{12}	.0676873	.0223459	.0176084	.0047364	.0690969	.0225878	.0175133	.0039873	.0702777	.0451379	.0150913	.00319773
A_{13}	.0715515	.225021	.0472044	.0226465	.0988901	.0341193	.0506419	.039768	.107403	.0140393	.0475498	.00671544
A_{21}	4.2259	8.74737	2.65064	7.27135	5.17248	10.3437	1.52651	2.46125	3.36566	10.9476	1.2043	1.7465
A_{22}	3.48963	1.72032	1.87412	.67937	3.44267	1.82030	1.68142	.643310	3.14288	1.85309	1.71444	.547259
A_{23}	3.74261	1.19961	3.81811	.980342	4.21782	1.64998	4.08704	3.82625	2.96529	.73773	3.3577	.611424
L^b	46.5532	28.6454	47.6304	31.5527	42.3281	32.3091	42.9552	21.0256	41.1587	16.0455	47.0984	20.1773
K^a	1805.51	869.789	4031.70	1842.43	1854.86	1376.79	3584.00	1526.36	1405.89	546.248	3783.69	1132.9
population	463.511	314.691	456.283	252.626	350.703	219.093	357.627	173.629	371.667	183.757	423.115	173.533
T	47		46		64		67		63		61	
Actual number of kibbutzim	57		56		72		72		67		73	

Source: Calculated from the survey data

[a] In thousands of 1958 IL.

[b] In thousands of days.

14

The Performance of Small-Scale Producer Cooperatives in Developing Countries: Capital Starvation and Capital Management

Peter Abell and
Nicholas Mahoney

Many less developed countries, in one way or another, are supporting the establishment of cooperatives; the greatest support has been forthcoming for agricultural cooperatives though there has been some encouragement of industrial-producer cooperatives (IPCs) also. The latter are sometimes deemed to offer a "third way" between "capitalist" and "planned socialist" development and as such have been encouraged and supported by governments, which frequently make available capital loans at concessionary interest rates and provide tax concessions. The motivation for these policies appears to lie with the belief that IPCs find it difficult to muster sufficient capital to operate competitively and effectively—that is, that they suffer from "capital starvation." Indeed, since IPCs seem to attract members who have insufficient capital individually to finance industrial enterprises, this is not an unreasonable assumption, especially in the less developed countries. It does appear, however, that, despite official support and encouragement, the rate of formation of IPCs is low; in some countries cooperatives that are registered never begin to operate, and overall their economic record is not particularly impressive. Compared with their capitalist counterparts the relatively few IPCs that do operate appear to have lower levels of profitability and inferior productivity.[1] Why should this be so—especially when, by their very nature, IPCs purportedly have a comparative advantage attributable to enhanced motivation (Meade 1972) and reduced overheads associated with a reduction in surveillance? Is it that these advantages are an illusion, or is it that any returns to them are more than offset by other intrinsic or extrinsic comparative disadvantages?

Vanek (1971, 1977) and Furubotn (1971) have also singled out capital starvation as the major contributory factor accounting for the poor performance of industrial cooperatives. In their view, this results from the cooperative practices of *saving collectively* and *limiting returns to capital*. It is argued that both these practices inhibit cooperative investment and reinvestment because self-interested members will seek more remunerative (and less risky[2]) investments external to the cooperative.

287

In the case of collective savings, since there is no individual entitlement to the invested capital (that is, the principal), rationally self-interested members will only plow back funds s into the cooperative, in the face of a rate of interest i elsewhere, if

$$s(1 + i)^t < s[(1 + r)^t - 1] \qquad (14.1)$$

where r is the rate of return (productivity of capital) inside the cooperative and t is the time horizon for returns from the investment. It is clear that the inequality will favor internal (collective) investment only if either r is significantly greater than i and/or t is lengthy. Limited returns to capital can have similar consequences. Here, there is a de jure entitlement to the principal invested[3] but the rate of return is limited. This can be an impediment to investment if the rate is significantly below that of alternative investment opportunities, though it should be noted that since members of a cooperative can choose how to remunerate themselves—either as returns to their work or as returns to capital—it seems that limited return to capital will have a deleterious effect only when capital holdings are unequally distributed.[4]

It is argued by those who favor the capital-starvation thesis (as we shall call it) that industrial cooperatives will suffer from poor investment, operate with a lower capital-labor ratio, have lower output, and in general be less efficient[5] than their (equilibrium) capitalist counterparts (Vanek 1971).

In addition, it is sometimes also suggested that the members of IPCs (being characteristically drawn from the less affluent) will have a comparatively strong consumption preference. This again would lead to "under-"investment but, in this case, not because investment is being made elsewhere but rather because there is a general disinclination to invest in the first place.

In the rest of this chapter we will provide some evidence pertinent to the above considerations derived from a study of small-scale producer cooperatives in developing countries.[6]

It should be emphasized, however, that the study is in a pilot phase only and the results should be treated with corresponding caution. Though the eight cooperatives studied in no way constitute a representative sample, they were selected in both countries by those conversant with the problems that cooperatives characteristically face. We would be surprised if our results were not generalizable to a wider population, but we cannot, of course, be sure of this. Given that the cooperatives were selected for study on the basis of whether or not they were successful and not as representative of the population at large, we have avoided any reference to a statistical inference (such as significance tests).[7]

Measuring the Economic Performance of IPCs

In developing countries most of the statistical summaries concerning the performance of IPCs take profitability as the yardstick of their success. However, it is our view that in emphasizing this measure one can seriously underestimate the actual economic viability of IPCs. This is for the simple reason that the members of a cooperative can, for one reason or another, manipulate the profit level downward by paying themselves a "high" wage or salary. Thus, residual profitability bears no necessary relationship to the underlying viability and performance of the enterprise.[8] It seems, therefore, in assessing the performance of cooperatives, that an emphasis on value-added is a more appropriate strategy. There is, of course, also theoretical justification for so doing in the work of Ward (1958) and Vanek (1970) though, in his turn, Horvat (1975) has cautioned against the models developed by these authors.[9]

In table 14-1 we have given a summary of the economic performance of 8 cooperatives in terms of value added per unit of labor and capital. The first 4 cooperatives listed were located in Peru and the second 4 in India; the designations VS (very successful), S (successful), MS (moderately successful), and F (failure) indicate, in qualitative form, the general (economic) performance of the cooperatives. It can readily be seen that average value added per unit of labor tends to correlate with this qualitative categorization, though value added per unit of capital is less so. If we consider profit, however, it appears from table 14-2 (columns 1 and 2) that there is a poor correlation (over time) between recorded profit and both the absolute magnitude of the value added generated and value added per unit of labor. One suspects that the correlations are particularly low in India, for there cooperatives are taxed in recorded profit and there is thus a strong disincentive to show a profit. This detail aside, the correlations give some support to our contention that profitability is not necessarily a guide to economic viability. We will therefore use value added-based concepts in the rest of our analysis.

Cooperative Savings and Investment

IPCs can generate funds internally in three ways: (a) by collective savings; (b) by member loans and deposits; and (c) by the issue of individually owned share capital. They can also obtain funds from external sources—loans, bank overdraft, trade credit—but these are not our principal concern here.

Collective Savings. The cooperatives studied did to some extent invest through collective savings—savings that generally took the form of a reserve fund created out of profit. The propensity to save in this way seems higher in Peru than in India, except for the unsuccessful cooperatives, but then the rates of profit (though not necessarily value added) were higher in Peru too.

Table 14-1
Economic Performance of the Cooperatives (over the Period Specified)

Cooperative		Value added/Labor[b]				Value added/Capital			
		Maximum	Average	Minimum	Time of Study	Maximum	Average	Minimum	Time of Study
Peru									
Peruprint 1970-1977[a]	(S)	84,000	68,000	57,000	57,000 [84,000][d]	1.40	1.00	0.67	1.00 [1.3][d]
Cobblers 1969-1977[a]	(VS)	99,542	71,403	40,839	43,007 [82,519][d]	2.18	1.17	0.46[c]	0.74 [1.51][d]
Metal FRN 1971-1977[a]	(F)	98,239	51,100	29,540	28,523 [24,540][d]	1.41	1.07	0.83	0.68 [0.83][d]
Clothing 1976-1977[a]	(F)	32,679	—	10,735	32,679	0.40	—	0.06	0.40
India									
Shuttlemakers 1962-1977[a]	(S)	5,601	4,330	3,454	5,279	1.46	0.74	0.44	0.72
Engineering 1970-1977[a]	(S)	7,047	5,137	3,075	5,383	0.58	0.36	0.14	0.30
Village 1971-1977[a]	(MS)	5,500	4,664	2,396[c]	4,997[e]	0.84	0.55	0.39[c]	0.37
Commercial 1966-1977[a]	(F)	11,431	1,494	0	0	2.47[f]	0.62 (0.4)[f]	0	0

[a]Indicates period over which data were collected.
[b]The figures are calculated in real terms, the base being the first year for which data is available for each cooperative.
[c]Indicates a figure for the first year of operation of the cooperative.
[d]Figures in brackets are for 1976, the year before the study. 1977 was a particularly bad year economically in Peru.
[e]The figures for Village Cooperative underestimte its performance. A "model" of its performance based upon production figures would give a value added-labor figure of 12,351 for 1977.
[f]This may be regarded as a freak figure; the average value added-capital given in brackets excludes this figure.

Table 14-2
Correlation of Profit and Value-Added and Use of Capital

Cooperative		(1)	(2)	(3)	(4)	(5)	(6)	(7)
Peru								
Peruprint (1970-1977)	(S)	0.63	0.58	17.3	9.8	0.1	46	51
Cobblers (1969-1977)	(VS)	0.68	0.62	16.2	10.5	3.0	37	45
Metal FRN (1971-1977)	(F)	0.51	0.67	0	0	1.0	19.?	37
Clothing (1976-1977)	(F)	—	—	0	2.7	1.0	25	25
India								
Shuttlemakers (1962-1977)	(S)	0.31	0.18	3.5	0	0	56	79
Engineering (1970-1977)	(S)	0.20	0.20	9.4	0	2.5	29	45
Village (1971-1977)	(MS)	0.00	0.00	0	0	0	68	91
Commercial (1966-1977)	(F)	0.00	0.1	2.6	0	0	70	70

Note: (1) Correlation recorded profit/value added; (2) correlation recorded profit/value added per laborer; (3) average percent capital in use from collective savings; (4) average percent capital in use from redundancy fund; (5) average percent capital in use from member loans; (6) average percent capital in use from individual shares; (7) average percent capital in use from internal savings.

It is, of course, imperative from a theoretical point of view to distinguish those collective savings that are made voluntarily by the members from those that are enforced by statute.[10] In table 14-2 (column 4) we have also given the average percentage of capital in use deriving from statutory redundancy-retirement funds. Clearly in one sense these funds are earmarked for individuals in the case of retirement or redundancy, and they are thus not quite on the same footing as the reserve funds.

Not surprisingly, by comparing tables 14-1 and 14-2 we can detect a positive association between the propensity to save in collective funds and the economic performance of the cooperative (measured either qualitatively or in terms of value added per unit of labor).

Attempts to test this association using the time-series data for each cooperative are not terribly revealing, though the correlations are always positive. This is, we suspect, because of various possible lagged effects; these will be explored in a subsequent publication when the pilot data have been further supplemented.

Member Loans and Deposits. Although member loans and deposits are not in the strict sense of the term *collective*, in the cooperatives studied they are in practice similar to the extent that they rarely bear a direct dividend return to the individual saver. Where they are made, they are regarded as mandatory sacrifices that members make for the sake of the cooperative. Inspection of column 5 of table 14-2 shows that such savings are by no means universal but that they do occur; it is noteworthy that Cobblers' cooperative (VS) made significant savings though loans and deposits as well as collectively. The average figures in column 5, however, underestimate the use made of member loans and deposits, for the cooperatives often raised loans in times of distress to a much higher degree than the averages would indicate.

Individual Shareholding. Inspection of column 6 in table 14-2 indicates that all the cooperatives generated savings and investment through the issue of share capital. We found, however, that in most of the cooperatives studied the direct dividend returns to share capital were either negligible or nonexistent. Moreover, in most cooperatives it was extremely difficult for members to redeem their shares or withdraw their investment. In practice and from the point of view of the individual member, therefore, there was little to choose between collective savings and individual shares since neither bore an immediate direct dividend to the individual member.[11]

Total Internal Savings. It seems reasonable, therefore, to take all the "internally" generated savings together, and this is accomplished in column 7 of table 14-2. Inspection of this column seems to indicate that, in Peru, the average percentage of internally generated capital in each cooperative is associated with its degree of success, but that in India no clear relationship seems evident. It would be interesting to explore this difference more systematically, but again this must await a more adequate data base. If one studies the average yearly increment in internal savings (again as a proportion of total capital in use) then there is no simple relationship. In Peru, Cobblers Cooperative and Print have figures of 12 and 15 percent, respectively, though the corresponding figure for Metal Furniture (a failure) is 19 percent; in India, Commercial Cooperative (a failure) has the highest figure (9 percent) for all the cooperatives there.

The conclusions we can tentatively draw from these figures seem to be twofold: (1) that IPCs do seem to show a propensity to save either in general collective funds or quasicollective funds; but (2) there is no simple relationship between this propensity and the performance of the cooperatives (why this should be so we return to later).

Performance of IPCs Compared
with Capitalist Firms

The nonavailability of statistics prevented comparisons being made between the cooperatives and similar capitalist enterprises in India, so the analysis in this section is confined to Peru.[12]

In table 14-3 the performance of the cooperatives is compared with the average for all enterprises in the same industry and size range. As the number of cooperatives in the sample is very small, the comparison can be regarded as one between the individual cooperative and the average similar capitalist enterprise. Incidentally, from the table it can also be seen (column 7) that Cobbler (VS) and Metal Furniture (F) are larger than average for all firms in their respective industries in terms of the number of employees; Peru Print (S) is just below the average, and Clothing (F) is significantly so.

The comparison of performance, though, in each case has not been made with all firms but with the class of capitalist firms in the same size range. The comparison of revenue, value added, and capital in use is not very revealing for the size of the four cooperatives varies around the respective comparative class averages. What is revealing is to take capital per unit of labor, value added per unit of labor, and value added per unit capital; it is then clear that (a) capital per workplace in Peru Print (S) and Metal

Table 14-3
Comparisons of IPCs with Capitalist Enterprises, 1975

Cooperative	Size	(1)	(2)	(3)	(4)	(5)	(6)	(7)	(8)
Peru print (S)	22.2	0.36	0.33	0.65	0.46	0.88	0.52	23.6	1.3
Similar capitalist (Ave)	30.4								
Cobblers (VS)	42.4	1.6	1.7	2.21	1.2	1.65	0.78	27.0	1.2
Similar Capitalist (Ave)	30.9								
Metal FRN (F)	40.5	1.3	1.2	1.33	0.86	0.90	0.94	25.6	1.1
Similar capitalist (Ave)	27.4								
Clothing (F)	14.5	0.20	0.07	2.27	0.00	2.66	0.03	20.4	7.9
Similar capitalist (Ave)	17.0								

Notes: For purposes of comparison, capital = Value of Fixed Assets + Value of Stock. All figures (except seventh column) are ratios of the figures for the cooperative to similar capitalist enterprises. (1) Revenue; (2) value added; (3) capital; (4) value added/labor; (5) capital/labor; (6) value added/capital; (7) all industries average size; (8) percent value added distributed to labor.

Furniture (F) is just below the respective class averages; in Cobblers' (VS) it is above, and in Clothing (F) it is substantially above the averages; (b) Value added per unit of labor is below average in Peru Print (S), Metal Furniture (F), and Clothing (F), and above only in Cobblers (VS); (c) Value added per unit of capital is below average in all four cooperatives and is particularly so in the case of Clothing (F). Again, we will discuss these findings below.

Consumption Preference

Do the members of cooperatives tend to consume an inappropriately large proportion of the value added generated? The final column of table 14-3 seems to indicate that in Peru they do, on the average, consume somewhat higher proportions than is paid to employees in similar capitalist enterprises.[13]

Comparative figures were not available for India, but the average percentages of value added allocation of labor in the four Indian cooperatives were as follows: Shuttlemakers 77 percent, Engineering 66 percent, Village 58 percent, and Commercial 61 percent.

Capital Starvation or Capital Management

The evidence we have amassed in the previous sections casts considerable doubt upon the thesis that would promote capital starvation as the central problem facing small-scale IPCs in developing countries.[14] We have shown that members will save either collectively or through the issue of share capital despite the "irrationality" of the former and the limited returns to capital. Furthermore, we find little evidence to associate the incidence of these sorts of savings and overall economic success (that is, value added per member). It is true that successful cooperatives do save internally, but so also do some unsuccessful ones. Thus, at best internal savings effort can be a necessary condition of successful performance.

Moreover, it appears that cooperatives characteristically have a higher capital-labor ratio than similar capitalist enterprises through their value added per unit of capital employed is lower.

The conclusion we wish to draw from these rather surprising findings is that the problem that small-scale IPCs face is not so much one of investing sufficient capital but one of managing it effectively.

Let us consider the propensity for members to save internally (that is, through collective (reserve) funds, individual loans, and deposits, and share capital) in more detail. It may be that members are, according to the canons of neoclassical economics, simply "irrational"—wanting to invest in their cooperatives even when more remunerative and less risky alternatives exist; this might spring from a sense of altruistic commitment to the cooperatives. Be this as it may, it is important to recognize also that through investing in their cooperatives, members are joining their own capital with their labor, which has the consequence of boosting the value of r in formula 14.1. It is surely not unreasonable to suppose that with a high r and perhaps a relatively long t (consequent upon a commitment) that the inequality in formula 14.1 will favor intenal investment. An assessment of the situation facing the members of many cooperatives in developing countries suggest that they often face unemployment or severe underemployment if their cooperative fails. This certainly seems to account for the propensity they have to invest—even if their cooperatives appear to be failing—and the lack of any relationship between internal investment and overall success.

The relatively high capital-labor ratio (that is, compared with similar capitalist enterprises) but low value added per unit of capital give indirect evidence for the above reasoning and points to capital management as the key problem facing small-scale IPCs.[15]

A caveat should be inserted here, however—summary statistics, especially in India, show that many IPCs fail outright or are "dormant." It may be that these failed to raise sufficient capital (internal and loans) to stay in existence. Nevertheless, this would not detract from our conclusion that had they managed to continue operations then they would have been likely to encounter problems of capital management.

We found much additional evidence to support this thesis, namely, unused or underutilized capital, overstocking, and an inbility to manage the cooperatives in conditions of fluctuating market demand.[16] This conclusion does, of course, call into question prevailing policies whereby cooperatives are encouraged by loans at concessionary interest rates. If poor capital management is the problem they have to overcome, then capital made available on easy terms hardly meets their real needs. What is more, it brings the cooperative movement into disrepute and enables critics to point to high failure rates despite the favorable capital terms.[17]

Finally, our conclusion seems to lend support to Vanek's (1970) idea that a support organization will be necessary to propagate a viable cooperative sector.

Notes

1. As far as we know there is no published work comparing the average life expectancy of IPCs with capitalist enterprises.

2. Although neither Vanek nor Furubotn explicitly bring the risk attached to investment into their deliberations, this risk is clearly pertinent,

and one suspects that investment in IPCs is often much more risky than, say, investment in a savings bank.

3. Individual share capital is in practice not always easily redeemable and there is usually no secodary market in cooperative shares. The de facto situation may thus depart significantly from the de jure one.

4. A group of members providing equal capital endowments will not be materially affected by limited returns to capital, for they can choose to remunerate themselves through work. External members (if any) cannot, of course, do so, and limited returns could inhibit them. Further, if internal-member capital holdings are unequally distributed, conflict can arise over returns to work and returns to capital.

5. Assuming the existence of positive efficiency returns to capital.

6. The research was funded by the Overseas Development Administration (United Kingdom) under the auspices of the International Cooperative Alliance. It involved the detailed study of a number of IPCs, some "successful," some not, in India, Peru, Indonesia, and Senegal during 1977 and 1978. The results are only partially reported here. The full report on the research will appear shortly in book form. All the cooperatives had less than 50 worker-members.

7. The qualitative categorization of the cooperatives as successful or otherwise derives from their a priori selection for inclusion in the pilot study. In this respect we took the guidance of local experts, who were asked to select cooperatives that, by local standards, either had been successful over a reasonable number of years or that seemed to have run into more than temporary difficulty.

8. There are other reasons why IPCs will not wish to show a profit. In many countries cooperatives are subject to a profit tax. Clearly, from the government's viewpoint, a turnover or value-added tax might be considered more appropriate.

9. Profit maximizing and maximizing value added per member are, of course, identical with a fixed membership (that is, in the short term).

10. Legally obligatory collective funds could not, of course, contribute to capital starvation.

11. But one should bear in mind what we said earlier concerning returns to work and returns to capital. Further, there is always the possibility of a dividend in the future.

12. The comparisons were made with the average figures for all enterprises of approximately equal size in the same sector. They therefore presumably contain both the successful and unsuccessful enterprises.

13. The all-industry average (1975) proportions of value added going to labor in capitalist enterprises are Print 45 percent, Cobblers 32 percent, Metal Furniture 42 percent, Clothing 37 percent. The ratios of the cooperative figures to these figures (for 1975) are, respectively. 1.1, 2.2, 1.4, and 6.0.

14. It must be borne in mind that we are dealing here with 8 cooperatives; whether or not our findings are generalizable is a moot point though our broader but less intensive investigation of a wider range of cooperatives seems to suggest that they are.

15. This conclusion may not be generalizable to larger cooperatives, especially when the production is capital intensive. In such cases capital starvation and management both may be problematic.

16. These factors are explored in more detail in the report already mentioned.

17. Perhaps we may single out the Mondragon Group of cooperatives in northern Spain as a case supporting our thesis. There the Caja Laboral Popular not only provides credit to the individual cooperatives, but also links this to the provision of advice and supervision; it thereby ensures that the capital is used effectively (see the chapter by Thomas in this volume).

15 Institutional and Economic Aspects of the Jamaican Sugar Cooperatives

Vincent Richards and
Allan N. Williams

During the 1970s the English-speaking Caribbean witnessed the emergence of a number of producer (worker) cooperatives (PCs) and other forms of participatory organizations. The PC was seen by many as an effective organizational form in the process of economic development.[1] By far the most significant case are the Jamaica sugar PCs, which sought to transform the organization and management of the Jamaican sugar industry, the core of the country's agricultural sector.

In this chapter we review the experiences of the Jamaica sugar PCs and offer an assessment of their performance.[2] We argue that the sociopolitico-economic environment and the institutional constraints within which the PCs function may be as vital to the results they achieve as are their internal structure and functioning. This is done in the following section of this chapter. In the third section we highlight key features of the PCs' internal organizational structure and attempt to place them in typologies suggested by Jaroslav Vanek (1975) and Derek Jones (1980). An account and evaluation of the economic performance of the Jamaica sugar cooperatives constitute the following section. Using ratio analysis we establish that their profitability and productivity experiences compare favorably with earlier performance under traditional capitalist plantation arrangements. In a concluding section we summarize our findings and relate them to results of other researchers in this field.

Historical and Environmental Settings

In assessing the performance of an individual production unit, an industry or indeed an economy, it is now well recognized that in situations involving structural changes and differences, as opposed to marginal adjustments, the historical and environmental contexts should be explicitly taken into account. The conceptual framework proposed by Koopmans and Montias (1971) for comparing economies or their systems is one in which outcomes *o*

Part of the research on which this paper is based was carried out while Vincent A. Richards was a Visiting Research Fellow at the University of the West Indies with financial support from the Inter-American Foundation. The support of both institutions is acknowledged but the authors take full responsibility for views expressed.

depend upon the environment e, the economic system s, and policies developed and pursued by actors under the system p. Formally

$$o = F(e,s,p). \qquad (15.1)$$

In addition, the results of a comparative analysis depend critically upon the norms and criteria utilized. This is equally applicable for the comparative evaluation of enterprises particularly in developing countries like Jamaica, where many of the changes are structural. Similar ideas are suggested by Espinosa in this volume. It is therefore instructive to review the environmental setting within which the Jamaica sugar PCs developed.

In 1968 government policies were conceptualized to respond to the desire of the major sugar manufacturers to divest themselves of the least productive part of sugar manufacture, the production of sugar cane. However, given the substantial assets tied up in sugar factories, it was essential that adequate quantities of sugar cane be forthcoming to ensure financial viability of the sugar factories. The high cost feature of sugar cane production by factory operators had been highlighted by the government-appointed Sugar Industry Enquiry Commission, which reported in 1967. In 1965, while cane farmers were paid $5.74 per ton for canes delivered to the factories, the cost of production on factory-operated estates was $7.17. The effect of this substantial differential on sugar-production costs was that estimated total cost of sugar manufacture was $74.08 per ton using farmers' canes compared to $87.88 using estate canes—a difference of 18.9 percent.[3]

Partly in response to the divestiture intentions of some segments of the industry, and certainly as a result of growing popular demand for national ownership of land resources, a substantial amount of lands—about 74,000 acres—that were previously under foreign control were to be in the government's hands at the end of the 1973-1974 crop. In 1972 the government established the Frome Monymusk Land Company (FMLC) to manage the lands. This company incorporated into its structure the technical and managerial staff who were previously engaged in the field operations of sugar-cane production on the purchased estates.[4] Almost all the productive acreage of these lands had been used to produce sugar cane. From the standpoint of the dominant interests of the industry, particularly the sugar factory owners and government, it was desirous to maintain these lands in sugar. Indeed, the approach to land use by the FMLC was simple and singular. It rotated around the requirement that the factories be supplied with adequate amounts of cane to make their operations profitable. This requirement gained added significance when within a year or two the sugar factories became government property.

What factors accounted for the decision to maintain the inherited land-use patterns? (1) As we shall demonstrate shortly, the financial viability of three of the major sugar factories depended upon this. (2) The sugar industry was a major employer of labor and its employment contribution was well recognized in an economy with an unemployment rate officially estimated at 23.2 percent in 1972.[5] (3) There were many communities on the periphery of, and some barracks on, the three estates involved, which housed working-class families. The members of these communities depended primarily on the sugar industry for their livelihood. Its abandonment, it was felt, would lead to severe social and economic dislocation. (4) The sugar industry provided, in varying degrees, community and health services, recreational facilities, water, and electricity to the surrounding communities. A significantly different land utilization program would in the short term affect the industry's capacity to deliver these services and consequently worsen the situation of the communities.

Of importance to the national standpoint, (5) the sugar industry was a significant and comparatively reliable earner of foreign exchange. The export price of sugar was determined primarily, if not exclusively, by international agreements so that independent action geared to maintain or increase foreign exchange earnings revolved around domestic output factors. For the period 1968-1972 only in one year did the share of sugar in the value of the main agricultural exports fall below one-half. When molasses earnings are added, earnings were above 50 percent for every year. The associated rum industry also accounted for modest export earnings.[6]

(6) The administrative and technical personnel who oversaw the field operations of the estates were integrated into the organizational structure of the FMLC. Assuming that their skills and power had some elements of specificity, it might be expected that any plan emanating from this group would have a bias toward maintaining the lands in sugar. In so doing their jobs and most likely their dominant position in the decision-making processes of the industry would be maintained. In other words, we contend that while the administrative and technical personnel may claim that their proposals are based on an assessment of national priorities and that they are in the national interest, the proposals are not likely to be in conflict with the interests of the administrative personnel.[7] Finally, (7) the attitudes of the trade union movement, particularly its leadership, were a factor. An alternative use of the lands that would threaten the traditional role of the trade unions would be resisted. Given the strength of the trade unions, any resistance on their part had to be treated seriously if a stable outcome was envisaged.[8]

To return to the first factor identified as affecting the land-utilization plan, there were three sugar factories involved, Bernard Lodge, Monymusk, and Frome. Bernard Lodge was the smallest. Government planners estimated that at full capacity throughout the grinding season it could take 525,000 tons of cane assuming 10.5 tons of cane to a ton of sugar. At the breakeven point, estimated to be 70 percent, the factory would require 367,500 tons of cane. The yearly average supply of sugar cane from independent farmers in the area was about 200,000 tons. Consequently the lands acquired by the government would have to supply between 167,500 and 325,000 tons to ensure a no-loss position for the factory. In 1972 there were 10,383 acres under cane production at the Bernard Lodge estate. This meant that given factory profitability imperatives, and in particular production at 90 percent of capacity, 84 percent of the lands in sugar cane had to remain in that use.[9]

The official picture takes an overly optimistic view. In particular, the assumed cane yield of 35 tons per acre does not tally with historical performance. During the 10-year period 1965-1974 not a single year experienced such a favorable productivity, the highest being 33.23 tons per acre (1965), the 10-year average being 28.09 tons per acre.[10] If we use the latter yield, land requirements for factory operation at 90 percent of capacity are 9,701 acres net (10,865 acres gross). In short, there would be no scope for the new occupants of the lands to engage in nonsugar-cane production.

The situation at both Monymusk and Frome was similar. Analogous calculations indicate that breakeven operations of the two factories would permit at most 8 percent of Monymusk's land and 24 percent of Frome's land to be used for alternative purposes.

The overall situation for 90 percent capacity operations is summarized as follows. Combined, the three factories were expected to process 2,065,500 tons of canes and produce 209,351 tons of sugar, 55.4 percent of Jamaica's production in 1972.[11] The input-output relationship implies 9.87 tons of cane to a ton of sugar. It is instructive to note that the industrywide productivity ratios for the period 1969-1974 reflect a less favorable situation. For the 12-year period 1964-1975 only 5 years experienced tons cane-sugar proportions better than or equal to the projected ratio. Hence if the industrywide ratios reflect closely conditions at the three factories, then the projections were certainly optimistic.

Another observation about the productivity of sugar lands is in order. The industry experience over the 12 years from 1964 to 1975 was consistently below the 35 tons assumed. Indeed, a downward trend over the period is clearly discernible, the average for the 5 years 1964-1968 being 30.50 while that for the 5 years 1971-1975 was 26.44. If the latter figure is used the acreage requirements for sugar-cane production to keep the factories at 90 percent capacity will be increased.

It should also be noted that the three factories are old, which partly accounts for their breakeven levels being about 70 percent of capacity. In addition, breakdown of factory equipment and machinery during the grinding season reduces their effective capacity from the levels given.

With the foregoing considerations relating to the three factories and the necessity to maintain the lands in sugar cane, the question arises as to the choice of organizational form to carry out farm operations. It may be useful to consider two schemes. In the first, the property relations in the industry are that government, through the FMLC, will have control over the lands while the foreign private interests maintain ownership and control over the three factories. In the second, as currently holds, government through the FMLC and the National Sugar Company has ownership and control of both the lands and the factory operations. The important distinction between the two systems from an organizational-management standpoint is that integrated operation of the lands and factory is not likely under the first, while under the second it could be a very attractive—perhaps the most attractive—arrangement. In both schemes, however, it should be understood that the overriding interest of the management-technical group is the profitability of the factories.

In the case where the organizational-management structure for the lands is separate from that of the factories, how can estate-cane production be organized? It appears that three alternatives were evaluated by the management-technical personnel.[12] First, the lands could be run as state farms. The old dehumanized plantation relations would continue, the management structure would be strongly hierarchical, sugar workers would continue to do their narrowly defined tasks, and widespread functional illiteracy among them would remain. Choosing this option would run counter to the widespread national call for destruction of plantation production relations and more particularly would receive strong resistance from sugar workers, who through their grass-roots organizations were demanding an end to existing structures in the industry. Equally important was the fact that questions were raised as to whether the oppressive features that the state farm structure implied in the presence of strong trade union activity could ensure the necessary amount of sugar cane for the factories—which, after all, was the goal. Would not the state-farm system breed additional industrial action by the working class?

Second, the lands could be subdivided and sold to nationals, who would organize production along capitalist plantation lines. Enterprises would be smaller than earlier arrangements for the first option, but organizational and management practices would remain unchanged.

The third option was to structure cane production along PC lines. Grass-roots organizations clamored for this option on the grounds that it would release sugar workers from dehumanized production relations and increase their economic benefits from the industry. Government leaders at all levels saw the PC and other participatory forms as key instruments in the country's economic and social transformation.[13] For these and other reasons cooperatives were chosen as an experiment.

Some caution was exercised in the establishment of cooperatives. In 1974 three pilots were set up, one on each estate, with government support and supervision. The experiences of these were to guide the development of subsequent ones. (All three reported a profit in the first year, Barham $348,641, Morelands $154,000, and Salt Pond $323,112; these figures have subsequently been questioned by the United Sugar Workers Cooperative Council (USWCC) and other officials). Their initial financial success (real or contrived) served as a fillip to the creation of others and demands by grass-roots organizations of the sugar workers for more cooperatives were granted.

Organizational Structure of Sugar Cooperatives

In all there are 23 sugar-cane-producing farm cooperatives, 5 at Bernard Lodge, 8 at Monymusk, and 10 at Frome. In addition to these primary production cooperatives, there are three branch cooperatives, one on each estate, providing tractor, transport, and irrigation services to the primary cooperatives.

The primary cooperatives function on the basis of worker self-management. The chief policy-making and executive body is a management committee, which is comprised of democratically elected cooperative members and the general membership participates in the annual elections. The management committee is supported by a management staff (numbering about three at each cooperative); management personnel are not members of the cooperative.

The farm cooperatives on each estate are grouped into a second-level estate cooperative. This facilitates coordination in the provision of services and the execution of production plans of the farm cooperatives. Each estate cooperative is managed by a management committee elected from the membership of the primary cooperatives, supported by technical and administrative staff (nonmembers).

The third level of the three-tier cooperative structure is the USWCC, whose members are the three estate cooperatives. USWCC coordinates the activities of the estate (and by extension of primary farm) cooperatives in the areas of technical and managerial personnel, finance, marketing, education and training, and planning. The policy-making body of USWCC is a management committee comprised of cooperative members democratically elected each year. Day-to-day management functions are carried out by a nonelected staff headed by a general secretary.

While the organizational structure of the sugar cooperative reflect some of the essential features of self-managment, there are several constraints limiting its full practice. Because of the pivotal role of the sugar industry and because the industry experienced serious financial difficulties prior to the advent of the cooperatives and thus handed them a fragile financial structure, the Sugar Industry Authority, the government agency that regulates the industry, plays a dominant role in the provision of finance. Also, the cooperatives are constrained to remain in sugar cane production and sell their output to a sole factory, which is state-owned and controlled; they have little or no say in price determination or output mix. In order to preserve jobs initial membership levels were set too high. Finally, given the strong influence of labor unions for all categories of workers in the industry, adjustments through cuts in labor incomes were not feasible.

In several respects, the sugar PCs are similar to the American self-help PCs analyzed by Jones and Schneider (forthcoming).[14] Both exhibit significant government influence and were seen as tools of government policy. In terms of the typology of PCs suggested by Jones (1980, pp. 142-143), the sugar PCs would be classified as type II; workers have majority control, the majority of workers are members and all members are workers. But important restrictions limit the ability of workers to full management and control. With respect to Vanek's (1975, pp. 13-16) typology of worker-managed and labor-managed cooperatives and PC, the sugar cooperatives would constitute a hybrid of the second and third categories.

An assessment of the cooperatives should recognize the educational and skill levels of their members in relation to their ability to assume effectively the expanded role that the new self-management arrangements imply. While estimates for all cooperatives are unavailable, it is known that cooperative members have low levels of literacy. For example, on the basis of a survey conducted in 1976 on 10 cooperatives, Stone (1976) reports that of the 340 cooperators questioned only 155 claimed they could read and write. Further, a substantial proportion of cooperative members have already completed more than half of their working life in manual tasks.[15] An intensive and ongoing educational program will be vital for the successful implementation of self-management under these social and demographic conditions.

Economic Performance

Given the historical background to the formation of the cooperatives, their performance cannot be evaluated on purely economic lines. The changes brought about in social and political relationships and structures are just as important as those in the area of production and management. Preliminary assessment of the cooperatives along social and political lines has on balance been positive.[16] Here we concentrate on economic performance.

Given the poor financial situation of the industry, it is not to be expected that the cooperatives would generate any profit in the short term. Indeed prior to the establishment of the cooperatives, sugar-industry officials forecast substantial losses on the farm operations of the Frome, Monymusk, and Bernard Lodge estates. The projections are shown in table 15-1.

Even excluding interest payments, which were quite substantial, overall losses were projected for the entire period 1974-1979, the loss for the last year alone being $1.7 million.

With this background, the relative economic performance of the sugar cooperatives has not been bad. First, the three pilot cooperatives, Barham at Frome, Morelands at Monymusk, and Salt Pond at Bernard Lodge, were established in 1974 and recorded profits of $348,641, $154,000, and $323,112, respectively during their first year of operation. However, there has been serious questioning of these figures, for this performance has not been repeated by any cooperative.[17]

The relative satisfactory performance can be inferred from the behavior of production costs. At Frome unit production costs fell 16.6 percent from $25.32 in 1975-1976 to $21.11 in 1976-1977. The reduction was due partially to increased yields. Average production costs at Bernard Lodge decreased 20.1 percent from $28.12 in 1975-1976 to $22.48 in 1976-1979. In contrast, Monymusk cooperatives collectively experienced an increase in unit production costs from $26.72 in 1975-1976 to $36.44 in 1976-1977. This substantial rise was due primarily to low yields consequent upon the record drought that afflicted the Monymusk area. Details are provided in table 15-2, in which it is seen that all Frome and Bernard Lodge cooperatives posted cost reductions ranging from 7.2 percent to 22.1 percent. All Monymusk cooperatives had cost increases ranging from 24.2 percent to 93.3 percent. While detailed estimates of production costs for subsequent years are unavailable, the estate figures for 1977-1978 indicate continued success in controlling increases in production costs during a period when fuel, power, fertilizer, and transportation costs have markedly increased.

It is instructive to look also at the profit-and-loss experience of the cooperatives. While the short time period precludes definitive conclusions on trends, it is not insignificant that the profit-and-loss position has improved

Table 15-1
Financial Projections of Farm Operations

Year		Profit (Loss) before Overheads			General Overheads	Profit (Loss) before Interest Payments
	Frome	Monymusk	Bernard Lodge	Total		
1974	(111)	(466)	509	(48)	(182)	(230)
1975	203	(1417)	(31)	(1245)	(300)	(1545)
1976	275	(1331)	107	(949)	(360)	(1309)
1977	247	(1256)	229	(780)	(414)	(1194)
1978	250	(1258)	182	(826)	(470)	(1302)
1979	175	(1447)	127	(1145)	(548)	(1693)

Source: USWCC Position Paper, no date.
Note: All figures are in thousands of dollars.

at the Bernard Lodge and Frome estates. The peculiar problems of drought
and absence of proper irrigation at Monymusk are such that natural conditions dominate the outcome there.

Table 15-3 presents the profit experience of the cooperatives at Frome
and Bernard Lodge. It will be observed that at the former the actual operating
loss per ton of cane produced fell from $5.73 to $3.13, or by 45.4 percent between 1976 and 1977—a remarkable improvement. However, *recorded* performance in 1978 worsened over 1977, the unit loss being $5.45, implying an
increase of 74.1 percent. We emphasize that this is recorded performance.
Had the Frome cooperatives harvested all of their mature sugar cane, it is
estimated that the result would have been a unit loss of $1.90; that is, unit
loss would have *fallen* by 39.3 percent. Although the 1978 harvesting season
at Frome extended for more than a month beyond its scheduled end, 65,885
tons of sugar cane, or 14.9 percent of total production by the cooperatives,

Table 15-2
Cooperative Production Costs

| Cooperative | Cost per Ton Sugar Cane | | Percentage Change |
	1975/76	1976/77	
Frome			
Shrewsbury	$25.37	$20.78	− 18.1
Barham	N/A	19.23	—
Blue Castle	24.94	19.99	− 19.8
Frome	25.63	23.89	− 6.8
Bella Isle	N/A	19.09	—
Meylersfield	26.42	23.86	− 9.7
Albany	N/A	19.69	—
Masemure	24.95	23.09	− 7.5
Mint	N/A	23.91	—
Georges Plain	24.89	22.49	− 9.6
Bernard Lodge			
Half Way Tree	27.61	23.15	− 16.2
Salt Pond	N/A	26.58	—
Ried's Pen	30.63	23.87	− 22.1
March Pen	26.70	21.91	− 17.9
Windsor Park	27.47	25.49	− 7.2
Monymusk			
Springfield	24.01	32.95	37.2
Exeter	25.35	31.48	24.2
Mumby	30.76	44.07	43.3
Greenwich	31.29	58.82	88.0
Salt Savannah	31.29	58.82	88.0
Morelands	N/A	38.19	—
Hillside	26.12	40.19	53.9
Bog	23.87	37.91	60.2

Source: USWCC financial records.

was not reaped due to continuing poor performance by the factory, a three-week work stoppage by factory workers and a three-week protest by cooperative members, among other factors. The result was a revenue loss estimated at $1.25 million.

The favorable financial performance of the Frome cooperatives was outstripped by their Bernard Lodge counterparts. Actual operating loss per ton of cane fell from $9.45 in 1976 to $4.53 in 1977, a dramatic 51.9 percent. Even this substantial improvement would have been better if all the mature sugar canes had been reaped. About 29,000 tons, or 15.7 percent, of total production was not harvested. Further massive decline in unit loss was recorded in 1978, equivalent to 38.6 percent. Like Frome, the harvesting activities of the Bernard Lodge cooperatives during 1978 were frustrated by factory difficulties. There were several equipment breakdowns and four work stoppages by factory operatives. The consequence was an estimated 43,000 tons of stand-over cane or 17.1 of total production. This meant loss in revenue of $817,000. The bottom-line estimate adjusted for this gives a small unit profit of $0.94.

The primacy of factory economic viability in policy discussions and decisions on the sugar industry has been discussed in an earlier section. This has affected the results of their performance. The issue of stand-over cane was just mentioned, and it was noticed that the result was reduced revenue for a given level of production. It has been estimated that for all cooperatives, the inability to reap all mature sugar cane caused in 1978 a loss of gross revenue of $2.73 million of $1.46 million net of associated harvesting expenses.

Three other factors should be mentioned: harvesting at times of premium labor rates, cane production on marginal lands; and long harvest

Table 15-3
Profit/(Loss) Performance of Cooperatives

Cooperative	1976	1977	1978
Frome			
Actual profit (loss)	(5.73)	(3.13)	(5.45)
Adjusted profit (loss)[a]	(5.73)	(3.13)	(1.90)
USWCC-SIA 5-year plan		(3.51)	(1.57)
Bernard Lodge			
Actual profit (loss)	(9.42)	(4.53)	(2.78)
Adjusted profit (loss)[a]	(9.42)	(2.55)	0.94
USWCC-SIA 5-year plan		0.50	1.84

Source: USWCC financial records.
[a]Adjusted for standover cane.
[b]All figures are $ per ton of sugar cane.

time. The cooperatives have inherited the legacy of acting as raw-material supply buffers to the sugar factories, a role the factory-owned plantations fulfilled under the previous ownership-organizational arrangements. Private cane farmers tend to supply the factories primarily during weekdays, when standard labor rates apply. To keep the factories operating on weekends the factory-owned estates provided the bulk of the sugar-cane needs, paying premium labor rates in the process. While organizational relationships have altered, the cooperatives claim that through the quotas decided by the various harvesting committees, cane deliveries by the cooperatives have been biased toward times when premium rates apply. The result is that in 1978 it costs the cooperatives an estimated $2.16 million in added harvesting expenses.

Cane production on marginal lands in order to conform to factory needs, as outlined in the second section of this chapter, also results in higher unit production costs. Research by one of the authors on the historical productivity performance of the cane lands at the cooperatives suggests that a sizable proportion of the fields have consistently given poor results. In table 15-4 sample findings for the Windsor Park Cooperative at Bernard Lodge are presented. Productivity experience for 11 years (1956-1974 and 1976)

Table 15-4
Productivity of Windsor Park Lands

A. By Fields[a]

Average Yield (tons/acre)	Number of Fields	Percentage	Cumulative Number	Cumulative Percentage
40.00-	4	1.3	4	1.3
35.00-39.99	10	3.3	14	4.6
30.00-34.99	44	14.4	58	19.0
25.00-29.99	121	39.7	179	58.7
20.00-24.99	91	29.8	270	88.5
15.00-19.99	25	8.2	295	96.7
0.00-14.99	10	3.3	305	100.0

B. By Acreage[a]

Average Yield (tons/acre)	Acreage of Fields	Percentage Acreage	Cumulative Acreage	Cumulative Percentage
40.00-	32.25	0.9	32.25	0.9
35.00-39.99	85.50	2.4	117.75	3.3
30.00-34.99	520.25	14.7	638.00	18.0
25.00-29.99	1,560.05	44.0	2,198.05	62.0
20.00-24.99	1,047.50	29.5	3,245.55	91.5
15.00-19.99	300.50	8.5	3,546.05	100.0

Source: Author's research files.
[a]Calculations are based upon results for 11 years, 1965-1974 and 1976.

was such that only 18.0 percent of the acreage had an average yield of 30 tons per acre and above. Of the acreage, 38 percent produced on average below 25 tons per acre. Of the 305 cane fields, 41.3 percent produced under 25 tons an acre. Similar results obtain for the March Pen Cooperative, as seen in table 15-5. The extent of production on marginal lands is not small. But the conditions under which the cooperatives lease the lands from the government do not permit adequate flexibility in land use.

The last factor with serious economic impact on the cooperatives is the irregular duration of the harvest season. The cooperatives get paid not simply for tons of cane but in relation to its sucrose content. Irregular harvesting seasons lead to reaping at times of low average sucrose content, resulting in a low effective price for a ton of cane. One estimate of this cost in 1978 is $1.3 million.

In summary, the results discussed above suggest a measure of economic performance that is satisfactory. If the reductions in unit production costs recorded by the Frome and Bernard Lodge cooperatives are not one-shot but are sustained, then the economic viability of these cooperatives is a real prospect.

Caveats and Conclusion

While the limited evidence presented above gives a picture of modest relative financial success, several limitations should be noted. First, the period covered by the data is rather short and as such it cannot be said that the favorable results noted are the beginning of a continuing trend. Second, certain outcomes have been identified but no attempt was made to isolate the causative factors. To refer to the earlier mentioned Koopmans-Montias conceptual framework, we have a rough idea of outcomes but we cannot attribute specific ones to the environment, the economic-management system, or the particular policies implemented by the sugar cooperatives. Third, as Yotopoulos and Nugent (1976, chapter 5) cogently demonstrated, output per acre, input per acre, and related productivity ratios do not lead to straightforward valid economic efficiency comparisons.

Nevertheless, the results to date indicate a generally improved position with respect to unit-production costs. With no evidence of significant favorable environmental or other external factors, it seems reasonable that the cooperative organizational form and the efforts of the cooperators should be among the determining factors.

It is useful to compare our findings with those of other researchers on other developing countries. In his study of Peruvian reform enterprises, Horton (1976) found that in the early years of their establishment, sugar and other cooperatives were able to maintain or modestly improve upon pre-reform levels of production while making sizable productive and social investment. Initial favorable economic performance by the Castle Bruce

Table 15-5
Productivity of March Pen Cooperative

A. By Fields

Average Yield (tons/acre)	Number of Fields	Percentage	Cumulative Number	Cumulative Percentage
40.00-	0	0.00	0	0.00
35.00-39.99	7	4.55	7	4.55
30.00-34.99	42	27.27	49	31.82
25.00-29.99	63	40.91	112	72.73
20.00-24.99	33	21.43	145	94.46
15.00-19.99	9	5.80	154	100.00
0.00-14.99	0	0.00	154	100.00

B. By Acreage

Average Yield (tons/acre)	Acreage of Fields	Acreage	Cumulative Acreage	Cumulative Percentage
40.00-	0.00	0.00	0.00	0.00
35.00-39.99	80.55	4.54	80.55	4.54
30.00-34.99	473.05	26.68	553.60	31.22
25.00-29.99	743.65	41.93	1,297.25	73.15
20.00-24.99	390.85	22.04	1,688.10	95.19
15.00-19.99	85.25	4.81	1,773.35	100.00

Source: Authors' research files.

Cooperative in Dominica is also reported by Williams (1980). The early satisfactory results of the Castle Bruce Cooperative have, however, given way to less favorable outcomes. This suggests that caution should be exercised in extrapolating the initial modestly successful performance of the Jamaican sugar cooperatives.

Notes

1. Vanek and Espinosa (1972) make a strong theoretical case for the PC as an effective organizational form in an underdeveloped context. For its relevance to Jamaica, see Manley (1974) and (Jamaica) Advisory Committee on Worker Participation (1976).

2. For a review of cooperative experiences in another Caribbean country, see Williams (1980).

3. These costs are computed from data in (Jamaica) Sugar Industry Enquiry Commission (1967).

4. Higgins (1980) provides some discussion on the historical background.

5. The figures are based on data in (Jamaica) National Planning Agency, *Economic and Social Survey*, (various years).

6. Derived from data in National Planning Agency, *Economic and Social Survey* (various years).

7. This argument is akin to the voluminous literature that emphasizes goals and preferences of managers in enterprise decision-making.

8. Evidence reported by Stone (1977) indicates significant trade-union loyalty among members of the sugar cooperatives.

9. The data and conclusions drawn on the sugar factories are based upon the authors' analysis of planning memoranda related to the establishment of the cooperatives.

10. These and other historical performance records are computed from (Jamaica) Sugar Industry Research Institute, *Annual Report* (various years), and National Planning Agency, *Economic and Social Survey* (various years).

11. This targeted production of the three factories was 62.1, 56.3, and 59.0 percent of actual national production for 1973, 1974, and 1975, respectively.

12. For another discussion, see Higgins (1980).

13. The case for the PC in the agricultural sector is strongly stated by Michael Manley, Jamaica's Prime Minister from 1972 to 1980 in Manley (1974) especially pp. 113-122.

14. The sugar cooperatives are also somewhat similar to the Scottish Daily News case from the standpoint of government sponsorship and support and the employment maintenance goal. See Bradley and Gelb (1980b).

15. A survey undertaken at Barham cooperative in 1975 revealed that the average age of its members was 46.6 years. There was little variation around the mean, the standard deviation being 9.8 years. Barham had a membership of 163 at that time (Patterson et al (no date)).

16. See Higgins (1980), and Stone (1977, 1978).

17. Several USWCC position papers have questioned the financial arrangements governing the sugar cooperatives, and in particular certain costs assigned to the cooperatives when the transfer of responsibility from the FMLC to the cooperatives took place. See, for example, USWCC background paper to the press conference held March 27, 1979.

Part VI
Postscript

16 Toward a Forward Step in Empirical Self-Management Research

Jaroslav Vanek

In this chapter, I argue that many researchers in the field of self-management have been talking too much to each other, for the most part repeating to ourselves what we are convinced of already and for which by and large we already have theoretical and empirical proofs, while at the same time not convincing anyone else. If we want to move closer to what we all believe in, I feel that the traditional procedures of economic science and Western social science in general are a dead end street and we must seek new paths. All this is related to some broad issues concerning the state of social science and going well beyond the concrete problems of empirical verification in the field of self-management.

I will first address myself to these broader critical issues in the following section and then turn in the fourth and fifth sections of this chapter to more positive considerations and solutions, whether potential or actual. The division between the fifth and sixth sections is one between constructive observations on the state of our discipline or science on the one hand, and constructive considerations with respect to the practice and praxis of self-management on the other. To the issue of praxis as it pertains to our scientific work I will return in the third section. Also as we will see later the structure of this paper itself is one given by what I refer to as the praxis progression.

From a Primitive to a Critical Consciousness

The basic problem that we are facing is that socioeconomic systems, broadly defined, develop their own systems of thought, or paradigms, or scientific structures corresponding to them. The sociopolitical-economic system to which we refer as self-management, however, is fundamentally different and thus its corresponding paradigm is different from the Western capitalist paradigm. To judge or evaluate a new system from the vantage point of the old capitalist paradigm and to be in some sense objective is exceedingly difficult if not impossible. Yet most of the literature we have on the subject of self-management looks at the subject matter from within the capitalist system of thought. What we as scientists work with and in is by and large the old system of thought.

For example, the very foundation of the neoclassical theory of self-management contains a significant element in this sense and in fact a warning to the scientists. Here I speak of the Ward backward-bending supply function: an impossibility resulting directly from the neoclassical myth and totally disregarding empirical evidence or the common sense of normal social conduct. And yet most of the theoretical work on self-management in economics bears precisely the same marks. Going beyond this in one's analysis, as I have done in many mostly unpublished papers and by now some four or five book-size manuscripts, meets with considerable resistance.

As far as I am concerned these "contributions" are far less true contributions in some objective sense, and far more results of the distorted state of the economic profession in general. To paraphrase, using Biblical terminology, the majority of our profession will not believe even if the dead would return from their graves. On the contrary they will keep proving ad nauseam that their ship is headed for the promised land even if it were sinking (as it is).

The voluminous theoretical prediction of inefficiency of self-managing firms by such authors as Alchian and Demsetz (1972) and Jensen and Meckling (1979) is another example of shooting of paper balls from the cannons of the ship of fools of the economic profession. One reads such glaring terms as "shirking"—"premiums of managers to be grudgingly shared with workers"—"effect of size on control with increasing labor force". As if it were not a notorious fact that in the capitalist world workers hate, resent, or fear the employers and foremen, and thus they maximize shirking when possible and protect their fellow workers: whereas when the factories are their own domain they protect them collectively, always fulfilling themselves the roles of "dialogical" supervision. Or, how can one blame effects of size when even very large factories can and are being decentralized in the real world into smaller and functional autonomous working collectives? This is the same decentralization that would seem to be the organization of production least conducive to decentralization.

The funding of scientific research by Western and especially American national and private foundations proceeds very much along the same lines. Here I do not imply malice but simply a fairly honest, sometimes self-righteous, evaluation of a new subject by people who wear the old glasses or into whose mind the superiority of the profit-maximizing capitalist system has been inculcated by years of drilling in undergraduate and graduate classes.

I do not have to elaborate further on these matters. Much that is more positive, constructive, and objectively valid can be offered even at this stage of a critical evaluation. One must remember that it is precisely by arresting the process of praxis—or what I shall define later in this paper as praxis progression—at an inferior stage that the establishment impedes forward motion. This maintainance of myth in substance and method is what I refer to, at least for our discipline of economics, as the ship of fools. The problem is that we in the discipline of economics of self-management still are, at least with one foot, on the ship of fools, especially in the domain of methodology.

If we are truly concerned with democratization and self-determination in the economic sphere, we must first and foremost separate ourselves from the old paradigm. The costs in personal terms may be considerable, but the benefits in the social sense are enormous. I have noted already that it is difficult if not impossible to convince any one operating strictly from within the academic world.

Leaving the ship of fools means transferring to another means of transportation; which above all should bear the characteristics of the land to which we want to travel. I will return in more practical terms to this in the subsequent two sections. The leaving of the old ship is not antisocial behavior toward those whom we are leaving. In fact our departure is potentially beneficial to them because if there is a way toward mental sanity on their part it must be assisted by others than fellow travelers. The vehicle of correction for them cannot be an arrogant and abstract theoretical monologue; the vehicle must be practical and tangible, if there is a vehicle at all.

Three Fundamental Instruments of Self-Management Research

In the course of my own work, I have become aware of what I consider to be three instruments that are the essence of optimal self-management, whether in research or in any other human endeavor. The first is a fundamental law of participation, as a matter of establishing an optimal structure. The second is a process that I call the praxis progression, as a matter of an optimal procedure. The third is dialogue as the only possible form of social reflection.

There is an organic unity among the three principal instruments not only in the context of dialogue but in several other respects as well. There is no logical order or hierarchy among the three; but perhaps as a matter of simplicity of exposition it is good to begin by explaining what I mean by optimal participation. I have written extensively on this subject[1] so that here I can concentrate on the general ideas and rely more on intuitive reasoning.

Let me begin with an example. The domain in question is factory production, wherein we may say that capitalist control and profit-making by stockholders is also a form of participation. Indeed, it is participatory production in which all the votes are given to those who own capital and no votes are given to those who work, and similarly for distribution of profits.

It does not take much argument to be convinced that there is something incorrect, or certainly suboptimal, in this form of participatory decision-making. Of the many things wrong with this kind of participatory management, one seems to be most central: that different people and different groups of people are treated unequally. Implicitly or explicitly somehow we all have the idea that people are equal and in some sense, perhaps difficult to define, they ought to be treated equally. This we may call the axiom of equality. It is indeed an axiom because while we may all feel its correctness, it is difficult to prove. It is this axiom that I take as my point of departure, relying on the willingness of the reader to concur with or accept it. If the reader disagrees I feel that the burden of proving the contrary ought to be on him or her.

Of course the axiom of equality, while intuitively appealing, is not directly applicable without proper qualifications. If I want to speak about equality in the context of participation, I obviously must mean some kind of equality of power or of decision-making weight. But the question immediately arises, power over what, over what domains of decisions? For example, should a resident of The Hague have a voice in deciding on issues of public safety in Amsterdam equal with someone living in Amsterdam? Obviously not. What this example brings out immediately is the question of involvement. In some way the degree of involvement must be brought into consideration.

The axiom of equality with respect to participation can now be more clearly stated: different people ought to have equal weight or power in decision making provided that their involvement is similar. For example, two workers who work eight hours a day on similar jobs ought to have similar decision-making power. By contrast, if someone has a heavier involvement, however defined, he or she ought to be given a greater weight or power.

Of course, there is the problem of measuring and expressing the degree of involvement, but that problem is not insurmountable. In some situations, as in our example of working hours, there are objective measures of the degree of involvement. In other situations there is no reason why people themselves could not self-determine their degree of involvement over specific segments on the assumption that aggregate involvement is the same among individuals. A good example here is the participation by the teaching staff on the one hand and the technical staff on the other of an educational institution. Both of them *in total* have aggregate equal involvements per person; but they themselves may self-determine that the teaching staff's involvement is relatively heavier within the domain of educational matters, whereas the technical and other staff of the school may self-determine that their involvement is heavier in their own domain of interest.

What I have said thus far is that in order to attain a social optimum, participation in decisions and in power ought to conform to intensity, that is, the aggregate decision-making power over some well-defined area, ought to be the same for all individuals. This participation according to the involvement suggests another important law that takes us out of the customary unidimensionality of socioeconomic analysis: involvement can differ among people not only in intensity, which can be measured in terms of hours or degrees or percentages, but also, more fundamentally, in terms of quality. For example, take a drug that can at the same time serve to preserve someone's life, and to be just an opiate or alcohol to give someone else a more or less pleasant sensation. Obviously the two persons' involvement is fundamentally different in kind and not only in intensity. One may say that the first person is involved vitally because his or her life depends on the drug, while the second person is involved superficially or even pathologically.

The real world of human beings is full of similar (although not as extreme) instances, of such differential involvement. In the area of industrial organization I immediately think of the involvement of stockholders as compared to that of the workers. Stockholders of a factory can be scattered around the world, never even having seen the factory. By contrast, workers who spend eight hours a day, thirty or forty years of their lives in that factory are involved in quite a different manner. Their own involvement is infinitely more direct and approaches the vital involvement of the person in our example regarding medication and survival.

It is immediately apparent that if participation according to involvement is to vary with intensity there is a far stronger reason to let participation and decision-making power vary with the nature of involvement. While it is simple to match involvement with participation according to some exact index of degree of intensity, the matching of quality of nature of involvement with the quality or nature of participation is less straightforward. But it happens that there is always some kind of internal (organic) logic that in some sense confirms our notion of multidimensionality. For example, the internal logic in our case of vitally or nonvitally needed drug is that the person who needs it vitally ought to have some king of absolute preference over the other person or persons, irrespective of how many others there are and irrespective of how rich they may be.

Thus I have introduced in our concept of the optimal participation the notions of first, involvement; second, intensity of involvement; and third, nature or quality of involvement. There are three other very important considerations that must be brought in: first is the dialogue, in the sense that I have elaborated on already; second is decentralization; and third is constitutionality. All are interrelated: I will elaborate on them briefly.

The fact of life is that social preferences—the crux of participation—are not a result of some kind of adding of individual preferences. Rather they result from a very complex process involving learning, education, dialogue, emulation, feelings of sympathy or antipathy, among other things. Central to all these is a dialogue among people that not only transmits but also and above all creates knowledge and preferences.

People involved in a dialogical relationship form something quite different from voting democratic groupings. Dialogical groups cannot be very large. This brings us to the issue of decentralization of larger social bodies and to the issue of the optimal decentralization and optimal size of dialogical groups. The decentralization as much as the introduction of decision making by intensity of involvement and by nature of involvement brings in the issue of long-range constitutional decisions as distinct from short-range parliamentary-type decisions. For example decentralization or restructuring of an enterprise or of a political entity is something that is done constitutionally with reference to decades and not on an ad hoc parliamentary basis. A lasting constitutional basis also has the effect of purifying the decision-making process from possible problems of strategizing or pretending in that process. Dialogue in itself is also the best protection against strategizing and dishonesty. Dialogue is also much more likely to lead to consensus and homogeneity as compared to secret blind voting.

All I have done here is to sketch some principal characteristics of an extremely complex process. But even such a sketch does not leave any doubt about the necessity of introducing these factors into the design of an optimal participatory process. All these considerations lead to a formulation of what I refer to as the *fundamental law of participation,* which also summarizes the first long-range instrument for a new global order. To attain an optimal order and fullness of life in society the following is necessary:

In all areas of human endeavor all those, and only those who are involved, should participate in all decisions, and their participation must be according to both the intensity and the nature of their involvement. The participation should be democratic, and there should be a flexible constitutional framework for this democracy. Decision making should be optimally decentralized by application of devolution of power to such levels that dialogue and direct participation are always possible.

I now turn to the other two elements: dialogue and what I have termed the praxis progression. Not much space need to be devoted to the former, because we have just elaborated on it in connection with the optimal law, and because there are writings on the subject, especially those of Paulo Freire, as well as my own.[2]

The remaining element is procedural and constitutes what one may call the dynamic essence of optimal participation. We have referred to this third component as the process of *praxis progression.* As the term indicates the matter is related to and in fact constitutes a formalization of what Marxist writers refer to as *praxis*—interpreted by Paulo Freire as a combination of action and reflection.

I will begin unwinding my argument from a simple proposition. The proposition is not a definition of praxis progression or proof of social sanity (which also occurs in the proposition) but rather a cornerstone or a point of departure of a discussion leading to both such a definition and such a proof that everyone must, in the final analysis, "create" dialogically for himself. As we will see, the proof of social sanity also relies on the analogy and on the reader's introspection. The proposition is:

> All intelligent and sane (nonpathological) life of individuals, societies, or of all humanity over short periods of time or very long ones, covering many generations, can be seen as one or more concurrent and/or consecutive "praxis progressions."

By praxis progression I understand a series of seven consecutive states or stages of consciousness or action. This progression can be identified with the following seven general stages:

1. No consciousness
2. Naive or primitive consciousness
3. Critical consciousness
4. Denunciation
5. Enunciation
6. Testing and experimentation
7. Change or revolution

These terms are largely self-explanatory. All have been used, even if perhaps with somewhat different meanings, in the literature. The praxis progression can be arrested temporarily or permanently. When that happens, we are facing a case either of insanity (pathology), either individual or social, or of absence of intelligence; that is, cessation of intelligence if a praxis progression has been begun and then interrupted. But let us now move on to some concrete examples that will illustrate our argument and at the same time suggest how this type of analysis can become useful.

The first example involves individual rather than social praxis progression. It has significant elements of "skipping" of stages because of repetition, and it is normally very short in duration, lasting perhaps ten or twenty seconds for the whole process. The domain or context of this progression is driving an automobile. In fact, the whole action of driving an automobile from one place to another can be visualized as a very large number of strictly consecutive praxis progressions. A typical one may be described as follows.

I am an experienced driver driving on a straight stretch of the road. The activity is quasi-automatic, and I am in a state of naive consciousness in which I was (with respect to driving the car) before I entered the car and started driving. Suddenly a curve occurs in the road, and I first acquire a critical consciousness in the sense that I realize that if I continue the preceding action of driving the car straight ahead, something very bad will happen.

That critical consciousness, of course, does not suffice and I acquire a state of mind that I refer to as denunciation, attaching so to speak a value to the fact that there is a curve and that if nothing is done I will have an accident. From that state of denunciation I form a theoretical abstract model (project) of what should be done and the corresponding state I refer to as enunciation; I enunciate—although only mentally in the concrete example of driving an automobile—that what I am going to do is to turn the wheel to adjust to that curve. If I were driving the car for the first time in my life, I would not know by how much to turn the wheel and I would have to enter a state of testing and experimentation. But since I learned to drive the car years ago, I have learned by experience and have automatized that stage in the praxis progression—that is, I can omit it. And thus I proceed immediately to the action, the revolution—that is, the revolution of the wheel. Thereafter I again find myself on a straight stretch of the road, and when new curves occur I repeatedly apply similar praxis progressions. Ultimately I stop and leave the automobile, whereby I again return to a state of no consciousness in the context at hand.

With the example of this individual praxis progression I am illustrating not only the case of "skipping" with repetitive activities and situations. By it I can also see in concrete terms what is meant by insanity, or lack of intelligence. An insane person starting from naive consciousness might progress to any one short of the final seventh stage of a progression and not progress to the next, thereby ultimately causing an accident.

Similarly—and this has significant analogies for the praxis progressions in the social context—the driver might be prevented from moving beyond that state of naive consciousness or held back at any one of the junctures between two stages by some external agent or as a matter of some side effects of the process of driving itself. The latter can be illustrated by car sickness resulting from the motion or gasoline fumes in the particular case of driving.

Of course, all such interruptions of the free flow of the progression interfere with and conceivably can entirely destroy what I have termed before a sane (nonpathological) and intelligent life. While an obvious and perhaps trivial observation in the context of our driving example, the notion of pathology can become less trivial and far more useful in understanding what is going on in the world when we come later on to the social forms of praxis progression.

Before I proceed to examine social situations, another one from the individual domain ought to be briefly noted. As compared to the driving example it stands at the other end of the spectrum in terms of duration, involving the entire life span of an individual. And because we all have our own lives and life experiences, our exposition can rely heavily on mere suggestion and the reader's introspection, or experience from his or her environment.

The praxis progression that I have in mind here is a human lifetime itself as each of us experiences it. Note that we all pass at birth from no consciousness to naive or primitive consciousness; we accept things uncritically as we receive them from our parents or our teachers. And in many respects many of us remain in that stage for all of our lives. But a fully lived, intelligent, and sane life really must involve a complete praxis progression reaching stages of critical consciousness formation, denunciation of imperfections, followed by an enunciation of what one wants to do with one's life in view of such a critical consciousness. That stage of enunciation really corresponds to and is nothing else but what is usually referred to as vocation or calling. The rest of life then corresponds to the last two stages of experimentation (searching) and actual change or revolution in one's life.

The fact that many remain in the state of naive consciousness, believing the myth that making money is their purpose in life, is probably less their own fault than that of the environment and social system in which they live. Education, social consensus, and certain self-conserving mechanisms of the established order often obstruct the individual's life praxis progression. In this, these factors act very much like the gasoline fumes, or more appropriately, an exorbitant uncontrollable speed in the case of car driving.

The obstruction of an individual's life praxis progression coming from other progressions in the social domain suggests a very important principle: it is very difficult to have unobstructed progression in some domains if significant obstructions occur in other domains. This is so especially with the dependence of individual progression domains on higher (broader) social domains.

Let me now turn to the social domains that lie at the heart of my interest. First I must note a fundamental difference and make a subsidiary definition. The fundamental difference is that the "reflection" part of praxis in the context of an individual cannot be directly transposed into the social context of two or more individuals. But the transposition can be effected by introducing the notion of *dialogue*. The process of dialogue among involved members of society, which we define with Paulo Freire as a process not only transmitting but also creating knowledge, now becomes *social reflection* in the process of social praxis progression. With that in mind all the above discussion of individual praxis progression can be extended to and become useful in the context of social praxis progression.

In particular I note that Paulo Freire's process of social conscientization or formation of critical consciousness in the context of literacy education or otherwise is nothing but a beginning of a revolutionary process of praxis progression (if brought all the way to its seventh stage). Freire's experiences with conscientization in northeast Brazil and his personal difficulties with the Brazilian government also illustrate a kind of an arrestation—like the fumes in my car-driving example. While perhaps rational from the point of view of the ruling generals, from the social point of view of praxis progression of the Brazilian nation that episode indicates a social pathology.

In a broader context—in a prospective sense the context is global—what I have spoken of elsewhere as accumulation is probably the most serious pathology of a (potentially) global social praxis progression. By terminal accumulation I understand accumulation of human capital, which is basically not self-determined but originates in the profit motive of capitalism, and which is bound to lead ultimately to a grave social pathology. As in the tower of Babel, the excessive non-self-determined knowledge must end in a "confusion of tongues" (pathology of communication): as in television, advertising, political propaganda, capitalist education, and so forth.

It follows from the discussion thus far—and the reader can realize it even more clearly by himself or herself—that the social and individual praxis progression can indeed occur over a virtual infinity of domains (or within a virtual infinity of contexts) defined in terms of duration, number of persons included, and concrete contexts such as production, consumption, formation of history, or driving an automobile. Of particular interest for us are the domains defined by social groups according to size or contiguity. It often happens that a lower (smaller) contiguous group, such as a class or enterprise, can engage in social praxis progression whereas the corresponding higher group (such as the economy, the nation as a whole, or global population, respectively) cannot do so, being engaged in a fundamental conflict situation, such as class struggle or world political crisis in the last two of the three instances.

In the context of our notions of intelligence or sanity of social life (see the initial proposition) such conflicts constitute an arrestation of the progression—an insanity or lack of intelligence.

Marxist class struggle and class conflict is an arrestation or a pathology of the global or national praxis progression; and its cure and termination, in my view, is a consistent global application of the fundamental law of participation. And indeed that application first and foremost implies abolition of capitalism. The only difference as I see it is that the task of renewal is much more than just the abolition of capitalism, and that the process leading to the solutions must be much more a deliberate global praxis progression than an automatic or autonomous process of deterministic forces of history.

It should be noted, and it will probably be better understood now that I have gone through my discussion of the three components, that there is a certain tri-unity of the three. The fundamental law of participation, true dialogue, and the process of praxis progression are three distinct matters, yet they mutually contain and support each other, and indeed any one is impossible without any other one.

Positive Paths: In the Real World

Relying on the extensive discussion in the preceding section, I can conclude my paper very briefly, dealing first with the real world and next with our scientific discipline.

When I leave the old ship or descend from the ivory tower I must have some general principles to follow. These are as I see them. Follow the method of praxis by means of true dialogue, that is, social reflection. While in our cabin on the ship of fools we were able only to reflect and we are starved for action; hence it is the latter that must be given priority at first. Because the new ship must resemble the new world we must be as fully participatory as possible in our scientific method—to which I come in the next section—as much as in our action.

Where, then, lie the practical approaches? Obviously the answers can be only partial: probably they will be too much influenced by the fact that the immediate reality of the observation for me is the United States. I appreciate in a general sense concrete work done by and on behalf of worker communities in closing down plants in the United States and elsewhere, although I may disagree on some essential specifics of that work. It is good to save workers' jobs wherever this is possible by reorganizing a failing capitalist firm into a self-managing one. This is so not only for the jobs saved, but also for the by-product of education and conscientization on the part of workers and the local community.

The procedure may be less desirable because these firms already are failing and often have very little chance of survival as self-managing firms. In addition this procedure most of the time gives the capitalists undue reward in compensation for assets and very often leaves them in the end with the argument, "you see, self-management does not work." I like to use the allegory of operating a social revolution in collaboration with only those in iron lungs or otherwise near death. The social and other costs of this procedure very likely exceed any social or private benefits from the point of view of transition to a democratic economy.

We ought not to condemn this procedure of shut-down plant takeovers because of the intrinsic worth to the workers who otherwise would become unemployed. But many and much more positive avenues must be sought. To recognize a failing firm as a human community rather than as a collection of assets with defined products will help: normally it may be better to preserve the community as a working collective by moving to other products and even other technologies.

More generally, the main attack in our quest for self-management in the

Western world ought to be not failing firms or communities but new communities, new products, and new technologies already in the general spirit of self-management and participation. In doing this, important lessons can be taken from an expansion of Paulo Freire's ideas: if we can operate a change of consciousness and corresponding revolutionary changes it must be within the domain of what we might call the principal problems or principal contradictions of individuals and society—in our case, of Western society. And what else in the immediate socioeconomic sphere but inflation, unemployment, the energy crisis, and an enslaving technology and form of organization are such principal contradictions? For all of them, the self-management and a participatory mode of organization is the cornerstone of a solution.

In addition to this role of self-management "in the large context" there is also the cooperative and self-managing form that I have been working with now for about a year and half as my own principal focus "in the narrow context." It consists of developing cooperative self-managing production at all levels of solar energy. This approach resolves directly the above-noted four contradictions: of price inflation, with about 1,000 percent greater efficiency per installed watt of heat than atomic power stations and thus lower price of energy; problems of employment, with about $100 or $200 (of capital equipment) per job as compared to a national average in the United States of about $50,000; obvious problems of energy such as import of oil, air and atomic pollution, and many others. In addition this solution resolves my own principal contradictions in the field of economics and social science of self-management by promoting democratic organization, organic and democratic technology, and decentralization to the point where true dialogue and self-management are possible.

Finally, I would like to address a concrete and personal question concerning us in the field of social science of self-management and participation. The natural first reaction of most of us—to some extent an inheritance from the ship of fools—is, how can "academics," men and women of science, "descend" to actual work with workers, building of new productive units and even manual work? My answer is, who else will if we do not? We may be the only ones with a sufficiently strong motivation and consciousness as well as comprehension of the problems involved to do it. In Mondragon it took precisely such a move of the five or six founding fathers, who left the technical university in Saragoza and returned to their home town to do practical work. I feel that only then will we have the hope to become true scientists in the sense of praxis progression and in the sense of a new ship distinct from the ship of fools. Only with interaction with the workers and with soiled hands can we serve our main objective while remaining scientists.

Positive Paths: In Scientific Discipline

I now turn from the action to the reflective part of self-management research involved in the leaving of the ship of fools and descending from the ivory tower.

At a recent "Energy Day" during which hundreds of working-class people visited our solar installations, I realized that they really were as apprehensive of big business and big government as I am, and shared my concern with energy, prices and employment; that is, their principal contradictions and problems. At the same time we spoke about workers' cooperatives: many of the installations were marked with the sign of our students' cooperative *ENSOL solar Cooperative* and a number of the students were wearing t-shirts with the same inscriptions. The 500 or so visitors certainly were not schocked or displeased by our idea of worker cooperative organization.

This experience and general reflection convinces me that the best way of generalizing self-management in our country and in the West in general is to do education and popularization work and research showing how the principal problems of our Western societies can be resolved. Here I mean the principal problems as perceived by the majority of people. The absence of self-determination and self-management is not yet perceived by the majority as their principal problem, and thus popularization along these lines is virtually impossible. In summary we must earn the confidence and good will of the majority by helping them through self-management.

My conviction that we need a lot of popularization and education related to research is further strengthened by the fact that in the long run, irrespective of what are today's principal problems of the majority, this majority of 95 percent or more will definitely benefit from the introduction of self-management and economic self-determination. It is primarily the absence of consciousness of this fact in basically democratic societies that explains that self-management is not with us as a dominant form of economic organization. But if this is so, education and popularization, linked to practical experiences as much as possible, become the principal instruments of a peaceful revolution.[3]

What I have said thus far in this section is more a matter of strategy than substance. But substance is very important in the context of our analysis, especially because here we encounter probably the greatest violations of the spirit of participation on the part of self-management researchers. In fact I feel that in many instances our research methodology still belongs to the ship of fools.

In principle we agree that research on and leading to self-management and participation should also be participatory, but do we really understand what it means, and do we really practice that principle? First we must realize that research involves at least five stages: research project selection, design, carrying-out, evaluation, and reaping of fruits. If we want to have participatory research, all those involved must participate as much as possible in all five stages. They must participate according to the nature and intensity of their involvement. And here is the stumbling block in the social sciences. Those involved are a group or groups about whom the research is conducted: normally they are infinitely weightier, both in intensity (numbers) and vitality of involvement, than the minute group of researchers themselves. This means that according to the principle of participation we researchers or scientists cannot be anything but faithful and dedicated servants of the majority. It is true that in the earlier stages, especially in selection of research projects, we may be sometimes too distant from that majority, but it is precisely the action-part of research in praxis that must bring us close to the majority so that we could organically consult with them on what research should be done. Only in extremis when such contact is absolutely impossible must we practice what I call the principle of "others' shoes," that is, putting oneself into the place of those with whom we cannot communicate and take decisions on the researched, so to speak, on their behalf according to our best conscience. It will take only a minimum of reflection to realize how much all of us in our scientific work violate such principles. The top-down arrogance of the Western establishment scientists is still much too much with us.

The nonparticipatory nature of research is not the only flaw of our work inherited from the ship of fools. Note that on that ship, at least in economics, probably the widest-spread disease is that of irrelevance of excessively technical, theoretical suprastructures. But we must realize that within the established order irrelevance is a second-best solution, which the establishment is led to support with prizes and grants. Irrelevance is a barrier against being relevant and rocking the boat. But in our (for the moment) tiny life-raft in which we want to reach the new world, irrelevance is an impermissible luxury. I would like to note that this qualification by no means pertains only to theory. A good deal of our empirical research may be fundamentally irrelevant or redundant. Only an honest consultation with the majority of those involved on the subject can give the correct direction.

In conclusion, I would like to call for broadly based and conceived research, on the part of those seeking a participatory society, embedded in praxis, true dialogue, and the fullest application of fundamental principles of a participatory society. These three precepts are as necessary for research as they are for any other aspect of optimal human existence.

Notes

1. See Vanek, J. (1977). Some of the substance of this chapter is taken from and builds upon arguments developed in other manuscripts that I prepared, Vanek and Emmerij (1979, chapter 7), Vanek (1980).

2. See Freire (1973), Vanek (1977a), and Vanek and Emmerij (1979).

3. In the developing countries, which are not our principal concern here, further analogous arguments can be made that bring together issues such as development, education, self-management, and technology.

Bibliography

Aigner, D.J., and Chu, S.F. "On Estimating the Industry Production Function." *American Economic Review* 58 no. 4 (September 1968):826-839.

Alchian, A.A., and Demsetz, H. "Production, Information Costs, and Economic Organisation." *American Economic Review* 62 no. 5 (December 1972):777-795.

American Economic Association. *Publications of the American Economic Association* 2 vols., Baltimore: Guggenheim, (1887), (1887).

Antonovsky, A., and Arain, A. *Hopes and Feats of Israelis*. Jerusalem: Jerusalem Academic Press, 1972.

Aoki, M. "A Model of the Firm as a Stockholder-Employee Cooperative Game." *American Economic Review* 70 no. 4 (1980):600-610.

Arrow, K. "Control in Large Organizations." *Management Science* 10 no. 3 (1964).

√ Atkinson, A.B. "Worker Management and the Modern Industrial Enterprise." *Quarterly Journal of Economics* 87 (1973):375-392.

Bajt, A. "The Girl in Illyria." Paper presented to the Second International Conference on Economics of Self-Management. Forthcoming in *Economic Analysis and Workers' Management* (1981).

Balassa, B., and Bertrand, T.J. "Growth Performance of Eastern European Countries." *American Economic Review* (proceedings) 60 (1970): 314-320.

Barkai, H. *Growth Patterns of the Kibbutz Economy*. New York: North-Holland, 1977.

———. "Incentives, Efficiency, and Social Control: The Case of the Kibbutz." Discussion Paper 7815. Jerusalem: The Maurice Falk Institute for Economic Research in Israel, 1978.

Barkin, D., and Bennet, J.W. "Kibbutz and Colony: Collective Economics and the Outside World." *Comparative Studies in Society and History* 14 (1972):456-480.

Barrera, M. "Participación de los Trabajadores en la Gestion de las Empresas en Chile. Una Experiencia Historica." Paper presented at a Conference at the Latin American Centre, Oxford, and Institute of Development Studies, Sussex, 1978.

Barthel, D.L. *Sandotone Utopia: Mystique and Politics in the Amana Colonies*. Mimeo, State University of New York at Stony Brook, Department of Sociology, 1979.

Bartlett, W.J. "Economic Development, Institutional Reform and Unemployment in Yugoslavia, 1945-1975." Ph.D. thesis, Liverpool University, 1979.

Bartlett, W.J. "A Structural Model of Unemployment in Yugoslavia, and Alternative to the Institutional Hypothesis." Manuscript, University of Southhampton, 1980a.

―――― . "Economic Development and Institutional Reform: The Introduction of Workers' Self-Management in Yugoslavia." *Economic Analysis and Workers' Management* 14 no. 4 (1980b):429-443.

Barton, M.F. "Conditional Logit Analysis of FCC Decisionmaking." *Bell Journal of Economics* 10 no. 2 (1979):399-411.

Basevi, A. *Studi Cooperativi*. Rome: Edizioni de "La Rivista della Cooperazione," 1953.

Batstone, E., and Davies, E.L. *Industrial Democracy: European Experience*. London: Her Majesty's Stationery Office, 1976.

Becker, G.S. *The Economic Approach to Human Behavior*. Chicago: Chicago University Press, 1976.

Bellas, C.J. *Industrial Democracy and the Worker-Owned Firm: A Study of Twenty-One Plywood Companies in the Pacific Northwest*. New York: Praeger, 1972.

Ben-Ner, A. "On Cooperatives and Hired Labor: Two Step Optimization and Instability." Mimeo, Yale University, Institution for Social and Policy Studies, October 1980.

―――― . "On the Economics of Communalism and Self-Management: The Israeli Kibbutz," Ph.D. dissertation, State University of New York at Stony Brook, 1981.

Ben-Ner, A., and Neuberger, E. "The Kibbutz." Forthcoming in Stephen F., (ed.). *The Performance of Labour-Managed Firms*.

Bennett, J.W. "The Hutterian Colony: A Traditional Voluntary Agrarian Commune with Large Economic Scale." In Dorner, P. (ed.), *Cooperative and Commune*. Madison, Wisconsin: The University of Wisconsin Press, 1977.

Berle, A., and Means, G. *The Modern Corporation and Private Property*. (rev. ed.), New York: Harcourt, Brace and World, 1968.

Berman, K. "Comparative Productivity in Worker-Managed Cooperative Plywood Plants and Conventionally Run Plants." Mimeo. University of Idaho, 1976.

Berman, K. "Worker Management in U.S. Plywood Manufacturing Cooperatives: A Cooperative Model for Labour Management." Forthcoming in Stephen, F. (ed.), *The Performance of Labour-Managed Firms*.

Berman, K.V. *Worker-Owned Plywood Companies*. Pullman: Washington State University Press, 1967.

Berman, K.V., and Berman, M.D. "The Long-Run Analysis of the Labor-Managed Firm: Comment." *American Economic Review* 68 no. 4 (September 1978):701-705.

Bernstein, P. *Workplace Democratization: Its Internal Dynamics.* Kent, OH: Kent State University Press, 1976.

Bićanić, J. *Economic Policy in Socialist Yugoslavia.* Cambridge: Cambridge University Press, 1973.

Biedenkopf, K. *Mitbestimmung in Unternehmen.* Mitbestimmungskommission, Bonn: Deutscher Bundestag, 1970; reprinted by W. Kohlhammer GMBH: Stuttgart, 1970.

Bilderbeek, J. *Financiele Ratio-Analyse.* Leiden: Stenfent Kroese, 1977.

Bjelćić, B., Penezić, D., Sarać, S., and Stavrić, B. *Ekonomika Jugoslavije.* Bosnia, Elas, Banja Luka, 1974.

Blackburn, R., and Mann, M. *The Working Class in the Labor Market.* Cambridge: Cambridge University Press, 1979.

Bluestone, B., and Harrison, B. "Why Corporations Close Profitable Plants." *Working Papers for a New Society* 7 no. 3 (May-June 1980): 15-23.

Bluestone, B., Harrison, B., and Baker, L. *Corporate Flight: The Causes and Consequences of Economic Dislocation.* Cambridge, Massachusetts: Progressive Alliance, 1981.

Blumberg, P. *Industrial Democracy: The Sociology of Participation.* New York: Schocken Books, 1968.

Blumenthal, W.M. *Codetermination in the German Steel Industry.* Princeton University, Industrial Relations Section, 1956.

Borda, F.O. *El Reformismo por Dentro en America Latina.* Mexico: Siglo Veintiuno Editores S.A., 1976.

Bornstein, M. (ed.). *Plan and Market.* New Haven: Yale University Press, 1973.

Bowles, S., and Gintis, H. *Schooling in Capitalist America.* New York: Basic Books, 1976.

Bradley, K. "A Comparative Analysis of Producer Cooperatives: Some Theoretical and Empirical Implications." *British Journal of Industrial Relations* 18 (July 1980):155-168.

Bradley, K., and Gelb, A. "The Radical Potential of Cash Nexus Breaks." *British Journal of Sociology* 31 no. 2 (June 1980a):188-203.

———. "Worker Cooperatives and Industrial Policy." *The Review of Economic Studies* (July 1980b):665-678.

———. "Motivation and Control in the Mondragon Experiment," *British Journal of Industrial Relations* 19 no. 2 (1981).

Brannen, P. et al. *The Worker Directors.* London: Hutchinson, 1976.

Braverman, H. *Labor and Monopoly Capital: The Degradation of Work in the Twentieth Century.* New York: Monthly Review Press, 1974.

Brown, A., and Neuberger, E. (eds.). *Internal Migration: A Comparative Perspective.* New York: Academic Press, 1977.

Brown, C., and Medoff, J. "Trade Unions in the Productive Process." *Journal of Political Economy* 86 no. 3 (1978):355-378.

Brus, W. *Socialist Ownership and Political Systems.* London: Routledge & Kegan Paul, 1975.

Bruyn, S.T., and Nicolano, S. "A Theoretical Framework for Studying Worker Participation: The Psychosocial Contract." *Review of Social Economy* 37 no. 1 (1979):1-24.

Buber, M. *Paths in Utopia,* Boston: Beacon Press, 1958.

Buchannan, R.T. "The Economic Conditions for Industrial Democracy." *Economic Analysis and Workers' Management* 12 nos. 3-4 (1978):291-301.

Bullock, L. *Report of the Committee on Inquiry on Industrial Democracy.* London:.Department of Trade, Her Majesty's Stationery Office, 1977.

Cable, J., and Fitzroy, F. "Productivity, Efficiency, Incentives, and Employee Participation: Some Preliminary Results for West Germany." *Kyklos* 33 no. 1 (1980a):100-121.

_____ . "Cooperation and Productivity: Some Evidence from West German Experience." *Economic Analysis and Workers' Management* 14 (1980b):163-180.

Carnoy, M., and Levin, H.M. "Workers' Triumph: The Meriden Experiment." *Working Papers* (Winter 1976):47-56.

Carnoy, M., and Shearer, D. *Economic Democracy: The Challenge of the 1980's.* White Plains, New York: Sharpe, 1980.

Carson, R.G. "A Theory of Cooperatives." *Canadian Journal of Economics* 10 no. 4 (1977):565-589.

Chenery, H.B. "Patterns of Industrial Growth." *American Economic Review* 50 no. 4 (1960):624-654.

_____ . *Transitional Growth and World Industrialization.* Washington, D.C.: World Bank Reprint Series no. 61 (1977).

Chenery, H.B., and Syrquin, M. *Patterns of Development, 1950-1970.* Oxford: Oxford University Press, 1975.

Clarkson, K.W., and Martin D.L. (eds.). *The Economics of Non-Proprietary Organizations.* Greenwich, CT: JAL Press, 1980.

Clayre, A., (ed.). *The Political Economy of Cooperation and Participation.* Oxford: Oxford University Press, 1980.

Coase, R.H. "The Nature of the Firm." *Economica* 4 no. 16 (1937):386-405.

Coch, L., and French, J.R.P., Jr. "Overcoming Resistance to Change." *Human Relations* 1 no. 4 (1948):512-532.

Coddington, A. *Theories of the Bargaining Process.* Chicago: Aldine, 1968.

Comisso, E.T. "Yugoslavia in the 1970s: Self-Management and Bargaining." *Journal of Comparative Economics* 4 (1980):192-208.

Commons, J.R, et al. *History of Labour in the United States.* New York: Macmillan, 1918.

Conte, M., and Tannenbaum, A.S. *Employee Ownership: Report,* to the Economic Development Administration, U.S. Department of Commerce, Ann Arbor: University of Michigan Survey Research Center, 1978.

Cooperative Union. *Cooperative Statistics.* Manchester: Cooperative Union. 1945-1973.

Coyne, J., Chiplin, B., and Sirc, L. *Can Workers Manage?* Hobart Paper 77, London: Institute of Economic Affairs, 1977.

Dahl, Jr., and Henry, G. *Worker-Owned Plywood Companies in the State of Washington.* Dissertation, Everett, WA: Pacific Coast Banking School, April 1957.

Dal Pane, L. *Nullo Baldini Mella Storia della Cooperazione.* Milano: Gingre, 1966.

Department of Employment and Productivity. *British Labour Statistics, Historical Abstract, 1886-1968,* London: H.M.S.O.

Dimitrijević, D., and Maćešić, G. *Money and Finance in Yugoslavia.* New York: Praeger, 1973.

Dirlam, J.B., and Plummer, J.L. *An Introduction to the Yugoslav Economy.* Columbus: Merrill, 1973.

Domar, E. "The Soviet Collective Farm as a Producer Cooperative." *American Economic Review* 56 no. 4 (1966):737-757.

Don, Y., "Dynamics of Development in the Israeli Kibbutz." In Domer, P., *Cooperative and Commune.* Madison: The University of Wisconsin Press, 1977.

Downs, A. *An Economic Theory of Democracy,* New York: Harper, 1957.

Dreze, J.H. "Some Theory of Labour-Management and Participation." *Econometrica* 44 no. 6 (1976):1125-1139.

Duncan, G. "Earnings Functions and Nonpecuniary Benefits." *Journal of Human Resources* 11 (Fall 1976):462-483.

Eisenstadt, S.N. "Traditional and Modern Social Values and Economic Development." In Eisenstadt et al. (eds.), *Integration and Development in Israel.* New York: Praeger, 1970.

_____ . "Some Observations on Historical Changes in the Structure of Kibbutzim." *The Kibbutz: Interdisciplinary Research Review* (Special Issue: *Development of the Kibbutz Federations*) 6-7 (1978-1979):xvi-xx.

Eisenstadt, S.N. Yosef, R.B., and Adler, C. (eds.). *Integration and Development in Israel.* New York: Praeger, 1970.

Ekonomska Politika. Belgrade: Borba, various issues.

Ellerman, D. "Workers' Cooperatives: The Question of Legal Structure." Palo Alto, CA: Center for Economic Studies, 1980. Forthcoming in Jackall and Levin (eds.), *Producer Cooperatives in the U.S.*

Espinosa, J.G. "The Building of a Self-Managed Sector in a Capitalist Underdeveloped Economy." Paper presented at the Walton Symposium, University of Strathclyde, Glasgow, 1979.

Espinosa, J.G., and Zimbalist, A.S. *Economic Democracy: Workers' Participation in Chilean Industry 1970-1973*. New York: Academic Press, 1978.

Estrin, S. "An Explanation of Earnings' Variation in the Yugoslav Self-Managed Economy." *Economic Analysis and Workers' Management* 13 nos. 1-2 (1979a):175-199.

_____ . "Self-Management: Economic Theory and Yugoslav Practice." D. Phil. thesis, Sussex University, 1979b (forthcoming Cambridge University Press).

_____ . "Income Dispersion in a Self-Managed Economy." *Economica* 48 (1981):181-194.

_____ . "The Effects of Self-Management on Yugoslav Industrial Growth." *Soviet Studies* 32 no. 3 (January 1982).

Fabbri, F. (ed.). *Il Movimento Cooperativo nella Storia d'Italia 1854-1975*. Milano: Feltrinelli, 1979.

Fals Borda, O. *El Reformismo por Dentro en America Latina*. Siglo Veintiuno Editores S.A., Mexico, Coleccion Minima numero 48, 1976.

Farrell, M.J. "The Measurement of Productive Efficiency." *Journal of the Royal Statistical Society* 120 (1957): Series A (general), part 3, pp. 253-281.

Felix, D. "De Gustibus Disputandum Est: Changing Consumer Preferences in Economic Growth." *Explorations in Economic History* 16 (1979):260-296.

Fellner, W. "Prices and Wages Under Bilateral Monopoly." *Quarterly Journal of Economics* 16 (1947):503-532.

Fleming, J.M. *The International Monetary Fund, Its Form and Function*. Washington, D.C.: International Monetary Fund, Washington, 1964.

Franković, V. "Cene Produckcijskih Tvorcev in Alocacija Resursov v Naśem Ekononskem Sistemu." Manuscript, Ljubljana, Institut za Ekonomska Raziskovanja, 1974.

Freire, P. *Pedagogy of the Oppressed*. New York: Seabury Press, 1973.

Frieden, K. *Workplace Democracy and Productivity*. Washington, D.C.: National Center for Economic Alternatives, 1980.

Friedlander, A.F. "Macro Policy Goals in the Postwar Period: A Study in Revealed Preference." *Quarterly Journal of Economics* 87 (February 1973):25-43.

Frobel, F., et al. *Die Neue Internationale Arbeitsteilung: Strukterelle Arbeitslosigkeit in Industriellandern und Industrialisierung in Entwicklungs Landern*. Hamburg: Rowohlt Taschenbuch Verlag, 1977.

Fürstenberg, F. "Workers' Participation in Management in the Federal Republic of Germany." *International Institute for Labor Studies Bulletin* no. 6 (June 1969).

_____. "West German Experience with Industrial Democracy." *Annals of the American Academy of Political and Social Science.* May (1977).

Furubotn, E. "Toward a Dynamic Model of the Yugoslav Firm." *Canadian Journal of Economics* 9 (1971):182-197.

_____. *The Economics of Property Rights.* Cambridge, MA: Ballinger, 1974.

_____. "The Long-Run Analysis of the Labor-Managed Firm: An Alternative Interpretation." *American Economic Review* 66 no. 1 (March 1976):104-123.

_____. "The Economic Consequences of Codetermination for the Rate and Service of Private Investment." In Pejovich, S. (ed.), *The Codetermination Movement in the West.* Lexington, MA: Lexington Books, 1978.

Furubotn, E., and Pejovich, S. "Property Rights and the Behavior of the Firm in a Socialist State: The Example of Yugoslavia." *Zeitschrift für Nationalokonomie* 30 (December 1970):431-454.

Gallant, A. "Seemingly Unrelated Nonlinear Regressions." *Journal of Econometrics* 3 (1975):35-50.

Gamson, S., and Levin, H. "Obstacles to Survival for Democratic Workplaces." Palo Alto, CA: Center for Economic Studies, 1980. Forthcoming in Jackall and Levin, (eds.), *Producer Cooperatives in the U.S.*

Gazit, Z. *Values and Value Changes in Kibbutz Society.* (2 parts) Israel: Histadrut Olamit Hashomer Hatzair, 1972.

Graaff, J. de V. *Theoretical Welfare Economies.* Cambridge: The University Press, 1957.

Greenberg, E.S. "Producer Cooperatives and Democratic Theory: The Case of the Plywood Firms." Palo Alto, CA: Center for Economic Studies, 1978. Forthcoming in Jackall and Levin, (eds.), *Producer Cooperatives in the U.S.*

_____. "Participation in Industrial Decision Making and Work Satisfaction: The Case of Producer Cooperatives." *Social Science Quarterly* 60 no. 4 (March 1980):551-569.

Griliches, Z. "Specification Bias in Estimates of Production Functions." *Journal of Farm Economics* 39 nos. 1-3 (February 1957):8-20.

Griliches, Z., and Ringstad, V. *Economies of Scale and the Form of the Production Function: An Econometric Study of Norwegian Manufacturing Establishment Data.* Amsterdam: North-Holland, 1971.

Gunn, C. "Toward Workers' Control." *Working Papers for a New Society* 7 no. 3 (May-June 1980):4-6.

Gyllenhammar, P.G. *People at Work*. Reading, MA: Addison-Wesley, 1977.

Halevi, N., and Klinov-Malul, R. *The Economic Development of Israel*. New York: Praeger, 1968.

Hallet, G. *The Social Economy of West Germany*. London: Macmillan, 1973.

Hallett, H.A. "Approximating Unknown Objective Function with Known Optima: An Error Control Theorem for a Class of Variable Metric Algorithms." Rotterdam: Erasmus University Institute for Economic Research, discussion paper 7816/G, October 1978.

Hart, P.E., and Prais, S. "The Analysis of Business Concentration: A Statistical Approach." *Journal of the Royal Statistical Society*. Series A, 119 (1956):150-181.

Hawrylyshyn, O. "Yugoslav Development and Rural-Urban Migration." In Brown, A., and Neuberger, E. (eds.), *Internal Migration: A Comparative Perspective*. New York: Academic Press, 1977.

Heilbroner, R. *The Economic Problem*. (3rd ed.), Englewood Cliffs: Prentice-Hall, 1972.

Hewitt de Alcantara, C. *Modernising Mexican Agriculture: Socio-Economic Implications of Technological Change, 1940-1970*. Geneva: United Nations Research Institute for Social Development, 1978.

Higgins, W. "Worker Participation in Jamaica Sugar Production." *Rural Development Participation Review* 1 no. 2 (Winter 1980):11-14.

Hoch, I. "Estimation of Production Function Parameters Combining Time-Series and Cross-Section Data." *Econometrica* 30 no. 1 (January 1962):34-53.

Horsefield, J.K. *The International Monetary Fund 1945-1965: Twenty Years of International Monetary Cooperation*. Washington, D.C.: International Monetary Fund, 1969.

Horton, D.E. *Haciendas and Cooperatives: A Study of Estate Organization, Land Reform and New Reform Enterprises in Peru*. Ph.D. dissertation, Ithaca: Cornell University, 1976.

Horvat, B. "Yugoslav Economic Policy in the Post-War Period." *American Economic Review* 61 (1971):71-169.

———. "Fundamentals of a Theory of Distribution in Self-Governing Socialism." *Economic Analysis and Workers' Management* 10 nos. 1-2 (1976a):24-42.

———. *The Yugoslav Economic System*. White Plains, NY: International Arts and Sciences Press, 1976b.

———. "On the Theory of the Labor-Managed Firm." In Horvat, et al. (eds.), *Self-Governing Socialism: A Reader*. White Plains, NY: International Arts and Sciences Press, 1975.

Horvat, B., et al. (eds.), *Self-Governing Socialism: A Reader*. White Plains, NY: International Arts and Sciences Press, 1975.

IDE International Research Group. *Industrial Democracy in Europe*. Oxford: Oxford University Press, 1981.

Ireland, N. "The Behavior of the Labour Managed Firm and Disutility from Supplying Factor Services." Paper presented to the Second International Conference on the Economics of Self-Management. Forthcoming in *Economic Analysis and Workers' Management*, 1981.

Israelsen, L.D. "Collectives, Communes, and Incentives." *Journal of Comparative Economics* 4 (June 1980):96-124.

ISTAT. *Censimenty Generali dell'industria e del Commercion*. Roma: 1951, 1961, 1971.

————. *Il prodotto lordo e gli investimenti delle imprese industriali*. Supplemento al *Bollettino mensile di Statistica*. Roma: various years.

Jackall, R. "Paradoxes of Collective Work: A Study of the Cheeseboard, Berkeley, California." Palo Alto: Center for Economic Studies, 1980. Forthcoming in Jackall and Levin, (eds.), *Producer Cooperatives in the U.S.*

Jackall, R., and Crain, J. "The Shape of the Small Producer Cooperative Movement." Palo Alto, CA: Center for Economic Studies, 1980. Forthcoming in Jackall and Levin, (eds.), *Producer Cooperatives in the U.S.*

Jackall, R., and Levin, H.M. (eds.), *Producer Cooperatives in the U.S.* Forthcoming.

Jamaica. Advisory Committee on Worker Participation. *Report on Worker Participation*. Kingston: 1976.

————. National Planning Agency. *Economic and Social Survey*. Kingston: various years.

————. Sugar Industry Enquiry Commission. *Report*. Kingston: 1967.

————. Sugar Industry Research Institute. *Annual Report*. Kingston: various years.

Jamison, D., et al. (eds.), *Education as an Industry*. New York: National Bureau of Economic Research, 1976.

Jay, P. *A General Hypothesis of Employment, Inflation, and Politics*. London: Institute of Economic Affairs, 1976.

Jenkins, D. *Job Power*. Baltimore: Penguin Books, 1974.

Jensen, M.C., and Meckling, W.H. "Rights and Production Functions: An Application to Labor-Managed Firms and Codetermination." *Journal of Business* 52 no. 4 (1979):469-506.

Jerovśek, J., and Mozina, S. "Efficiency and Democracy in Self-Managing Enterprises." In Obradovic, J., and Dunn, W.N. (eds.), *Workers' Self-Management and Organization Power in Yugoslavia*. University of Pittsburgh, University Center for International Studies, 1978.

Johansen, L.F. *Production Functions: An Integration of Micro and Macro Short Run and Long Run Reports*. Amsterdam: North-Holland, 1972.

Jones, D.C. "The Economics of British Producer Cooperatives." Ph.D. dissertation, Cornell University, 1974.

———. "British Economic Thought on Associations of Laborers, 1848-1974." *Annals of Public and Cooperative Economy* 47 (1976):5-37.

———. "The Bullock Report." *Economic Analysis and Worker's Management* 11 nos. 3-4 (1977):245-279.

———. "Producer Cooperatives in Industrialized Western Economies: An Overview." *Annals of Public and Cooperative Economy* 49 no. 2 (April-June 1978):149-162.

———. "U.S. Producer Cooperatives: The Record to Date." *Industrial Relations* 8 no. 2 (Fall 1979):342-356.

———. "Producer Cooperatives in Industrialized Western Economies." *British Journal of Industrial Relations* 18 (July 1980):141-154.

Jones, D.C., and Backus, D. "British Producer Cooperatives in the Footwear Industry: An Empirical Test of the Theory of Financing." *Economic Journal* (September 1977):488-510.

Jones, D.C., and Schneider, D. "Self-Help Production Cooperatives: A Case Study of Government Administered Producer Cooperation." Forthcoming in Jackall, R., and Levin, H. (eds), *Working Cooperatively. Producer Cooperatives in the U.S.*

Kanovsky, E. *The Economy of the Israeli Kibbutz*. Cambridge, MA: Harvard University Press, 1972.

Kanter, R.S. *Commitment and Community, Communes and Utopias in Sociological Perspective*. Cambridge, MA: Harvard University Press, 1972.

Kapteyn, A., Wansbeek, T., and Buyze, J. "The Dynamics of Preference Formation." *Journal of Economic Behavior and Organization* 1 (1980):123-157.

Kaser, M. (ed.), *Economic Development for Eastern Europe*. New York: Macmillan and St. Martin's Press, 1968.

Katzell, R.A., Bienstock, P., and Faerstein, P.H. *A Guide to Worker Productivity Experiments in the United States 1971-1975*. New York: New York University Press, 1977.

Kavčić, B., Rus, V., and Tannenbaum, A. "Control Participation and Effectiveness in Four Yugoslav Industrial Organizations." *Administrative Science Quarterly* 16 (1971):74-86.

Kendrick, J.W., and Vaccara, B.N. (eds.), *New Developments in Productivity Measurement and Analysis. Studies in Income and Wealth*. Chicago: University of Chicago Press, 1980.

Kester, G. *Transition to Workers' Self-Management. Its Dynamics in the*

Developing Economy of Malta. The Hague: Institute for Social Studies, 1980.

Klein, B., Crawford, R.G., and Alchian, A. "Vertical Integration, Appropriative Rents and The Competitive Contracting Process." *Journal of Law and Economics* 21 no. 2 (1978):297-326.

Kleindorfer, P.R., and Sertel, M.R. "Value Added Sharing Enterprises." Discussion Paper 79-81. Berlin: International Institute for Management, 1978.

Kleindorfer, P.R., and Sertel, M. "Labor-Management and Codetermination." In Mitchell, B., and Kleindorfer, P., *Regulated Industries and Public Enterprise.* Lexington, Massachusetts: Lexington, 1980.

Kmenta, J. "On the Estimation of the CES Production Function." *International Economic Review* 8 (June 1967).

Knight, P. "Problemas de la Comparacion Internacional de la Eficiencia Economica al Nivel Microeconomico en Industrias Manufactureras: La Experiencia del Estudio ECIEL de Eficiencia Industrial." *Ensayos ECIEL* Numero 1, Rio de Janeiro, Brasil y Brookings Institution, 1974.

_____ . "Peru's Social Property Sector: Development Through December 1975 and Prospects for Expansion." Washington, D.C.: The World Bank, 1976.

Knight, P., et al. *Self-Management in Peru. Program on Participation and Labor-Managed Systems.* Ithaca: Cornell University, 1975.

Koopmans, T.C., and Montias, J.M. "On the Description and Comparison of Economic Systems." In Eckstein, A. (ed.), *Comparison of Economic Systems.* Berkeley: University of California Press, 1971, pp. 27-78.

Korać, M. *Analiza Ekonomskog Polozaja Privrednih Grupaciha na Bazi Zakona Vrijednosti.* Zagreb, 1968.

Korać, M., and Vlaśkalić, T. *Politicka Ekonomija: Osnovi Teorijske Analize, Kapitalisticke, i Socialisticke Robne Proizvodne.* Rad: Beograd, 1975.

Krengel, B., Baumgart, E., Boness, A., Pischner, R., and Droege, K. *Produktionsvolumen und—potential, Produktions—factoren der Industrie in Gebiet der Bundesrepublic Deutschland.* Deutsches Institut für Wirtschaftsforschung, 1973, 1975, 1977.

Krueger, A.O., and Tuncer, B. *Estimating Total Factor Productivity Growth in a Developing Country.* Washington, D.C.: World Bank Staff Working Paper 422, October 1980.

Laidlaw, A. "Cooperation in the Year 2000." Paper presented at the 1980 ICA Congress, Moscow.

Lane, R. "The Hegemony of the Market." Forthcoming in *Personality, Economy, Polity.* Yale University, Institution for Social and Policy Studies.

Lange, O. "The Foundations of Welfare Economics." *Econometrica* 10 (1942):215-228.

Lau, L.J. "Applications of Duality Theory: Comment." In Intriligator, M.D., and Kendrick, D.A. (eds.), *Frontiers of Quantitative Economics*, vol. 2 (Contributions to Economic Analysis Ser.: vol 87). Elsevier: North-Holland, 1974:176-199.

Lau, L.J., and Yotopoulos, P.A. "A Test for Relative Efficiency and Application to Indian Agriculture." *American Economic Review* 61 (March 1971):94-109.

Law, P.S. "The Illyrian Firm and Fellner's Union-Management Model." *Journal of Economic Studies* 4 no. 1 (1977):29-37.

Lawler III, E.E. *Motivation in Work Organizations*. Monterey, CA: Brooks/Cole, 1973.

Leibenstein, H. "Allocative Efficiency versus X-Efficiency." *American Economic Review* 56 no. 3 (June 1966):392-415.

_____ . "Organizational or Frictional Equilibria; X-Efficiency and the Rate of Innovation." *Quarterly Journal of Economics* 83 no. 4 (1969): 600-623.

Levin, H.M. "Concepts of Economic Efficiency and Educational Production." In Jamison, D., et al. (eds.), *Education as an Industry*. New York: National Bureau for Economic Research, 1976.

_____ . "Workplace Democracy and Educational Planning." *Education, Work and Employment II*. Paris (Unesco International Institute for Educational Planning, 1980): 1980a, pp. 123-216.

_____ . "Improving the Creative Potential of Human Resources with Producer Cooperatives: Employment, Productivity and Self-Actualization." Invited paper presented at the Sixth World Congress of the International Economic Association, Mexico City, August 1980b.

_____ . "Raising Employment and Productivity with Producer Cooperatives." Forthcoming in Streeten P. and Maier, H. (eds.), *Human Resources in the Long-Run Perspective*.

Lissak, M. "Patterns of Change in Ideology and Class Structure in Israel." In Eisenstadt, S.N., et al. (eds.), *Integration and Development in Israel*. New York: Praeger, 1970.

LNCM (Lega Nazionale della Cooperative). *Indagine su 225 cooperative 1975-1977*, "Quaderni di Cooperazione e Societa." Roma, 1979.

_____ . *Indagine su 304 cooperative 1975-1978*, "Quaderni di Cooperazione e Societa." Roma, 1980.

London and Cambridge Economic Service. *The British Economy, Key Statistics 1900-1966*. London: Times Newspaper.

Long, R.J. *The Effects of Employee Ownership on Job Attitudes and Organizational Performance: An Exploratory Study*. Ph.D. dissertation, Cornell University, 1977.

Long, Richard J. "The Effect of Employee Ownership on Organizational Identification, Employee Job Attitudes, and Organizational Performance: A Tentative Framework and Empirical Findings." *Human Relations* 31 no. 1 (1978):29-48.

_____. "The Relative Effects of Share Ownerships vs. Control on Job Attitudes in an Employee-Owned Company." *Human Relations* 31 no. 9 (1978):753-763.

Lowin, A. "Participative Decision Making: A Model, Literature Critique, and Prescriptions for Research." *Organization Behavior and Human Performance* III (February 1968):69.

Lucas, R. "Hedonic Wage Equations and Psychic Wages in the Returns to Schooling." *American Economic Review* 67 (September 1977):549-558.

MacFadden, D. "The Revealed Preferences of a Government Bureaucracy: Theory." *Bell Journal Economics* 6 no. 2 (1975):401-416.

Maddison, A. *Economic Progress and Policy in Developing Countries.* London: George Allen and Unwin, 1970.

Maier, N.R.F. *Problem-Solving Discussions and Conferences: Leadership Method and Skills.* New York: McGraw Hill, 1963.

Maier, N.R.F., and Hoffman, L.R. "Using Trained 'Developmental' Discussion Leaders to Improve the Quality of Group Discussions." *Journal of Applied Psychology* 44 (1960):247-251.

Maksimović, F., and Panić, Z. "Price Problems in Yugoslav Theory and Practice." In Kaser, M. (ed.), *Economic Development for Eastern Europe.* New York: Macmillan and St. Martin's Press, 1968.

Malinvaud, E. *Statistical Methods of Econometrics.* Amsterdam: North-Holland, 1966.

_____. "The Consistency of Nonlinear Regressions." *Annals of Mathematical Statistics* 41 (1970):956-969.

Manley, M. *The Politics of Change.* London: André Deutsch, 1974.

Margolis, R. "Collectives in an Urban Environment: Critical Notetaking." Palo Alto, CA: Center for Economic Studies, 1980. Forthcoming in Jackall, R., and Levin, H.M. (eds.), *Producer Cooperatives in the U.S.*

Markusen, J.R. "Profit Sharing, Labour Effort, and Optimal Distributive Shares." *Economica* 46 (1976):405-410.

Marschak, T.A. "Centralized and Decentralized Resource Allocation: The Yugoslav Laboratory." *Quarterly Journal of Economics* 82 (1968): 402-428.

Marshall, A. *Industry and Trade.* London: Macmillan, 1919.

_____. *Principles of Economics.* 8th edition. London: Macmillan, 1964.

Marx, K. *Capital.* Vol. 1. New York: Charles H. Kerr, 1906.

Massell, B.F. "Elimination of Management Bias from Production Functions Fitted to Cross-Section Data: A Model and an Application to African Agriculture." *Econometrica* 35 nos. 3-4 (July-October 1967):495-508.

McCain, R.A. "Critical Note on Illyrian Economics." *Kyklos* 24 no. 2 (1973a):380-386.

———. "The Cost of Supervision and the Quality of Labor: A Determinant of X-Efficiency." *Mississippi Valley Journal of Business and Economics* 8 no. 3 (1973b):1-16.

———. "On the Optimal Financial Environment for Worker Cooperatives." *Zeitschrift Für Nationalökonomie* 37 nos. 3-4 (1977a):355-384.

———. "Codetermination: A Formal Theory." Manuscript, 1977b.

———. "A Theory of Codetermination." *Zeitschrift für Nationalökonomie* 40 nos. 1-2 (1980):65-90.

———. *Markets, Decisions, and Organizations: Intermediate Microeconomic Theory.* Englewood Cliffs, NJ: Prentice-Hall, 1981.

Meade, J.E. "The Theory of Labour-Managed Firms and Profit Sharing." *Economic Journal* 82 (1972):402-428.

Mediobanca. *Dati cumulativi di 856 società italiane (1968-1978).* Milano: Mediobanca, 1979.

Meller, P. "Efficiency Frontiers for Industrial Establishments of Different Sizes." *Explorations in Economic Research* 3 no. 3 (1976):379-408.

Melman, S. "Industrial Efficiency Under Managerial Versus Cooperative Decision-Making: A Comparative Study of Manufacturing Enterprises in Israel." In Horvat, B., et al. (eds.), *Self-Governing Socialism: A Reader.* White Plains, NY: International Arts and Sciences Press, 1976.

Merhav, M. *Technological Dependence, Monopoly and Growth.* London: Pergamon, 1969.

Meyer, D. *Participative Decision: An Analysis and Review.* University of Iowa, Center for Labor and Management, College of Business Administration, monograph series 15 (September 1970).

Milenkovitch, D.D. *Plan and Market in Yugoslav Economic Thought.* New Haven: Yale University Press, 1971.

Mill, J.S. *Principles of Political Economy.* Ashley Edition. London: Longman, 1909.

Miović, P. "Determinants of Income Differentials in Yugoslav Self-Managed Enterprises." Ph.D. dissertation, University of Pennsylvania, 1975.

Mood, A.M., Graybill, F.G., and Boes, D.C. *Introduction to the Theory of Statistics* 3rd edition. New York: McGraw-Hill, 1974.

Moore, B. *Injustice: The Social Bases of Obedience and Revolt.* White Plains, NY: Sharpe, 1978.

Moore, J.H. *Growth with Self-Management: Yugoslav Industrialization, 1952-1975.* Stanford, CA: Hoover Institution Press, 1980.

Mundlak, Y. "Empirical Production Function Free of Management Bias." *Journal of Farm Economics* 43 no. 1 (February 1961):44-56.

National Center for Employee Ownership. *Employee Ownership* 1 no. 1 (June 1981):1-10.

Neuberger, E. "The Yugoslav Visible Hand System: Why Is It no More."
State University of New York at Stony Brook, Department of Economics, Discussion Paper 23, 1970.

Neuberger, E., and Tyson, L.D'A. *The Impact of International Disturbances on the Soviet Union and Eastern Europe*. New York: Pergamon
Press, 1980.

Niv, A. "The Survival of Social Innovation: The Case of the Commune
and the Kibbutz." *The Kibbutz: Interdisciplinary Research Review*
(special issue: Development of the Kibbutz Federations) 6-7 (1978-1979):
115-130.

Niv, A. "Organizational Disintegration: Roots, Processes and Types." In
Kimberly, J.R., Miles, R.H., and Associates. *The Organizational Life
Cycle, Issues on the Creation, Transformation and Decline of Organi-
zations*. San Francisco: Jossey-Bass, 1980.

Oakeshott, R. *The Case for Worker Co-Ops*. London: Routledge & Kegan
Paul, 1978.

Obradović, J. "Participation in Enterprise Decision Making." In Obradović, J., and Dunn, W.N. (eds.), *Workers' Self-Management and
Organization Power in Yugoslavia*. University of Pittsburgh, University Center for International Studies, 1978.

Obradović, J., and Dunn, W.N. (eds.). *Workers' Self-Management and
Organization Power in Yugoslavia*. University of Pittsburgh, University Center for International Studies, 1978.

Olson, M. *The Logic of Collective Action*. New York: Schocker, 1965.

Pack, H. *Structural Change and Economic Policy in Israel*. New Haven:
Yale University Press, 1971.

Pateman, C. *Participation and Democratic Theory*. Cambridge: Cambridge University Press, 1970.

Patterson, O., Biron, N., and Woods, D. *Report on the Barham Sugar
Workers' Cooperative*. Harvard University, Department of Sociology,
no date.

Payer, C. *The Debt Trap, the IMF and the Third World*. New York: Monthly
Review Press, 1974.

Pejovich, S. "The Banking System and Investment. Behavior of the Yugoslav Firm." In Bornstein, M. (ed.), *Plan and Market*. New Haven: Yale
University Press, 1973.

Pejovich, S. (ed.). *The Codetermination Movement in the West*. Lexington,
MA: Lexington Books, 1978.

Peleg, B., and Yaari, M.E. "On the Existence of a Consistent Course of
Action When Tastes Are Changing." *Review of Economic Studies* 40
(1973):391-401.

Peltzman, S. "The Effects of Automobile Safety Regulation." *Journal of
Political Economy* 83 no. 4 (August 1975):374-379.

Pen, J. "A General Theory of Bargaining." *American Economic Review* 42 (1952):24-42.

Pfouts, R.W. "The Theory of Cost and Production in the Multi-Product Firm." *Econometrica* 29 (1961):650-658.

Pigou, A.C. (ed.). *Memorials of Alfred Marshall*. London: Macmillan, 1925.

Pollack, R.A. "Endogenous Tastes in Demand and Welfare Analysis." *American Economic Review* 68 (1978):374-379.

Popov, S. "Kretanje Produktivnosti Rada i Ličnih Dohodaka u Pojedinim Granam u Periodu od 1952 do 1966 Godine." *Obračun i Raspodela Osobnih Dohodaka u Radnim Organizacijama*. Zagreb, 1968.

Popov, S., and Jovičić, M. *Uticaj Ličnih Dohodaka na Kretanja Cena*. Belgrade: Institut Ekonomskih Nauka, 1971.

Potter, B. *The Cooperative Movement in Great Britain*. London: Allen and Unwin, 1890.

Powell, A.A. *Empirical Analytics of Demand Systems*. Lexington, MA: Lexington Books, 1974.

Primorac, E., and Della, Valle. "Unemployment in Yugoslavia: Some Structural and Regional Considerations." *Jahrbuch der Wirtschaft Osteuropas* 4 (1974).

Pryor, F.L. *Property and Industrial Organization in Communist and Capitalist Nations*. Bloomington: Indiana University Press, 1973.

Publication of the American Economic Association, American Economic Association, New York [etc.], 1886.

Putterman, L. "Voluntary Collectivization: A Model of Producers' Institutional Choice." *Journal of Comparative Economics* 4 (June 1980): 125-157.

Reich, M., and Devine, J. "The Microeconomics of Conflict and Hierarchy in Capitalist Production." *The Review of Radical Political Economics* 12 no. 4 (Winter 1981):27-45.

Rhodes, S. *The Relationship Between Worker Ownership and Control of Organizations and Work Attitudes and Behaviors*. Report, U.S. Department of Labor, Employment and Training Administration, Office of Research and Development, September 1978.

Rhomberg, R., and Heller, R. "Introductory Survey." In *The Monetary Approach to the Balance of Payments*. Washington, D.C.: International Monetary Fund, 1977.

Rivera-Batiz, F.L. "The Capital Market in Yugoslavia: A Theoretical and Empirical Note." *Quarterly Journal of Economics* 44 (1980):179-184.

Rocco, F., and Obraz, R. *Tržište i Marketing*. Zagreb: Informator, 1968.

Rockwell, C.S. "An International Comparison of the Size and Efficiency of the Yugoslav Plant." Mimeo. New Haven: Economic Growth Centre, 1968.

Rockwell, C.S. "Growth and Technical Progress in Socialist Enterprises of Yugoslavia: A Cobb-Douglas Analysis Using Extraneous Estimators." Discussion Paper 91, Yale University Economic Growth Center, 1970.

Rosner, M., and Avnat, A. "After Seven Years—Changes in the Perceptions and Attitudes of Kibbutz-Born Members and Their Causes." *The Kibbutz: Interdisciplinary Research Review* (special issue: *Development of the Kibbutz Federations*) (Hebrew with English summary) 6-7, (1978-1979):162-192.

Rothschild-Whitt, J. "The Collectivist Organization: An Alternate to Rational-Bureaucratic Models." *American Sociological Review* 44 (August 1979):509-527.

Ruiz-Tagle, J. *Reforma de la Empresa y Cambio Social. La Experiencia Chilena: 1964-1973*. Ph.D. dissertation, Université Catholique de Louvain. V. 2, 3rd Part, 1979.

Rus, V. "Enterprise Power Structure." In Obradović, J., and Dunn, W.N. (eds.), *Workers' Self-Management and Organization Power in Yugoslavia*. University of Pittsburgh, University Center for International Studies, 1978.

_____ . "Limited Effects of Workers' Participation and Political Counter-Power." In Burns, T., Karlsson, L.E., and Rus, V., (eds.), *Work and Power: The Liberation of Work and The Control of Behavior*. London: Sage, Studies in International Society (18), 1979.

Rusinow, D. *The Yugoslav Experiment, 1948-1974*. London: Hurst, 1977.

Sacks, S.R. "Changes in Industrial Structure in Yugoslavia, 1959-1968." *Journal of Political Economy* 80 (1972):561-574.

_____ . *Entry of New Competitors in Yugoslav Market Socialism*. Berkeley: University of California Institute of International Studies Research, Series 19, 1973.

_____ . "Regional Inequality in Yugoslav Industry." *Journal of Developing Areas* 11 (1976):59-78.

_____ . "Divisionalization in Large Yugoslav Enterprises." *Journal of Comparative Economics* 4 (1980).

Salter, W.E.G. *Productivity and Technical Change*. Cambridge: Cambridge University Press, 1960.

Samuelson, P.A. *Foundations of Economic Analysis*. New York: Atheneum, 1965.

_____ . "Thoughts on Profit Sharing." *Zeitschrift für die Gesamte Staadtswissenschaft* (special issue: *Profit Sharing*) (1977).

Sapelli, G. (ed.). *Il Movimento cooperativo in Italia. Storia e problemi*. Torino: Einaudi, 1981.

Sapir, A. "Economic Growth and Factor Substitution: Whatever Happened to the Yugoslav Miracle?" *Econonic Journal* 90 no. 358 (1980):294-313.

Scherer, W. *Industrial Market Structure and Economic Performance*. Chicago: Rand McNally, 1970.

Scitovsky, T. *Welfare and Competition*. Homewood, Illinois: Richard D. Irwin, Inc., Revised edition, 1971.

Seashore, S.E., and Bowers, D.G. "Durability of Organization Change." *American Psychologist*. (March 1970):227-233.

Sector de Propiedad Social (Asamblea del Sector), "Propiedad Social Seis A; os Despues." Paper presented to the International Conference on Self-Management and Participation, San José, Costa Rica, June 23-28, 1980.

Shirom, A. "The Industrial Relations Systems of Industrial Cooperatives in the United States, 1880-1935." *Labor History* 13 (Fall 1972):533-551.

Siber, F., Sverko, B., Kljajić, S., and Magdić, M. "Perceptions of Enterprise Power Structure." In Obradović, J., and Dunn, W.N. (eds.), *Workers' Self-Management and Organization Power in Yugoslavia*. University of Pittsburgh, University Center for International Studies, 1978.

Sirc, L. *The Yugoslav Economy Under Self-Management*. London: Macmillan, 1979.

Slot, R., and Vecht, J.M. *Zicht op cijfers*. Agon: Elsevier, 1975.

Solis, A.E. *Central de Empresas Campesinas del Valle Sagrado de los Incas*. Paper presented to the International Conference on Self-Management and Participation, San José, Costa Rica, June 23-28, 1980.

Staellerts, R. "The Effect of Capital Intensity on Income in Yugoslav Industry." Forthcoming in *Economic Analysis and Workers' Management* (1981).

Statistical Yearbook of the Federal Republic of Germany. (Statistisches Jahrbuch der Bundesrepublik Deutschland). Statistisches Bundesamt: Wiesbaden, 1950-1978.

Statistički Godišnjak Jugoslavije. Belgrade: Savezni Zavod za Statisticku, various issues.

Steinherr, A. "On the Efficiency of Profit Sharing and Labor Participation in Management." *Bell Journal of Economics* (Autumn 1977): 545-555.

———. "The Labor-Managed Economy: A Survey of the Economics Literature." *Annals of Public and Co-Operative Economy* 49 no. 2 (April-June 1978):129-148.

Stephen, F.H. "Bank Credit and the Labour-Managed Firm: Comment." *American Economic Review* 70 no. 4 (1980):796-803.

———. (ed.). *The Performance of Labour-Managed Firms*. London: Macmillan. Forthcoming.

Stern, R.N., Wood, H., and Hammer, T.H. *Employee Ownership in Plant Shutdowns*. Kalamazoo, MI: W.E. Upjohn Institute for Employment Research, 1979.

Steward, J.H. *Theory of Cultural Change: The Methodology of Multi-linear Evolution.* Urbana: University of Illinois Press, 1955.

Stiglitz, J. "Incentives, Risk and Information: Notes Toward a Theory of Hierarchy." *Bell Journal of Economics* 6 no. 2 (Autumn 1975):552-579.

Stockton, F. "Productive Cooperation in the Molders' Union." *American Economic Review* 21 (June 1931).

Stone, C. "Socio-Political Aspects of the Sugar Cooperatives." Kingston, Jamaica: Department of Government, University of the West Indies, 1976.

———. "Socio-Political Aspects of the Sugar Cooperatives." In Stone, D., and Brown, A. (eds.), *Essays on Power and Change in Jamaica.* Kingston: Jamaica Publishing House, 1977, pp. 140-170.

———. "An Appraisal of the Cooperative Process in the Jamaican Sugar Industry." *Social and Economic Studies* 27 (1978):1-20.

Streeten, P., and Meier, H. *Human Resources in the Long Run Perspective.* Proceedings of the International Economic Association, 1980 (forthcoming, Macmillan).

Sturmthal, A.F. *Workers' Councils.* Cambridge, MA: Harvard University Press, 1964.

Svejnar, J. "The Effect of Employee Participation on Bargaining Power and Wages: A Generalized Nash Solution and Econometric Evidence from West Germany." Working paper 106, Princeton University, Industrial Relations Section, 1977.

———. "Employee Participation in Management, Bargaining Power, and Wages." *European Economic Review* 18:3 (July 1982), pp. 291-303.

———. "The Bargaining Problem with Variable Bargaining Powers: Theory and Empirical Evidence from U.S. Industry." Paper presented at the Annual Meetings of the Econometric Society, Denver, September 1980b.

———. "Relative Wage Effects of Unions, Dictatorship and Codetermination: Econometric Evidence from Germany." *Review of Economics and Statistics* 63 no. 2 (1981):188-197.

———. "On the Theory of a Participatory Firm." *Journal of Economic Theory* 21:2 (August 1982), pp. 313-330.

Talmon, Y.G., and Stup, Z. "Sector Asceticism: Patterns of Ideological Change." In Eisenstadt, S.N. et al. (eds.), *Integration and Development in Israel.* New York: Praeger, 1970.

Tanić, Z. "Yugoslavia." In Krane, R.E. (eds.), *International Labour Migration in Europe.* New York: Praeger, 1979.

Tannenbaum, A. *Hierarchy in Organizations.* San Francisco: Jossey-Bass, 1974.

Tannenbaum, A.S., Kavćić, B., Rosner, M., Vianello, M., and Weiser, G. *Hierarchy in Organizations, an International Comparison.* San Francisco: Jossey-Bass, 1974.

Taylor, R. "Labor-Managed Firms and Capital Subscriptions." *Revista Internationale di Scienze Economiche e Commerciali*, 21 (1) (1974):75-81.

Theil, H. *Principles of Econometrics*. New York: John Wiley and Sons, 1972.

Thimm, A.L. *The False Promise of Codetermination: The Changing Nature of European Workers' Participation*. Lexington, MA: Lexington Books, 1980.

Thomas, H., and Logan, C. *Mondragon Producer Cooperatives*. The Hague, The Netherlands: Institute of Social Studies, 1980.

Thomas, H., and Logan, C. *Mondragon: An Economic Analysis*. London: Allen and Unwin, 1982.

Thornley, J. *Worker Cooperatives in the Western World*. London: Heinemann, 1981.

Timmer, P.C. "On Measuring Technical Efficiency." Food Research Ininstitute Studies in Agricultural Economics, Trade and Development, 1970.

_____ . "Using a Probabilistic Frontier Production Function to Measure Technical Efficiency." *Journal of Political Economy* 79 no. 2 (July-August 1971):776-794.

Triffin, R. *Monopolistic Theory and General Equilibrium Theory*. Cambridge, Massachusetts: Harvard University Press, 1940.

Tyson, L. D'A. "The Yugoslav Inflation: Some Competing Hypotheses." *Journal of Comparative Economics* 1 no. 2 (1977):113-146.

_____ . "A Permanent Income Hypothesis for the Yugoslav Firm." *Economica* 44 (1977a):393-408.

_____ . "Liquidity Crises in the Yugoslav Economy: An Alternative to Bankruptcy?" *Soviet Studies* 2 (1977b):284-295.

Tyson, L. D'A., and Kenen, P.B. "The International Transmission of Disturbances: A Framework for Comparative Analysis." In Neuberger, E., and Tyson, L. D'A., *The Impact of International Disturbances on the Soviet Union and Eastern Europe*. New York: Pergamon Press, 1980.

Uca, M.N. "The Turkish Road Toward Self-Management." *Economic Analysis and Workers' Self Management* 13 no. 4 (1979):537-550.

United Nations (UNCTAD). *Current Problems of Economic Integration*. New York: United Nations, 1973.

University of Michigan, Institute for Social Research. *Employee Ownership*. Report to the Economic Development Administration of the U.S. Department of Commerce, Project 99609433, 1979.

U.S. DHEW (Department of Health, Education and Welfare). *Work in America*. Cambridge, MA: The M.I.T. Press, 1973.

U.S. Senate Subcommittee. *Economic Concentration, Part 7*. 90th Congress, 2nd session, 1968.

Vahčić, A. "An Econometric Analysis of Post-War Performance of the Yugoslav Economy." Ph.D. thesis, Cornell University, Program on Participation and Labor-Managed Systems, 1976.

Vanek, Jan. *The Economics of Workers' Management: A Yugoslav Case Study*. London: George Allen and Unwin, 1972.

Vanek, Jaroslav. *The General Theory of Labor-Managed Market Economies*. New York: Cornell University Press, 1970.

——— . "The Basic Theory of Financing of Participatory Firms." Cornell University, Department of Economics, Working Paper 1971. Reprinted in Vanek, Jaroslav (ed.), *Self-Management, Liberation of Men*. Baltimore: Penguin, 1975.

——— . *The Participatory Economy: An Evolutionary Hypothesis and a Strategy for Development*. Ithaca: Cornell University Press, 1971.

——— . "The Yugoslav Economy Viewed Through the Theory of Labor-Management." *World Development* 1 no. 9 (1973):39-56.

——— . (ed.). *Self-Management, Economic Liberation of Men*. Baltimore: Penguin, 1975.

——— . "The Absurdity of the Rich Man's Trade Doctrine." Cornell University, Department of Economics, Working Paper 125, 1976.

——— . *The Labor-Managed Economy: Essays*. Ithaca: Cornell University Press, 1977.

——— . *Through Participation and Dialogue to a World of Justice*. Ithaca: Cornell University, 1977a.

——— . "Yugoslavia as the Pathbreaker for the Global Society." *Economic Analysis and Workers' Management* 14 no. 4 (1980):445-463.

Vanek, J., and Emmerij, L. *From the Old to a New Global Order*. The Hague: Institute of Social Studies, 1979.

Vanek, J., and Espinosa, J.G. "The Subsistence Income, Effort and Development Potential of Labour Management and Other Economic Systems." *Economic Journal* 82 (1972):1000-1013.

Vanek, J., and Jovičić, M. "The Capital Market and Income Distribution in Yugoslavia: A Theoretical and Empirical Analysis." *Quarterly Journal of Economics* 89 (1975):432-443.

Vanek, J., and Miović, P. "Explorations Into the 'Realistic' Behavior of a Yugoslav Firm." Cornell Department of Economics Working Paper no. 7, April 1970. Reprinted in Vanek, Jaroslav (ed.), 1977.

Virtue, G.O. "The Cooperative Coopers of Minneapolis." *Quarterly Journal of Economics* 19 (August 1905):527-544.

——— . "The End of the Cooperative Coopers." *Quarterly Journal of Economics* 46 (May 1932):541-545.

Vollmer, R.J. "Industrial Democracy in Germany." London: Embassy of the Federal Republic of Germany, June 1976.

——— . "Labor Relations and Industrial Democracy in the Federal Republic of Germany." Washington, D.C.: Embassy of the Federal Republic of Germany, December 1979.

Vroom, V.H. *Some Personality Determinants of the Effects of Participation*. Englewood Cliffs, NJ: Prentice-Hall, 1960.

Wachtel, H.M. "Workers' Management and Inter-Industry Wage Differentials in Yugoslavia." *Journal of Political Economy* 80 (1972):540-560.

_____ . *Workers' Management and Workers' Wages in Yugoslavia*. Ithaca: Cornell University Press, 1973.

Walters, A. "Production and Cost Functions: An Econometric Survey." *Econometrica* 31 nos. 1-2 (January-April 1963).

Ward, B.N. "The Firm in Illyria: Market Syndicalism." *American Economic Review* 48 (September 1958):566-689.

_____ . *The Socialist Economy: A Study of Organization Alternatives*. New York: Random House, 1967.

Webb, S. and B. *A Constitution for the Socialist Commonwealth of Great Britain*. London: Longman, 1920.

Weisbrod, B.A. "Private Goals, Collective Goals: The Role of the Non-Profit Sector." In Clarkson, K.W., and Martin, D.L. (eds.), *The Economics of Non-Proprietary Organizations*. Greenwich, CT: JAL Press, 1980.

Whyte, W.F., and Blasi, J.L. "From Research to Legislation on Employee Ownership." *Economic and Industrial Democracy* 1 (1980):395-415.

Wiles, P. "The System of Permanent Employment in Yugoslavia and Japan." Mimeo. London School of Economics, 1977.

Williams, A.N. "Self-Management, Social Transformations and Development: The Experience of the Castle Bruce Workers, Dominica, West Indies." *Economic Analysis and Workers' Management* 14 no. 1 (1980):149-162.

World Bank. *Yugoslavia: Development with Decentralization*. Baltimore: John Hopkins University Press, 1975.

Yatchew, A. "The Design of Econometric Choice Models." Ph.D. dissertation, Harvard University, 1980.

Yotopoulos, P.A., and Nugent, F.B. *Economics of Development: Empirical Investigations*. Harper & Row, 1976.

Zellner, A. "An Efficient Method of Estimating Seemingly Unrelated Regressions and Tests for Aggregation Bias." *Journal of the American Statistical Association* 57 (1962):348-368.

Zwerdling, D. *Democracy at Work*. Washington, D.C.: Association for Self-Management, 1978.

Index

About the Contributors

Peter Abell is a professor of sociology at the University of Surrey. He is the author of several books and numerous articles, including a forthcoming book on industrial producer cooperatives in less-developed countries.

William Bartlett is a lecturer in economics at the University of Southampton. He is the author of several articles dealing with the issue of unemployment and institutional reforms in Yugoslavia.

Avner Ben-Ner is an assistant professor of economics at the University of California at Davis. He is the author of several articles published in the *Journal of Comparative Economics* and *Economic Analysis and Workers' Management*.

Keith Bradley is a lecturer in industrial relations at the London School of Economics and a visiting professor at the University of Pennsylvania. He has published extensively in journals such as the *Review of Economic Studies, British Journal of Industrial Relations*, and *British Journal of Sociology*.

Michael Conte is an assistant professor of economics at the University of New Hampshire. He is a contributor to various journals including the *Journal of Comparative Economics, Economic Analysis and Workers' Management*, and *Monthly Labor Review*.

Juan Guillermo Espinosa is a senior economist at the Centro Interamericano de Enseñanza de Estadística (CIENES) in Santiago, Chile. He is the coauthor of *Economic Democracy: Worker Participation in Chilean Industry,* and a contributor to various economic journals including the *Economic Journal* and *Economic Analysis and Workers' Management*.

Saul Estrin is a lecturer in economics at the University of Southampton, England, and a visiting assistant professor at Cornell University. He is the author of several articles published in *Economica* and *Economic Analysis and Workers' Management*. He is also the British correspondent for *Economic Analysis and Workers' Management*.

Alan Gelb is an economist in the Development Research Center of the World Bank. His research articles appeared in the *Review of Economic Studies, British Journal of Sociology*, and the *British Journal of Industrial Relations*.

357

Hank Levin is the director of the Institute for Research on Educational Finance and Governance in the School of Education at Stanford University. He is the coeditor of *Working Co-operatively* and author of several books and numerous papers.

Nicholas Mahoney is a member of Hackney Co-operative Developments and a former research Fellow at the International Co-operative Alliance. He is a coauthor with Peter Abell of a forthcoming book on producer cooperatives in the less-developed countries.

Roger A. McCain is a professor of economics at Fordham University. He is the author of several articles published in the *American Economic Review, Kyklos,* and *Zeitschrift für Nationalökonomie* as well as of a new micro-economics text.

Vincent Richards is head of the Antigua office of the Association for Caribbean Transformation and a former Fellow of the Institute of Social and Economic Research at the University of the West Indies.

Stephen R. Sacks is an associate professor of economics at the University of Connecticut. His written work has appeared in the *Journal of Political Economy, Journal of Comparative Economics, Economic Analysis and Workers' Management,* and *Journal of Developing Areas.*

Henk Thomas is associate director of the Institute of Social Studies in The Hague. He is the author of a forthcoming book on Mondragon producer cooperatives and of various articles published in such journals as *Economic Development and Cultural Change, Economic Analysis and Workers' Management,* and *De Economist.*

Jaroslav Vanek is the Carl Marks Professor of Economics and International Relations at Cornell University. He is also director of Cornell's Program on Participation and Labor-Managed Systems (PPLMS). His numerous books include *The General Theory of Labor-Managed Market Economies, The Participatory Economy,* and *Self-Management: Economic Liberation of Man.*

Allan N. Williams is secretary general of the Association for Caribbean Transformation and a consultant to various United Nations agencies. Before assuming his current position, he taught at Miami University in Ohio. His written work has appeared in *Economic Analysis and Workers' Management,* and he also serves as the Caribbean correspondent for this journal.

Alberto Zevi is a lecturer in economics at the University of Rome and author of several articles published in various Italian journals.

About the Editors

Derek C. Jones is an associate professor and chairman of the Economics Department at Hamilton College. He received the B.A. from the University of Newcastle upon Tyne, the M.Sc. from the London School of Economics, and the M.A. and Ph.D. from Cornell University. He has published widely in journals including the *Economic Journal, British Journal of Industrial Relations, Economic Analysis and Workers' Management, Industrial Relations,* and *Annals of Public and Cooperative Economy.* He is currently engaged in a research project on the economic performance of producer cooperatives in various countries including Italy, Poland, and France.

Jan Svejnar is an assistant professor of economics and industrial and labor relations at Cornell University. He is also acting director of Cornell's Program on Participation and Labor-Managed Systems. He received the B.S. from Cornell University and the M.A. and Ph.D. from Princeton University. His written work can be found in journals such as the *Journal of Economic Theory, Review of Economics and Statistics, Industrial and Labor Relations Review,* and *Annals of Public and Cooperative Economy.* At present he is collaborating with Michael Conte on a research project examining the economic effects of employee participation in management, employee stock ownership, and profitsharing schemes in U.S. manufacturing.